Captain of the Queen

Captain of the Queen

Robert H. Arnott, R.D., R.N.R.
and
Ronald L. Smith

NEW ENGLISH LIBRARY

483008771

02875642

From Bob Arnott to my dear Joan
for all her years of wonderful support.

Copyright © 1982 by Captain Robert H. Arnott and Ron Smith

First published in Great Britain by New English Library,
Mill Road, Dunton Green, Sevenoaks, Kent, in 1982.
Third impression January 1983.

Printed in Great Britain by
The Thetford Press Limited, Thetford, Norfolk

Bound by Robert Hartnoll, Limited.

ISBN: 0 450 04891 8

Chapter 1

The cluster of stone jugs of ginger beer standing on the back of my father's dray cart clinked together in cheerful rhythm with the clip-clop of our horse's hooves as we trundled through the streets of Hamilton, New South Wales, more than half a century ago.

My father, Fred Arnott, was manager of the local mineral-water works. In the hot months of his peak selling season, he would go out on the rounds himself. When I was just a few months old, Dad would prop me up on the hard wooden bench seat of the cart, wedging me tightly between himself and my mother. One day we would deliver our cool, fizzy cargoes among the bustling docks district of nearby Newcastle, and the next day we would be out in the sleepy settlements that lay along the banks of the sprawling Hunter River.

And so, on those early explorations, my first views of the world were seen perched only a few feet above the dusty Australian roadways and across the sturdy haunches and swishing tail of our stocky draught horse. Half a planet and half a lifetime away from those mineral-water meanderings was to come the moment in October 1976 when I stood the bridge of the fabulous *Queen Elizabeth II* – at a height of a thirteen-storey building – and realised that this flagship of the Cunard fleet, the world's acknowledged super-ship, was now mine to command.

More than forty years at sea, many of them spent as Master of other glamorous floating palaces in the historic Cunard fleet, had, I felt, led me inexorably to that sublime moment when I looked out over Southampton Water. Those earlier commands and senior service on other queens of the Atlantic had already made me friend and confidant to reigning royal families and their cousins seeking solace in exile through the floating pleasures of the luxury liner.

I was – and am – shipboard adviser to many of the Hollywood greats, to the world's political super chiefs, and father-confessor

1

figure to tens of thousands of ordinary folk who have travelled on my ships. I know every corner of the world's seaways. In taking over command of the *QE2*, I knew I was reaching the professional seaman's highest pinnacle. I had been handed the 'Keys of the Ocean Kingdom'.

The true-to-life sea-yarns of my voyages across the world during war and peace, the untold tales of the fantastic people I have met, all pour from the pages of my own personal sea-log like a spell-binding adventure story – one that started out on those primitive Australian roads in the far-off 1920s.

Both my father and mother were born near Bury, Lancashire, England. It is a cotton manufacturing town, much more famous for the quality and flavour of black puddings sold in the local market than for the wealth of career opportunities open to its young folk, and my father, on his return from his service at sea after the First World War, quickly decided he needed more out of life than his job of working on the company books in a cotton mill's offices. So the eager, ambitious Fred Arnott set sail at age twenty-two with his brand new bride to make a fresh life 8000 miles away in Australia. My parents moved in with relatives named Taylor who lived in a wooden, white-painted house in the Broadmeadow district of Hamilton, New South Wales. And it was there that I first saw the light of day on 17 July 1923.

Both my father and mother eventually succumbed to a severe attack of homesickness, and they brought me back as a toddler to Bury, Dad returning to the Manchester office of the firm he had left to emigrate to Australia. But that proved far too tame for Dad – a future war-time squadron leader – and in the early 1930s the Arnott family moved out to within splashing distance of the Irish Sea.

We took over a roomy private hotel on the promenade at Fleetwood, a Lancashire fishing port and holiday resort. There I breathed in the tingling fragrance of sea and ships. It was a delicious infection that burst into my blood when, as a small boy, I used to watch the heavily laden trawlers heading into port from the chill, sub-Arctic waters. From a very early age, I knew that my future lay out there on the waves rather than in the warm, shore-bound security of helping in the family hotel, or perhaps working in a shipping company office.

But Dad had other ideas. World trade was depressed in the 1930s and he couldn't honestly see any worthwhile prospects on board ship for his only son. He would say, 'Now look here, Bob lad. You're a big young feller and we should get you into some solid, steady sort of job where you can use that height and those shoulders.' So it was decided. The obvious choice, according to Dad, was a job in the police. At fifteen, I was well over six feet tall, played second row forward for the school rugger team and weighed in at 217 lb. My masters at Fleetwood Grammar School agreed with the parental prognosis, and I was soon launched into a special study programme geared toward my entering the Police Training College at Hendon.

I hated it. From my bedroom overlooking the Irish Sea, I would glance up from my special police swotting and think that I belonged out there on the water, not behind some police station desk. It was blue seas and not blue uniforms that drew me. I just had to tackle my father.

My cause was helped by the fact that war had just broken out. Dad himself was thinking of volunteering for the services, so he could hardly refuse me the chance to get into my own line of action. We had a deep, heart-to-heart talk. At the end of it, Dad said, 'All right, Bob. You can go to sea, but not on any of these Fleetwood trawlers.'

I wondered what was coming next. My father always had the ability to see several moves ahead in any particular game, and he had already worked out just how he would allow me out there on the waves. He said, 'I have a friend on the Blue Funnel Line in Liverpool. I'm pretty sure I can get you a place as a midshipman there, then you can train for a proper officer's career.' I gave him a rough bear-hug. I wouldn't have minded if he had said I was to join the Black Chimney Line as a stoker; I just wanted to get out there to sea, and there was no way I could do that without his permission. Now I'd got it. Ecstasy for a sea-struck sixteen-year-old!

Within a month I'd been accepted by the Blue Funnel Line as a midshipman. My father took me to the Sailor's Home Outfitters in Liverpool and bought me dark sea jackets, reefers, oilskins, white shirts, a couple of tropical suits and, joy of joys, a peaked midshipman's Merchant Navy cap. A couple of days later I signed my indentures and waved farewell to my anxious-looking parents at Fleetwood railway station.

3

I set out for the Blue Funnel Line midshipman's hostel, the Holm Lea, sited in Riversdale Road, Dingle, in South Liverpool. Right next door lived the formidable Mr Heathcote, the Blue Funnel's 'man in charge of midshipmen', who ruled: 'Everyone back inside by 10 p.m., and lights out at 11.30 p.m.' For young men who might be sunk at sea within weeks, that ten-o'clock curfew seemed most unfair. Even an innocent night out at the cinema could result in the punishment penalty of being confined to quarters for several evenings if one happened to arrive back just a few minutes after ten. And some of the lads had local girl friends who couldn't quite understand the Heathcote curtailment on 'kissin' and cuddlin'' hours.

So we decided to beat the system by arranging for one lad to stay in each evening and leave a living-room window open. Late-comers could then climb back inside without having to use the hostel's front door. It didn't work. One after another, middies returning around midnight were caught and hauled before Mr Heathcote.

It was years afterwards when I found out how he consistently snared late-comers. The Heathcote secret was that he never oiled the front gate. Said the now-benign gentleman, 'It was so rusty, it almost screamed whenever it was opened. I deliberately kept that gate without oil, and as soon as it squeaked, I looked out from my window and saw the culprit. Simple, but totally effective.'

In the early days of 1940 terrifying tonnages of Allied shipping was plunging daily to the bed of the Atlantic under the fierce maraudings of the U-boat fleets; hence my course of training for entering sea service was destined to be short and sharp. There were twenty of us in the Dingle Hostel, and for just over a week we all took a tram each day to India Buildings in Water Street, Liverpool, where the shipping line ran its seamanship school. I was then just seventeen and looking forward to learning all about the theoretical side of my new profession over the coming months. Latitudes, longitudes, knots, flag signals – how I had dreamed about being initiated into these wonderful mysteries. And here I was actually being paid to learn it all – at the rate of exactly £9 a year. But the shore-based lessons suddenly ended. Ships were being sunk and lives lost so rapidly that the twenty of us were posted immediately to various vessels in the Blue Funnel fleet.

4

My particular chum was Les Allen, a sixteen-year-old, cheery-faced youngster from Nottingham, and like myself, he was besotted with the sea. We went to the local fleapit cinema in the odd hours when we were off duty; he loved sport, loved life, and we got on wonderfully well. After our so-short crash course, the postings went up on the classroom notice board at India Buildings. I was to join a Blue Funnel cargo liner called the *Antilochus* bound for Australia. Les, standing beside me, noted with disappointment that he was to join a different ship, the *Euryalus*, sailing from Liverpool Docks the same day as mine. He gripped my hand and shook it, saying, 'We'll always be pals, Bob, no matter where we have to go. And we'll keep in touch.' I vowed that we would indeed, then off we went to the India Buildings snack bar and celebrated our postings with cups of tea.

The Blue Funnel Line named all its ships after heroes of Greek mythology. I'm no 'Brain of Britain' when it comes to Greek legend, but I do know that some of those Grecian superstars came to very sticky ends. Perhaps Blue Funnel were risking the wrath of the gods in taking the names of their favourite sons.

The next day I carried my sea bag up the gangplank of the *Antilochus* and was assigned quarters high over the engine room with several other midshipmen. Within a few hours we were cutting through the grey-green waters of the Mersey estuary to join our convoy escort north of Ireland. Right ahead of us, I saw with intense interest, was the *Euryalus*, and I wondered how Les was faring.

I thought little of the dangers from U-boats. One of my fellow middies told me, in an educated Southern accent, 'They'll be waiting for us like a pack of hungry wolves when we get out into the Atlantic.' Being naturally suspicious, like any other good Northern lad, of anyone with an accent marking him from south of Birmingham, I didn't take too much notice. In any case, I was far too busy thinking just how lucky I was to be exactly where I wanted to be – on the deck of a cargo vessel heading ultimately for the land of my birth. 'I must be dreaming all this,' I told myself. 'It's all too good to be really true.'

It was true all right. Ship after ship joined our convoy until there were more than fifty vessels heading out into the North Atlantic. I wasn't even dismayed to find that our 'escort' comprised in total just two armed trawlers: in September 1940 it was as bad as that. But I could still see the *Euryalus* just a few hundred feet away, and as long as I knew where my chum Les was, well, that made me feel a lot happier.

A few days out, I heard 'Action stations' for the first time in my young life. What a thrill. I tingled with excitement, not afraid at all. I was humiliated to find that my part of the action was to be carrying cups of hot cocoa to the officers and men on the bridge. I wondered what sort of a job they had given Les – probably something much more exhilarating. It was mid-morning. The men on the bridge were sipping the steaming cocoa I had just carried up from the galley. Suddenly there was a screaming, shattering explosion. Instantly I thought, 'We've been hit.' Then, as I looked out across the water, I saw smoke and flames belching amidships on the *Euryalus*.

The torpedo had searched out, I believe, the freighter's explosives cargo. In a brief, unforgettable instant in time, men and chunks of ship were blown indiscriminately into the heavens.

'God,' I thought, 'poor Les is in that lot. Surely we'll stop and start picking up people.' We didn't. Orders, apparently, were to get away from the scene of a U-boat attack just as fast as our engines could carry us. It could have been our turn next.

I saw heads bobbing about in the deathly cold Atlantic waters. I whispered a prayer for Les, realising that it could so easily have been me dying out there. I don't think anyone from the *Euryalus* survived the attack; no swimmers were picked up. For a few moments it didn't seem such a wonderful adventure after all. I watched the smouldering hulk sink swiftly as the sea silently swallowed her. Our Chinese firemen heaped coal frantically into the ship's boilers, and we sped away bound for South Africa and then on to Australia, the land of my birth.

Chapter 2

Billows of smoke and steam surged from the broad single funnel of the *Antilochus* as she churned her rugged course through the heaving swells of the autumn North Atlantic. Built in 1906, our sturdy ship had had a maiden voyage speed of 13 knots, and such was the excellence of her original design, she had no trouble at all thirty-five years later in thrusting her 10,000 tons bulk across the seas at a steady, persistent 12½ knots.

The midshipmen's quarters on the *Antilochus* were cramped, but efficiently comfortable. Our home at sea was known as the halfdeck, and amid the fragrances of freshly scrubbed mahogany, brass porthole metal polish and salt spray, four of us slept, ate, swotted and played bridge for matchstick stakes. Furnishings in the halfdeck were simple and solid. There were two bunks on each side of the quarters, a wooden table in the middle, screwed firmly into the bare wooden deck, two tiny settees, two chairs and a single ship's wardrobe which we all shared. The halfdeck was on the port side of the *Antilochus*, within whistling distance of the bridge. Three short blasts on the mate's pea whistle summoned us up there, ready to read flag signals from other ships in the convoy or perhaps to take our turn watching out for the long-distance Fokker reconnaissance planes shadowing our westward progress.

The three other young midshipmen were all just a few months older than myself, and had been at sea a few months longer. It was a vital advantage. When Tom Edwards, the senior middie, handed out the daily chores, it was usually the junior middie who was elected 'Peggy'. And that was me.

'Peggy' was the nautical nickname for the fellow who got to scrub the deck, polish our three brass portholes until they gleamed, and clean out the ancient bathroom and toilet rooms. The nickname dates from the old sailing ship days when there were many sailors around with wooden legs. These unfortunate 'peg-leg' gentlemen were given the deck-chores simply because they couldn't climb riggings or move swiftly on the decks. Happily, after I had suffered a full week as the wretched Peggy, Edwards relented and assigned the next in line up the middie ladder, one Jack Coventry, to be chore leader.

Before we had left Liverpool docks, Neil McLean – second in the midshipmen command chain – had announced he was planning a treat for us in mid-Atlantic, saying, 'It will be my eighteenth birthday. And I've brought something special for us all the way from South Africa.' McLean was a young blond Springbok giant, who had joined Blue Funnel from the Simonstown training ship, *General Botha*. Normally a taciturn sort of chap, he seemed quite elated as his 'big day', or rather 'big night', drew near; we were kept far too busy during our days at sea to sit down to a birthday feast, so McLean's momentous moment was fixed for midnight.

Afterwards, the whole affair gained fame in Blue Funnel folklore as the 'Case of the Walking Birthday Cake', but at the time, all we knew was that McLean was planning to give us a pleasant surprise. We hoped it would be an edible one. Blue Funnel shipboard fare was adequate, but we felt at times that it lacked the imagination of our mums' home cooking.

There we were, gathered excitedly round the halfdeck mess table, a dim electric light from the cabin's two small bulbs reflecting a shining anticipation in our faces. McLean reached into his locker, and brought out a huge, dark blue chocolate tin. 'This is it,' he announced proudly. We leaned forward, eager to see and sample the contents. He lifted off the lid, and his shovel-like hand groped in the tin. Out came a giant, rich, dark brown fruit cake. The young South African placed it squarely in the centre of our table.

And then, as if the four of us were at a Spiritualist seance, the cake started to move. It wasn't the rolling of the ship that caused it: that cake began its own steady, slow march towards the edge of the table.

I was too amazed to speak. Edwards exclaimed, 'Hell, McLean, what sort of a joke is this?' I looked across at the birthday boy. His jaw had dropped open in complete shock. He was as thunderstruck as the rest of us. But the cake's progress went on: left, right, left, right, left – in perfect precision.

It was, after all, McLean's cake. It was up to him to make it behave. His huge fist reached out and lifted up the magical confection. 'Watch it,' called Coventry. 'Your mum has put a spell on it.' As McLean raised the cake in the air, we saw what looked like fat black capsules dropping from its base onto the table. The South African's face broke into a grin. 'Ah,' he said, relieved, 'they're only copra bugs.'

McLean assured us the itinerant insects were quite harmless. They were simply partial to his mother's cake recipe and somehow they had invaded the tin between Simonstown, South Africa, and the central waters of the North Atlantic. We swept the still-marching bugs from the table onto the floor, squashed them with our feet, and then tucked into the cake. The bugs had left us plenty. We washed down the 'walking birthday cake' with a bottle of bitter beer each from our secret stock. It had to be secret because, according to our articles of indenture, Blue Funnel midshipmen were 'not to drink alcoholic beverages, frequent taverns, or resort to houses of ill repute.' The indentures said nothing about playing jokes on each other, or the rest of the crew. Sinkings, drownings, submarine attacks, tellings-off from the mate – none of these vanquished our excited, schoolboy enjoyment of those early weeks at sea.

The halfdeck was right next to the section housing the steering engine of the ship, and below that was the main engine room. A voice-pipe ran from the steering engine room to the engineer's platform in the main engine compartment many feet below. I noted with mischievous interest that, as one engineer blew into the voice-pipe, it was possible to look below and see another answer it.

I couldn't resist. I waited until there were no officers around, filled a jug with water, then blew into the pipe. I heard the high-pitched squeak echo below, and saw a burly engineer lift the pipe from its mounting in the engine room. *Woosh*! I emptied the full quart jug down the narrow shaft. I stayed for a split second to watch him catch it full in the face, then I ran as fast as my long legs would take me to a neutral corner of the ship. The phantom water chucker was never caught.

Another time the joke was on me. It was in the early hours of the morning, and I was pulling on my trousers to go up on deck to take my turn on watch. Suddenly, a heartless Atlantic wave crashed against the ship's port side where we were housed, roared along a ventilator shaft, and spewed itself, still foaming, into each of my trouser legs as I drew them upwards. Dripping

9

and indignant, I choked back a startled shout. I decided that three midshipmen, sleeping solidly, could inflict more damage if suddenly awakened than a rogue wave. I swore, but silently, and closed the culprit ventilator before creeping out on deck in my spare pair of trousers.

Essentially, our task was to become professional seamen and ship's officers worthy of the Blue Funnel Line, and we had been set homework in the academic side of seamanship before we left the Blue Funnel college in Liverpool's India Buildings. Our efforts were to be assessed and marked when we returned there at the end of the voyage. In spite of our daily high jinks, the four of us swotted long and hard, and we rapidly became young experts in reading the signals sent out by flag or semaphore from the convoy's command ship to the other vessels steaming across the Atlantic. It was a point of honour for the *Antilochus* to be first in acting on the commands, such as a switch in course, before any of the other vessels were able to transcribe and start to obey the Commodore's orders.

I was keen, too, on all aspects of navigation. At home, my father was interested in astronomy and had lots of books on the stars and planets, and I had read every one several times long before I even went to sea. Here, in the crystal-clear ocean nights, I would sneak out on deck and gaze at the Orion constellation with its shimmering jewels of Betelgeuse and Rigel, or perhaps look in wonder at Sirius the Dogstar, the brightest body in our heavens, sending its ageless guidance to sailors from a distance of more than 50 million million miles. Later, in the warm southern oceans, I would lie on the hatch outside the halfdeck and watch the wonders of the Southern Cross, spangled on the blue-black silk tapestry of tropical night skies. Celestial navigation was a truly romantic affair then; not so the instant, electronic satellite 'fix' I can call up today on the bridge of the *QE2*. Efficient, accurate, but soul-less.

In those early days, if we midshipmen couldn't work out our own position on the high seas, we would have had no idea where we were until we actually docked. Shipboard security was tight. The officers obviously knew our day-to-day course, but they didn't deign to tell the lowly middies where we were heading. But they didn't need to, as we had it all worked out from our atlases, stars and sextants.

It looked to us as if the *Antilochus* was steaming full ahead towards the island of Bermuda. Our navigation was spot on. After my first ever Atlantic crossing, we anchored off St George's Island, north-west of Bermuda, to await sealed orders for the next stage of the voyage; these said – I found out much later – 'Proceed to Cape Town.' The *Antilochus* weighed anchor, and we headed for the southern seas.

Chapter 3

If you have a world map, draw an imaginary line diagonally south across the Atlantic, from Bermuda to the southern coast-line of South Africa. In a few seconds, you have covered more than 6000 miles to anchor in the shadow of Table Mountain at the port of Cape Town.

It took us rather longer than that in the *Antilochus*. Drably decked out in her grey war-time camouflage paint, the old freighter followed a zig-zag course southwards at a steady 12 knots, steaming first on one short track, then suddenly veering to another. The idea was that a shadowing U-boat would find it extra hard to set us up as a target for its torpedoes.

Perhaps it was our zig-zags that brought us safely across the North and South Atlantic, or maybe the roaming German subs just didn't see us. Either way, we sailed into the sunny security of Table Bay having avoided any sort of attack. I swapped my working dungarees for the all-white tropical uniform I had treasured since sailing from Liverpool. I carefully fastened up the five buttons on my tunic, checked the knife-crease on the long white trousers I was putting on for the first time, and headed ashore.

I was allowed only a few hours to take in some of the tradi-tional Cape Town sights. And it wasn't just a matter of time; I had little money. But it was wonderful to step onto South Africa's warm, rich soil after so many days at sea. Britain, the hazards of the North Atlantic, and the world at war meant little as I gazed skywards in boyish amazement at the awesome, cloud-topped bulk of Table Mountain. Years later, as Master of Cunard's super-ships, I had ample time and tides to explore the Cape. Not so in 1940. I had little to tell my mother on the card I posted in the dockland postbox beyond the brief message that I had taken a bus ride through Cape Town to see Cecil Rhodes' house, and that I believed the Prime Minister now lived there. Then it was back on board. Soon we were steaming around the

Cape of Good Hope into the rolling swells of the Indian Ocean, and Junior Officer Arnott was back in dungarees.

Blue Funnel Line treated its youngsters well, and it had a deserved reputation as one of the world's finest cargo-carrying companies. Yet the working hours were long and tiring. In the sweaty heat of the Indian Ocean, we washed down the decks and companionways, scrubbed whitewood until it shone, and painted overhead wires and stays with Stockholm tar from the precarious comfort of the bosun's chair. We had no gloves and the thick black mixture stuck to our palms and fingers. It could resist the onslaughts at sea of sun, salt and storms, and despite diligent washing, it clung to our hands for days. At times, the plentiful, plain Blue Funnel food took on from our fingers the pungent and exotic flavouring of Stockholm tar, but we ate it all up anyway.

Zig-zagging across the Atlantic might have saved our lives, but it had also eaten into our coal stocks. With vast ocean wastelands ahead, it was decided to bunker at Durban, and *Antilochus* steamed gratefully into that busy Natal harbour to replenish her stocks. Long trains of coal wagons brought our supplies to the dockside; then the precious black chunks of fuel poured like an ebony avalanche into the gaping mouth of our hungry ship.

It was my job simply to stand there and see that everything went smoothly. It didn't. The docker directing the flow of coal momentarily missed his aim. Right next to the bunkering hatch was the ship's radio cabin. Suddenly it was engulfed in a dense black cloud and a moving mountain of coal burst down the cabin door. Radio Officer Smith, sitting inside, was buried up to nose level in coal lumps.

I plunged into the black mass, shouting for help and clawing desperately with bare hands to exhume our freshly buried Sparks. It took two or three of us nearly an hour to get him out. He looked like an unwashed coal miner, was understandably furious, and surprisingly unhurt. Reward for the rescue came instantly. With the other midshipmen, I had to shovel the deck clear of coal, sweep it clean, then scrub it until there was no trace of the near-lethal deluge. The bosun stood over us as we worked, his face wearing a crimson, outraged glare as he muttered, 'How could such a cock-up happen on *my* ship?'

After the Durban debacle, *Antilochus* swung her grey bows

13

eastwards, heading, I hoped, for Australia. I intended, if I could, to visit my birthplace in Hamilton, and look up my relatives along the shores of Australia's great Hunter River. But first we had to sail a lone passage across one of the remotest ocean regions on earth.

The ship's Master decided to follow a 'composite great circle', a course between 40 and 45 degrees south. He was following a traditional route which was not quite the shortest sailing distance, but which avoided the more ruthless of the Roaring Forties, those perpetual, gale-force winds that sweep unchallenged across the ocean brink of earth's most southerly frontiers.

For days we churned our solitary passage towards my birthplace. The only thing alive between ourselves and the desolate peaks of Antarctica seemed to be the huge, black and white bird which glided along mournfully sea-mile after sea-mile over the wake of our ship.

It was the first time I had seen the legendary albatross. This amazing bird must have stretched more than twelve feet from wingtip to wingtip, and I saw with surprise and wonder that it never flapped its wings. With gentle but powerful undulations that pulled in the power from the salt-sprayed air currents, the albatross floated ceaselessly just a few feet adrift of our stern. I have since seen hundreds of these strange, enormous creatures during my voyages across the southern oceans, but I'll always remember my first albatross; it left the ship one night as I slept, but the memory of the bird's haunting grace still stays vividly with me. I am not surprised that the Ancient Mariner believed that to kill one would instantly becalm a ship; I don't know of a single sailor who has tested the legend.

My first sighting of Australia for fifteen years came as *Antilochus* steamed into Fremantle harbour. Like my midshipman chums, I worked a seven-day week learning the basic crafts of my profession, but the first mate decided that a couple of us could have half a day ashore simply because I was, as I told him, an Australian citizen returning proudly to the land of his birth. Delighted, and just a little wet-eyed at my homecoming, I headed with a pal into Fremantle. The place surely was in Australia, but to the Aussie man-of-the-world – myself – it seemed disappointing.

There was one main street, close to the docks, and wooden

shacks with occasional overhanging balconies lined the side-walks. But Fremantle had one fine feature – a single-room, dockside bar where I drank my first, throat-cooling Australian beer. It tasted delicious, and I have loved Aussie brews ever since. After the beer, which of course broke company rules, it was back to the ship, up anchor, and away to Sydney.

The first mate had promised me weeks earlier that if we ever reached Sydney – he wouldn't say whether or not we were going there – I could have a whole day off to see my uncles, aunts and cousins who still lived in the house where I was born. I had written to the Taylors, at Boreas Road, Broadmeadow, earlier in the voyage to say how much I wanted to see them whenever my ship reached Sydney. Now was the time to remind the first mate of his promise. 'Arnott, you are not speaking to a man who breaks his word,' he chuckled. I laughed too, but it was really with excitement at the thought of going back to the white, wooden house where my parents had themselves laughed and loved.

Since that heady morning, I have sailed into most of the great harbours of the world, but I believe Sydney has the finest of them all. As the ocean-weary *Antilochus* steamed under the superb sun-arch of Sydney Harbour Bridge, I caught my breath at the splendid vista ahead. I was glowing with inward pride – here was my birthland.

However *Antilochus* had not steamed half-way round the world solely for its junior midshipman to stand and admire the scenery. We were bringing thousands of tons of machinery, motor parts, metal tools, whisky and general consumer goods for the Australian market. All that first day was spent unloading, and I played my part in keeping a close eye on our priceless British exports going ashore. Every penny of return was needed for the war effort, and like every other port in the world, the Sydney docks had their share of petty thieves ready to pounce the moment a ship's officers relaxed their guard.

Next morning I caught a train around 10 a.m. from Sydney to Newcastle. It was November, and by mid-morning the summer Australian sun made the air stifling and uncomfortable in the crowded, stop-and-start coastal carriages. Blue Funnel decreed that midshipmen went ashore in uniform, but whoever wrote that regulation had never sat in a packed Aussie train in a shade temperature of 90 degrees. Fortunately, I had decided that an

15

open-necked white shirt and grey flannels would be a lot more sensible, so I left the rule book on board ship.

My father had told me, before I left England, that Broadmeadow was the local station for Boreas Road. I asked the man sitting opposite me if we were getting near Broadmeadow. He said, 'I'm getting off before then, but you just watch out for the Broadmeadow racecourse. Then leap for the door, or you'll be past it.' Everyone, it seemed, knew Broadmeadow because of the racetrack. I was to learn that my Australian cousins loved to gamble on the track almost as much as they enjoyed sinking gallons of their bubbling beers. Of those traits, in a modest sort of way, I absolutely approved.

I left the Broadmeadow station, and wandered along a narrow, unmade road. The place didn't seem to have changed at all from what I could remember as a very small boy. Everywhere was hot, and sullenly silent. It was the absence of people that worried me; no Dad, no Mum, no uncles and aunts. It wasn't anything like the shouting and kissing homecoming I had dreamed about.

Suddenly I heard a loud 'Hi, Bob!' It was Old Man Taylor, my great-uncle, who had with his own hands built the house where I was born. He threw a gaunt, powerful arm around me as he came up from behind, and his warm 'Wow, you've grown, son,' instantly swept away the lonely doubts that had been creeping into my mind. From under his giant stetson, he explained that he had come to the station, but must have missed me there. He pointed over the brow of the hill. 'That, Bob, is where you were born.' I saw the house's white wooden walls, reflecting the sizzling noon sunshine. I knew I was truly home.

My great-uncle led me into the house, where I was hugged, kissed and cuddled by relatives I never knew I had. They gave me a kind of welcome Australians keep for their own folks, and rarely lavish on visiting 'pommies'. The whole Taylor clan declared I couldn't go back to Sydney that night; there was so much to do, so many friends to meet after fifteen years away. I had to agree. I despatched an urgent telegram to *Antilochus* asking for three days' leave and, surprisingly, I got it.

During those days, I felt and lived like a visiting king. The Taylors and their friends fed me up with their choicest beef steaks, best cuts of lamb, finest fresh vegetables, and lovely local beers. I put on more than half a stone in less than half a week – and there was no Stockholm tar relish added to those marvellous menus.

I was eager to see the picturesque Hunter River country where my father had trundled me as a toddler on his 'pop' delivery rounds, and I borrowed a horse for my sightseeing. Happily, it was a quiet, pleasant-natured animal, for I'm no cowboy. I felt both proud and humble, a true son of my native land, as Ben, my mount, carried me through the Hamilton lanes where my dad had travelled in his horsedrawn carts so many years earlier.

I was glad when the sun went down after a day on horseback in fierce heat. In the cool evenings, I sat with the Taylor family on the wooden verandah outside the house and swapped stories about the years between. Sitting outside was the only sort of air-conditioning the Taylors had, but it was all so friendly and peaceful that I felt totally at home.

It was a weepy farewell all round. Still wearing his tall stetson, Old Man Taylor walked with me to the railway station. 'Son,' he said, 'we're going to miss you here. Don't let it be too long before you're back with us.' He gripped my shoulders, hugging me to him for a moment, and then I was stepping, red-eyed, onto the Sydney-bound train.

As I arrived back on board *Antilochus*, her massive holds were being crammed with thousands of bales of raw wool. It wasn't a cargo likely to appeal to petty thieves, but it had to be stowed exactly right, or valuable shipping space would be wasted. With my fellow midshipmen, I stood on deck in the shadow of the dockside derricks, watching and learning just how the wool should be stowed away. My thoughts wandered to the up-country sheep stations where the prosperity of my native land had all started, and then to the Yorkshire and Lancashire woollen mills which would turn the rough wools into fine suits, or into uniforms for our servicemen.

'Hey cobber, are you with us or do you want to go ashore and join the sheep?' The heavy humour of the bosun brought me back from daydreams. It was time to finish loading, weigh anchor and sail back into the seas of war.

The homeward run took us back across the Indian Ocean to Cape Town, round the African coast to the deep water anchorage off Freetown, Sierra Leone. *Antilochus* sat out there for a few days as ship after ship joined us to form a convoy for the next, dangerous stage of our passage. Then we sailed into mid-Atlantic, away from the German-occupied coastlines, around the north of Ireland and into the Mersey to Liverpool.

An hour's train ride took me on leave to the sixteen-bedroom Kingston Hotel at Fleetwood, where Mum was now staying alone. Dad had volunteered for the Royal Air Force, where he became a squadron leader. Many thousands of airmen were training in nearby Blackpool, and they packed the coast's hotels and boarding-houses. But because my mother was living alone, the authorities wouldn't turn our hotel's fine accommodation into RAF billets. They obviously didn't know Mum very well: at 4 ft 10 in, she could make strong men shrink with just a few words. I still remember the quiet telling-off she gave me when, a couple of years earlier, she heard that, with a school pal, I had built a still to brew up potato hooch. Both Dad and I had long realised who was boss at the Kingston Hotel.

One thing Mum couldn't do was drive a car. When he went off to the RAF, my father left his blue Triumph Gloria standing forlornly in the hotel garage. In those days, there was no driving test; you just filled in a form for a licence and immediately got one. I had been driving Dad's cars since I was eleven – unofficially – and now that I was old enough at seventeen to go out on the roads, I started up the Triumph and edged her out carefully.

'Come on, Mum,' I called, 'we're going for a ride.' She got in beside me, giving me a stern 'be careful' look. I drove across the lovely, hilly Lancashire countryside around Preston and Bolton to the mill town of Bury, where my parents had been brought up. As I looked at the grey mill chimney smoke, hovering like an ashen blanket over the town centre, I wondered just how many of our Australian woollen bales would end up there being spun and woven on the local looms.

Chapter 4

It wasn't always my mother sitting in the low-slung, comfortable leather seats of the little Triumph. In the fourth form of the co-ed Fleetwood Grammar School, I had met a pretty fourteen year old by the name of Joan Hardern. Now, after my months at sea, she seemed to have changed mysteriously into a darkly attractive beauty. And that wasn't just my opinion. The discerning officials of Fleetwood Corporation had recruited Joan to feature as a cover girl on the resort's holiday brochure. She was a warm and delightful adornment to the pale blue Gloria as we drove cheerfully along Fleetwood's picturesque promenade, or slipped away to splash out the precious petrol ration on a trip to the Lake District.

Joan and I are now grandparents with more than a quarter of a century of marvellous marriage, but in courtship I was something of a slow starter. Romance was a condition I drifted into with Joan at a very slow rate of knots. As school chums, we had occasionally taken an evening out at the pictures, and Joan had been faintly surprised when I took along trigonometry problems to work on during the intervals, rather than chatting to her over an ice cream. But Joan was a patient sort of girl. She turned up to support the school cricket team in its meanderings around Lancashire playing other grammar schools, and she cheered loudest of all when I took eight wickets for seven runs against St Joseph's College, Blackpool – one of our traditional summer enemies. With her form friends, Joan had shivered on windswept rugby touchlines to give her faithful support to Fleetwood Grammar's XV, in which I played second row forward. She was a fine young sportswoman herself, playing a graceful but devastating flow of tennis shots at the local St Peter's Club courts, where we were both members.

Now Joan Hardern had come home on her first leave from the Auxiliary Territorial Service with which she had been posted to the Isle of Man to learn how to intercept enemy radio signals.

Having quickly mastered that delicate and vital war-time art, Joan had returned to Fleetwood in her smart khaki uniform just as I arrived home from my six months' round-the-world voyage on *Antilochus*.

'And what happened to all the letters from the lovely far-away places you visited?' asked Joan suddenly as we zipped along the A6 towards the Carnforth turn-off for the Lakes. The question interrupted my concentration on the powerful, purring performances of the Gloria's Coventry Climax engine.

'Letters, what letters?' I mumbled vaguely.

'Well, you know, the things you pop into postboxes in overseas ports to let people know how you're getting on. I don't seem to have had any.'

My memory ranged rapidly over the blue waters and anchorages between Bermuda and Sydney, and I realised with a sudden pang of guilt that I had left the harbour lights of exotic ports across the world without sending so much as a picture postcard to this laughing, lovely girl who was, I supposed, my first-ever girl friend. 'Sorry, Joan,' I answered shamelessly. 'You know how I hate writing letters. If I was sitting down to plot a course, well that's different.'

Joan shook her pretty head ruefully. 'Thanks for making me feel wanted,' she smiled. 'It would be nice once in a while to hear from dear Bob in English rather than listening to all those boring radio messages from Hitler.' I chuckled, and lowered my head a little over the wheel.

That evening we drove back to Fleetwood for a dance at the seafront Marine Hall. I held Joan's slim young body close to mine as we moved around the floor. Yes, perhaps I should have written to her after all. There was definitely more to Joan than cricket, rugger, tennis and trigonometry. Yet in that February of 1941, I had only one intense, true love in my life – the sea.

Joan kissed me briefly on the lips as I stepped aboard the Liverpool-bound train at Fleetwood station. We waved to each other as the old black steam locomotive drew the clattering carriages noisily on their way. I drew my head back inside, closed the window by its thick leather strap, and sat down thoughtfully. I was going to miss Joan's sparkling eyes and her friendly, refreshing warmth. Through the carriage window, the soft, peaceful contours of the Fylde coastland slipped rapidly away. The oceans and the war were waiting for me at the other end of the tracks.

Within hours, I was carrying my gear on board the *Denbighshire*, a recently built motor vessel of around 9000 tons gross. Owned by Glen Lines, the ship was operated during the war by Blue Funnel out of Liverpool. For this trip, hundreds of closely packed bunks had been built in every available bit of space below decks, while on top carpenters had fitted dozens of small wooden sheds: the latrines for the 600 or so troops we were taking out to the Middle East.

Soon we were heading around the north of Ireland to join other troop ships packed with courageous men in khaki destined to fight in the hot and bloody North African campaigns. Ship after ship cruised into view at the North Atlantic rendezvous area. Through my binoculars, I read off some of the names of the world's most famous vessels. There was the giant French passenger liner *Pasteur*, the first ship before the war to have lawn tennis courts; now she had joined Cunard for war service. Then I saw the huge, yet graceful bulk of the *Empress of Canada*, the giant P and O ships *Strathaird* and *Strathnaver*, the Union Castle liner *Warwick Castle*, and, from Holland, the pride of their merchant fleet, the enormous *Johan van Oldenbarnevelt* – named after one of that country's legendary patriots. I also noticed in the cluster of naval escorts the mighty predominance of HMS *Nelson*, the sixteen-inch guns of which ranged protectively across the chill Atlantic horizons.

Overhead, the prowling, long-distance Fokker-Wolfe reconnaissance planes skirted the fringes of our immense convoy. The aircrafts' crackling radio sets must have been hard-pressed to transmit all the detailed intelligence on the one hundred or so vessels that finally steamed resolutely westwards, carrying a combined cargo of more than 100,000 fighting men. I wondered if the German fliers reported to their HQ that the smallest ship in that vast fleet was MV *Denbighshire*. Probably not, for we were dwarfed beside the ocean leviathans, and I learned with some chagrin that our orders were to 'Stay in the centre of the convoy for your own protection.'

The commanding officer of the troops on our ship appealed to us to keep them busy. This wasn't easy on a smallish cargo vessel never intended for passengers, but we appointed successive squads of soldiers as extra look-outs at strategic points around

21

the decks, and on the wings of the bridge, men from the Royal Corps of Signals quickly gained their maritime merit marks by spotting and transcribing at high speed the flashing morse signals from the command ships. They didn't, of course, understand the close-range flag signals, but we did and between us we made a first-class team which, as on *Antilochus*, more often than not beat the rest of the convoy in recognising and acting on urgent ship-to-ship orders.

'Well done, lads,' said our own captain. 'We're not the biggest but, believe me, we're the best.' A simple compliment, but it helped to keep shipboard morale high as we switched course south towards Africa.

As *Denbighshire* surged across the South Atlantic, through warmer and safer waters, HMS *Nelson* peeled away with some of her own smaller naval escorts, like so many mother hens leaving their fast-growing chickens to fend for themselves. Cheerful signals wishing 'God Speed' and 'Good Luck' flashed across the waves, and our salt-sprayed, sunburned soldiers cheered staunchly on deck as they watched the sleek, grey shapes slide swiftly over the horizon. Then we were almost alone on guard duty, with just the odd naval ship here and there along the leviathan length of the convoy on its way round the Cape of Good Hope to Alexandria.

Crossing the Equator brought a welcome break from daily shipboard routine. With my midshipmen chums, I spread the word among the army boys that, as the ship crossed the line, there would be a definite and noisy bump. Then, we added, water in bathtubs and toilets would flow straight down for a few minutes before swirling round the opposite way to the direction it did in the Northern Hemisphere.

Most of the lads had never been further to sea than in a rowboat in their local park lake, and to a man, including the officers, they swallowed our tall tales. They waited on deck nervously as we neared the magic moment. A blast on the hooter signalled we were there, but after a half an hour of tremulous trepidations and anxious inspections of the ship's waterworks, our khaki friends came to the good-natured conclusion that they'd been had. Then, for extra measure, we threw most of them in a makeshift swimming pool in the traditional crossing-the-line dunking ceremony.

Off the South African coast, the convoy split into two groups for refuelling; our half headed for Durban, the other for Cape Town. German subs had left us alone, but the giant Dutchman *Johan van Oldenbarnevelt* narrowly missed inflicting lethal damage on the ships closest to her – and the little *Denbighshire* was closest of all. Our eagle-eyed boys of the Royal Signals suddenly saw the flashing morse message: 'Our engines have jammed and cannot slow down or go astern.' The Dutch ship was less than half a mile away, and slewing round towards her nearest and dearest at a truly alarming rate. Our look-out lads had been the first to spot her signal, and passed it on to the first mate in time for us to take instant evasive action. Happily, the *Johan van Oldenbarnevelt* was able to break out of the convoy without hitting anyone, but it took an hour for her huge bulk to slow down, clear of the main body of ships. Later, she limped into Durban for extensive engine repairs.

One or two refurbishments in the port itself were also necessary after our soldiers hit town. They had been at sea for three weeks, and went ashore while their vessels took on fuel. Some 50,000 troops were let loose on the unsuspecting South African citizenry. I had been looking forward to a couple of days ashore, but I was reluctantly recruited to help the army provost staff break up fights in dockside hostelries, return the intemperate khaki heroes to their ships, and generally try to retain the South African populace as our allies. It was hectic, but reasonably good natured. The only real casualty I came across was a major from our ship, not at all liked by his men, who was ambushed ashore by a number of masked troops, who severely dented his military pride by slicing off half of his moustache.

As the ships' bunkers were filled, each vessel left independently to make its way northwards. Sailing through the Mozambique Channel along the Madagascar coastline, we came across a British cruiser on patrol. She steamed alongside for an hour or two, and brought her Royal Marine bandsmen on deck to play Souza marches and 'Rule Britannia', our soldiers clearing away the last of their hangovers by joining in lustily with words all of their own. It was a brief, colourful and emotional meeting between passing ships at war.

We were due to deliver our troops to Alexandria, at the eastern end of the Nile delta, but sunken ships at both ends of the Suez Canal trapped us for a few days in the Great Bitter

Lake. I helped to keep the men cheerful and busy by taking them on swimming and sailing trips in the ship's lifeboats until news came through that the waters behind us had been cleared. Then it was back to Suez with our troops and cargo of war materials.

It took us about a week to unload men and stores, with German dive bombers roaring overhead several times a day. They swooped down like fearsome falcons spewing their explosive eggs of death. Whenever air-raid sirens sounded, the men from the Royal Pioneer Corps, who were in the ship's hold helping the Arab stevedores to unload, were under orders to hurry ashore to the nearest air-raid shelter. One day the Captain looked at me thoughtfully as I joined him on the bridge. 'Arnott,' he said, 'it seems to me that not many of the army lads are going ashore when the sirens sound. Next time, take a look below and see what's happening.'

I didn't have long to wait. Within minutes the sirens blared their warning shrieks. I decided to take a look down Number One hold, where thousands of bottles of Guinness, destined for NAAFIs throughout North Africa, were being unloaded. As I swung down into the hold, I heard, sung softly, 'Bless 'em all, bless 'em all, the long and the short and the tall.' The chink of glasses and the pungent, Irish tang of Guinness hit me as I approached the songsters. In a corner of the hold, in almost complete darkness, the resourceful members of His Majesty's Pioneer Corps had built a bar, complete with dates and tiny clementine oranges in wooden dishes on the counter. I shone my torch on the cheerful scene.

'Will you be joining us, sir?' enquired an anxious Pioneer private. Regretfully I had to say no. I called 'Time, gentlemen, please' on that unique little pub with its unlimited supplies of free Guinness.

Our troops went westwards overland to the battle zones. *Denbighshire* headed south down the Red Sea, then out into the Indian Ocean towards the steamy waterways of Malaysia and my first glimpse of the night lights of Singapore, before they were suddenly switched off by the Imperial Japanese Army.

Chapter 5

The rowdy, daily shipboard hubbub of shouted commands from sergeant-majors, of tommies laughing, grumbling, snoring, had all suddenly slipped away as our small slice of the North African Army disembarked at Suez. I missed the din from our human cargo, now safely delivered in port. But *Denbighshire* still had to earn her keep. We would have to seek out and cart across the seas more commonplace loads.

I heard on the ship's almost infallible word-of-mouth telegraph system that we were to fetch a cargo of tons and tons of rubber, waiting for us at the southern tip of the Malay peninsula. *Denbighshire*, scarcely two years old, surged southwards through the Red Sea at a beefy 18 knots. We made swift passage to the Strait of Malacca, called briefly at Penang, looked in at Port Swettenham, the port of Kuala Lumpur, then on to the scorching, sweaty island colony of Singapore, founded by Sir Thomas Raffles in 1819.

As the huge bales of rubber were swung into our holds, I meditated on the cool, elegant idea of taking a taxi to the swish hotel bearing Raffles' name on the other side of town, and relaxing in one of the wicker armchairs with an iced gin and tonic or perhaps a cold mint tea. Musing never became reality until years later. In the summer of 1941, I wasn't quite in the big league of lavish, Far Eastern spenders; my midshipman's pay was still £9 a year, plus a war-risk booster of £5 a month. Hardly a buccaneer's riches. Instead, with a couple of shipmates, I took a penny rickshaw ride to Singapore's sunset strip of nightclubs.

The rickshaw boys handed out the lore of the local night spots for no extra charge. 'You see New World, Great World, Happy World,' said my charioteer. 'Nice girls, nice beer and nice ice.' The nightclub owners hadn't gone in for too much originality in naming their booze bazaars. These various 'worlds' were dimly lit, pleasantly cool, drinking and dancing clubs; the New World,

I found, lived up rather better to its expansive title than the other two.

After a hot, shirt-drenching day on deck, it was totally refreshing to relax over a three-penny half pint of beer, cooling off under the ever-swishing fan blades set in the New World's low, dark ceiling. The chilled airstreams wafting around the club came from huge blocks of ice standing in drip-trays sited liberally around the bar and dance floor. Occasionally we danced with the lovely Malaysian nightclub girls to the surprisingly professional beat of the club's own small band. Just how much it would have cost to buy an aftermath of more intense pleasures from the dark-skinned beauties, I never got round to asking. I had a feeling that all my War Risk wealth and a year's Blue Funnel pay wouldn't quite have matched the bill.

In any case, there were more serious sea-going adventures at hand. Our shipping agents had booked aboard *Denbighshire* a live cargo of more than 1000 *hadjis* – pilgrims bound for Mecca – complete with dozens of goats destined for ritual Moslem slaughter each day of the voyage. The migrant Moslems took over the ship's centre castle accommodation so recently vacated by troops. The midshipmen got a joint retainer of a penny per pilgrim for seeing to their daily food and water needs, plus a few extra shillings for looking after the goats. The land-based agents who fixed that rate did not, I felt, take into account the pervasive pong from the poor animals penned up in stifling heat on the ship's afterdeck.

Half-way across the Indian Ocean, the senior midshipman and myself decided enough was enough, both for us and for the goats. When we saw that the daily list of chores handed out by the first mate included 'Clean out goat pen', it seemed a fine chance to shift the animals out for a spell, hose them down, and literally clear the decks. But the goats wouldn't co-operate when I took a hundred-foot heaving line, and put a clove hitch around each horn. The animals unanimously pointed up their objections by trying to butt me over the side of the ship. The riot of snorting, heaving, kicking goats became even worse when we dragged them out of their enclosure and hosed them down. The goats' leader at once tried to dive into the sea, taking his entire roped-up chain gang with him. It was all a most unholy mess.

Happily, the senior midshipman headed off the suicide squad while I pulled at the other end of the line with the desperate

26

strength of a whole tug-of-war team. There were no casualties, and the first mate never found out just how near we came to wrecking the whole pilgrimage, for the daily fresh meat ritual is a crucial feature of a journey to Mecca.

The patient and piously quiet pilgrims left *Denbighshire* at Jeddah, the Saudi Arabian port forty miles west of Mecca. We executed a rapid about-turn to head for Durban and re-fuelling.

On a velvety, moonlit African night, as *Denbighshire* raced swiftly along the Mozambique Channel – she was one of the fastest cargo vessels around at the time – I spotted the silhouette of a surfaced submarine standing silently between ourselves and the Cape Province coastline. The lean, wolfish outline etched sharply against the shimmering black tropical sky told me instantly this was a German U-boat.

Our Captain decided to press on southwards at full speed. He could do little else. I watched the submarine through my night binoculars and whispered an anxious prayer. If the U-boat commander had decided to attack, the brief career of *Denbighshire* and perhaps that of Robert Arnott and his chums would certainly and swiftly have come to a watery end. But the German hunter allowed an easy maritime meal to slip away. Perhaps he was waiting to swallow bigger fish.

Still thankful for that moonlit reprieve, we sailed across the Mersey Bar to reach Liverpool on a sunny August afternoon in 1941. I had been at sea since March, and now left *Denbighshire* to spend a few days' leave with my mother and father near Ipswich, where Dad was then serving in the Royal Air Force, running the RAF station fire service at Woodbridge. He had taken over a house at the edge of the aerodrome, and I saw, a little sadly, that he had brought along the little Triumph Gloria. I polished up its familiar bodywork, chrome headlamps and bumpers until they shone, and maybe I did too well, for my father quickly recruited me to do a similar job on his fire engines.

Then it was across Britain to Avonmouth to join the old freighter *Glenogle* in Bristol docks. Built in 1920, she had no running water system, and as we headed out across the North Atlantic for New York, I reluctantly became accustomed to drawing water for the midshipmen's quarters by using a farm-type hand pump which stood, with incongruous rustic charm, outside the galley. It was a full thirty-yard walk from that wretched cold water pump to the halfdeck, where *Glenogle*'s two midshipmen were housed. As the heaving grey Atlantic swells threw our decks around, it was not uncommon to reach the shelter of the halfdeck with just a few inches of water in the bottom of a bucket. Sometimes I lost the lot.

My senior midshipman was Tony Orchard, a young ex-public school southerner who stood even taller than myself. We got on well. When I arrived, fuming, back in the halfdeck with an empty bucket, Tony would grin cheerfully: 'Well done, Bob. Now try again.' He was the first fellow I met at sea who drew an allowance from home. It enabled us to swagger grandly down Broadway after we reached New York, stopping at every hotdog stand to devour the scrumptious novelties. At one stand, Tony had paid with a ten dollar bill. Half an hour later we realised we had walked off without getting change. Even with his allowance, Tony couldn't absorb such a cash leakage. Apprehensively, we located the hotdog seller. He laughed: 'Here's your greenbacks, young buddies. I'd have chased after you, but who would have looked after the stand?'

New York seemed much friendlier after that fiscal encounter. The piers and docks were then bursting with lend-lease activity. Today, the big jets have reduced the ocean terminals to a forlorn, despondent desert, but then, in the gathering tides of war, the New York waterfront was an exciting, bustling mecca for two sea-struck midshipmen. Soon, loaded with lend-lease war materials for Britain, we were churning through a westerly gale as we headed for Halifax before braving the sub-infested Atlantic seaways.

Our Master decided I should join the ship's gun crew, and I practised long hours on the 20-mm Oerlikon cannons that made up much of our meagre armaments. My early fusillades were scattered like sunbeams across the skies, but disciplined training quickly brought potting proficiency, a skill that was lying in wait for the Japanese pilot we shot into the sea off Batavia some months later.

On leave after *Glenogle* arrived at Avonmouth, I found my chums at Fleetwood Rugby Club – where I now played second row forward – were genuinely inquisitive about my first trip to the States. In those pre-jet days, travel across the Atlantic was still much of a rarity. 'Will they come into the war?' and 'Is it true everyone earns twice as much there as we do over here?' and 'Can you let me have any nylons for my girl friend?' – these were the sort of anxious queries thrown at me over pints of Lancashire ale in the club bar.

As a very junior midshipman, I didn't really have the close confidence of the United States Government on their military intentions, nor had I carried out any market research on American salaries. And the few pairs of sleek Dupont stockings I had been able to afford were strictly for Joan Hardern. But I found that opening the bar chat with 'When I was on Broadway the other day,' or describing the succulent delights of the hamburger, still known in Britain only as a morsel of the movies, rapidly brought the beer talk back to the universally interesting and undemanding topics of entertainment and food. That I could handle.

These rugby club reveries were sharply interrupted when orders arrived for me to report to Victoria Dock, Birkenhead. Awaiting my tread up the gangplank was a tough old lady of the sea, who had been around since the days of Edward VII. Apart from showing a few more grimy smoke-streaks across her grey camouflage, SS *Antilochus* hadn't changed at all.

Nor had her halfdeck. As I swung my sea-gear through the well-worn doorway of the midshipman's quarters, I half expected to see a giant fruit cake marching serenely across the familiar centre table. 'Welcome aboard,' came a warm, unknown voice from one of the darker corners of the communal cabin, and the slim, dark frame of Senior Midshipman John Chapman emerged. He shook my hand. None of my old mates in the halfdeck from my last voyage on the old freighter was still aboard, he told me, but he had more cheerful news. I was no longer lowest of the low, a junior midshipman; now I was number three. That small step upwards on the promotion ladder thrilled me almost as much as taking over the *QE2*. Maybe now I wouldn't be elected 'Peggy' quite so often. And now that I was eighteen, my War Risk money had just been raised to £10 a month. On that cold November morning, with a chill Mersey fog swirling across the decks, the outlook seemed positively sunny.

Chapman, a year or two older than myself, told me he didn't intend to stay with Blue Funnel after the war. 'Going into the pilotage, you know,' said John. 'Lot less whizzing round the world.' He kept his word: when I took *QE2* to Melbourne on her 1978 world cruise, the chief pilot and harbourmaster there was a bulkier, greyer but still warmly welcoming John Chapman. He came on board the super-ship to greet me. We sipped Scotch and water, and talked about that *Antilochus* adventure of '42.

Westerly gales whipped the North Atlantic into a seething, heaving mass of sea-mountains as the old steamer crossed that sub-infested ocean. Decks were awash with freezing, swirling foam spewed from the stormy depths. In all my career at sea, I have never been seasick, but on that violent crossing I felt heartily sorry for many of my shipmates, who lurched about their daily tasks with faces a hue of bilious green. And yet no one complained. We knew that storm-tossed seas generally gave better protection from U-boat attack than one or two Royal Navy escorts. It was better to suffer than sink.

So we came safely to Cristobal, at the northern end of the Panama canal. As *Antilochus* sailed into Limon Bay, I tingled with as much excited expectation as a disciplined, up-and-coming young navigator could reasonably show at the prospect of negotiating for the first time the forty miles of canal waters between Atlantic and Pacific oceans.

By way of a bonus, I had heard the USO club at Cristobal served up the finest banana splits anywhere in the Western world. Having just left a rationed and hungry Britain, where bananas were as rare as air on the moon, I couldn't wait to taste the fruity delicacy. The USO club was a superb, land-of-plenty version of our British NAAFIs, and the banana splits were breathtakingly enormous and quite delicious. As *Antilochus* took on coal stocks for the Pacific crossing, I ate the creamy confections until quite suddenly I felt sick, and I decided I never wanted to see the succulent yellow prime product of the Panama republic again.

With coal bunkers and banana appetites well filled, we edged forward into the canal's locks that would lift our ship more than eighty feet above sea level for its ocean interchange. United States security forces came on board at Cristobal and took over the whole vessel; armed guards stood on the bridge, uniformed sentries took up posts around the decks and big men with bulky hip holsters climbed noisily down to our engine room. When I heard the American officer in charge give the command 'Raise nets', I wondered briefly if they mistakenly believed we were some sort of outsized trawler. In fact, he was talking about a huge net that came up from the floor of the lock to brush the bottom of our hull, ensuring that no one threw overboard anything likely to blow a hole in the walls of the canal – a further impressive facet of the ruthlessly intensive American security system. This time the net raised nothing more dangerous than our discarded Panamanian banana skins.

From the Gatun lake, on the northern end of the canal, we emerged to head out into the Gulf of Panama bound for the island of Pitcairn. Thousands of blue Pacific sea-miles later, I saw the cloud-topped peaks of the lonely volcanic isle climb over the westerly horizon. I felt something of Pitcairn's stark, surf-drenched appeal that must have gripped Fletcher Christian when he landed with his mutineers from the *Bounty* more than 150 years earlier. Now descendants of Fletcher and the other mutineers drove their high-powered craft through the cruel breakers to board our steamer which stood safely out in deeper water. Light-skinned, cheerful and claiming convincingly that the copper trinkets they offered us were from the old *Bounty* metalwork, the islanders traded carved fishes, cleverly made wooden boxes with trick locks and their dried leaf collections. It seemed that most of the one hundred or so inhabitants had come on board with mementoes made 'from the *Bounty*'. Said the bosun: 'From all the years they've been selling bits of the *Bounty*, she must have been bigger than the *Queen Mary*.'

It was, however, unwise to doubt the veracity of those tough seafarers while enjoying the hospitality of their home waters. So we happily bartered our own civilised trinkets such as razors, blades, cigarette machines and papers, wads of tobacco and old copies of books in return for booty claiming direct descent from the ship of the unfortunate Bligh.

The islanders eagerly read the letters we had brought from the mainland, and we took on board their sack of mail for our next port of call at Wellington, New Zealand. Among the letters were a dozen or so from a New Zealand schoolteacher and his wife, the only non-mutineer people on Pitcairn. We watched the islanders' surf-boats making precarious landings on their harsh, precipitous shores, then we upped anchor and made full speed across the vast stretches of the blue Southern Pacific towards my first-ever landfall in New Zealand.

In my top ten of the world's most stunningly beautiful harbours, I would certainly include Port Nicholson, the deep-water anchorage for the New Zealand capital. *Antilochus* came in through Cook Strait and I marvelled at the navigational feat of the Royal Navy captain who first saw that sublime bay set against towering hills after bringing his ship half-way round the world under simple sail. This lovely sight reminded me of the wilder landscapes of northern England, and I wondered if that supreme seaman, Captain James Cook, had visualised the contours of his native Yorkshire as he caught sight of that same vista from the bridge of the *Endeavour*. Whitby and Wellington, I mused, shared a mutual natural magnificence.

But I had little time for scenic admiration on that trip. Trucks, guns, tank parts and desperately needed war materials were already stocked in our hold for delivery to Japanese-threatened Singapore. At Wellington, we loaded NAAFI supplies, including thousands of packs of chocolate, and headed through the Bass Strait to top up our bunkers at Fremantle before starting out on a frantic, boiler-bursting clip through the Java Sea. We had to try to reach Singapore before the gentlemen from Japan. We lost the race.

Chapter 6

We were just twenty-four hours out of Singapore when the Japanese swarmed in. Our officers didn't tell us what it was all about as *Antilochus* suddenly changed course, but the halfdeck's 'brotherhood of navigators', chaired by Third Midshipman Arnott, quickly worked out the game we were playing on the dangerous waters of the Java Sea.

The situation must have been desperate to call for such a complete turn about. This was one time, we felt, when the middies should be told what was happening, and I was elected as spokesman to put a straight question to the mate. 'Sir,' I ventured, 'we wondered why we're now steaming directly away from Singapore when we were only a day out of the port?'

The mate gave me a quizzical look. 'Young sir,' he said, 'I know full well that you and your pals in the halfdeck probably know as much about the ship's position as we do on the bridge. But what you don't know is that we've just had a "hurry up" signal to get away from Singapore just as fast as we can. The Japs are already in there.'

What a difference just one day can make, I thought, between a free life on the oceans and imprisonment in a Japanese lock-up. 'Thank you, sir,' I replied politely, moving away towards the halfdeck, where my chums were eagerly waiting to hear if our calculations had been right. We had come up with our exact position without any charts. Star sightings, dead reckoning and a few school atlases were all the navigational aids we needed.

I pulled up my chair to the halfdeck's solid table. 'Right lads,' I said. 'Now let's see where we're running to escape from these Japs.' The unanimous verdict of the 'brotherhood' was that *Antilochus* was steaming towards Batavia (now Djakarta), on the island of Java. Again we scored ten out of ten.

Batavia's huge harbour was already filling up rapidly with ships from many Allied nations; like us, they were fleeing from the scorching rays of the Rising Sun. But the sultry harbour waters offered no hiding place, we found, as the Japs sent their carrier-based fighter-bombers screeching in after us. For five days, *Antilochus* lay alongside under a daily cloudburst of bombs. Between attacks, units from assorted Allied armies turned up to raid our holds for jeeps, pick-up trucks, guns and shells originally intended for the now-captive garrison at Singapore.

At that time, the Mitsubishi company were not turning out cars and superb hi-fi equipment. In 1941 and 1942, their top models were the A6-M Zero fighter-bombers and the G3M torpedo-bombers, and these had obliterated, in waters not very far from us, the battleships *Prince of Wales* and *Repulse*.

Now it was our turn. The Mitsubishi menaces chased in each day's dawn. Ships' sirens, hooting 'Action stations' in communal consternation, echoed across the crowded harbour's waters from first light to dusk as the Japanese pilots swooped on sitting targets they could hardly miss. Against brand new cannons and machine guns spitting stacatto death from freshly built aircraft, many of the anchored merchantmen could fight back only with aged armaments rescued from the First World War. All around us, the Japanese were blasting ships, crews and still-smoking antique guns to the bottom of the Java Sea. I sat in my canvas harness, exhilarated beyond fear by the thrill of battle, squeezing relentlessly the trigger of my 20-mm Oerlikon cannon.

From the heavens, a Zero screamed in at mast-top height. Its shining silver wings, gleaming in the sun, hurtled towards me like fine steel blades that seemed about to slice me from the face of the earth. Then somewhere a voice called: 'Hold your fire.' For me, the order wasn't necessary. As the Zero hurtled across *Antilochus*, my cannon jammed, but not before I saw smoke pouring from the plane's fuselage. The Zero plunged into the sea, exploding as it hit the water, just yards ahead of our ship.

'That, my lads, was definitely one for us!' The shout came from our ship's Royal Marine. Many merchant vessels were carrying a marine to look after their weaponry, and our bloke, like the rest of us, was beaming with excitement. I lifted my tin hat to wipe steaming sweat from my forehead.

The Marine called out to me, 'Did you hear me order the crew of the 12-pounder to hold their fire until the plane was point-blank? They couldn't miss.'

34

So that was what I'd heard. Maybe the old World War One 12-pounder had downed the Zero, but I knew that my own Oerlikon had been hurling high-explosive shells at the fighter-bomber at the rate of more than 500 rounds a minute – until the gun jammed a split second before the Jap hit the waves. It didn't really matter who killed the Zero. We had fought together as underdog sea-dogs and had, for an instant, come out on top. It was beers all round on *Antilochus* on that evening.

In their fantastic, careering conquests, Japanese troops were rarely far behind their naval carriers. Sure enough, we heard by radio next morning that landing craft were pouring hordes of battalions into Surabaja on Java's eastern flank. We'd tackled fighters and torpedo-bombers with shells from antique cannons, and were still afloat, but now the general feeling was that we should quit while we were ahead. The bare backs of our Chinese stokers glistened as they hurled coal lumps into the boiler fires. We fled through the Sunda Strait towards the solid safety of Australia.

Sea and sky were black as tar. *Antilochus* vibrated with the power of her surging steam pistons, sending her at full speed into what should have been the safer waters of the Indian Ocean. I dropped into my bunk, totally exhausted while Java and Sumatra slipped away astern. A shattering, violent bang tossed me cruelly out of sweet sleep. 'Oh God,' I exclaimed, 'we've been torpedoed!' I plunged into a pair of trousers and ran barefoot across the dark decks to join officers already gathering anxiously on the bridge.

It wasn't a torpedo. A mystery ship, perhaps Japanese, had hit us amidships on the starboard side. It had ripped a huge gash in our half-inch-thick steel plates before escaping into the darkness. Water was already pouring into our holds. I had no time even to cover my bare feet with sea boots before I had to race below to help set up the pumps.

Complete black-out was the commonsense rule for staying alive at sea, but for just a few minutes the Captain ordered all lights switched on. It was, he decided, vital to check the damage. The ship's searchlights focused on the crash area as I stood in a cargo hold just above the waterline. I looked through the jagged tear right out across the dark, heaving ocean. No more sleep that night. Only pump power would keep us afloat until first light, when the crew craftsmen could start desperate repairs. The pumps huffed and wheezed, but managed to throw out the

35

swirling salt seas as fast as they were pouring into the wounded belly of *Antilochus*.

The fierce dawn of another tropical day burst over the horizon. Light streamed through the enormous gap. It looked as if someone had launched a huge battering ram at the side of the ship and punched a hole some ten feet square through her steel plates. With pumps working every second of the day and night and planks rigged over the lower part of the gash, we crept like a wounded animal into Fremantle.

Repair men there looked dubiously at the damage. It was, they decided, too severe for them to tackle, so we crawled at an even slower rate to the Cockatoo Dry Dock at Sydney. I wasn't too depressed when I was told that the job of putting *Antilochus* right would take about six weeks – what a marvellous chance to get to know my birthplace quite a bit better. This was, I decided, a positively happy backlash to that Indonesian pile-up. As the Aussie welders worked with white-hot torches on our starboard plating, I set out each evening for one of the coolest spots in the city. With three pals from *Antilochus*, I made for the Glaciarium Ice Rink at the top of Sydney's George Street. From being an absolute duffer on the ice, I quickly learned to cruise confidently round the rink with the local 'Sheilas' to the latest records of Glenn Miller, Tommy Dorsey and Paul Whiteman.

The good Sydney folks often invited us home for meals during that long summer semester. Sometimes, with my buddies David Alcock, John Chapman and wee Derek Wood, I would take a bus out to Chatsworth in the north of the city for a delightful Sunday lunch with the Geddes family. Perhaps their beautiful daughters, Margot and Pam, attracted my pals as much as Mrs Geddes' wonderful cooking. I had to agree that the Geddes girls were gorgeous, but my own number-one girl was still the sea, with the delectable Joan a short head away at number two.

However, the Cockatoo Dry Dock ship repairers wasted no time, and my days of ice skating, tennis and eating ice cream at downtown picture shows faded out after just six weeks. Then, it was back to loading giant bales of wool from the sheep stations and hundreds of cases of canned fruit sent by a cannery in Tasmania. A short call at Auckland for coal, and we headed out into the Pacific for the lengthy sea voyage to the Panama Canal.

It was exactly 3.55 a.m. We were in mid-ocean. I had just left the slumbering shelter of the halfdeck to go up on deck for my watch, which started at four. *Antilochus* was, as usual, under complete black-out. By way of an early breakfast, I munched an apple as I walked towards the bridge.

S-w-oo-sh, a huge black shape hurtled past on the port quarter. Another ship, I saw, also in total darkness, was racing past us in the opposite direction. There were no more than 30 yards between us. I hurled my apple in disgust at the dark stranger. How many other near misses, I wondered, were there between ships playing blind man's buff, even on the earth's vastest stretch of ocean?

With no more similar shocks, we arrived at the southern approach to the Panama Canal, passed through the Miraflores and Pedro Miguel locks into the main section, down through the Gatun locks and then bunkered at Cristobel before poking our bows out warily into the Caribbean, where German subs had been sinking Allied ships with dreadful, depressing frequency. Steaming towards the Florida Keys, *Antilochus* regularly sliced through chunks of drifting wreckage from slaughtered vessels. We scanned the seas around *Antilochus* with anxious eyes for signs of subs setting us up as the next victim. My binoculars ranged over the far waters and came upon what looked like a rag waving in the wind from a wedge of floating wood. At once I told my officer of the watch, who called the Captain.

As we steamed nearer, the mystery object took on the unmistakable shape of a Blue Funnel lifeboat. These were huge, sturdy craft, built specially for the Line by a Hong Kong firm of boatbuilders. This particular lifeboat told its own silent tale of a recent sinking. I wondered if the 'Old Man' would follow strict war-time orders and flee from the scene as quickly as possible. But loyalty to Blue Funnel shipwrecked comrades swept away caution. We were soon throwing rope ladders over the side to the cheering seamen packed closely together on the lifeboat thwarts.

Captain Peter Jackson, then fourth officer of the sunken ship, was one of the men I helped up the ladders onto the sun-splashed deck of *Antilochus*, and he later told us what had happened. On 27 May 1942, the Blue Funnel Line ship *Mentor* was bound from New Orleans to Bombay. At 6.22 p.m. the vessel was struck amidships by a torpedo, and a second torpedo a few minutes later quickly sank it, most of the crew managing to scramble into lifeboats and on two rafts.

They had sent out distress calls, giving the position of the sinking, hoping that they would be picked up by the US Coast Guard. Other Allied ships would not normally come near a distress call, knowing there was an enemy submarine in the vicinity. No Coast Guard rescuers showed up. The men of the *Mentor* learned later that their radio had been faulty and had not sent out the transmissions. They decided to make use of the slightly northerly breeze and head south-east, in the hope of making the nearest land, the island of Cuba, which was some 300 miles away.

Several days later Peter Jackson was at the lifeboat tiller when he noticed a faint smudge of smoke on the horizon and, with mounting hope of rescue, the men aboard the lifeboat watched *Antilochus* slowly approach. In view of the many ploys used by U-boats to entice ships, the Captain of *Antilochus* would have been quite justified in sailing in the opposite direction as soon as he saw their sail, but he went over to investigate and took the risk of stopping to pick them up.

Since that first meeting so many years ago, Peter Jackson and I have met many times, and after hostilities ended, we both joined the Cunard Line. Much later, I took over command of Peter's ship, *Cunard Adventurer* so that he could join the *Queen Elizabeth II*. That first meeting in 1942 was very much in both our thoughts as Peter handed over command to me in such different circumstances.

Back in 1942, a fierce tropical storm lashed *Antilochus* with stinging rain torrents soon after we brought Peter and his shipmates in from their open boat. They slept, warm and dry, as the Caribbean clouds burst their bouncing raindrops across our decks. With the forty survivors, we hugged the Florida coastline to make passage north, and at Key West, we joined a convoy also moving in the general direction of our trans-atlantic assembly point at Halifax, Nova Scotia. The ships sailed only by day, for in a series of devastating night-time attacks, the German subs had been sinking scores of merchantmen. At last it had been realised that the blacked-out moving ships were seen by the U-boat commanders as sharp silhouettes set against the glaring lights of the American coastal cities. All the submarines had to do was sit out at sea and wait for their unsuspecting prizes to steam into neon-lit torpedo range.

Our coastal fleet anchored for the night as we reached the Chesapeake Bay. That night a heavy fog enshrouded the coast, sealing off the wide estuaries that normally carried busy, round-the-clock traffic in and out of the bay. At first light, the fog billowed away in a freshening breeze. I had an instinctive feeling that something was wrong, and I looked across at Third Mate Mathias, my watch officer on the bridge. 'Mr Mathias,' I ventured, 'I think we are aground.'

The officer's brow creased with sudden concern. 'Don't be ridiculous, Arnott,' he frowned. 'How on earth can we be aground?'

I didn't know how, but I was sure that we were. 'Look over there, Mr Mathias.' I pointed out into the bay. All the other ships at anchor were heading in the opposite direction to us. I took a sounding. 'I think we'll float off with next tide,' I told the crestfallen officer.

'I should bloody well hope so,' he muttered. Happily for the career of Mr Mathias, we did.

Antilochus chased after the long-gone coastal convoy to the next overnight anchorage in Delaware Bay, then it was onto the Staten Island refuge of New York harbour, up the East River, through Long Island Sound, Rhode Island Sound, across Buzzard's Bay and a hurried dash to Halifax through the Cape Cod canal. There we anchored well clear of hostile submarines in the sanctuary of Dartmouth Bay. Over the next couple of days, another fifty ships joined us for a mass burst eastwards across the Atlantic.

It was, as it turned out, such a routine crossing that as we came into the North-West Approaches off Ireland, our convoy commander decided he needed to waken everyone up, so he ordered a brisk session of target practice, a welcome break from the ship's daily round. Gun crews throughout the convoy blasted away lustily at imaginary overhead targets. Off duty next morning, I was sitting on the hatch outside the officers' saloon sipping orange squash when I noticed the woodwork had been ripped open by a line of small, jagged pockmarks. I took a closer look: the cavities were brand-new bullet holes.

Our old ship crossed the Mersey Bar to arrive in Liverpool on 2 July 1942. In a nine months' round-the-world voyage, we'd been machine-gunned by Japanese planes, holed by a hit-and-run mystery ship, run aground, and been at the wrong end of a barrage from 'one of ours'. And between times *Antilochus* had earned her keep as a workaday freighter. As we tied up in her home port, I thought that she still looked much younger and sprightlier than her thirty-six years.

I walked down the gangplank of *Antilochus* for the last time, took a tram to the railway station and booked a ticket for Fleetwood. But ten days later I was back again in Liverpool to join another vessel bound this time for the sweltering latitudes of equatorial Africa.

Chapter 7

For many years, the sturdy freighters of the Elder Dempster line had worked along the old slave routes carrying cocoa, groundnut oil, timber and precious metals from the ports of West Africa. Blue Funnel then took over these routes using their own ships, including the 6,000-ton motor vessel *Prometheus*, in which I sailed from Liverpool bound for these exotic lands.

Captain Kerr, Master of the *Prometheus*, was a tall, dour Scotsman. Like most sea captains of this era, he presented a remote, austere figure, rarely bothering to speak to any of the crew, apart from his chief officer and chief engineer. It was only in the 1950s that a social revolution at sea transformed Captains into approachable human beings. Then the formerly godlike creatures, especially those on cruise liners, began to play their now-familiar role of ambassador, host, raconteur and public relations officer. Captain Kerr was undoubtedly from the earlier breed of strong, silent men of the sea, but like many other old Masters, he displayed the odd foible. I have known a Captain who walked along the decks at midnight reciting Shakespeare, one who believed he could see into the future and another who wrote romantic poems. Captain Kerr had a catapult.

Perhaps imagining that his domain of the bridge was a castle turret, the good Captain peppered the decks with bombardments of small lumps of coal delivered with ferocious velocity from his catapult. Now and again, he let fly at a passing seagull. The midshipmen were the Captain's ammunition carriers. He sent orders that we were to keep his special box on the bridge well topped up with pieces of coal from the galley fire stocks. I felt that humping coal from galley to bridge did little for my progress in seamanship, but because the Captain's commands were law, I said nothing and did my share of the coal chores. The enigmatic Master never offered any reason for frequently making the ship's well-scrubbed decks take on the look of a coal mine face. He was boss, and did not need to explain himself.

Another unusual facet of shipboard life on the old West African freighter was that the officer's smoke-room boasted an upright, walnut honky-tonk piano. I never heard of any other ship sailing the perilous summer seas of '42 to the accompaniment of a plink-plonk one-finger version of 'Roll out the Barrel'. The finger was mine. I rolled out that particular tune incessantly until my shipmates vehemently advised me to put a sock in it. Eventually I managed to broaden my repertoire by one or two other ditties.

We were carrying crated aircraft for the Middle East war, and these were unloaded at Takoradi in the then Gold Coast, the first West African port of call. Royal Air Force men there had built their own artificial harbour, enclosing the breakwater so that the bulky, yet delicate loads would reach the shore undamaged. After supervising unloading all day, the two other midshipmen and I took a taxi ride to nearby Sekondi, where we wandered around the local bars, putting away a respectable number of pints. At the end of the evening, we had only a few shillings left between us, so we had to thumb our way back to the ship. Luckily, it seemed, an old Dormobile pulled up for us almost immediately.

As the battered vehicle got near to the docks, the driver demanded a fare that was far more than we judged the trip to be worth and, besides, we didn't have that sort of cash. Some large, black gentlemen travelling with the driver lent their support to his ransom demand. Beefy and fit as we were, we were outnumbered, outweighed and far from home. I kept up a verbal bargaining battle with the driver until we came in sight of the dock gates. RAF police on duty there saw arms waving in the mini-bus, and hastily climbed aboard to our rescue. 'In future, do your drinking in our own bars,' advised the RAF police sergeant.

Back in our quarters, the three of us decided we would take that advice and curtail our explorations of the African hinterland. When we sailed into the waters of the Niger delta to pick up Britain-bound cargo at Port Harcourt we wandered no further inshore than to the bar of the sergeants' mess in the British services' camp.

It was a sheer delight at the end of a day's loading under the scorching African sun to swap dungarees for white drills and head for the smoky shade of the mess where the steward served up deliciously chilled English beers at the sort of prices we could afford. My own favourite brew, cold Worthington, had a wonderfully refreshing tonic effect as the first pint of the evening gushed into my parched throat. Perhaps the resuscitation was enhanced by the view through the bar-room windows of the beautiful profusion of hibiscus splashed against a background of palm and mangrove.

Laden with palm oil, *Prometheus* picked up her homeward convoy at Freetown, where forty vessels had mustered for mutual support and safety in one of Africa's finest natural harbours. Then we swept out into mid-Atlantic to face the steel pack waiting hungrily beneath the waves. On watch in the cool night hours, I saw red, flaming spumes spurt across the deep black waters. Each brief holocaust spoke of the terrors of torpedoes and agonies of drowning men. With morning light, gaps in the convoy line computed the cost in ships and blood.

Off Africa, day-time attacks were rare, but as we drew abreast of Gibraltar, the signal came: 'Scatter! Scatter! Scatter!' The stalking U-boats were launching an impudent noonday assault. Splinters of merchant ships and bodies of the men who sailed in them were blasted into the skies. For those still alive as they hit the water, there was no help from convoy comrades: we fled.

As our ships wearily grouped up again several hours later, I saw a Belgian freighter moving into the convoy line just a few hundred yards ahead. Without warning, she suddenly veered to port. A smaller British steamer, thankfully regaining her own particular place, was sliced amidships by the Belgian, whose steering gear had probably been damaged during the earlier attack. The British ship plunged to eternal oblivion with all her crew in less than ten minutes. *Prometheus* made all speed northwards to reach Liverpool unharmed on 23 October 1942.

It was to be five months before I sailed in another Blue Funnel ship, when at last the tides of war were starting to turn in the Allied nations' favour. The Japanese had been halted in New Guinea, General Montgomery's Eighth Army had just smashed the German and Italian desert armies at El Alamein, and the Americans had landed on Guadalcanal. After Monty's troops had chased Rommel's Afrika Korps across hundreds of miles of North African desert, the Allied armies linked up with the American and British forces coming in from the sea. In Europe, a Combined Operations raid on Dieppe pointed the way for the big invasion across the Channel. And that was why I stayed ashore.

Every merchant ship has detailed plans of its cargo holds, essential when the Master and his officers are working out where to stow the many varied items on a typical ship's manifest (inventory of cargo). But when the Allied commanders began planning the assault on Europe, it was vital to check every measurement on these plans against the actual interior of the ships to see if the plans were accurate; this helped to decide which spaces would carry tanks, guns, trucks and men. I was assigned to the Sea Transport Department in Liverpool, the division of officers, mostly from the Royal Naval Volunteer Reserve, who went down into the holds with tape measures and notebooks.

These old sea dogs had spent all their working lives in the Merchant Navy and knew every corner of a ship. My own pre-invasion role was primarily to stand holding the end of a tape measure while the RNVR chaps did most of the calculations. It wasn't as easy as it seemed; a pillar or stanchion in the centre of a hold might not be shown on the ship's plans, and could mean that the space was not wide enough to hold a huge tank or piece of field artillery. Day after day, we worked in the ships of many nations, and I came to realise, as I groped around in the holds of some of the foreign freighters, exactly how trim and tidy were the cargo compartments of the Blue Funnel ships.

My normally ruddy cheeks were turning quite pale from the many hours I had to spend in the gloom of ships' cellars, but working in Liverpool had its compensations as I was able to travel home to Fleetwood for Christmas. My father had been posted to India, but my mother had been saving up her food-ration coupons to produce a Christmas Day lunch of roast turkey, sage and onion stuffing, apple sauce, Brussels sprouts, roast potatoes followed by a rum-soaked Christmas pudding heavy with fruit and topped by a delicious white sauce. To bring such a spread to the table in the middle of the war was, I felt, a small miracle of domestic management, and I told my mother so. For a moment tears clouded her eyes. 'Bob, lad,' she said, 'with all of you away in the war, and me just sitting here at home, it's the least I can do.'

It seemed, too, as if Joan had been saving up her kisses for those few Christmas-leave days. She looked lovelier than ever, and the sweet warmth of her lips plus, I suppose, the fresh Irish sea breezes as we walked briskly arm in arm along the deserted promenade, began to put back some of the rosy glow into my pallid face. The hours, alas, flashed by in the way that pleasurable times will, and too soon I was again waving goodbye to Joan, to journey not this time to Liverpool but to North Wales – and back to school.

The Outward Bound Sea School in two large houses at Aberdovey in Merionethshire (now Gwynedd) had opened a month or two earlier, the Welsh extension of the famous Scottish public school of Gordonstoun where Prince Charles later spent his early years. The Blue Funnel Line helped Gordonstoun with the finances at Aberdovey, and sent their midshipmen there, a dozen at a time, to sample the establishment's Spartan delights. True to the Gordonstoun pattern, these included showers every morning in cold mountain spring water, a strict early to bed, early to rise regime, no smoking or drinking, treks across the mountains and swimming in the freezing currents in Cardigan Bay. The school owned a waterfront shed and from there, in a small fleet of cutters and lifeboats, we tried out our seamanship skills in much closer contact with the waves than was ever possible on large cargo ships.

Courses at Aberdovey lasted a month. During my spell there, apart from the twelve middies from Blue Funnel there were also a dozen or so officer cadets from the training ship HMS *Conway*, a similar number from Gordonstoun itself and a mixed group of deck lads and apprentices from industrial towns. Most of the 'other ranks' on my course were boys in the leather trade from Northampton, a marvellous bunch, always ready to tackle the toughest assignment. Some of the more polished public school customers from *Conway* were already adept at evading any task they didn't fancy, but our officers in charge, including some Blue Funnel men, cut away their veneer by the end of the first week.

In the second week we were all becoming good pals, growing leaner and fitter as the disciplined demands on our minds and bodies began to bite. If I had been ordered, when I arrived at

45

Aberdovey, to undertake a two-mile run, followed the next day by a five-mile run, then by a marathon 32-mile walk, I would probably have replied, 'You must be joking.' Before the end of the first month, I had done them all, and in near record times. But it wasn't always work and sleep, although we were generally so healthily tired that it was sheer relief to climb into our bunks at ten each night and collapse into instant sleep. Sometimes we played the odd prank on our officers, such as taking the screws from their beds so that frames, sheets, blankets and man hit the stone cold floor in a cursing, tangled heap. And once we filled the pillows of Third Officer Martin, from Blue Funnel, with coke dust from the stocks for our open fires. His head was lost in a grey cloud of foul smelling powder, but perhaps this discomfort provided some sort of counter-irritant to the pain inflicted by the claws of Aberdovey beach crabs, which we had planted at the same time among Martin's bedclothes.

After successfully surviving the first month of Spartan torments, I decided to stay on a second month as a 'guardian' or group leader. Now it was my own bed that was dismantled, or filled with crabs and starfish. By day, I led treks across the mountains or carted the boys by car for miles to hike back across the Welsh countryside. Sometimes I used the Ford V8 owned by the school's manager, a Mr Hogan. I would fill up at the village garage and tell the owner, 'Mr Hogan will call in with the coupons,' but when I mentioned this to Hogan after several fill-ups, he became, I thought, quite unnecessarily agitated. 'Good God, Bob, I've no bloody petrol coupons,' he shouted with flushed face. 'I thought you had some.' I hadn't.

Ration coupons were as rare and precious as the gold mined in the Merionethshire mountains north of Aberdovey. Fortunately, Mr Hogan secured a fresh supply of the priceless paper tokens in time to save our reputations.

As a school guardian, I occasionally had access to rather more exotic food than was available to first-month novices. Somehow Mr Hogan had acquired the services of a Chinese servant, one Mr Wong, who had been officers' steward on the *Denbighshire* when I was there. From him, I learned the appetising way in which our Chinese friends celebrate New Year. Magically, Mr Wong produced for the officers and myself a feast of more than twenty individual Chinese dishes. It was the start of my life-long love affair with Chinese food. Succulent spare ribs, sweet and sour pork, bean sprouts, fried rice, bamboo shoots, mushrooms and lots of other Chinese delicacies made me realise that there must be some resourceful Oriental system of getting round the British rationing scheme.

Sometimes on marches into the far hills behind Aberdovey we would call at a remote farmhouse. There, the buxom farmer's wife sold delightful ham-and-egg tea for a few coppers, and as a special treat for the hungry youngsters, she would prepare an after-tea titbit of small, hot pancakes – as many as the boys could eat. On one famous occasion, a Northampton leather apprentice in my party put away more than seventy. I think the good farmer's wife had to revise the terms of her offer soon after that.

From time to time, the majestic, two-masted Gordonstoun schooner *Prince Louis* would sweep into Cardigan Bay with sails billowing under fresh breezes tumbling down from the Welsh mountain peaks. She looked magnificent, but wasn't quite the sort of ship in which to send raw beginners out into the bay's bumpy waters. Nevertheless, lads with little sea experience climbed cheerfully aboard the schooner at Aberdovey, with no idea of the sufferings ahead. Twelve of us would help to crew *Prince Louis* across the bay to anchor at Abersoch. At that time, the Aberdovey lads had no official uniform, and our baggy RAF denims were in sharp contrast to the smart grey shorts and shirts worn by the Gordonstoun boys on board. But these stylish outfits were no defence against seasickness. The Scottish public school youngsters were just as sick as the rest. On average, nine of the twelve young crewmen would be really ill from the moment we set sail until *Prince Louis* anchored.

Their misery brought a bonus beano to those of us who were immune. Our eating tables were two stout planks slung from the deck head with, at mealtimes, six lads sitting on each side. The cook always sent food for twelve up from the galley. The steaming plates would start to slide up and down the planks as the bows pitched into the waves – and suddenly there were only three of us sitting at the 'table'. Catering at the Aberdovey school was nutritious, but sparse, and those of us remaining downed the extra three meals each in rather less time than would have been taken by a starving shark.

Those short trips on *Prince Louis* set me longing to return to sea. I enjoyed the rough, tough days at Aberdovey Sea School, but I had long since realised that my destiny was out there on the oceans. With a clutch of silver medals for Outward Bound achievements wrapped carefully between jerseys in my duffle bag, I climbed onto a north-bound train. In Liverpool, I signed on the steam-turbine freighter *Asphalion*, which was to take me to the region of koala, kangaroo and full-bodied foaming beers.

Chapter 8

Taking over *QE2* was still a little way off, but I made just a small advance along the promotion path when I joined *Asphalion* on 1 March 1943. Now I was senior midshipman of the four lads making the trip to South Africa and Australia. At nineteen, with my own 'crew' of junior midshipmen in the halfdeck, I cheerfully and optimistically reckoned that my career at sea was making swift headway.

Two of my middies were youngsters whose seaboots later followed mine onto the Cunard decks. Bill Deslands, an old boy of the Merchant Taylors school at Crosby, later became assistant marine superintendent with Cunard in Liverpool, while the second lad, one K. T. Jones – nicknamed Katie – served, as I did, on the *Franconia*, the first *Queen Elizabeth*, the *Queen Mary* and a host of other Cunard passenger liners.

The third midshipman, another K. Jones, had been torpedoed on his first voyage. 'It's all right for you chaps,' he said. 'You don't know what it's like to be thrown into the sea. I don't mind telling you I'm worried to death it's going to happen again.'

'Come off it, Jonesy,' I answered, with more confidence than I felt. 'You're not going back into the drink on this trip. Tell you what, I'll stand you all a meal when we get to Cape Town.'

However, when we were abeam of Gibraltar, it seemed young Jones's anxieties were only too well founded. The twenty-year-old *Asphalion* was carrying a terrifying cargo of shells, bombs and high explosives, as were most of the other ships in our southbound convoy. When torpedoes hit them, they didn't go down. They went up. German subs lurked beneath the waves until darkness shrouded the convoy; then they blasted us. The crash of a nearby explosion hurled me from my bunk. I raced up to the bridge, flying metal and glowing lumps of red hot coal spattering me as I ran. Had we caught it this time?

I looked across the white-hot waves. An ammunition ship sailing next in line to *Asphalion* had vanished into the sky, searing through the heavens like a moon rocket. Burning coal from her boilers and jagged splinters of hot metal raining down from the sky onto our decks were all that remained of our companion ship. The sheer force of her leaving the water had lifted our own vessel, too, but so far as I could see, *Asphalion* herself had escaped that first vicious torpedo attack.

The ocean sky burned like a red dawn across the Indies, yet it was still only midnight. Incandescent violent death was hitting ships and sailors indiscriminately and, in my first hour on the bridge, I watched half a dozen ships disintegrate around us. I wondered how young Jones was taking it in the halfdeck below. Then, another British freighter and her men, spared like ourselves from the earlier torpedoes, suddenly erupted into a flaming, melting mass.

I would have stayed on the bridge until morning light, but Captain Evans told me in his slow, Cornish drawl, 'Try to get some sleep, Arnott. There's nothing either of us can do for those poor chaps out there.' It was galling, but the good Captain was absolutely right: our only hope of escape was to make full speed, some 12 knots, to get away from those hellish waters around Gibraltar. I fell into my bunk, fully dressed, and prayed that we would see another dawn.

Mercifully, we did, but twelve of our fifty-ship convoy would never greet daylight again. I helped my own team of youngsters with the melancholy chore of sweeping up shrapnel, coal and occasional splinters of blackened bone that had fallen from night skies to turn our decks into a gory shambles.

We reached Cape Town on my twentieth birthday, and young Jones reminded me of my promise. I said, 'We'll ask the mate if we can go ashore together. If he agrees, then you're on.' I knew that normally the mate would allow middies off the ship only a couple at a time, and I felt my cash was safe. But the mate let me down, saying 'OK, it's been a rough ride. You can all take a half day off.'

As well as a birthday celebration I decided to make the occasion a sort of thanksgiving dinner for our safe arrival. I took the lads that evening to Delmonico's, a steak restaurant in the centre of Cape Town, and my chums decided, perhaps because I was paying, they would do me the honour of eating their way through the menu. As we sat on the ornate balcony of Delmonico's, the hungry midshipmen waded through fresh

mealies (corn on the cob), boerewors – a sort of spiced sausage –
then chased their huge steaks with pineapples, bananas and
paw-paws. I began to worry whether the £20 savings I'd brought
with me would cover the bill as it mounted mercilessly, mouthful
by mouthful. In those days, it did, with even enough left over for
a few South African beers.

Earlier in the day, we had taken a bus to the foot of Table
Mountain to catch a cable car to the summit, but suddenly the
wind had freshened and ascents were banned for the rest of the
afternoon. I've tried several times since to get up that mountain,
but the view from its flat top still eludes me; bad weather sweeping across the Cape Peninsula highlands has somehow always
managed to arrive just as I was setting foot into the cable car.

Before we left Cape Town for the eastward crossing to
Australia, I bought a couple of books to while away the warm
hours on the Indian Ocean. *Mathematics for the Millions* and
Science for the Citizen would, I felt, help me along with my
self-teaching – a vital necessity for someone spending most days
of his young life away from any sort of classroom discipline. I
didn't look upon the hours of swotting at sea as any sort of
imposition. Strangely, perhaps, for someone who loved playing
rugger, tennis, cricket and squash as much as I did, I also
enjoyed solving the most way-out mathematical problems, and
often took my trigonometry work with me when I went on
watch through the night.

Asphalion arrived at Hobart, Tasmania, and I put away the
textbooks for a while to explore the gentle greenery of the lovely
island. With its orchards and farmlands, rolling hills and quiet
countryside, I found Tasmania reminded me very much of
England in springtime. We might well have been walking into
an English yacht club, too, when we visited the Royal Yacht
Club of Tasmania. Their commodore, a Mr Battie, shook the
four of us warmly by the hand with the always welcome words:
'Now, lads, what can we get you to drink?' Over large schooners
of beer, he invited us out for a cruise the next day aboard his
ocean-going yacht *Weenie* and, delighted, we accepted at once.

I told the first mate it wouldn't help Anglo-Australian
relations at all if we welshed on our invitation. Thrusting his
hands deep into his uniform trousers, the mate looked at me,
perplexed. He asked, 'Do you know what a *fait accompli* is,
Arnott?'

51

Feigning innocence, I replied, 'No, sir, what does it mean?'

The mate grinned. 'It means, you crafty devil, that I've had it, chum. You'd better be off with your pals.'

Weenie sailed sweetly across Hobart Harbour as the midshipmen from *Asphalion* hauled on halyards, tied down reefs and tried to look as if crewing the creamy white *Weenie* was just an everyday skill. All went well until *Weenie*'s swelling sails suddenly crumpled and we were becalmed. Mr Battie told us, apologetically, that he had no auxiliary motor. But he did have three lovely daughters who were crewing *Weenie*, I'm afraid, much more professionally than the four hands who had signed on for the day. We were lucky to have run out of breeze with such salubrious shipmates, and the next three lazy hours passed rather pleasantly, their father serving up cold beers while the girls rustled up salad sandwiches from below decks. It seemed something of a shame when the winds returned to clip us back to the yacht club.

Then, it was back to an irate mate ('So you haven't jumped ship, then?') and our own professional task of sailing *Asphalion* up the coast to Melbourne and Sydney. There, we loaded up supplies for Britain, set out on the long, and this time peaceful, voyage home, to arrive back in Liverpool at the beginning of September.

British losses in ships and men in the first years of war had left an acute shortage of certificated officers. Blue Funnel decided that I could now sit for my second-mate's exam after only two years at sea instead of the usual four, but first I had to take a stiff course at the Technical College, Liverpool, in navigation, ship construction, English and general seamanship subjects. For the weeks at college, I found digs with Mrs Jones, a landlady who 'served' the Blue Funnel line. She laid on a comfortable bed, breakfast and a generous evening meal for just 30 shillings (£1.50) a week. Saturdays and Sundays, of course, I spent at home in Fleetwood.

I heard on the Blue Funnel grapevine that my main examiner was to be one Captain Keeting, a man with a ferocious reputation dating back to his service in the First World War. He had, I found, mellowed somewhat between the wars and turned out to be quite a kind-hearted old chap. Perhaps that was because I knew most of the answers to the questions he was putting.

My first paper was for the lifeboat certificate. It involved describing how to launch the boats, illustrating how they were built and demonstrating how to box a compass. It is all a vital part of seamanship, particularly since the *Titanic* disaster, and even today the young men and women who are making their careers on the giant ocean liners such as the *QE2* take a similar sort of lifeboat exam.

I managed to pass this and all the other papers, and just a week later I was handed a slip of paper at Fleetwood Mercantile Marine Office which said simply Robert Harry Arnott was now the holder of a second-mate's certificate. I think that day I was the proudest man in the whole merchant service. The many hours I'd put in at sea with my nose in books had paid off. My mother was delighted, and I knew that when my airmail letter reached Dad in India he would be over the moon, too. Another boost was that I got an immediate company pay rise, and my War Risk allowance doubled to the fantastic figure of £20 a month – real riches in 1943.

My days in the halfdeck were over when I was posted to Glasgow as fourth officer on the motor vessel *Ajax*, in January 1944. I now wore one officer's stripe on my dark-blue jacket, and for the first time ever took over a cabin of my own. I felt I'd joined the ranks of ocean swells as I unpacked my sea bag in a compact cubby hole on *Ajax*'s port side just below the bridge.

I still have the little green notebook in which I recorded every fact I could find out about MV *Ajax*, the first vessel on which I could truly call myself a ship's officer. She was built by Scott's of Greenock in 1930 and had a war-time cargo capacity of 12,628 tons. Flipping through the pages, I see she had special compartments for fruit and meat, and carried six lifeboats plus a motor boat. I drew up detailed plans of the ship, and altogether amassed some 500 facts on her build and performance. This type of miniature survey is something I've continued to do from ship to ship. It's a valuable, instant working guide, but I must admit on the *QE2* I have to rely as well on official statistics because the ship's mammoth catalogue of facts and figures is truly mind-boggling.

Captain Kersley of the *Ajax* told me that part of my job as Fourth Officer would be spent looking after the welfare of the passengers. I wondered why he chuckled, but I quickly found out. The only passengers travelling turned out to be fifteen horses, two rams, seven sheep and one pig – all bound for Australia.

British racing was still in the war-time doldrums, but the sport was flourishing in Australia and New Zealand. The British Bloodstock Agency had sent aboard *Ajax* at Glasgow the stallions, First Edition (by Early School out of Atmosphere), and Whirlaway (Bahram–Jury), bound for the Kooba Stud at Riverina and the Widden Stud at Kerrabee respectively. The stallion Fortunate Trial (Fair Trial–Fortunate Lady) was going for transhipment to South Australia. Three other stallions, Ruthless (Hyperion–Correa), Lord Bobs (Nearco–Sister Sarah) and Pictavia (Nearco–Lovely Rosa), were booked to travel on from Melbourne to New Zealand.

Brood mares on board included Good Abbess (Robin Goodfellow–Buchaness), in foal to Pherozsha, Rayberry (Rameses the Second–Berystede), 'expecting' to Admiral's Walk, and Mrs Pipchin (Papyrus–Florence Dombey), in foal to Felstead. Also in the stables specially built for the consignment was the filly Fearless Flight (Fearless Fox–Fugit), as well as an unraced colt by Sol Oriens, a son of Hyperion, and a colt by Brumeux out of Laurel Wreath. There were fillies by Sir Cosmo, one of the fastest horses of his day, by King Salmon, and by Foxhunter, whose 'mum', Good Abbess, was the matriarch of our party.

I'm sure you'll forgive me for going into such detail about the ancestry of our equine emigrants. But I reckoned myself a knowledgeable student of horse breeding, and it's noteworthy that the progeny from our *Ajax* horses have since won hundreds of races on Australian and New Zealand tracks, right down to the present day.

All our animals were a friendly lot, especially the pig who had the grand title of Roundhill Proud Prince, with his breed number of 212 notched in an ear. But my favourites were the horses, and I spent many off-duty hours nuzzling their noses, talking quietly into their ears to soothe them or treating them to carrots I had 'borrowed' from the galley. There were two grooms on board to care for this valuable bloodstock, and I did everything I could to help them keep the horses contented in such strange, restless surroundings.

Ajax was fully capable of 16 knots, and because of her fairly high speed it was decided she would sail unescorted across the

Atlantic on her way to the Panama Canal. It was the first time I had ever ventured to the other side of the world without some sort of naval escort, and I worried as much for the safety of the horses and other livestock as I did for my shipmates. After all, the poor animals had absolutely no choice in being hoisted into this unfamiliar contraption that was our ship. Crossing the Atlantic, *Ajax* had to zig-zag on varying tacks and at full speed. This may have mystified the U-boat commanders, but it did not do much for our horses. They were often wretchedly seasick and their legs tended to swell because they could never settle down in their boxes. The incongruously named stallion, Ruthless, a most placid fellow, suffered agonies; as he brushed my cheek with his nose, I saw in his eyes the sort of wild, worried unhappiness I've seen so often in human victims of seasickness. Even when we had arrived in the calm safety of the Panama Canal and nausea subsided, one of our stallions – First Edition – became ill with colic. An American veterinary surgeon had to work on the poor horse the whole way through the locks. He pronounced him on the road to recovery only as *Ajax* was about to nose her bows into the Pacific.

Despite all these problems, when we arrived in Melbourne the local paper was able to run a banner headline proclaiming 'ENGLISH BLOODSTOCK COMPLETES LONG VOYAGE – ARRIVES HEALTHY'. It had been almost a full-time job for myself as well as the two grooms to achieve such a happy ending.

As fourth officer on *Ajax*, I took the 4 a.m. to 8 a.m. watch with Chief Officer Glynn Williams. I kept a close eye on the well-being of the lifeboats, took frequent star sightings and supervised work on the general cargo. This included, to the dismay of the Melbourne port authorities, hundreds of tons of high explosive. An official who came on board as we approached the port exclaimed, with real concern, 'Do you know, you're a bloody floating bomb?'

I knew this was absolutely true, but I said with as much nonchalance as I could muster, 'Oh, come off it. It's not as bad as that.' But it was. Throughout the voyage, no one had been allowed near the explosives deck in anything but soft rubber shoes or bare feet. Ordinary boots, which could have caused a fatal spark, were banned.

Melbourne port authorities decreed that *Ajax* could not take her explosive cargo into the harbour, and they diverted us into a remote anchorage off Port Melbourne, where the explosives were off-loaded. About half our livestock also left us at Melbourne, with the other animals staying on until Sydney.

One of the benefits, I reckoned, of working on watch through the night was that it gave me a lot of time off during the day for sightseeing or, when in Sydney, for going to the races. Jimmy, one of the horse grooms, claimed he knew all about Australian racing. 'All right, then,' I suggested, as we went ashore, 'see what you can come up with for tomorrow's meeting at Randwick.'

To me, Jimmy signalled his total lack of knowledge of the Australian racing scene by tipping an absolute outsider for the opening contest at the popular Sydney track. He said, 'Have a good bet on Royal Gem. It's going to be a star performer.'

I suffered delusions of grandeur about my own forecasting abilities in those days, and I told Jimmy, 'The animal has about as much chance of winning as I have of swimming back to England.' When we arrived on the track I saw the first race odds against Royal Gem were 100 to one. 'Told you it had no chance,' I said to Jimmy. 'Let's back something else.' But Jimmy was adamant about his selection, and eventually I agreed to place a five-shilling bet on his horse, and as soon as I had put my money down I wished I had followed my own good sense.

It was a maiden race, in other words, none of the entrants had ever won, and it seemed to me most unlikely that Royal Gem was about to lose his maiden status. But he did. I watched, open mouthed, as Jimmy's selection romped home. At 100 to one, I raked in £25, then tormented myself with typical gambling perversity that I should have staked a jolly sight more. After all, during the long hours that Jimmy, the other groom and I had watched over the thoroughbreds on *Ajax*, I'd come to respect their knowledge of horses. Why hadn't I remembered that a few moments earlier?

I congratulated Jimmy as if I had never doubted him, and bought him a couple of pints of foaming Australian brew by way of celebration. In the next few years, the nobly named Royal Gem lived up to his name by winning a whole host of races, including the valuable Melbourne Cup. But never again did he start at 100 to one.

Tragedy hit us in Sydney. One of our midshipmen, putting

the cover over *Ajax*'s number three hatch, slipped and fell forty feet into the hold below and was killed at once. One afternoon a few days later, I stood silently with Captain Kersley as the lad's coffin was lowered in the grave which was, I reflected sadly, so many thousands of miles away from his English home.

On the way back from Australia, we dropped off cattle at Colombo, Ceylon. Anchored there, I passed my watch one afternoon mending flags on the ship's 'monkey island' – the platform on top of the bridge – sitting shirtless in the hot overcast Ceylon sun with my legs crossed in native fashion. After my watch ended, I ate dinner, and an hour later was prostrate with pain. Luckily for me, we carried a ship's doctor, Dr Rowlands, who diagnosed acute sunstroke; apparently my pulse was racing and my temperature topped the hundred mark. It was into the sick bay for Fourth Officer Arnott. Then jaundice set in.

For the next six weeks I couldn't leave my cabin, and I grew to dislike thoroughly the sight of my cabin's walls which had so delighted me a few months earlier. As part of my treatment, I had to drink lots of fluid. I had no toilet in my cabin, but the doctor brought me bottles by the crate to pee in – and emptied them for me each day. As the south-west monsoons lashed *Ajax*, I cursed my stupidity for sitting out in the sun in the tropics.

Ajax plied her trade as a cargo carrier up and down the Indian coastline, but I stayed and sweated indoors. When the ship arrived in Bombay, the gateway to India, for me that gate was closed. It was only when we reached Calcutta that I was able to step ashore, somewhat shakily, onto the warm red soil of West Bengal. I didn't walk very far that day, but the next morning I decided to test the strength now returning to my wasted leg muscles and venture a little further into the city.

I particularly wanted to see the famous Maidan, a great open area containing the huge white marble Victoria Memorial. My long legs stood up to their test surprisingly well. I turned out of the Maidan and strolled into the adjoining street of Chowringhee. It seemed that most of Calcutta's crowded millions were there that morning, jostling and pushing each other – and me – as they hurried in and out of the street's shops, hotels, clubs and imposing public buildings. I decided I had better head for quieter meadows, and I was about to turn off the street near St Paul's Anglican Cathedral when I felt a tap on

57

the shoulder. Surprised, because I knew no one in Calcutta, I looked round. A broad, handsome figure in the unmistakable uniform of an RAF officer stood smiling at me: it was my father. I hesitated for a second, totally amazed. Then I flung my arms around him in a tearful embrace.

To say 'What are you doing here?' was absolutely inadequate at that moment. Yet they were the first words that sprang to both our lips. We stepped back, and laughed at each other. White-robed, hurrying Indians slowed down briefly, then moved to one side to pass these two big crazy Englishmen, shaking hands furiously, and completely blocking the pavement. My father had always been as keen on mathematics as myself, and we worked out that, roughly, the odds against us meeting on Chowringhee, at that precise second among the three million plus people in Calcutta that morning, must have been well over a billion to one.

Dad, it turned out, was spending a few days' break in Calcutta from his squadron leader's duties at Imphal, on the plain of Manipur. When I told him how ill I had been for the past few weeks, he was silent for a few moments. Then, looking thoughtful, he asked, 'Do you really think, Bob, that this meeting is just a wild chance?' I'm no fatalist, but I had to agree that it seemed most unlikely.

Dad and I ate Bengali freshwater prawns for lunch, washed down with fresh lime juice, and for 'afters' we kept cool with chilled custard apples, lychees and papayas. Then I took him back on board ship to meet my fellow officers. Captain Kersley shook his head in disbelief: 'First a 100 to one winner in Sydney and now this, Arnott. What are you going to do for the hattrick?'

Dad was staying at Calcutta's Grand Hotel with RAF friends, and as I still wasn't back on full duties, I spent many pleasant hours in the lounge there, sipping gin. He, in turn, often came to the ship where it was my privilege to pay for the gin sips. At only five shillings a bottle, our excellent ship's gin was well within my price range.

A few months later, when *Ajax* again docked in Calcutta, I decided on the spur of the moment to call at the Grand to see if by some remote chance my father was again staying there. I asked at the reception desk for Squadron Leader Arnott, but the sari-clad girl there said 'Sorree – the officer gentleman not booked in.' It seemed a pity to waste my taxi fare to the hotel, so I bought a gin and relaxed in the cool shade of the foyer lounge. I wondered exactly where Dad was, for the Manipur plain had been the scene of violent clashes with the Japanese.

My glass was empty. Should I have another? A familiar, wide pair of shoulders was silhouetted by the sun in the hotel doorway. Yes, I would order again. 'Waiter, over here please. And a gin for you, Dad?'

Chapter 9

A few days later, my father came down to wave goodbye as *Ajax* again left the Calcutta dockside. He was due to be posted to Ceylon, and was hoping to be there by the time *Ajax* called in on her way to Australia. I had calculated this should be around the time of my twenty-first birthday, which would be as good an excuse as any for another party.

When we reached the port of Colombo, I went to the nearby RAF station – a massive establishment – and asked if Squadron Leader Arnott had arrived. My good luck was still running: Dad had reached Colombo just a few days earlier. That night, the eve of my birthday, we launched into yet another reunion booze-up. This time we were joined by Ken Pemberton, a regular RAF officer from Fleetwood. Ken's father was the sergeant-major of the Officers' Training Cadet Unit at Rossall Public School, just a few miles along the coast from my parents' hotel, while Ken himself had been at the local grammar school only a few years ahead of myself. In just the few days since they had met he and Dad had become firm friends, and we all had a lot of nostalgic Lancashire tales to swap as the birthday evening went on.

Amazingly, Ken conjured up a bottle of fine Scotch whisky, a rarity scarcer than diamonds in war-time Ceylon, and I still don't know how he came by it. Armed with the precious bottle, the three of us set out for a little Chinese restaurant near the camp where we ordered three curried chickens and three dozen hard-boiled eggs – a combination which, Ken vowed, would enhance the tang of his whisky.

As we polished off the food, we sipped the golden liquid as delicately and slowly as its rarity deserved. Then, a group of young officers from the aircraft carrier *The Attacker* walked into the restaurant and, with a keen naval nose for good Scotch, came straight over to our table. More glasses were produced, and in minutes the navy men had seen off all our priceless

Scotch. By way of reparation, they invited us back to their mess on *The Attacker*. Whisky stocks after weeks at sea were low, but we all switched quite happily to the Navy's cool, clear gin, and the party tippled along until 5.30 in the morning. *Ajax* was sailing on the 6 a.m. tide, and I arrived on the bridge, shaved, bathed and humming 'I'm twenty-one today', only minutes before she weighed anchor. 'God, Arnott,' declared Captain Kersley, 'you must have the stamina of an elephant.'

I modestly denied the assertion, but even after the all-night party my head was clear and there was no sign of a hangover – the sort of attribute that is still fairly valuable to the Master of the world's largest floating hotel.

Our first call in Australia was at Port Pirie in the Spencer Gulf, to pick up a cargo of lead ingots from the works of the Broken Hill Mining Company. I walked up the port's main street; like many other small Australian towns, it could have been an old Wild West Hollywood film set. There was just one line of faded, white-painted wooden houses with fenced balconies that hung out over the street. This was cut by a single railway line running down to the dockside. A tall, leather-faced mining man who turned up at the ship in a steeple stetson to discuss loading cargo could have walked right out of an old black and white Buck Jones cowboy movie.

After loading the ingots straight from the smelting works, we sailed out of the Spencer Gulf towards Adelaide. Some of the ingots weighed more than 90 lb and caused problems in handling the ship, for such a heavy cargo in the holds makes a vessel 'stiff' and unresponsive. As we left the gulf for open seas, a heavy swell hit *Ajax*, sending her rolling like a drunken elephant. The ship's officers, including myself, had just sat down to dinner when the first huge wave hit us. Plates, cutlery, drinking glasses and tureens of hot food were bounced into the air, splattering our white uniforms and then smashing to the deck. I ate dinner later that night from an inelegant but unassailable Australian billy can.

Ajax returned to Britain laden with butter and wool at the beginning of October 1944. The Allied invasion forces were already biting into northern France, and in the south of that country, American armies had landed to initiate a nutcracker crush on Hitler's Wehrmacht. Two of my fellow *Ajax* officers had fallen into a trap, too – the tender one of matrimony. I was

61

best man at each of their weddings, and trotted out roughly the same speech at both receptions. This worried me afterwards and I mentioned it to my father months later. 'Don't let it get to you, Bob,' he told me. 'Politicians do that sort of thing all the time.'

We turned the ship round quickly, and by Christmas I was back in Australia. On Christmas Day, one or two of us went surfing and swimming at Coogee beach, Sydney, next door to the famous Bondi. It was a lovely hot summer's day, and I forgot the power of those great, rolling crested waves. One of them picked me up like a toddler's toy, spun me round and hurled me heavily onto the sands. Not a very pleasant Christmas experience, particularly after the generous helpings of food and strong Australian beers we had just been putting away.

Those Aussie beers seemed to follow me around. In Sydney, we picked up hundreds of tons of bottled Richmond lager for the troops in India, and before we unloaded it in Calcutta it was only fair to test out a few sparkling specimens from the chilled cargo holds. We also opened several cases for the stevedores streaming with sweat under the punishing Indian sun; it saved them the trouble of having to break into the cases themselves.

Before reaching Calcutta, we put in at Trincomalee in Ceylon to unload carcases of frozen lamb onto waiting barges. Unlike *Ajax*, the barges had no refrigeration and the scorching sun seemed – from the aroma wafting across the channel – to be cooking the lambs on the vessels' sizzling open decks. It was so overwhelmingly hot that I decided to cool off by swimming ashore through the crystal clear water. I was churning along in a style I liked to imagine resembled closely that of Johnny Weismuller when an inquisitive school of grey mullet brushed along my face and neck. Ah, this was far better than frying on *Ajax*. Without warning, I felt as if somebody was punching me hard in the stomach. Hell, had a shark been following the mullet and switched to making a meal of me? The pain in my midriff was intense, but I thrashed along as best I could; vaguely remembering that sharks hated commotions in the water, I splashed noisily with each forward stroke.

I hit the beach and looked down at my bare belly. It was blackened and burned, but certainly not the bloody mess I'd expected. A naval policeman ran up. What did I mean, he asked testily, by swimming when underwater charges were being dropped to deter Japanese frogmen. Did I realise how lucky I was not to have been killed? Yes, I did realise how lucky I had been, and would it be all right to collapse now? Shaken but intact, I decided next time to come ashore by boat.

The Trincomalee harbour explosive charges were not needed much longer, for the war was ending around the world. *Ajax* was in Fremantle for VE Day, and as officer in charge of the ship's flags, I unearthed a Nazi tricolour that had been stored since one of the ship's pre-war visits to Germany. We dressed up a protesting junior engineer as Adolf Hitler, and alarmed him even more by giving him a ceremonial 'burial' beneath the flag and a mound of hundreds of bottles of beer.

On VJ Day we found ourselves moored off Taronga Park, Sydney. Our celebrations were somewhat curtailed by a signal from the commander-in-chief banning us, and other ships moored nearby, from letting off rockets. The authorities of the densely wooded Taronga Zoo area feared that an errant rocket might start a devastating blaze, endangering their rare animals. So, although rockets were out, we still went generally mad on board all the ships in the harbour. The port police ran a twenty-four-hour launch service around the moored vessels, picking up visiting revellers reduced to a coma by the day and night parties, and returning them to their own ships.

Ajax headed for home, this time through the Red Sea. I went ashore at Port Said with Dr Rowlands, and by way of diversion we decided to hire a horse apiece from one of the Arabs offering 'rides' in much the same way donkeys are rented out on British holiday beaches. We had only covered a couple of hundred yards when an ear-splitting whistle brought the animals to a full stop. Then they did an about-turn and trotted back towards their master.

I wasn't having any of this, and wheeled my horse round to move off again. But another whistle blast abruptly stopped him. I was determined to have my money's worth, and turned the now thoroughly confused animal away again. This time, there was no whistle, but when I finally rode back, the Arab was spitting with rage. 'Now my horses don't know who is master,' he accused.

'Well, that's tough,' I retorted, 'but big white jockey can't stand screech in ears. You go get stuffed.' I thought for a moment that the Arab was coming for me with his riding whip, but he only turned angrily, shouting at his horses. As the Doc and I made for our ship, I could only hope the Arab wasn't venting his wrath on those unfortunate animals.

By early December 1945, *Ajax* was docking at Birkenhead, and I set off to Fleetwood to spend the Christmas holidays at home with my mother; Dad, still out east, was now Commanding Officer of an RAF unit operating between India and the Seychelle Islands. With the war over, I began to think about how I would tackle the years ahead. Although I still saw my future stretching away to sea, the voyages that lasted many months far from the lovely Joan no longer excited me. That Christmas Eve, we held each other tightly in the warm fireglow, and I whispered, 'Darling, I miss you all the time I'm away,' and I vowed to her that, if I could, I would try to join a shipping line that operated briefer voyages.

Joan smiled. 'Let me know when you get round to doing something about it.' She knew me well enough to realise I wouldn't be jumping onto the first short-haul ship that sailed along.

In fact, my next trip was out to the Far East once more. In February 1946 I signed on in Liverpool as third officer – another step up – on the *Glenartney*, a 9000-ton motor vessel leaving for China and Australia. She was a fairly new ship, completed in 1940, and as I went aboard I noticed radar fittings on her mast.

Compared to the sophisticated equipment carried by today's ships, *Glenartney*'s radar was primitive, but nevertheless it had what was known as a Position Plan Indicator, which pin-pointed on its screen objects up to twenty-five miles away. Before sailing I took a four-day radar course, and learned that, even at that elementary stage of evolution, radar gave us enormously enhanced anti-collision security in fog, as well as being a valuable navigational aid. Even now, *QE2*'s radar can 'see' for only forty miles – the approximate distance to the horizon – although she does, of course, have other advanced technological navigational and safety equipment unheard of in the early years after the war.

Shanghai, with a population as large as London's, struck me at once as a booming, bustling city of hurrying workers. No one, it seemed, stood at street corners watching the world go by. The people, the buses, the cars and even the harbour's hordes of sampans were buzzing around like so many earnest bees. Our Chinese who run the laundry on *QE2* today make a similar impression – busy, busy, busy from the moment they open their eyes, swallowing up the ship's daily tonnage of dirty washing and keeping at it until it is all crisp and white. The Chinese, I've noticed around the world, seem to be born with an inherent gift for sheer hard work.

The Shanghai authorities no doubt wanted to make sure that their artisans secured a good night's sleep after the day's toil, and they imposed a nightly nine o'clock curfew. Wandering round the city sightseeing with a couple of shipmates, we lost track of the time and had to retreat just after nine to our shipping agent's flat, where I spent my first night in China sleeping in an armchair.

From Shanghai, *Glenartney* headed for Australia in what turned out to be a record-breaking run to Brisbane. The fastest ship I had ever handled, with thousands of tons in her holds, she could surge across the oceans of the world with the ease and flair of a coast guard cutter. And her officers' cabins had running water – the peak of luxury for a working freighter. Lawrence Holt Senior, doyen of the Alfred Holt Line, had inspected the vessel before she left Liverpool. I was standing by my cabin when he asked, 'How's the accommodation?' I replied, 'It's fine,' which sent the old fellow off muttering, 'We spoil you chaps these days.'

Glenartney brought thousands of tons of Australian apples back to Britain on that trip, as well as many thousands of frozen lambs. We had developed a special way of packing the lambs into our holds, with fore-ends and hinds closely interlocked, that we reckoned just about doubled the quantity of lambs the ship could carry.

The ship had custom-built accommodation for a dozen passengers, and the cabins were always full. Most of the travellers were businessmen, anxious to build up their trade with the Far East again. The world's airlines hadn't yet started to schedule their long-distance services across Asia, so passenger places on fast ships like the 19-knot *Glenartney* were very scarce. As third officer, I considered myself lucky not to be spending time catering for the passengers' day-to-day needs. Their board and lodgings came under the domain of our purser, and I wished him the best of luck with the job, so long as he left me out. Captain Coates, Master of the *Glenartney*, took a similar line. A taciturn man, he didn't even say very much to his own officers.

Glenartney left Liverpool again, its holds bursting with British exports. There was everything from furniture to toothpaste – all eagerly awaited by countries starved of British manufactured goods. For a few golden years, the world markets were ours; the 'Made in Britain' brand mark guaranteed superb quality, and British shipping fleets were switching quickly from carrying high explosives to peaceful, currency-earning cargoes.

Just four years after I'd narrowly escaped the Japanese in Singapore, we were discharging *Glenartney*'s crates of Staffordshire pottery in the island's docklands. Later that night, I strolled along the seafront to watch fish being lured along a lamplit path of stakes (the *kelong*) into a net staked out at the other end by wily Chinese fishermen. As I walked inshore towards Chinatown, geckoes – tiny lizards – scuttled lightly across my feet. They're harmless and tend to make their homes in the walls and ceilings of Singapore's houses. I noticed one or two at the small Chinese restaurant where I celebrated my visit to the island with a plate of banana cakes washed down with a couple of pints of the local lager. Then, back to the ship and onwards next day to Hong Kong and Shanghai.

Throughout the voyage back to Britain, I reminded myself of my promise to Joan that I would try to join a short-haul shipping company. I fancied Cunard might be just the one, so after signing off *Glenartney* I popped into the famous Liverpool Cunard Building to see Cunard's Jerry Dalton, assistant to the company's marine superintendent. I told Jerry that I had a second mate's certificate, but needed another six weeks or so at sea before I could sit for my first mate's ticket. Jerry didn't beat about the bush. He simply told me, 'Come back and see us when you've got it.'

Having left Blue Funnel, who had looked after me really well, I was out of a job, and I needed more time at sea to qualify for that vital certificate. I tramped round Liverpool's shipping offices until I heard on the grapevine that Pacific Steam Navigation had a job waiting for a young officer on their motor ship *Santander*. It would be a three-month trip, to the west coast of South America, but I needed that extra bit of experience, so I signed on. She was carrying a gleaming cargo of British cars for Chile, pipes for oil installations in Peru and thousands of cases of expensive Scotch whisky destined for fastidious Latin palates in Colombia, Peru, Bolivia and Ecuador.

I was relieved to find that *Santander* carried a dozen or so passengers since that normally meant the food on board was better than on the average cargo-only boat. And as an extra home-from-home amenity, my cabin had hot and cold running water, with officers' baths and showers only a few yards away. After washing in stone-cold water from a farm pump out on an open deck just a year or two earlier, I reckoned I had dropped in the lap of real luxury on *Santander*.

In most South American ports, a heavy, relentless swell rolled in day and night from the Pacific, making the landing of heavy cargoes dangerous and difficult. But land them we must, and it was heartbreaking to watch our lovely new cars – mostly Vauxhalls – that we had cared for like babies across the Atlantic, now swinging and smashing against coamings and the ship's side as we unloaded them into lighters. Such damage is always a hazard at anchorage ports – those places where larger ships can't get into the docks. Today, it is the flesh and blood of passengers we have to watch out for as we disembark them into tenders from our big liners at tourist anchorages. Wrecked cars could be written off under insurance, but that's not possible with men, women and children, which explains why ships' Masters always prefer to land their passengers on quaysides rather than into tenders bouncing around offshore.

As *Santander* cruised southwards through the warm Pacific swell, I wondered what had happened to my resolve to make shorter voyages. This trip, I decided, would definitely be the last time I went meandering for months on end many thousand of miles away from home and Joan. But meanwhile, I had to admit that it was agreeable to sail along the sea-paths first marked out by Columbus. There was an abundance of lush, exotic, old Spanish ports along the way, and I went ashore as often as I could to soak up the Latin atmosphere that has always intrigued me.

In Columbia I sipped the excellent local beers in the garden city of Cali, just a short train ride from our calling port at Buenaventura. Always an avid trencherman, I enjoyed munching through Columbian *fritanga*, a tasty offering of potatoes, popcorn, pork and bananas, which I followed with juicy pineapples and nutty avocados. Later, in the archaeological park south of Cali, my guide showed me squat, mysterious carvings of the god Chimichagua, creator of the world and father of the sun, worshipped by the Chibcha Indians thousands of years before the birth of Christ.

On to Peru, where I took a train from Callao to the capital Lima, 'city of kings'. There I sampled the local *pisca*, a powerful but palatable hooch distilled from grapes. Western skyscrapers, I noted, were already soaring here and there along the sub-tropical skyline, although the Spanish Colonial architecture, which really appealed to me, still dominated the city. As we sailed away from Peru, leaving behind its citizens well stocked with the Scots spirit they prized above all others, I saw giant black clouds sweeping down towards *Santander*. We had had no hurricane warnings, so perhaps this was an outburst of ash from an Andes volcano smouldering far away in the Peruvian hinterlands.

In minutes, we found out just what was in the enormous wheeling, circling, and screeching mass that blacked out the sky over *Santander* – many millions of birds were migrating northwards along the cooling path of the Humboldt current. Amazingly, the swirling cloud opened up just as *Santander* ploughed her bows into it, but the black veil never parted above mast-top height. Still, I was glad to see, not one of the migrants hurt so much as a wingtip as the ship's massive bulk surged through them.

Valparaiso was the last stop on our South American ride. Sweeping the north-east horizon with my binoculars as we approached the port, I could just make out the awesome, snow-capped peak of Aconcagua, at almost 23,000 feet the highest mountain in the Andes and indeed in the whole of the Americas. Aconcagua's remote vastness contrasted sharply, I thought, with the friendly warmth of the Chilean folk living on the rich green coastal plains below.

Santander's officers were frequently invited out to meals by the hospitable people of both Valparaiso and Santiago, the Chilean capital just a short journey inland from the port. Prominent in the fare were some of my fish and sea-food favourites, such as rainbow trout, oysters, shrimps and crayfish. I was surprised to find that the quality of Chilean wines was so highly regarded that its vineyards had built up quite an export trade with France. The local beers, on the other hand, I judged to be only one grade above rubbish, and my first pint there was also my last.

In the outskirts of Valparaiso, our shipping agents showed me the beautiful garden city and holiday resort of Vina del Mar. I would have loved to have played cricket on its fine, spacious ground, or perhaps watched the Chilean Derby being run at the Vina del Mar track. I did manage to play and win a contest of wits outside the cricket ground against two Chilean spivs trying to sell cold tea dressed up as Scotch whisky. Unfortunately for them, their 'brand' was the same as we had so recently and liberally distributed to liquor enthusiasts all along the west coast of South America. Our agents translated my remarks for the benefit of the swarthy spivs. Briefly I told them: 'Labels forged, bottle contents faked. You very stupid crooks. Now get lost.' Muttering angrily, they did.

On the way home, *Santander* called at Santiago de Cuba to collect a cargo of unrefined brown sugar for Britain, packed in 300-lb bags. It amazed me to watch the small, wiry Cuban labourers carrying the huge sacks across their shoulders. I took my own personal Cuban cargo onto the ship in the form of several boxes of fine Havana cigars. My father, now back from the war, would really enjoy puffing away on them with his chums in Fleetwood.

Chapter 10

When *Santander* reached Liverpool on 26 November 1946, I had achieved the necessary time as officer in charge of a watch to be able to take the exam for first mate's certificate. Being in charge of a watch generally means that, under the Captain's supervision, you undertake full navigational steering of the ship, checking on speed and location at least once an hour in the open seas, and once every twenty minutes in narrow waters.

Today, we have echo sounders that, at the touch of a button, show the depth of water, but years ago it was literally a case of 'swinging the lead'. Nearing harbour or in shallow water, a crewman would lean out over the side from a special platform called 'the chains' under the bridge and heave a lead and line ahead of the ship. As the momentum of the ship brought it level with the submerged lead, the sailor would call out the depth to the Captain or officer of the watch.

This ancient style of sounding had a language all its own. The lead line was marked off with pieces of leather, red bunting or white linen along its length. The sailor didn't need to see which 'mark' came into his hand; he knew at once, by the feel of the material, just how much water lay beneath the ship. And he never shouted anything so simple as 'one fathom' or 'thirty feet'. His cry might be 'half less seven' (six-and-a-half fathoms), 'by the deep four' (four fathoms) or 'by the mark seven' (seven fathoms). And so it went on, through a complex ritual of sea shouts.

For a short time after *Santander* came home, I stayed with the Pacific Steam Navigation Company on relief port duties over Christmas. Soon afterwards I resigned to give my full attention to brushing up on sea-subjects ready for the first mate exam. I passed and got this prized certificate in April 1947.

Meanwhile, I had applied optimistically to a number of shipping companies. Canadian Pacific, Cunard, Lamport and Holt and one or two others had nothing going at the time, so I stayed at home and signed on the dole. Then, one morning a telegram arrived from Lamport and Holt saying, 'Report on board ship tomorrow.' As I was reading this, the postman popped the morning mail through our letter box. A plain buff envelope postmarked Liverpool held a letter which was to chart my career course for the next four decades: Cunard were offering me the chance to join the passenger liner *Samaria* on stand-by duties in Liverpool. My shout of 'Whoopee!' brought my mother running into our hotel's breakfast-room. I just couldn't believe my luck. Here, on one of Cunard's unassuming letterheads, was my invitation to walk the decks of the world's most illustrious shipping fleet.

Nova Scotian Samuel Cunard had founded his transatlantic line in 1840 with the wooden paddle steamer *Britannia*, followed by three sister ships *Acadia*, *Caledonia* and *Columbia*. On her maiden voyage, *Britannia* arrived to a tumultuous welcome in Boston just fourteen days and eight hours after leaving Liverpool. Within ten years, the fleet had doubled. As I read the letter from Cunard's Liverpool office, I recalled some of their famous passenger liners which had reigned over the North Atlantic.

By 1884, *Umbria* and *Etruria* – with velvet curtains throughout, plus pianos and an organ – were already crossing at 18 knots. In the early 1900s came the fast steam-turbine liners *Carmania*, *Mauretania* and then the *Lusitania*. The fine pedigree extended through the years to those royal ladies of the oceans, the *Queen Mary*, 'born' in 1936, and the *Queen Elizabeth* who arrived just one hundred years after the *Britannia*.

Now, in May of 1947, Cunard were asking me to step aboard. I sent two telegrams. My first said 'sorry' to Lamport and Holt. The second one was to Cunard. Its simple wording – 'I accept' – hardly reflected my joyous exhilaration.

Naturally, my father was as gleeful as I was with the Cunard offer. 'I'd like to be coming with you, Bob,' he said. He took a draw on his Havana and added ruefully, 'It's going to be a bit tame here in Fleetwood after the excitement of two world wars.' Dad was, of course, at sea in World War I, and to this day I wear on my white *QE2* captain's uniform the five brass buttons from my father's World War I tunic, which he had given to me on the day I left home at seventeen to go to sea.

After all my excitement, I didn't sail anywhere on my initial assignment with Cunard. The 20,000-tonner *Samaria* was docked in Liverpool between trips to Canada, and my task was to keep a watchful eye on her until she went to sea. Two officers were detailed for the job, myself and Phil Reed. Phil, known to his chums as Pip, was senior man, and afterwards he, too, became a Cunard captain.

The one thing my memory throws up about my initial reaction to *Samaria* isn't her gigantic size compared to the cargo ships I had been roving the world in, but the fact that all the *Samaria*'s bunks, including mine, had eiderdowns. I asked Pip if all the passengers on Cunard liners enjoyed such luxuries.

'Why, yes,' he answered.

'Don't tell me you haven't come across eiderdowns at sea before.'

'Gosh, no,' I had to admit. 'Blue Funnel didn't go in for that sort of thing.'

My *Samaria* sojourn lasted only a week or so. Then orders came through for me to travel to Southampton and join RMS *Queen Mary*. I knew there was no chance of my sailing on this ocean leviathan – yet – for all her officers had to hold a Master's Certificate and I was a couple of years away from that. But even on stand-by duties it would be fantastic, I reckoned, to serve as an officer on one of the two most famous ships in the world.

During the war that had just ended, *Queen Mary* and *Queen Elizabeth* had carried more than 1.2 million Allied troops. More than one million of these came and went across the North Atlantic, but the two *Queens*, drab in their grey warpaint, were also in action on the other side of the world, carrying Australian and New Zealand contingents to Suez. At one stage of the war, the 80,000-ton *Queen Mary* was carrying 15,000 troops a trip, having been stripped and fitted out for that mammoth task in Sydney, Australia. Now, at Southampton, the final ornate furnishings were being installed to restore the *Queen* to her peace-time majesty.

It was my first-ever visit to Southampton, and I joined *Queen Mary* at Berth 101 in the port's New Docks. A satellite town of marquees, caravans, wooden cabins and camping tents had mushroomed on the wastelands around the docks, housing carpenters, plumbers, cabinet-makers, painters and engineers who were recreating the graceful elegance of this great lady. I was one of fourteen officers who patrolled the ship night and day to try to protect the craftsmen's finished efforts from thieves, vandals and fire raisers.

Despite our best efforts, an enormous furniture van drew up at the dockside one weekend when quite a few officers were away on leave. An army of white-coated gentlemen went aboard the ship, brandishing passes from a non-existent London furnishing company. Three hours later, wardrobes, beds, mirrors, priceless wood panelling from all over the world and many of the tables and chairs from the largest restaurant ever built in a ship had vanished into the van. Neither the onshore pirates nor their royal booty were ever seen again.

I left *Queen Mary* a few weeks before she was due to resume her crossings of the North Atlantic in tandem service with *Queen Elizabeth*. I knew in my heart that I would be seeing the *QM* again when I had climbed a little further up the Cunard rigging. And I did, some five years later. Meanwhile, one of my last tours of inspection on board centred on the sports deck. There I had been asked to take a look, not at the fine tennis or badminton courts, but at the 'doggy hotel' adjoining them.

Many sea-going dog lovers couldn't bear to be separated from their pets, and on the *QM* they didn't have to be, for Cunard had built a complete doggy complex. I couldn't believe the sheer luxury of the lay-out. There were, I saw, twenty-six ample-sized dog houses (I wouldn't demean them by calling them kennels). Each had a removable teakwood floor, a skylight to admit warm sunshine, plus the ultimate 'mod-con' of hot and cold running water. The dogs and their owners had exclusive use of an eighty-foot exercise paddock next door to the 'houses'. Now, I thought, I've seen everything.

Cunard comforts were rather less opulent on their 7000-ton ex-war-time Empire boat *Vasconia*. Formerly the *Empire Pendennis*, the ship had been built quickly with others of her class to replace the tonnages wiped out by U-boats. I joined her as second officer in Victoria Docks, London, on 17 June 1947. The War Risk payments had now ended, of course, and my gross pay for the new job was just £34 a month, yet, as *Vasconia*'s Captain George Morris reminded me on the day I joined his ship, my prospects were 'from now on, rather better than bright'. It was an encouraging turn of phrase from a future Captain of the *Queen Elizabeth* who also became Commodore of the Cunard fleet.

Vasconia earned her wages carrying people and cargo between London, New York, Halifax, Nova Scotia and St John, New Brunswick. In all, I made nine voyages aboard her. The Canadian ports of call were bitterly cold, and I often watched hot vapour from the steam winches crystallising into solid ice. I was intrigued, too, by my first glimpse of the reversing falls at St John's. The rise and fall of the tides there is one of the greatest in the world, more even than on Britain's Severn. Downriver, there is a waterfall and, as the incoming tide rushes upstream, the waterfall literally reverses its flow because of the tide's pressure. It's a sight I've never come across anywhere else.

By way of a contrast to the chilly coast of Canada, we had a hot time in New York on my second voyage in *Vasconia*. A deep-freeze hold containing hundreds of tons of meat caught fire. How the blaze started we couldn't imagine, although we did suspect foul play. New York's enthusiastic fire brigade asked questions only after they had flooded our holds with what seemed to be half the Hudson River. Of course, the water was polluted and washed away any ideas we might have had of extra rations of barbecued beef. The firemen did in fact confer upon our cargo of fine quality meat the somewhat reduced grading of floating petfood but, more importantly, they did a first-class job putting out the blaze.

Essentially, *Vasconia* was a cargo vessel that squeezed in three or four passengers. She carried only males in her passenger cabins, for no matter who the travellers were, they were allotted bunks at random. The banning of women, therefore, avoided a certain measure of transatlantic hassle.

By this time, the two *Queens* were criss-crossing the Atlantic with packed cabins. The close association between Britain and the United States during the war gave an enormous peace-time boost to trade and tourism between the two nations, and despite the monster capacity of the *Queens*, Atlantic berths were scarce and highly prized. Giant jets were years away, but occasionally I would see British Overseas Airways' Empire flying boats roaring over the ocean. I don't believe any of us sailing so nonchalantly below had the least idea just how big a hammering the liners would take from the descendants of the silver-winged amphibians.

Those early voyages with Cunard were truly golden days. I was away from home only weeks at a time, instead of many months, and I felt completely at ease with the Cunard style of seafaring. It was more relaxed and much more friendly than the austere days with Blue Funnel. Masters were still absolute monarchs, but ran their ships more in the style of paternal fellow-professionals than as aloof autocrats.

Early in 1947, my parents had sold the Kingston Hotel and had moved to the XL Hotel on the Watling Street trunk road at Garstang, between Preston and Lancaster. It was, I thought, a rather magnificent establishment with sumptuous bars, lounges and residents' bedrooms. Once when I was there on leave, the thought came into my head that it would be a good idea to move in and help them run the place. I spoke to Joan about it, but she said heatedly, 'You're not going to waste those years you've put in at sea. Get the idea right out of your head.' I did.

Joan's home at Fleetwood was now some ten miles from the hotel, but the drive didn't take long in my father's new two-litre MG. It was the first time I had ever driven at 100 miles an hour in any car, and I couldn't quite make out whether Joan was swearing or praying under her breath as we hurtled along the A6 on our way to a Ladies' Evening at the XL towards the end of 1947. The after-dinner speaker was one Owen Woodiwiss, a Fleetwood coach-builder and a long-standing friend of the family. Half-way through his rhetoric and wisecracks, Owen suddenly declared: 'And now I'd like to announce the engagement of Joan and Bob. Please join me in giving them a big hand.' The seventy or so guests broke into loud applause.

Dad, sitting near me, whispered fiercely, 'I knew nothing about this.'

Shocked, but not displeased, I hissed, 'And neither did I.'

Afterwards, Joan and I tackled an unrepentant Owen as he sipped his usual Scotches at the bar. 'Well,' he said, 'I reckoned you'd been courting long enough so I thought I'd give you two a bit of a push towards matrimony.'

Joan shook her head in dismay. 'I never thought I'd be proposed to by proxy.' Then her face cleared. 'But I don't think we should deny we're engaged, do you, Bob? It might confuse our friends.' That, I agreed, would never do. I bought another Scotch for Owen the Matchmaker.

Perhaps it was that old spring feeling, or maybe I was lonely as *Vasconia* neared London from Canada just a few months after that eventful night at the XL. With the ship safely tied up, I called Joan from a dockside kiosk. 'How about getting married next week?'

There was a long silence from the Fleetwood end of the line. Then Joan spoke softly. 'Bob, I think you're quite mad. But the answer, darling, is yes, yes, yes. Please hurry home.'

It was only then that I realised that there was the matter of calling banns at our parish church, of fixing my shipboard duties so that I could actually attend my wedding, and of letting all our friends know the time and place. I soon found it was too late to call the banns so I had to rush off to get a special licence. Precise and methodical in all transactions of the sea, I had navigated an impetuous course in this affair of the heart. Happily, *Vasconia*'s third officer, Tony Graham, agreed to stand in for me over the next couple of weeks in port, and I promised I would do the same for him one day. A first-class shipmate, Tony had an uncle who was a Scottish laird and also happened to be chief purser of the *Queen Mary*. A few years later, I also came to know Laird Alistair Graham extremely well when I returned to the *QM* as a sea-going officer.

But back to 1948. The Reverend Tooley, an ex-RAF padre and now vicar of St Helen's Church, Churchtown – our parish church – secured permission from his bishop for our almost instant marriage. Joan, now out of the ATS, spent hours on the phone inviting all our friends, and I spent quite a bit of time on the phone myself, persuading Owen Woodiwiss that, because it was he who started off all the commotion, the least he could do was come along and be my best man. It was an offer he couldn't refuse.

Joan, too, did an effective job of persuasion with her last-minute invitations. Perhaps the hint of free beer all day at the XL played some part in her success. Whatever the reason, it seemed to me that all our friends and relations from Fleetwood, Garstang and Lancaster turned up for the wedding on the last day of March 1948.

Sadly, Joan's father wasn't able to see his daughter's great day. A superintendent engineer with a Fleetwood shipping company, he lost his life at Milford Haven in a boiler-room accident on board an Admiralty trawler. But Joan's paratrooper brother, Major Alan Hardern, proudly took his sister's arm, backed up by her uncle and a cousin, both in army uniform.

Joan and I realised it wouldn't be the easiest part of the day escaping from the XL after the wedding reception. We spread the word around that we were travelling to Langwathby, which most of our friends took to be in Wales. Our honeymoon destination was, in fact, in the opposite direction but we decided – mistakenly as it turned out – that if folk thought we had to make the long trip to Wales they would let us leave quietly. The subterfuge was quite useless. Carloads of revellers chased our taxi to Lancaster railway station hours after we should have caught our north-bound train for Penrith. And the taxi's registration number of BED 504 didn't help. Some of our friends guffawed raucously as we climbed into the cab, then shouted and screamed through their car windows as BED 504 careered up the A6. Other friends, with more taste, sang to us the current hit song, 'In Room Five Hundred and Four'. I can still remember one of the lines: 'It was romance, a dream come true, that perfect honeymoon with you, in Room Five Hundred and Four.'

The porter at Lancaster told us, 'You're lucky. The last train to Penrith is just ready to leave.' Thankfully, Joan and I climbed aboard it. She murmured, 'At last, sweetheart, we're alone.' The train huffed and puffed twenty yards up the platform. It stopped. Our supporters' club rushed up to our carriage. Faces at the window shouted 'Surprise, surprise!' We tried to smile as the train rustled up enough steam to get going again. As it moved forward, we sank back in our seats again. Then, oh no! The train shuddered to another full stop. Faces at the window again. It was only after the honeymoon that I found out that some perverted genius had tipped the engine driver ten shillings to put on the start-stop routine.

Finally, we arrived at Salkeld Hall, a lovely Cumbrian stately home near the elusive Langwathby, where the owners catered for a few occasional guests. In those Elysian days of early spring, the place was enchanting and utterly peaceful. When we weren't making love in our enormous four-poster bed, the two of us wandered through the hall's acres of gardens, browsed through the magnificent library, or helped to bottle-feed orphan lambs on the nearby farm. It was as idyllic a honeymoon as either of us could ever have dreamed about.

Chapter 11

Now a newly married man of twenty-four, I was looking forward to spending lots of time with Joan between *Vasconia*'s quick cruises to the other side of the Atlantic. We had set up home at Joan's mother's house in Highbury Avenue, Fleetwood, and our matrimonial barometer was forecasting, I believed, only the shortest of separations whenever my Cunard voyages happened to interrupt leaves and loving. That this was altogether too optimistic an outlook hit me when I returned to London. *Vasconia*'s new Captain 'Tiger' Evans shook my hand. 'Welcome back, Bob, and many congratulations,' he said. 'Sorry to have to tell you that this time we're off to Australia and New Zealand.'

This was bad enough for a young bridegroom. But by the time we reached New Zealand, the dockers – or wharfies as they're known out there – were in the middle of a lengthy strike. We were stranded for weeks in the port of Dunedin. Most days I posted plaintive pages to Joan saying, 'I love and miss you every moment.' And I meant it.

On the way to New Zealand, *Vasconia* put in at Sydney to unload cargo. It was a Saturday, and with a couple of shipmates I took the afternoon off to pay a return visit to Randwick race meeting. It was more pleasant than profitable, and on the way back to the ship my chums told me in friendly yet forcible terms that I'd better stick to navigation and leave the finding of winners to people who knew what they were talking about.

And with the dockers' strike, I wasn't too lucky in New Zealand either. *Vasconia* reached Dunedin, harbour capital of the province of Otago, to take on frozen lamb and mutton for Britain, but the wharfies wouldn't load *Vasconia* or any other ship. We lay alongside in the harbour and waited day after expensive day as negotiations trickled along.

Sometimes, a few of us would club together to hire a car and explore the eastern coastal strip. Otago, we found, had been the scene of a hectic scramble for gold in the 1860s, and it was a bonus side-effect of the strike that we had time to take a look at some of the old mine workings. My pal Tony Graham even had the time to learn to drive, and during the lazy days at Dunedin took out a New Zealand driving licence. My own British licence landed me into a slight skirmish with the law when a traffic cop stopped our hire car and pointed out around a dozen regulations I had broken by not taking out a local driving permit. We all went down to the lock-up, where the policeman decided honour had been satisfied by a good telling-off. He tore up the infringement ticket and made us all a cup of tea. 'And where do I get this permit?' I asked the now-friendly officer. 'Right here, son,' he answered, fishing out a form from his desk. I quickly answered its twenty questions, handed him £1, and carried on driving round the island.

We could have been stranded in many worse spots. Dunedin, we were told, was founded by Scottish settlers who decided they would name their new home with the Celtic word for 'Edinburgh'. One rainy day we spent a fascinating afternoon at an Early Settlers' Museum, plentifully packed with the tartan clothing and hand-made cottage furniture of the MacPhersons, the MacTavishes and the Camerons of more than one hundred years before.

One day, the news came that the strike was over, and we sailed out of the lovely harbour whose tall surrounding hills we had often climbed to get a bird's-eye view of our ship. *Vasconia* sailed northwards up the Canterbury Bight to Christchurch. Our chief steward, 'See me later' Jones, had obviously been there before, because he knew just where to find a sack of my favourite New Zealand oysters. Mr Jones got his nickname from his habit of answering 'See me later' to any requests for action fired at him by the crew. This time, though, he got the oysters before I'd even asked. Their delicious flavour lingers over the years and, although since then I've feasted on some of the world's finest oysters, those I ate in Christchurch, from the beds at nearby Bluff, are right at the top of my mollusc league.

From the graceful cathedral city of Christchurch, we took *Vasconia* across the Cook Strait to bunker at Wellington ready for the voyage across the Pacific, through the Panama Canal and then to the Atlantic and home. It would be a long haul, so we built up the 'saddle-back' coal bunker by fitting boards on deck around the engine-room hatch and piling in it all the extra tons of coal we reckoned we would need for the non-stop marathon to the Panama Canal – 6500 miles.

We hadn't sailed far when *Vasconia* ran into a patch of the Pacific Ocean's foulest weather. Violent seas rampaged through our saddle-back boarding, smashing it into a thousand splinters, and catapulting our precious fuel into the depths. We ploughed on, but by the time we were crossing the Tropic of Capricorn in mid-Pacific our coal-stock situation was decidedly dicey.

As second officer, I was responsible for navigating the ship, and its sheer survival remained very much a matter for *Vasconia*'s skipper. As well as the storm, Captain Evans also had the bad luck to be challenged by persistent squalls sweeping across the Pacific. I was just half-way through my midnight-to-4 a.m. watch on yet another night of savage seas when Tiger Evans came up to the bridge.

'I can't sleep, Bob,' he began. 'You're the navigator, but I'm the one who will carry the can if we don't make it. Can we reach a South American bunkering port on the coal we've got left?'

'Sorry, sir, we're beyond the point of no return.' My answer meant that we were so far out in the Pacific that it would be better to try for Panama than to aim for South America which lay far to the east. Either way, we were surrounded by what seemed to be an infinity of hazardous ocean, and I knew that, unless a gift of good weather was coming our way, *Vasconia* could soon end up as a record-sized chunk of flotsam. Thankfully, the head-on storms took pity on us a day or two later and we scraped into Cristobal with just a few inches of coaldust in our bunkers.

After the strike, the Captain had been anxious to catch up on time, banning shore leave in Christchurch and now at Cristobal. This didn't suit some of our engine-room ratings, who had already been in trouble at Dunedin. There, our night watchman, an old able seaman named Foley, had caught some of them stealing ship's stores after an evening on the town, and he told the bosun. The next day, the young toughs blacked Foley's eyes, smashed his spectacles and threatened to do the same every day if he squealed on them again. Tiger Evans hadn't come by his nickname by accident, and he promptly had the gang thrown into Dunedin jail until the morning *Vasconia* sailed.

This sort of trouble, unusual on a Cunarder, didn't promote

a particularly happy atmosphere as we struggled across the Pacific. And when the engine-room roughnecks heard that they were to be confined to the ship, away from the more lurid delights of Cristobal, their growlings and grumblings could be heard right up to the bridge. The 'Tiger' roared back: 'Any more of this and I'll have you all tried for mutiny when we reach London.' Although hanging was no longer the popular punishment for open revolt on the high seas, the Captain's threat effectively cowed the troublemakers. Just how serious was the prospect of a latter-day *Bounty* incident can be judged by the fact that more than one loyal crew member slept with an iron bar beneath his pillow on the Atlantic crossing back to London. There, we paid off the miscreants with the sea-going equivalent of 'Don't call us, we'll call you.'

It was 3 October 1948 when *Vasconia* finally steamed up the Thames estuary into the Pool of London after six months at sea. I called Joan to say I would be home the following day. 'Have you been trying to prove that absence makes the heart grow fonder?' she enquired sweetly. 'Because you didn't need to, you know.'

'I'll deal with you, Mrs Arnott,' I retorted, 'when I hit Fleetwood tomorrow.' Twenty-four hours later, our exchanges were rather more tender.

Luckily, *Vasconia* had now reverted to her New York–London shuttle service, which enabled me to get home fairly frequently. When Joan and I weren't eating sandwiches in the Lake District on summer afternoons, we often turned out for tennis practice, and in the evenings I liked to put in a few badminton sessions at our old school's courts. By way of even more sport the Fleetwood Rugby Union Club team coach used to pick me up on winter Saturday mornings during my leaves to take me off to play second row forward at some of the many illustrious rugger grounds spread across northern England. It was a rough, physically ferocious sort of game and inspired an awesome thirst. It wasn't at all unusual for us to sink around ten pints each of powerful north-country bitter beer in the clubhouse after a match. Perhaps fortunately, because of my commitments at sea, I was only an occasional member of the valiant rugger rovers.

In the spring of 1949 I heard without too much enthusiasm that *Vasconia* was going out east again to Australia, but I was spared the pleasures of accompanying her by being transferred to Cunard's latest passenger ship, the 13,000-ton *Parthia*. It was a time when passenger licences for the North Atlantic were still hard to obtain from the British Government, but Cunard's associate cargo company, Brocklebanks, had laid down the keels of two ships which the Cunard hierarchy now decided to switch to the lucrative trade of carrying people to and from the United States. The new ships, the *Parthia* and the *Media*, still carried a fair amount of cargo, but they earned most of their bread by transporting 250 first-class passengers each across the Atlantic.

They were not, I'm afraid, the most comfortable of ships. Because their passenger cabins had been added high on their superstructure almost as an afterthought, *Parthia* and *Media* tended to roll and pitch around the Atlantic like a couple of sick sea horses. Because of her unruly antics, *Media* became the first ship to be fitted with stabilisers, made by the Denny-Brown company. These were huge lateral fins that retracted into the side of the ship, which stopped the ship rolling, but not pitching. There were also one or two teething problems when one of these 'wings' broke off on *Media*'s first voyage, but now these stabilisers have proved themselves invaluable and are fitted on the world's ships on a massive scale. *Parthia*, without stabilisers, was one of the most violently unstable ships ever to cross the Atlantic, and yet some regular passengers loved her tantrums. New Jersey warehouse owner Jimmy K. Burns once confided to me: 'I really feel I've been to sea on this old cow. On the *Queens*, you might as well be on Central Park Lake.'

I was second officer on *Parthia*, with a small but pleasantly furnished cabin just below the bridge. There was a general shortage of junior officers around that time, and I was the first second officer on a Cunard passenger ship who didn't hold a Master's Certificate, although I did, of course, have my first mate's ticket. The dire deficit in officers arose, I suppose, because so many young chaps who had served at sea through the war came home at the end of hostilities and took shore jobs. This was understandable, but no great help to the British Merchant Service.

Parthia was a Royal Mail Ship, and carried His Majesty's mail across the seas under Cunard's prized Royal Mail Charter. She used to dock in New York at her Fourteenth Street berth – derelict now, the huge Cunard sign that once proudly dominated the pierhead hanging forlorn and dilapidated. *Parthia*'s schedule allowed for a week in New York unloading and loading, a week crossing to Liverpool, another week there, and then a week back at sea on the westward crossing.

This sort of timetable allowed me reasonable spells ashore in New York, and often I would walk the four or five miles up to Central Park to listen to the band playing, or I would take a dime subway ride to the park from the docks and then walk back. Around Union Square I used to pick up the packs of butter, sugar and meats that were still tightly rationed in England, plus one or two pairs of the unrationed but equally scarce sheer Dupont nylons. These were one of Joan's few extravagances.

An agreeable aspect of serving on a passenger ship was that you could invite guests into the officers' wardroom for afternoon tea or a glass of beer. You didn't bring them in for gin sips, because our entertainment allowance comprised only one fifteen-shilling bottle of spirits each fortnight, but on the other hand, officers had a virtually unlimited ration of beers. The draught variety was supplied by the Wrexham Lager Company, and Mr Gresher Thomas, chief of the brewery group, often travelled on *Parthia*. He had a much appreciated custom of giving every seaman a voucher worth two free pints of beer, and Thomas the Brewery was therefore a very popular fellow with *Parthia*'s crew.

The weeks I spent to-ing and fro-ing on the *Parthia* didn't, for obscure technical reasons, count fully towards the service I had to accumulate to qualify for my Master's Certificate. I was anxious to put my name on one of these diplomas as quickly as possible, so I transferred back to Cunard's cargo division where every minute at sea counted towards the coveted certificate. In August 1949, I signed on the steamship *Fort Musquarro* in Trafford Docks, Manchester. In the war, Britain had built her Empire-class ships, the Americans their SAM boats, and the Forts came from the Canadian yards. *Fort Musquarro* was due to sail back to her birthland when I walked up her gangplank in the unique inland dock complex only a mile or so from Manchester's busy city centre.

Our mission was to collect grain from Montreal's huge silos and bring it back for grinding into flour by Britain's mills. It was a hot, sunny afternoon as *Fort Musquarro* eased her 7150 tons along the waterway that slices through the heartlands of Lancashire and Cheshire. Passing close to Warrington's town centre I reflected on the foresight of those Victorian city fathers who laid down the 35½-mile-long Ship Canal to make Manchester one of Britain's major ports. Now, unhappily, the shrinking of world shipping business has forced the Port of Manchester, like so many others, into serious contraction.

The St Lawrence River was enjoying its summer freedom from ice floes as we headed upstream, past Quebec, to Montreal. There, I set foot on Canadian soil for the first time. The sheer enormity of the city's inland harbour surprised me, but overall Montreal gave me the impression of a sophisticated, lively centre for the finest facets of both the French- and English-speaking cultures. However, I wasn't there to evaluate Montreal's multitude of attractive features; my immediate task was to supervise the loading of grain into each of the ship's five cargo hatches, the cereals pouring smoothly down the silo's overhanging conduits until our holds were bulging.

Grain has never been my favourite cargo. It has the malevolent capacity to transform itself into fine white dust in ever-increasing amounts during the days at sea, and this dust penetrates everywhere. Even when I kept my cabin door tightly closed, the wretched stuff blew in through the ventilation shafts. I was more than glad to take charge of off-loading our cargo in London's Victoria Docks.

Fort Musquarro was scheduled to sail round Britain's south-west coast from London to call at the port of Cardiff. On the way, I developed a severe throat infection and our skipper, Captain Armstrong, called in a Cardiff doctor who recommended that I should part company with my swollen tonsils, but I thought it would be better to hold onto them for another couple of days and have the operation nearer home. That's how I came to wake up one morning towards the end of October in 1949 in Blackpool's Victoria Hospital minus tonsils but with one very sympathetic wife holding my hand.

The routine stay after a tonsillectomy was at least ten days, but I was feeling so great after a week that, immediately after Joan's visit on a Saturday afternoon, I asked one of the doctors if I could go home. 'Only if you sign yourself out,' he answered, and ten minutes later I was standing in Blackpool's Talbot

Road bus station waiting for the Number 14 bus to take me home to Fleetwood, some eight miles away. Ahead of me in the queue, I caught the back view of a slim and fairly familiar outline: Joan. She insisted on putting me straight to bed and, under protest, I submitted – on condition that I could have a bottle of Guinness by way of medicine each morning and evening. The dark Irish brew had been prescribed for the chap in the next bed to me at Victoria Hospital to 'build up his strength', and that, I decided, was just the sort of tonic I needed, too. Nurse Joan brought in my daily dosage from the shop on the corner. The Guinness worked so well that in two or three days I was up and about. I took another couple of weeks' leave and re-joined my ship at Avonmouth Docks, Bristol.

People were walking the streets of St John, New Brunswick, in heavy fur coats by the time the *Fort* docked there just after Christmas. Even with extra winter woollies and my heaviest topcoat, I shivered dispiritedly on deck as the temperatures tumbled. The staple export of New Brunswick was timber from its magnificent forests, and the masts of Britain's once great sailing fleets had started life there. But the cargo I watched over as it went into *Fort Musquarro*'s holds had nothing to do with the province's fine timbers; again, it was the dreaded grain. I wasn't too depressed to hear, when we returned to Britain, that *Fort Musquarro*, complete with clouds of white dust, had been sold.

The ship's new owners asked me if I would take her round the coast to Leith in Scotland with a couple of engineers. Anxious as I was to wave goodbye to the floating fort, the offer from the buyers of £42 – more than a month's pay – plus a rail warrant home from the Scottish port quickly persuaded me to suffer just a little longer. The voyage from London to Leith took only three days, and I arrived home to Joan with the elation of a football-pools winner. That night we went out for a fish and chip supper, total cost five shillings, by way of celebration.

Next day I went to Fleetwood Navigation School to make arrangements to study there for the Master's Certificate examination. The grain days on the Canadian run might have tickled my throat a bit, but they had totted me up enough time at sea to qualify for the Master's ticket. The school was then in Fleetwood's Station Road, opposite the docks. It shared its red brick building with the local labour exchange; seamanship lessons were through the door on the left, dole money through the door on the right. I went in by the left for a month or so and studied with Captain MacFarlane, the veteran skipper who had headed the school for many years, and with other assorted vintage seafarers.

I met up with Captain MacFarlane's wife, and got to know his twin boys – now both Mersey pilots – quite well, but that didn't stop me failing the exam. I had passed every subject in the written part, and all that stood between me and the top ticket was a quite complicated Board of Trade oral quiz, held in Liverpool. I gave an instant but totally wrong answer to just one of these questions, and the examiner told me, 'Sorry, Bob, but you know as well as I do that a ship's Master can't afford the slightest error. I'm afraid I've got to fail you.' Gloomily, I went back to sea for another month.

Chapter 12

In October of 1947, the Princess Elizabeth – now Her Majesty Queen Elizabeth II – travelled north to Clydeside and cracked a bottle of champagne on the first liner Cunard had built especially for cruising after the war. 'I name this ship *Caronia*,' said the young princess. 'May God protect her and all who sail in her.' Three years later I became one of those for whom our heir to the throne had invoked the Almighty. During my sabbatical from the Fleetwood Nautical School, I joined the 34,000-ton *Caronia*, the largest ship I had ever sailed in and my first all-passenger liner.

Painted a bizarre shade of green, Cunard's now obsolete cruising colour, RMS *Caronia* was not unnaturally also known as 'The Green Goddess'. She was standing in on the Atlantic run for one of the *Queens* during her annual refit. In my few weeks aboard *Caronia*, I was something of a nobody – simply the night officer who patrolled the ship with her Master at Arms, the chief security officer.

Keeping an eye on the glittering restaurants, passenger cabin areas and bustling bars was a pleasant and routine operation. But in the below decks quarters for the crew of 600 we came across the occasional punch-up, and were expected to sort it out. A drunken sailor lashing out in a cramped corridor can inflict rather painful damage and the application of a hammerlock by way of a sedative wasn't always an easy or tidy manoeuvre. 'Tell you what, Bob,' wheezed our Master at Arms after we had put a fast finish to a boozy fracas, 'it's just the job to have a big, fit, young feller like yourself on this game.'

I rubbed a well-kicked shin. 'Perhaps it is,' I retorted, 'but I like to think I'm a professional navigator and not a flaming all-in wrestler.'

The scene in the officers' wardroom was rather more restful. I was off-duty through the daytime, and called in there most afternoons for a pot of tea and a plate of hot toast with butter.

Munching away steadily, I was wondering about the number of contests that might figure that evening on the below-decks boxing bill, when a deep, melodious voice from the wardroom doorway flowed over the three or four of us sitting inside. A tonnage only slightly lighter than that of *Caronia* moved into the saloon. I looked up at the man whose absurd antics had sent me limp with laughter twenty years earlier as I sat in the children's half-price seats at our local cinema. 'Do have a chair, Mr Hardy,' I said. 'Isn't Stanley with you today?'

'No, he isn't, son,' answered Oliver Hardy. 'With my bulk those chairs really won't do. Mind if I take the settee?'

There was no reason why I should mind, particularly as the settee was right next to my own table. 'Please do,' I told the great funny man. I wondered if he would tell us what had happened to Mr Laurel.

Our guest settled himself, rather elegantly for his size, in the depths of our Cunard settee. He drummed his fingers lightly along the upholstered arm and looked at me. I had seen that 'another fine mess' gaze in a hundred movies. 'Er, would you like a drink?' I asked him.

His face relaxed into a smile. 'Why, yes. May I join you in a cup of tea?' Sipping his tea with little finger outstretched, Oliver Hardy told me that he and Stan Laurel had been on the British music-hall circuit.

'How did it go?' I asked innocently.

Mr Hardy's chubby cheeks darkened. 'Not at all well, I can tell you. Can you imagine Stan and myself as stand-up comics?'

'Well,' I said, 'you could always make me laugh.'

'Ah, yes, dear boy, but that was in our film situation routines. Neither of us is a Bob Hope.'

I asked again about Stanley. 'Oh, he's travelled up to the north of England to the Lake District, I believe. He'll be along later.' Mr Hardy finished his tea, thanked the steward and raised himself carefully from the settee; he didn't seem any taller than my own 6 ft 1 in, but his beam was enormous. Much older, much sadder than the funny man of my boyhood, Ollie rolled towards the door. I half-expected him to twiddle his tie as he turned to say, 'Cheerio, chaps, and thanks for the tea.' But he didn't, and in another instant was gone. What a shame, I thought, that great comics have to grow old.

A few weeks later I picked up my Master's Certificate pass notice from Dick Willoughby, marine superintendent at Fleetwood Mercantile Marine establishment. 'No mistakes this time, eh Bob?' said Dick as he handed me that lovely slip of paper. Mistakes were something I could no longer afford. Joan and I were about to become parents.

I was now twenty-seven and the proud holder of the British Master's Certificate, and this took me straightaway to my first appointment on the *Queen Elizabeth*. I joined her on 28 August 1950 at Southampton as junior third officer for just £45 a month. Both the *Elizabeth* and her companion *Queen Mary* were running fast, packed voyages to and from New York. Our leave allotment was not as generous as it is today, but in October I managed to get home for a few days knowing that Joan's time was drawing near.

I arrived in Fleetwood on a Friday, and took Joan to the doctor's surgery for a check-up on the Saturday morning. While I was away at sea, Joan had already ordered the pram, a cot, baby linen and everything else she could think of for our new baby. Now, while she saw the doctor I popped into a local pub for a quick pint of beer. Fifteen minutes later I returned to the surgery. Joan came out of the doctor's office with a bewildered look. 'Oh Bob,' she said, 'you'll have to double up on everything I've ordered. It's twins!'

Three days later Joan drove me to Fleetwood station to catch the 9.30 p.m. train for Preston and London. While I was snoozing peacefully on the train, I became the father of twins – Roger weighing in at 4 lb 9 oz and his sister Janet tipping the hospital scales at 4 lb 14 oz. When I reached Southampton, there was a cable waiting from Joan telling me the good news with the words, 'Well done, Bob, you're now a dad as well as a Master.'

The next five days on the Atlantic were awash with champagne as the word went around my shipmates and even the passengers that Third Officer Arnott was a new father twice over, and it was just as well that, on that trip, I wasn't navigating the great *Queen*. In my heart I knew that the one who really should have been getting all the congratulations was my darling Joan. Then, and many times later during our life together, I have always seemed to be at sea when something crucial was happening back home. But at least when *Queen Elizabeth* came back to Southampton, the Captain sent me home on 'paternity' leave.

Like many seamen, I wasn't much help with baby chores; nappy changing was not really my scene. But Joan had wonderful support from her mother who was also our regular baby-sitter whenever we sampled Fleetwood's high life – two half-crown seats at the local cinema. In the years that followed two more babies came along, and Joan's lonesome motherhood was eased because of the care, love and sheer hard work of her mother. It's no joke being mother-in-law to a fellow who much of the time might just as well be the Invisible Man. But Mrs Hardern understood the ways of the sea and never once suggested that I should work ashore. From the beginning she simply rolled up her sleeves and helped her daughter with the double delights of bringing up our twins. I went back to the other lady in my life, RMS *Queen Elizabeth*.

The ship's longer-serving officers often whiled away the hours at sea telling me tales of the *Queen*'s earlier years. One of the best-kept secrets of the war concerned her maiden voyage. In March 1940 the newly-built *Queen Elizabeth* set out from Clydeside for final fitting out in Southampton. At least, that's the story that was spread around by Cunard and the British Admiralty. It was designed to bamboozle Hitler and his service chiefs, and it did. Swarms of Luftwaffe planes were reported along the *Queen*'s projected route and even in the approaches to Southampton waters. They were wasting their time. After short engine and compass trials downriver on the Clyde, plus the slapping on of more than twenty tons of grey camouflage paint, *Queen Elizabeth* set course for New York. On board were workmen, technical advisers and company officials who each carried only a spare shirt and a toothbrush for what they believed would be the short voyage to Southampton. It was years later when some of these unfortunate chaps managed to get home.

Even Captain Townley, then Master of the *Elizabeth*, wasn't sure where he was taking the ship until a King's Messenger arrived from First Lord of the Admiralty Winston Churchill with Top Secret orders to head out west. Only 400 of the usual 1200 crew were working as the grey lady raced across the North Atlantic, known then as U-boat Alley. By the time *Queen Elizabeth* was approaching New York, unscathed, all America had heard on the radio about her cloak-and-dagger break-out. Thousands of New Yorkers packed the waterfront on the West Side to acclaim with loud cheers the world's largest liner as she tied up at her Hudson pier. Moored nearby was the other mighty Cunarder *Queen Mary*. The royal ladies were about to go to war.

Now, some ten years later, the *Queen Elizabeth* was at the pinnacle of her Atlantic career. She weighed 83,673 gross tons, and her length of 1031 feet was only slightly shorter than the height of the Empire State Building; she was longer than the individual heights of the Eiffel Tower in Paris, the Washington Monument and Britain's Blackpool Tower. More than 1200 Cunard men and women on board looked after the 2200 passengers, who could spend their ocean hours in a 338-seater theatre, in lounges, smoking-rooms, swimming pools, ballrooms, libraries, cocktail bars, and superb restaurants – all of which seemed to me a long way removed from my first ship, the humble *Antilochus*.

From Southampton, *Queen Elizabeth* popped across the Channel to collect her French voyagers at Cherbourg, where the war-damaged quay had not yet been fully restored. Passengers, their cars, hundreds of bags of mail, first-class freight, and Parisian high-fashion dresses all had to cross from shore to ship by tender. The pounding seas were not as vicious as on South America's west coast, but the choppy Channel could occasionally put on quite a show. Once, I watched a highly expensive car part company with its overhead slings and plunge straight into the water. Its emotional French owner was quite uninhibited in his fit of screaming hysterics.

Out at sea, there was even more excitement in the first-class smoke-room. Gentlemen gamblers among the passengers organised an auction pool on the length of the ship's run the following day. Only twenty numbers were allowed to be sold, and a popular number thought to be somewhere near the expected mileage could often draw a bid of more than £1,000 from the fevered punters. The total pool would frequently top £5,000, and with so much gambling money around, the Cunard company wisely kept out of the action. All these on-the-spot arrangements were handled, discreetly and totally unofficially, by the smoke-room stewards who were given ten per cent of the winnings. When the wives of these marine Midases met them in New York or Southampton, they were more likely to drive up in Rollses or Caddies than old Chevies or Morris Minors.

Unhappily for the stewards, the tote pool vanished towards the end of the Fifties as wealthy passengers took to the planes. But, as Al Capone once said, it was good while it lasted.

The heavy gambling on just how many miles the ship would achieve in a day seemed to go hand in hand with a long run of heavy weather. I recall that, more than once, our ship's doctors had to give advice by radio to Captains of nearby ships on how to treat sick seamen, it being much too rough to send out the medicos in *Queen Elizabeth*'s cutter. I also remember when our Staff Captain Otto Lucas was looking out over the bows from the wheelhouse more than ninety feet above the sea, and a sky-climbing wave belted him across the back and drenched him where he stood. Said Otto: 'In all my years at sea, I've never seen anything like that one. It must have been waiting for me.'

There were no cricket or football pitches on the *Queen*, but the otherwise excellent sports facilities did include a new squash court. I had recently joined the British Squash Rackets Association, which didn't have too many members in its early years, and I was able to play every day on the ship and, through sheer practice, became quite adept. The court had a full-time attendant whose job was to look after it and occasionally give passengers a game. If he found that any of them were reasonably good, he would pass them on to me. One doughty opponent he sorted out was Captain Grettin, later a famous admiral and at that time the youngest captain in the British Navy, on board the *Queen* as chief of staff to Admiral Lord Bruce Fraser. Grettin and I put in some hectic games, and watching one of these from the spectators' gallery was new Wimbledon champion Doris Hart with her friend Shirley Fry – champion a few years later.

'Will you teach me how to play?' asked Doris.

'Of course I will,' I answered, rather flattered. The delightful Doris was, not surprisingly, a first-class pupil, picking up the game rapidly, and I often wondered if she kept up her interest in squash back home in the States.

In the Fifties, there wasn't the same urgency as there is today in either Southampton or New York to get the ship turned round back to sea, and this gave me lots of time ashore to indulge my passionate interest in sport. I joined Southampton's famous Trojans Club; founded originally in 1874 solely to play rugby, the club had evolved a fine broad sporting tradition, and in the Fifties also had cricket, squash and hockey teams. Hockey didn't appeal to me, but I played for Trojans in all the other club sports.

On *Queen Elizabeth* we had quite a useful set of cricketers and, as well as turning out for Trojans, I played with the ship's team against such opponents as the British & American Tobacco side, customs officers, Cunard's office eleven, the Midland Bank and quite a few other keen and competent ships' teams. I was, I suppose, what is known as a 'useful all rounder'. Plenty of wickets fell to my medium-paced left-arm deliveries, and I regularly knocked up thirties and forties with the bat. If it seems that I was spending more time playing than sailing, it's only fair to add that some of my rugby matches were during the *Queen*'s four weeks' winter overhaul at Southampton, and I had a similar excuse for my cricket matches when she came in for a ten-day summer check-up.

In the major winter refits, every inch of the vast floating palace was inspected and each item of equipment, from the three sixteen-ton anchors to the 200,000 horse-power main engines, was carefully serviced. Cunard's staff brought ashore 3500 pieces of furniture for checking and partial restoration and, one by one, they went through the ship's half million items of china, glassware and table silver, the 210,000 towels, 30,000 bed sheets, 31,000 pillow cases, 21,000 tablecloths and 30,000 electric lights. Surveyors and technicians went down to the dry-dock floor to inspect the entire hull, and the bottom plating of bilge keels and seawater inlets were gone over minutely. Altogether, 1000 men worked on the overhaul for a month.

Restored to pristine condition, the *Queen* sailed for New York. On the return trip, I came across Burt Lancaster taking the ocean breezes on the boat deck one morning. We had had a brief chat about the weather the day before, but now he obviously had something more serious on his mind. 'I've heard it around that you're something of an athlete,' said Lancaster. I was about to reply that playing amateur rugby, cricket and squash doesn't necessarily make a person an athlete, but the film star didn't give me the chance to say anything. He went on: 'Let's see if you can do anything like this.' I watched amazed as he then ran the full length of the boat deck on his hands, with legs waving in the air. He came back the same way, then called over his valet who was standing by looking totally bored at what I thought was an amazing performance. With one hand, Lancaster lifted up the poor chap to an overhead rail right outside the wardroom, left him swinging there, and walked off. Burt Lancaster, I mused, was a mighty strong, but mighty unusual sort of fellow.

Less energetic but equally fascinating travellers were the Duke and Duchess of Windsor, who had just restored their royal patronage to the two *Queens* after crossing with French liners for several years after the war. The couple invariably arrived at the quayside with unbelievable quantities of luggage. On one of their first trips after returning to the Cunard fold, I counted seventy-five suitcases going into their luxurious suite on the main deck, and they had seventy more trunks in the hold. What was in them all? It's fair to assume that many pieces of the luggage held the dazzling array of fashion shipped to and from the United States several times a year by the Duchess.

She dressed superbly in a quiet, cultured style and often changed her outfit several times a day. I had now reached the chosen ranks of navigational officers serving on the bridge, even though I was still very much a junior member of that élite echelon; perhaps that's why I was delegated to take the regular 8.30 a.m. phone call to the bridge from the Duchess. First, the telephone operator would come on the line and announce: 'The Duchess of Windsor for you.' The rather nasal, unmistakably American voice of the Duchess didn't vary its dialogue very much from day to day. 'Good morning, young man. And what's the weather going to be like today? Just so I know what to wear . . .' Anticipating that the Duchess would be calling, I would already have prepared a detailed forecast of whether it would be sunny, showery or windy as well as the probable temperatures for the rest of the day. When I had read it over to her, the Duchess would say, 'Thanks, young man, that will help me tremendously.'

The Duke himself occasionally came up on the bridge with the Commodore of the Cunard fleet, the stocky veteran George Cove. I thought the Duke appeared much shorter in the flesh than in Press pictures I had seen, and already his slight frame was beginning to bend with the years. He was always interested, in a courteous but friendly sort of way, in just what was happening on the bridge, and liked to inspect the charts to see exactly where we were.

The Commodore brought the Duke over to where I was working, and said, 'Show His Royal Highness our precise position, Arnott.' I pointed out on the chart the location of the ship at that moment.

'Thank you very much,' murmured the Duke, 'and now can I also ask you about the weather?' He was well qualified to discuss navigation and meteorology on the level of a professional seaman, but I suspected that his interest in the weather arose because, like his wife, he was wondering what to ask his valet to lay out next from his conservative yet fabulously extensive wardrobe. Having the appropriate clothing ready wasn't just a matter of fashion in the Fifties: there was no air conditioning on the ship, and passengers could roast in their cabins in a hot summer, and in winter there was no true central heating, although hot air could be blown through the ventilators. Even an ex-king couldn't enjoy the comforts of constantly controlled air temperatures which are commonplace on today's cruise liners.

Early in 1952, I left one great *Queen* to join her sister monarch of the North Atlantic. I switched to the *Queen Mary* as inter-third officer – just a little higher than junior third – after one voyage moving up to senior third. Masters of the *Queens* tended to swap posts with each other from time to time, but I think my favourite Captain of the *Mary* was Ivan Thompson – later Sir Ivan – a warm-hearted, big-bellied Liverpudlian. Six days a week, Captain Thompson appeared an easy-going sort of fellow who loved a pint and a joke as much as any of his crew, but Saturdays it was different. Then, the Captain's mood depended essentially on the success or failure of the Liverpool football club. He must have been one of their longest-standing members, and was certainly one of their most avid supporters. Towards tea-time on a Saturday, when the famous Merseyside club had no doubt just walked off the field after the final whistle, Captain Thompson invariably ordered: 'Go and find out how they've gone on.' Off I would troop to the radio room and wait until the British football results came over the air; the Master, meanwhile, paced the bridge in dire suspense. If the radio message was that Liverpool had won, I would hurry back at once to tell him the good news; if they had lost, I couldn't help but dawdle back to the bridge, for I knew that the normally genial face would turn a rich shade of purple at the sad tidings.

'What, what, Arnott, what's that you're saying?' was his immediate irascible reaction. And if the radio reported that the Captain's club had been really well beaten, it was a wise and immediate strategy to keep out of his way for a few hours, for by the next day, the thrill of anticipation over Liverpool's next game would have taken over, and our much-respected Commodore would again become an approachable human being.

In the first-class dining-room of the *Queen Mary* was a huge colour map of the North Atlantic. Chugging across it in opposite directions were little electrically driven models of the two *Queens*, so arranged that, on the same day that the big ships were passing each other in mid-Atlantic, the models almost touched, although the *Queens* were probably many miles apart and rarely visible to each other. That was because, at that time, ships crossed the Atlantic in well-defined sea-lanes, keeping east-bound and westbound traffic completely apart. With the coming of more sophisticated and effective radar equipment, such wide separation became less critical, the awful prospect of a head-on collision in mid-ocean receding into remote unlikelihood because all nearby vessels could be 'seen' on the *Queens*' radar screens.

Some of *Queen Mary*'s officers still recalled with horror the war-time crash disaster of 1942, when she was bringing to Britain an entire division of GIs, totalling some 15,000 men. Because of the *Queen Mary*'s speed and rudimentary radar, she needed no naval escort across the Atlantic, but as she slowed slightly in her approach to the Clyde, the Navy provided one to bring her through the undersea flotillas of waiting U-boats. Hitler had promised a cash reward of more than £200,000 plus Iron Crosses and oak leaves all round to the crew that sank the *Queen Mary*, and it was on her entry to the shallower, more enclosed waters of the Clyde estuary that she was most vulnerable.

The *Queen*'s escort was the 5000-ton cruiser HMS *Curaçao*. To foil the submarines, the two ships followed the well-established zig-zag evasion plan. Somebody on one or other of the British vessels miscalculated, and in five seconds the 81,000-ton *Queen Mary*'s bow had sliced into the cruiser and cut her in two. She sank instantly, drowning more than 300 of her crew. To safe-guard the lives of her own 15,000 troops, the Captain of the

96

Queen Mary did not dare stop to pick up survivors. She put out an immediate distress call, then limped away forlornly with a crumpled bow. The destroyers HMS *Bramham* and HMS *Cowdray* raced to the scene and managed to drag 100 survivors from the *Curaçao* out of the water, but for the missing 300, the destroyers arrived too late.

More than ten years later that sad story was particularly poignant because we had on board, travelling to the United States, the great war-time leader Sir Winston Churchill. He and Lady Churchill had one of the finest suites on the main deck, and right next door in another spacious suite was their daughter Mary, her husband Christopher Soames, and the Churchill grandchildren.

A quiet, close-knit family, the Churchill clan liked to eat a late lunch in the Verandah Grill, then take a short stroll along the open deck before going back to their suites. One afternoon, however, after finishing lunch around three o'clock, the Churchills and the Soames family didn't turn round as they usually did when they were half-way along the open deck, but kept right on walking towards the bridge. There I was on duty with First Officer Corpus Jones.

The bridge telephone rang sharply. 'Sir Winston and his family are heading your way,' said a rather alarmed voice at the other end.

'OK,' I answered, and immediately called Captain Thompson on the private line to his cabin.

'I'll be right up,' he said. 'Hold the fort till I get there.' In fact, the Captain arrived on the bridge seconds before Sir Winston and his family.

The aroma of the famous Churchill cigar filled the bridge. Sir Winston walked over to our radar equipment, commenting, 'Pity we weren't as far advanced as this in the war. How exactly does this equipment perform?'

Captain Thompson beckoned me over. 'You're the expert, Arnott. Will you explain the system to Sir Winston, please.' I wouldn't have described myself as an expert. It was true I had attended courses in operating our Metro-Vickers set, but radar technology was a game for the boffins. Still, I was able to show Sir Winston just what was happening on our radar screen and why. Sir Winston thanked me, moved to the engine-room telegraph system and asked me just how it worked, although I suspected that, as a former First Lord of the Admiralty, he must have known quite well.

The tireless Sir Winston then said, 'Let's take a look at the chart room to find out where we are.' Our Loran long-range navigation set flashed up, via its 'green snake' cathode-ray tubes, that we were steaming off Newfoundland's Grand Banks. 'Ah yes,' mused Sir Winston, blowing a fog of Havana smoke across the charts. Almost to himself he muttered fiercely, 'British for 500 years, now it's gone to Canada.' Tall, slim and handsome, Sir Winston's politician son-in-law nodded in sympathetic agreement. I assumed our legendary patriot was referring to the acquisition by Canada of Newfoundland and Labrador in 1949. The loss of Newfoundland didn't seem to worry Sir Winston's attractive daughter Mary unduly. She smiled at us reassuringly, and trooped off the bridge with her children, right behind her still-frowning father.

Chapter 13

As on *Queen Elizabeth*, there was a daily tote on the day's mileage on *Queen Mary*. The number of miles achieved in the previous twenty-four hours was officially declared at noon, and as I have described earlier, the fate of several thousands of pounds of passengers' money would rest on the ultimate mileage figure. In practice, sometime after 11.30 in the morning the navigating officer would decide on the figure he would quote, which gave us time on the bridge to type up notices to be displayed in various parts of the ship minutes after the stroke of noon.

However, one of the *Queen*'s Masters, Captain Harry Grattridge, occasionally caused chaos. Often he wasn't on the bridge when all this was going on but, wherever he was, the notice had to be approved by him before it went out. Grattridge had a naturally suspicious nature, and rarely accepted the mileage shown to him, invariably altering it by a mile or two. Once, I asked him why he did it. 'Cuts out fiddles,' he answered shortly. What he didn't know, or care about, was that by shamelessly altering the mileage, he disrupted our production run of typing and fast delivery to the various lounges. I was a fairly reasonable typist and could re-type the notices within minutes, but some officers became flustered at the Master's action, returned in confusion to the bridge and kept the gamblers waiting until they were almost screaming in frustration. It was a pointless exercise on the part of the Captain, I thought, because the fiddles he feared just didn't exist. Yet Grattridge was the boss, and if he decided *Queen Mary* had steamed 702 miles when she had in fact covered only 697, then the Grattridge version was the one announced.

An agreeable young man who came for tea in the wardroom with us one afternoon was the seventeen-year-old King of Iraq, Faisal II. He had just left Harrow public school in England and was on his way with half-a-dozen courtiers to tour the United States. The King chatted away easily in perfect English. 'I'm a little sad, you know, that I'm not going back to Harrow,' he told us. 'First when I went there, I had as rough a time as any other new boy. But I've come to love the place, and truly your England has made me most welcome.' Poor Faisal. His own country was not so hospitable. Six years later both he and his uncle, Emir Abdulillah, who sailed with him on *Queen Mary*, were brutally butchered when their own soldiers staged a *coup d'état* and overthrew the Iraqi monarchy. I shook hands with the smiling King as he left the wardroom and thought, 'What a fortunate young fellow.' Destiny showed how much I was mistaken.

Another illustrious occasional visitor to the wardroom was Bing Crosby. I had been a fan of his since, as a boy, I had seen him in *Pennies from Heaven*, and in later years, I had admired his acting skill in *Going My Way* and *The Bells of St Mary's*. But for me, he was at his peak as the cheerful con-man partnering Bob Hope in the famous *Road* film comedies. There was no trace of the comic in the Bing I met in mid-Atlantic; a smallish, shy and withdrawn man, he couldn't have been more different from the ebullient screen Romeo who chased after Dorothy Lamour in the *Road* classics. I learned afterwards from one of Bing's associates that there was a sad reason behind his shipboard reticence: back home, Bing's adored wife Dixie Lee was lying seriously ill, and not long afterwards I read that she had died. It wasn't so surprising that Bing had sipped his wardroom tea with such a melancholy air.

Although I was hobnobbing with the famous on the *Queens*, as soon as I stepped ashore I became just another young ship's officer – and a rather impoverished one at that. My monthly pay had crept up to £50, but nearly all of that went straight home to Joan and the twins. By way of entertainment, I had to shop around with my shipmates to find the best shows at the cheapest prices, and we found that New York's Radio City was tremendous value for money. The music hall put on a live show featuring the Rockettes, a high-kicking, glamorous chorus line, plus a varying array of cabaret stars, as well as a full-length film. We usually went along to Radio City in the afternoons, when the seats were even cheaper.

The prices of drinks in hotel bars were way beyond our pockets, too, and for a night's drinking in New York, my ship-board chum, Pat Morrish, and I usually called into either the

British Apprentices' Club or the Merchant Navy Officers' Club, which leased space on the first floor of a hotel overlooking Times Square. Looking out over the square on New Year's Eve, 1952, all I could see was wall-to-wall people, and I reflected that the singing, smooching mass of revellers could have been lifted right out of London's Trafalgar Square, except that the good folks celebrating New York's New Year weren't soaked to the skin. Times Square, unlike Trafalgar, had no fountains for the roisterers to jump into. At the stroke of midnight Pat and I, also dry externally but very well lubricated within, raised our glasses to welcome 1953, along with dozens of other merry-making youngsters from the world's merchant fleets, and I wondered if the babies were soundly asleep at home in Fleetwood. Someone flung open the club windows, and the hubbub from thousands of voices below welled up through the chill winter air. Pat and I led the seamen's League of Nations into the singing of 'Auld Lang Syne.'

Pat was a giant of a man. Once, in a slight difference of opinion, I saw him pick up a six-foot seaman and hurl him into a chair at the other side of the room. 'You sit there until I tell you to move,' said Pat. That was the end of the argument. But like most strong men, Pat didn't look for trouble. He was essentially a gentle sort of fellow, and sometimes used to bring his wife down from their native Scotland to join Joan and myself on car touring holidays in Southern England. The car, of course, was borrowed.

On most days on board the *Mary*, Pat and I used to work out in the gym with a huge medicine ball. It was the next best thing to squash, and I couldn't play that on the *Mary* because her former squash court was now part of the gymnasium and the squash spectators' gallery had been converted into the crew purser's office – an indication of how slowly the now ultra-fashionable game of squash progressed in its public appeal in the late Forties and early Fifties.

The medicine ball sessions came to an end for me when I was transferred to the *Parthia* in mid-January 1953, but from the way the top-heavy liner bounced up and down the Atlantic rollers, I might just as well have been back in *Queen Mary*'s gym. I was second officer and handled the 4 a.m. to 8 a.m. watch with the chief officer. It was now a more leisurely timetable to and from New York, largely because *Parthia* carried thousands of

101

tons of cargo as well as its 200 to 300 passengers. The loading and unloading of our main cargo of whisky took a week both in New York and Liverpool and, not surprisingly, the number of 'breakages' were way above average. In New York, making the rounds of the holds, I often came across cases of the finest Scotch 'damaged in handling' but with a longshoreman patiently holding a bucket underneath to catch the golden liquor as it dripped out. It didn't count as pilferage – just convenient accidental damage.

Around this time I became an acting lieutenant in Her Majesty's Royal Navy Reserve. I had applied to join while on *Queen Mary* and, after an interview at the Admiralty building in Whitehall, I was duly accepted. Normally, newcomers to the RNR joined up as sub-lieutenants, but because I held a Master's Certificate I entered at a slightly higher rank. Serving with the Royal Navy was something I had wanted to do since the war, when I had seen the Navy lads in action all over the world. At twenty-nine, I had thought that perhaps I had left it a bit too late, but the chaps at the Admiralty decided otherwise, and I was in. After a couple of short but hectic introductory courses I eventually served my first full year with the Senior Service, but first I left *Parthia* for the 20,000-ton Canadian-run liner *Franconia*, 'born' like myself in the summer of 1923.

Franconia was built by John Brown & Company of Clydeside, who in the next decade were to build the *QE2*. During the war *Franconia* carried troops around the world, and afterwards, in her middle age, she took many thousands of emigrants from Britain and Ireland to Canada. She wasn't the sort of ship where you would expect to find royalty or film stars; most of the passengers had few clothes and little money, but they had unlimited optimism for the new life waiting for them in the vast territories of Canada.

Sometimes, unfortunately, the realities of emigrant life did not match up to the feverish shipboard anticipation on the west-bound voyage. Newly promoted from second officer to junior first officer, one evening I was in charge of the 8 p.m. to midnight watch as we headed back across the Atlantic to Liverpool, when shouts from the stern area raised the alarm that a woman passenger had jumped overboard. Immediately I put in effect the 'Man overboard' procedure which involved blasting out the special 'overboard' signal on the ship's whistle, turning round and steaming back over the area. I also ordered a lifebuoy over the side, but it was all fairly hopeless from the start. A westerly gale was whipping up huge waves, the water was cold and the lookouts I posted around the ship reported: 'No sign of the lady.' A check of the poor woman's belongings showed she was one Rose Brennan from southern Ireland, and owned little more than the clothes she wore when she jumped into the Atlantic. Rose Brennan was eighty when she ended her life. For her, Canada just hadn't worked out.

In mid-summer of 1953, the Navy called me up for an officers' introductory training course and, wearing the dark blue uniform of the Navy, I reported to the naval barracks at Portsmouth. In the next few weeks I was initiated into the belligerent, hostile side of sea service. At HMS *Mercury* in Petersfield, Hampshire, I studied battle communications at sea, while in Portsmouth itself, at HMS *Vernon*, the Navy taught me minesweeping and their side of the torpedo and anti-submarine business. Then it was on to Lee-on-Solent to HMS *Daedalus* for a junior officers' flying course. The only other time I had been in the air was when I was six, when Sir Alan Cobham's air circus visited Bolton and Bury in Lancashire and my father took me up for a ten-shilling flip. This time was rather more serious. I sat behind the pilot in a dual-controlled plane and took the stick as we flew low over Spithead. The three-funnelled liner in the distance had, I thought, a familiar look. I could see the anxious, upturned faces of passengers as we buzzed over the masts of the homeward-bound *Queen Mary*. It was my turn to be worried when I tried formation flying, the wingtips of our three trainer planes seeming to touch as we scudded along the Solent. I found the experience exhilarating, but definitely so hair-raising that I decided privately to try to confine my future formation work to ballroom dancing.

As a seaman who had fired a few rounds in anger at the Japanese and other assorted enemies in the war, I took a particular interest in the gunnery section of the course, which operated at Chatham's Gunnery School. I was additionally happy to be there because Chatham was the centre for the United Services (Chatham) Rugby Football Club. The selectors quickly drafted me into the team at second row forward and we were beaten only once in a long run of matches. That was by the crack Old Merchant Taylors Fifteen, but we had good wins over Rochester, Old Blues, Bart's Hospital, United Services Portsmouth, Old Rutlishians, Brighton, Berkshire Wanderers and half a dozen other top teams. It wasn't easy getting into the United Services first fifteen. On selection day a dozen or so games started out on the various adjoining Services' grounds and, as they went on, the selectors moved around until they had chosen thirty players. These were split into two teams which played for half an hour on one of the central grounds until the final first fifteen was selected. It was a gruelling process, but well worth the struggle, I thought, when I battled as a first teamer against famous sides such as Harlequins, London Irish, London Scottish and Oxford and Cambridge Universities.

While I've never regretted a minute of my years in the Merchant Service, I believe that I would equally have enjoyed a career in the Royal Navy. The sporting facilities were certainly far better in the Navy and, as well as rugger, I played cricket for United Services, Portsmouth, and I turned out at squash for HMS *Osprey*, Portland. Between naval sporting sessions, I managed to fit in courses in chemical warfare, fire fighting, chasing submarines with depth charges and more gunnery with 4.7-inch weapons fired at moving targets.

Then I returned to more peaceful pursuits with the *Franconia*. As well as carrying some 1500 passengers, the Cunarder often brought cargoes of grain back to Britain which, as I've said earlier, was never my favourite freight. Occasionally, we shipped ice hockey teams to and from Britain, and like most sportsmen they could get pretty boisterous after a few drinks. One frolicsome team heaved the ship's piano into the Atlantic after a particularly hectic booze party. The ice men were pretty beefy customers, so we didn't provoke trouble by trying to stop them. But next day, as they nursed their hangovers, I rounded them up and exacted part-payment from each hockey player for the drowned piano.

I made an unscheduled dive underwater one summer's afternoon in 1954. The three daughters of a wealthy Canadian family were returning on *Franconia* after touring Europe. When we docked, they invited some of the ship's officers, including myself, up to their estate near Québec for a day out. The family's summerhouse was set on the banks of Lake Beauport, and came complete with canoes, sailing dinghies and speedboats. Tiring of small talk and drinks by the lakeside, I decided to take out a canoe. For the holder of a Master's Certificate, it looked easy. I sat in the stern and plunged the paddle deep in the water. Over she went, with the master mariner underneath. As I bobbed up, I heard loud, derisive laughter from the men and women onshore. 'Stroke the water, don't attack it,' shouted one of the girls. That, apparently, was the secret of successfully paddling a canoe, so I practised for an hour until I could guide the canoe round the lake almost as smoothly as I could bring *Franconia* into the St Lawrence estuary.

On another of *Franconia*'s voyages to Québec, the cruiser HMS *Sheffield* was in port as we arrived. She was the flagship of the Commander-in-Chief of the American and West Indies Station of the Royal Navy. My own induction into the Navy gave me a topical interest in the cruiser, and I was particularly pleased when invitations arrived for *Franconia*'s officers to attend the ceremony of Beating Retreat on the nearby quay in Wolfe's Cove where she lay alongside, just astern of the *Franconia*.

I've always found that a background knowledge of the origins of such ceremonies enhances appreciation of the actual occasion, so I looked up the brief history of Beating Retreat. Apparently, it began as part of a soldier's daily routine in the British Army in the early years of the sixteenth century. At sundown, regimental drummers went through the streets beating their drums in quick time to remind soldiers to return to their garrisons. The drum-beat also served as the official warning to local publicans to call 'Time, gentlemen, please.' British soldiers then serving in the Low Countries heard hostelry owners shout 'Tap, toe,' meaning 'turn off the taps', in response to the drums. The military men rendered this unwelcome phrase as something like 'ta-too', and soon 'tattoo' was the term used by the soldiers for the drummers' 'curfew' beat. On many overseas campaigns, a general drum and bugle call was also sounded to remind those outside the city walls to return inside for the night and, in the army's years in France, Belgium and Holland, this warning became known as *La Retraite*. By the eighteenth century, my brief research showed, it was the army's established custom at night to sound first the 'Retreat' and then send drummers around the garrison town beating 'Tattoo'.

The sunset ceremony near HMS *Sheffield* was colourful and impressive. It began with the Royal Marine Band stirring us all up with the ship's march, 'On Ilkley Moor Baht'at';

this traditional Yorkshire folk song was chosen because of the cruiser's association with its namesake city of Sheffield. Then, while the Retreat was beaten on the ceremonial drum, the red-uniformed Royal Marines marched and counter-marched to such blood-rousers as 'Lilli-Burlero', 'The Globe and the Laurel' and 'HM Jollies'. In contrast, the evening air stilled respectfully as everyone sang 'Abide with Me' and, as the sun vanished over the western horizon, the band marked its going with 'The Last Post', followed by the British and Canadian national anthems. Finally, the moving climax to the parade came with the ship's Guard and the Royal Marine Band marching past to the rollicking and appropriate bars of 'A Life on the Ocean Wave'. As the glittering ranks advanced on *Sheffield*'s gold-braided saluting base with a precise, patriotic panache, I felt proud to be wearing a British uniform.

It wasn't too long after that pleasant, memorable evening on the quarterdeck that Joan and I bought our first house, and some thirty years later we still live there. Number 47, Rossall Grange Lane, Fleetwood was close to the Irish Sea and to the local golf club. At least, that's what Joan told me in a letter, but I had never particularly noticed the property and, as usual when anything significant was happening at home, I was away at sea. Joan negotiated the sale, and, with the help of her mother and brother Alan – on leave from a foreign posting with the Gurkhas – she organised the removal.

The following year I reported to Portsmouth for my first long-term spell of training with the RNR. Was it just coincidence, I wondered, that I was assigned to the sloop HMS *Fleetwood*? Her fleet pennant number was 47 – the same number as my house – and before the war she had patrolled the waters of the Persian Gulf. In those years, she had also twice visited the Lancashire fishing port whose name she bore and, as a boy, I toured the sloop on one of these visits. I had been entranced, and decided then and there to go to sea.

I now joined HMS *Fleetwood* as she was nearing the end of a refit in Portsmouth Naval Dockyard and standing in the dock next door was a huge yet shapely grey monster I had last seen more than 3000 miles away. The gin was cool and clear that night in the welcoming wardroom of HMS *Sheffield*. Many of the officers who had been on the saluting base in Québec were ᶜtill serving with her, and one of the *Sheffield* veterans who had survived all the war years with the ship proposed a toast – 'To Bob Arnott. Now he's one of us.'

HMS *Fleetwood* was attached to Portsmouth Squadron and had been newly fitted out as an experimental radar ship. I was appointed officer in charge of her code books and confidential papers. At the end of their useful life, Top Secret documents and books were, according to the regulations, to be transported by myself to the local public incinerator and destroyed there; another officer was supposed to go along with me to the bonfire and sign a 'certificate of destruction'. In peace-time, all this seemed to be an excessive tonnage of red tape, but for some weeks I duly delivered HMS *Fleetwood*'s newly outdated paper secrets to Portsmouth's incinerator. One day, there weren't too many papers to be burned, and I decided there and then to update the whole system by awarding our custom to the ship's own boiler fires. I'd forgotten that on most naval vessels – including HMS *Fleetwood* – the funnel stands right next to the bridge. And as we steamed past Hayling Island, a fine white dust began to fall on the bridge's immaculate floors.

'Is it snowing?' asked puzzled First Lieutenant James Scott.

'I don't think so, sir,' I answered hastily. 'It's only the ship's secret papers going up in smoke.'

'What?' shouted Scott. 'Do you mean to say you've shoved them in the boiler fires?'

'Yes I have,' I explained stoutly. The boiler room, I added, was much handier than the Portsmouth incinerator.

'Well, in future,' said Scott, 'you'd better stick to the so-and-so rule book, or else.' I bowed to naval tradition, and restored our trade to the incinerator.

A couple of other jobs came my way. The commanding officer, Lieutenant Commander Stocken said to me one day:

'Is it right, Arnott, that your family keeps a pub?'

Wondering what was coming next, I answered warily, 'They do indeed.'

'Right then,' said the Captain, 'you're appointed wardroom mess secretary. It's like being the landlord of the officers' pub.'

It was rather more than that, I discovered. The job included supplying the wardroom steward with cash to buy produce at local ports of call, handing him money for such items as butter, coffee and tea from the on-board NAAFI, and keeping strict mess accounts for everyone using the wardroom. This was especially essential, I discovered, with the civilian radar boffins we took out to sea from time to time, one or two of whom were inclined to be absentminded and leave for home without settling up. These chaps found me blocking the gangplank, notebook in hand, as they prepared to abandon ship. 'If you ever want to get a debt collector's job ashore,' said Stocken, 'I'll give you a first-class reference.' I didn't take up his offer.

My third job, and possibly the most rewarding, was acting as quarterdeck divisional officer to a third of the crew – some thirty men. I looked after their general welfare, recommended them for promotion when I thought they deserved it and tried to sort out as best I could their frenzied depressions when wives didn't write or even went off with someone else back home. I often have to undertake the same sort of ticklish task today.

As well as cruising up and down the southern coast of England, HMS *Fleetwood* occasionally headed out to more fascinating waters. One weekend we took her down to Lisbon, and on the Sunday morning, I attended service at the Portuguese capital's English church. The following evening, I travelled north with some shipmates to visit the famous casino at Estoril, but roulette, I found, was far more costly and infinitely less satisfying than honest-to-goodness religion. Once or twice we called at some of the ports on the French coast which only a few years earlier had sheltered the U-boat wolf packs. I remembered nights of Atlantic horror as I looked down into the huge, concrete underwater submarine pens built by the Germans – and still intact – at St Nazaire.

Back in Britain, a letter was waiting for me from Portsmouth and Southsea Rugby Union Club. Their Irish international Con Griffin was organising an Easter tour, and had decided they needed a bit of extra beef in the second row. I joined the tour, and played matches in Birmingham and Manchester, but the plum fixture of the tour was a game at the Lytham St Annes ground of the famous Lancashire Fylde club. Con Griffin asked me how I reckoned we would get on with Fylde; I had known the seaside club since I was a boy, and I wasn't exaggerating when I told Con that we would get slaughtered. The tourists did their best, but for Fylde it was just a casual stroll to victory.

I should have been playing that day, but couldn't get through the packed Easter traffic between Fleetwood and Lytham St Annes in time for the game, even though I had set out half an hour early. The crowds were so dense that Blackpool police had to call in a helicopter on traffic control to get Burnley Football Club's team coach to Bloomfield Road in time for their match. When I finally reached Fylde's Woodlands Road ground, it was nearly all over. Vanquished and victors got together after the match in Fylde's fine clubhouse for the traditional jugs of ale. I hadn't played, but it wasn't my fault that the Lancashire coast had attracted half the motorists in Britain, so I reckoned I was fully entitled to join the jugging.

'Did you get thrashed?' asked Joan when I arrived home several hours later.

'Well, it's a long story. I didn't play. But yes, a good thrashing would be about right.'

Later in the year, the Navy celebrated the long, hot summer days with regattas, cocktail parties and guard-ship duties during Cowes Week. For HMS *Fleetwood*'s Midsummer's Day party, I took on the task, as mess secretary, of dressing up the quarter-deck. To be a little different, I decided to decorate the area on the lines of a ship visiting a tropical island, but that posed one or two problems, such as where to get palm trees and other exotic foliage. On the scrounger's grapevine I heard that Eastney Barracks at Southsea went in for such luxuries in their quite remarkable gardens and, within an hour, I was at the wheel of a naval truck bound for the barracks. Palms, equatorial bushes and white awning topped by a dazzling display of the ship's flags made, I thought, quite a devastating splash of colour on our normally sedate quarterdeck.

Cowes Week provided spectacular yachting, but the guard duties were fairly uneventful. No ships collided, and no one needed rescuing from drowning. By way of a mid-summer interlude, one or two officers from *Fleetwood* were invited onto a motor cruiser bound for a regatta garden party at the Royal Thames Yacht Club at Warsash on the Hamble River. Our hosts were Lord Mountbatten, President of the Club, and Lady Mountbatten. At the club's luxurious headquarters, there was a splendid saloon and lounge bar, supplemented on the river bank by a cool, canvas marquee. There, the cold chicken and salad, followed by strawberries and cream, and washed down with champagne, provided splendid regatta repast.

Most Saturdays around that time I played cricket for United Services, with occasional mid-week matches for the Portsmouth

Squadron. The Captain of the Services team was Instructor-Lieutenant Clive Woodcock, a National Serviceman who was proud to be a Yorkshireman. Said Clive 'You know, Bob, when I marry I'll make sure my sons are actually born within the county – so that they'll be eligible to play for Yorkshire. With the girls, it doesn't matter so much.' Clive was, of course, talking of the hallowed Yorkshire cricket tradition that only native-born sons of the county can represent it. I've met quite a few other Yorkshiremen since that time who made sure their wives gave birth to their babies in Leeds, Sheffield or York itself. Then, if the youngster turned out to be another Len Hutton, he'd be properly qualified to wear the White Rose on his county cap.

As winter approached, the rugger season returned and I decided to take up goal kicking seriously. As all rugger enthusiasts know, there is a free kick for goal after a try has been scored. This is known as 'converting' the try, and brings in extra points. I turned out to have quite a powerful goal kicking talent, and from 1954 onwards hit the target hundreds of times. I practised for hours to perfect my ability, using half a dozen rugby balls at a time for quick fire left footed goal shots. I felt that at thirty, my future scoring chances lay more in the realms of goal kicking than from the speed, skill and occasional brute force of full blooded forward play.

Getting back to reality, we now went off for exercises around the Azores, but the main purpose of the visit seemed to be for us to enjoy the exotic celebration of Mardi Gras. Non-stop dancing round the clock, in streets festooned with streamers and gaily-coloured balloons, was, I thought, far removed from the recent reserved and typically British celebrations I had seen during Cowes Week. After leaving the Azores, we came back north-wards to visit Stavanger in Norway, where we tested newly developed radar equipment in cold conditions.

One of my last 'official' engagements with the Royal Naval Reserve at the end of my twelve-month stint was to attend the United Services Rugby Club's annual dinner aboard HMS *Excellent*, the Whale Island gunnery school, after the annual match against London Scottish, and naturally included piping in the haggis. There were one or two wee drams afterwards, and many of the 200 diners who toasted the haggis – including myself – decided to stay the night at the school instead of braving the Whale Island night air.

Just before I returned north to civilian life, the captain of HMS *Boxer* – the largest ship in our squadron – challenged the rest of the squadron members to a game of soccer. I played in goal for 'the rest' one Saturday morning in early November, then walked straight across to the nearby rugby ground to turn out for United Services against Bournemouth. That was my final bow in services rugby for the time being, although a few days later I turned out at squash against Lieutenant-Commander Taylor in a hard-fought match at the Southsea Squash Racquets Club. It may appear that much of my Navy time was spent playing sport instead of being out at sea. It wasn't that way really – it's just that the British services do encourage sport in the belief that physical fitness encourages mental sharpness.

In mid-November, I put away my naval blues and began sorting out my long-stowed Cunard uniforms. A few days at home with Joan and the family, and I was heading south again to join the latest holder of one of Cunard's most famous appellations. Just before Christmas, 1955, I signed on in Southampton as senior second officer of RMS *Mauretania*.

Chapter 14

The latest *Mauretania* was completed at Cammell Laird's Birkenhead shipyard just before the war. The Admiralty decided, first of all, to convert her into an armed merchant cruiser, but this decision was soon overtaken by the priority to ship Allied troops around the world and, in 1940, *Mauretania* sailed for New York and then went on to Sydney to start her war service as a troop carrier. Her regular war-time run was between Australia and the Middle East, although she did do service elsewhere and, in 1945, went round the world in just eighty-one days; in her troop travels, *Mauretania* covered approximately 600,000 miles.

On one transatlantic trip, when the huge Cunarder was bringing 5500 American GIs to Britain, naval intelligence reported that two packs of U-boats off Northern Ireland were closing in on her course, one to the north and the other to the south. The gap between the submarine flotillas was narrowing by the minute, and the only practical course available to *Mauretania* was to try to dash through the fast-closing steel jaws. She surged to her maximum of 26 knots, and burst through to safety almost as the German commanders were sighting the mammoth target in their periscopes. Yet the troop-packed liner still wasn't out of danger. In the early hours of the next morning, her radar detected a submarine less than five miles ahead, sitting on the surface like a hungry cormorant. *Mauretania*'s Captain ordered an instant complete about-turn. Immediately, Western Approaches Command in Liverpool picked up a signal from the sub as it broke radio silence to flash out the exact position of *Mauretania* to the other submarines. Top speed and a bewildering zig-zag course outflanked the massed killers, and *Mauretania* eventually steamed breathlessly but unscathed into the safe haven of Clydeside.

That war-time yarn was recounted to me over a drink in the

wardroom of the Cunarder, which had just emerged from Southampton Dry Docks after a thorough refit. In the summer months of peace-time, *Mauretania* was sailing the Atlantic in routine service with the two *Queens*, but now, for the winter cruise season, she was about to transport citizens of the United States away from their climatic rigours into the soft warm breezes of the Caribbean. On Saturdays, we would sail out of New York in thick duffle coats, leaving the city firmly gripped by white winter, to arrive two days later in our tropical white drills at a sun-splashed Caribbean quayside.

The mid-Fifties saw the real start of the cruising scene as we know it today. The huge jets of BOAC, Pan Am and half-a-dozen European airlines were already lifting passengers by the thousand away from the cabins of transatlantic liners, and Cunard saw clearly that future prosperity – and perhaps even sheer survival – would depend on a successful switch to cruising. The custom-built *Caronia* was already shipping travellers around the world's tourist resorts, and even before the war the *Franconia* had pioneered world cruises. Ships of the Holland–American Line were also getting into the cruising game. Their liner *New Amsterdam* was almost a double for *Mauretania*, and she often followed our creamy wake through the blue Caribbean in whistle-stop tours of the islands. For passengers, cruising in the sun was a luxury pleasure, but for Cunard's ocean giants, the sombre choice was between cruising and the breaker's yard.

When *Mauretania* had arrived in New York, four of her lifeboats were taken off to make way for special cruise launches for landing passengers at ports too small to take the huge Cunarder at the quayside. As senior second officer, I went ashore ahead of our tourists to make sure that the launch arrangements were safe and secure. This was vital, because many of our American guests were senior citizens who weren't too adept at jumping in and out of heaving launches. The ten-day cruises were, I thought, a demanding exercise for the many elderly people aboard, especially as we called at a different port every day. Around the Dutch 'ABC' islands, for instance, one day we would be in Aruba, the next in Curaçao and the third in St Martin, or we might make a swift call to pick up duty-free liquor in the American Virgin Islands, then on to the breathtaking vista of Puerto Rico's San Juan Bay. I told Captain Charlie

Williams that it was all too hectic for even the fittest of our pensioners, but our approach to Cunard's marketing department brought the retort that the crowded schedule was exactly 'what sells'. The desk-bound planners hadn't, I felt, had to manhandle a twelve-stone old lady from the ladders of a liner standing out at sea into a launch alternately rising and plunging like a distraught Otis lift.

One gloriously sunny February day, *Mauretania* was visiting Curaçao, and we tied up at the berth of the local oil company to take on fuel. The British Mining Company, fortunately, had a private beach nearby, and threw it open to our crew for swimming from its silver sands. My own particular interest in the mining company was their renowned cricket team. *Mauretania* could muster a reasonably competent side from her 600 crew, and that afternoon we took a picnic tea from the ship's berth at Caracasbaai to the company's ground, just half an hour's drive away. We were well beaten, but the cool and potent Dutch beer provided by our opponents washed down our sandwiches beautifully, and we followed up with one or two glasses of the orange-flavoured liqueur bearing the name of the tropical island. It brought an early evening mellow glow to the whole sporting affair, and it didn't seem to matter much who had won or lost.

Meanwhile, back in frosty Fleetwood, Joan was enjoying the pleasures of coping with a young family all suffering from whooping cough. The twins were now four and a half, and our latest arrival, Gill, was just a year old. A couple of weeks earlier, I had sent Joan a letter from Paradise Beach, Nassau, enclosing a photograph of myself basking in the sun. 'It's always lovely to hear from you,' Joan told me later, 'but on that occasion with three babies whooping their heads off, I could have committed murder – on you.' Happily, and without my assistance, the children recovered completely.

I thought it better, just then, not to tell Joan about the Curaçao cricket jaunt, but the amounts of hooch put away there by the dispirited cricketers of the *Mauretania* were a mere puddle compared with the great lakes of the stuff shifted by the American Liquor Dealers when they came on board for a sales incentive cruise. Led by one Abe Shapiro, the booze barons brought their own stocks aboard in bottles, barrels and tanks. I don't think I've ever seen so much liquor sloshing around one ship. So many parties were going on during the ten-day cruise that no one, it seemed, ever finished a drink. The dealers downed half a tumbler of bourbon, Scotch, rum or gin at one cabin party, then left the rest to roll away to their next port of call. So much wasted liquor was poured down the ship's drains by stewards that one of them swore to me that he had heard a following school of dolphins hiccuping all over the Caribbean.

Occasionally we picked up passengers around the islands who preferred to sail rather than fly back to New York. One of these was a sun-tanned, black-haired and stunningly attractive woman who came on board in Barbados with a man she described as her butler. She was Joan Crawford and, as I escorted them to adjoining cabins, she stopped suddenly, remarking, 'I want this gentleman well looked after because, if he isn't, he won't be able to look after me, will he?' That was logical, I agreed, and I asked the couple's cabin steward to take very good care of both of them. Miss Crawford and her companion understandably kept apart from other passengers, but once or twice I talked to her briefly as she took an early stroll – alone – on the promenade deck. Joan Crawford was then, I suppose, in her mid-forties, but her superb eyes and boldly carved features were defying the onslaught of early middle age.

'Are you married?' was the unexpected query from the famous star on one of her morning walks.

'Why, yes,' I replied, 'and we've got three babies. They've just had whooping cough.'

'Your wife's a lucky girl,' said Joan sadly. 'I've always wanted children of my own, but could never have any. And as for husbands, well my latest, darling Alfred, is a real pain in the you-know-what. Of course, I've got adopted children, as you probably know.'

I didn't, but I ventured the hope that the sea voyage would help her sort out her problems. Said Joan, 'You know, young man, that's one of the reasons I'm aboard. I'm trying to stay away from problems. Are you psychic?'

'Not that I'm aware of,' I told the troubled lady.

'Ah well, never mind that,' she said. 'You just look after that girl of yours and the three youngsters. And tell them you talked to Joan Crawford.'

115

I promised I would. And I did. When I showed my own Joan the out-sized signed photograph the film star had given me, she declared, 'That will be a big help in bringing up the children.' Perhaps, I reflected, I should have kept the completely innocent picture locked away in my sea chest.

Invariably, when the *Mauretania* docked back in New York at her regular Pier 90 berth at the foot of Fiftieth/Fifty-First Street, a clutch of seedy-suited lawyers were hovering around the quayside. If they spotted any passengers coming ashore with an arm in a sling or perhaps limping slightly, they would pester them to sue Cunard on the basis of a 50/50 share out of any compensation they managed to win. It wasn't only the *Mauretania* that came in for this legal initiative; the quayside lawyers met every ship as it docked. Crews dubbed them 'the vultures', but so high was the success rate in securing substantial settlements, usually out of court, that most shipping companies, including Cunard, carried hefty insurance policies to protect themselves from the talons of these judicial predators.

One of them was acting for a woman claiming heavy damages for fracturing her ankle on *Mauretania* during a cruise to the Caribbean from New York. Fortunately for Cunard, one of our officers, 'Zulu' Thompson, from South Africa, had an eagle eye as well as a photographic memory, and he was able to recall that, as he stood on the quayside talking to friends while passengers joined the ship in New York, he saw the woman hobbling up the gangplank with her leg already in plaster. Case dismissed.

From the Caribbean I switched to the favourite European cruising waters of the Mediterranean, leaving one of the largest ships in the Cunard fleet to join one of the smallest – the 3800-ton *Brescia*. We weren't shipping film stars or even tourists around the Med; we carried motor cars, whisky and rolls of cloth from British ports to trading outlets in Italy, the Greek islands and along the Turkish coast to Izmir and Istanbul. For British housewives, we brought back grapes from Turkey, dried fruit and figs from Greece and tinned plum tomatoes from Italy.

Brescia was a tough little plodder. Her top speed was around 7 knots, and when she met a Mediterranean squall head-on – which happened more often than cruise companies ever admitted – it was a fairly even contest between *Brescia*'s pistons

116

and the challenging waves. Yet I was grateful to the ageing freighter because she gave me my initial appointment as a ship's chief officer, or first mate. And I was also thankful for the long Mediterranean experience of her Captain, Les Stant. I knew little about that sometimes treacherous stretch of sea, but Les showed me his way of trundling *Brescia* through the Strait of Gibraltar, and how to weave in and out of the Mediterranean jigsaw coastline where *Brescia* delivered and collected her work-aday cargoes. I quickly mastered the complexities of the almost landlocked sea, but Les was less successful in explaining to me his 'infallible' system for backing horses; we were both, I decided, far more adept at handling the Med than selecting winners at Ascot, Newbury or Newmarket. I left Liverpudlian Les still weighing up form when I left *Brescia* and the Mediterranean for the much larger motor vessel *Andria* and the broad rollers of the familiar North Atlantic.

MV *Andria* originally ran between London and South America for the Silver Line and was then known as *Silverbriar*, but in 1951 Cunard took her over and re-named her with the famous 'ia' fleet suffix. When I signed aboard, *Andria*'s Captain was Bil (only one 'l') Warwick, who later became the first Captain of the *QE2*. At that time, both Bil and I were concerned with rather more mundane matters than commanding the world's super-ship, for the 7200-ton *Andria* was just a general cargo vessel. Later in her career she carried coal so often that we jokingly referred to her as the only two-funnelled collier on the North Atlantic.

Nevertheless, she had spacious, comfortable accommodation for her officers. We lived in the cabins that had carried twelve passengers during the ship's South American days, and took our meals in a dining-saloon far too large and luxurious for an ordinary cargo ship. We didn't, of course, complain to the company.

Andria's cargoes went to New York and Baltimore, from where I went with a few shipmates on a Greyhound bus for a Sunday trip to Washington D.C. We found the usual long weekend queues at the Washington Monument for the lift to the top. I've never been one to queue, and I exclaimed, 'Blow this, I'll take the stairs!' Quite a few minutes later, I emerged panting from the stairway to the 556-foot high platform just as my more staid pals arrived there in the lift. 'Bravo, Bob,' said one, 'we thought we'd beat you up here, but you've run a great dead heat against Mr Otis.' I was too breathless even to reply, but I listened with interest a moment or two later when the guide told us that on no account should anyone drop a coin or anything else over the side. 'By the time it hits the ground, it will have built up the velocity of a bullet, and would kill,' he warned.

I was still working out the mechanics of that assertion when my pals hauled me into the lift to return to the earth. Later in the day we went to see the soaring dome of the Capitol and the splendidly imposing Lincoln Memorial at the north end of Memorial Bridge. Our grand finale was the White House itself. I had been looking forward to seeing the Presidential State Dining-room and the Red, Blue and Green Rooms which American liner passengers had often told me not to miss, but an official told us, 'Sorry guys, we're not open to the public on Sundays. Come back Tuesday, when we open up through to Saturday.'

A midweek trip back to the Federal capital was impossible, as our time was fully booked at Sparrow's Point, Baltimore, taking on steel that had been brought from the Bethlehem Steel Works in Pennsylvania. This deadweight cargo was stacked at the bottom of the holds, grain was poured on top and all of this was surmounted by 'shifting boards' specially fitted by carpenters. This was to stop the grain from moving around in Atlantic storms. More than one ship had been lost in the past through the movement of grain in mid-ocean, hence the vital need for the boards.

Not only did we find first-rate steel at Baltimore. Top-grade oysters grew in the local beds and our chief steward Dick Jones used to buy them for us at the wholesale rate of five dollars a bushel. Bil Warwick and I could demolish a full bushel between us over a couple of pints of beer at lunchtime. We were equally fond of the soft-shelled crabs which were a Chesapeake Bay speciality of Chief Steward Jones who battered them lightly – still alive – and dropped them in hot fat. One evening while he was preparing his fat, I was herding the crabs, dripping with batter, together on the galley table when some of the crew returning on board spotted the scene through the galley port-hole. 'You cruel so and so's,' they shouted, but that didn't put Bil and me off our eventual crustacean repast.

When we visited New York, Cunard's cargo interests there were looked after by Captain Bill Henshaw, superintendent with the associated company of Brocklebanks. He loved to yarn with me over a glass of gin, but he refused to touch my Old Tom brand, although he used always to drink tonic with his own gin. 'Wouldn't touch that stuff,' said Bill. 'It's nothing like as good as Gordon's.' I used to stock up with duty free Old Tom when we put in at Le Havre; it was certainly far cheaper there than Gordon's, and in my opinion was equally as good.

The Captain's preference for his favourite gin was renowned among officers who knew him, and one day I decided to test out his palate by decanting a full bottle of Old Tom into an empty Gordon's bottle. 'This is a drop of the real stuff,' chortled the Captain as we hit the halfway point on the Gordon's bottle. 'Don't know how you can drink that other muck.' It was years later before I told him how he had failed the taste test. 'Well, bless my soul, Bob,' he said stubbornly, 'I suspected you at the time. Gordon's was far too good to give away, but as for Old Tom, I still don't know how you drank it.'

The second skipper I served with as chief officer of the *Andria* was Joe Woolfenden, who later became Master of the liner *Carmania*. Occasionally *Andria* deserted the Atlantic to carry coal to Europe. Our normal unloading port there was Amsterdam, but once in a while we called in at Avonmouth to part-discharge before going to Kiel, via the famous canal that runs between the North Sea and the Baltic. The crane operators at Kiel didn't always aim their coal grabs too well, and were prone to hoist away parts of the ship instead of our black cargo. It was part of the delivery contract that the Kiel contractors had to make good any damage to our ship before we sailed, and as chief officer I had to watch every coal lump go ashore, then compile a list of 'accidents' and make sure repairs were completed before we left. Once at sea, there would have been no chance of recovering anything from the coal contractors.

I recall one of the Avonmouth sailings with some affection, for Joan came down to the West Country port around that time to spend New Year with me. We stayed at the Miller's Arms, near the Avonmouth Docks and, although it wasn't the Hilton, the turkey, roast potatoes, Brussels sprouts, roast chestnut and apple sauces, and the Christmas pudding served up by the landlord's wife on New Year's Day, tasted as terrific as any meal I've ever enjoyed in later years on the world's floating palaces. The coals glowed brightly in the hostelry's fire grates that Christmastide, and for a few wonderfully happy days with Joan, I forgot the thousands of tons of coal waiting for me in *Andria*'s holds just across the road.

But my days of chief officer of an ocean-going coal truck were coming to an end, for a couple of months later I rejoined Cunard's own Atlantic roller coaster RMS *Parthia*. We sailed out of Liverpool bound for New York, and when the vessel, renowned for her violence, reached the white-crested rollers of the open Atlantic, I could hardly believe the comparatively nonchalant way she moved into them. It turned out that *Parthia* had been fitted with stabilisers after I had left her in mid-1953. *Parthia*'s habit of hurling officers and crew indiscriminately from their bunks onto the cold floor in the middle of the night came to a sudden and welcome end.

The ship's second officer at that time was Charles Lucas, son of a former Captain, Otto Lucas. Young Charles's girl friend, whom he later married, lived on Long Island and was the owner of a blue and white Ford Fairlane. Charles used to arrive in style for duty in the powerful, wing-tailed automobile, and when our shipboard watches didn't coincide, he often lent it to me. It was my first experience of driving in the States, and although the four and six-lane highways initially bewildered me, I soon became accustomed to the roadways in New York State, chauffeuring my chums from the ship out as far as Poughkeepsie, or heading for the scenic beauties of Bear Mountain State Park. I don't know if Second Officer Lucas ever told his girl friend she was providing luxurious leisure transport facilities for *Parthia*'s rolling stones, but fortunately I always managed to bring back the Fairlane with no more damage than a few more miles on its clock.

Captain of the *Parthia* at that time was John Crosby-Dawson, from Wallasey, near Liverpool. A huge man, John loved his food even more than I did. His favourite dish, which he claimed to have invented, was oysters sewn inside an out-sized steak which he called the Crosby-Dawson Bay Steak. When we were in New York, he used to visit the chef at Jack Dempsey's restaurant to pick up the latest gourmet gossip. 'Do you know, Bob,' said the Captain one evening, 'I do believe I know as much about food as most of these professional eaters who write it up in magazines.' As I laid into his new creation, Supreme Crosby-Dawson Silverside, I agreed. The Captain was a widower, but he re-married when he retired from the sea, and I used to wonder how his new wife matched up to his lofty culinary standards.

Chapter 15

The 22,000-ton *Sylvania* was just a year old when I joined her as junior first officer. One Sunday morning, we were in mid-Atlantic on the way to Montreal when the ship ran into grey, swirling banks of fog. The Master and chief officer stayed on the bridge for several hours until *Sylvania* was well clear of the treacherous, billowing mists. As the ship's 'top two' scanned the seas, I was automatically elected, as third in line, to lead the religious service in the main lounge, a brand-new experience which I thoroughly enjoyed, joining the 200 or so passengers in hymns, psalms and the prayers set for that day. I was mightily relieved to find that I wasn't expected to preach during the cheerful, interdenominational service, and I hoped with all my heart, knowing the state of the weather, that there was nothing ominous in one of our hymns being 'For those in peril on the sea'.

Since that foggy Sunday, I've taken hundreds of shipboard services, including quite a few burials at sea. Even these sombre occasions bring a degree of consolation to the attending sailors, for most seafarers regard the cool ocean depths as a peaceful and perfectly natural resting place. And that includes myself.

On a happier aspect of religion at sea, people often ask me if I still marry couples on board ship. The answer, I'm afraid, is that I don't and I never have done. It's not because I don't want to – I have no particular feelings either way – but such a ceremony would be illegal under British law, which these days lays down that an authorised Registrar must always be present at a wedding. And since Cunard's fleet sails under British law, we can't marry people at sea.

Things were different in the old sailing ship days when young men and women emigrants might spend months packed quite closely in the ship's passenger holds. Falling in love was just one more hazard of the voyage, and the captain's power to marry his passengers was often a prudent blessing. The nearest we get to it today is when married couples taking a cruise on the *QE2* ask me to hear their renewal of marriage vows, sometimes twenty or thirty years after their wedding. I'm happy to 'officiate' at the short ceremony, and I'm sure the men and women who come along get a lot of emotional fulfilment from it.

Youngsters who meet and fall in love on *QE2* – and it happens as often as it does in TV's *Love Boat* series – are often in tears when I have to turn down their romantic requests to marry them. 'Can't you make an exception, just for us?' they plead. 'Look, if you want to consider yourselves married on board, that's OK by me,' I tell them by way of consolation, 'but the minute you step ashore, take my word for it, you're *not* legally hitched, and you might like to go along to see your priest, vicar or minister.' And apart from wishing the youngsters every happiness, that's as much as I can do to nurture the cause of blue water wedlock.

On summer crossings of the Atlantic, *Sylvania* often came across intermittent groups of icebergs, looking as large as floating Himalayan peaks. As the sunlight hit the drifting bergs they burst into all the colours of the rainbow, giving a mammoth prismatic display. Yet we never forgot they could kill. During ice alerts in darkness or in thick fog, the number of look-outs was doubled and watertight doors were closed. With radar, of course, an approaching iceberg could be spotted on the screen many miles distant; then, as it came nearer, the men on look-out were keen to be the first to sight it with the naked eye. At night and lit by the moon, the icebergs sailed silently by like towering and ghostly galleons and, day or night, we kept a distance of at least a mile from their menacing path. Now, some twenty years later, Atlantic icebergs are far fewer in the shipping lanes, tending to roam the seas in more northerly regions. That doesn't mean we ever relax our round-the-clock vigilance, for, as the *Titanic* found on the night of 14/15 April 1912, it takes only one iceberg to slaughter a ship. But with today's sophisticated radar, monitoring by satellite and electronic navigational aids, such an awful possibility becomes increasingly remote.

After *Sylvania*, I had a brief spell sailing to New York with the 13,300-ton *Media*. But an event on land takes priority over other *Media* memories. On 12 November 1958, Joan entered Milton Lodge nursing home, Fleetwood, and just a few hours later presented me with our youngest daughter Kate. Like her mother, Kate grew up to be tall, dark and beautiful. And just like everyone else in the Arnott family, she went to Fleetwood Grammar School. Kate was, in fact, among the last pupils there before the establishment was turned into a comprehensive.

Kate is now an executive officer with the British government's Customs and Excise Department based at Wakefield, Yorkshire. When I am on leave, I drive over with Joan to see her at the house she recently bought. Kate's a fiercely independent young lady, but she relies on her father for such tasks as making her doorlocks burglar-proof, maintaining her central-heating system, and rendering her house windows draught-proof. It's all a long way from captaining the *QE2*, but I've always enjoyed do-it-yourself jobs around the home. I installed the complete central-heating system in my own house, designed and built a new storeroom in the loft, and did all the carpentry and building for a large front porch that keeps us snugly warm in the face of chilling winds from the Irish Sea.

The motto of our old family school was *Cogitate Alte Ora* which, I believe, means 'think on higher things'. Maybe I had that lofty admonition in mind when I visited New York's Metropolitan Opera with Captain John Treasure-Jones, Master of the *Media*, to watch a performance of *Tosca*. We had seats in the stalls for Puccini's masterpiece, and I thoroughly enjoyed a night of coloratura culture; normally I wouldn't have been able to afford such affluent leisure, but we were lucky that a generous passenger had presented the tickets to the Captain. A Welshman from Haverfordwest, my good friend Treasure-Jones could himself put over quite a competent aria, and his fine voice can still be heard on record, welcoming visitors aboard the *Queen Mary* at her showpiece berth at Long Beach, California. Captain Treasure-Jones took the royal matriarch on her final voyage around Cape Horn to Long Beach in 1967.

The last voyage of any ship, whether she's destined for dazzling dockside display or simply bound for the breaker's yard, is something of a funereal experience for those who have served on her and have come to regard her as a vibrant, living entity. The only ship I ever took to the breaker's was the former White Star liner *Britannic*, a graceful vessel with an historic and distinguished career. Delivering her to a slaughterhouse for ships was a truly melancholy mission.

Britannic and her sister ship the *Georgic* were the first motor passenger liners on the North Atlantic, both built in the early 1930s by Harland & Wolff at their Belfast shipyards. By Atlantic standards, they weren't fast, their service speed being only 17½ knots, but perhaps because of this sedate rate of progress, they were renowned for their comfort. I never served on the *Georgic*, but her sister *Britannic* certainly gave her 1000 passengers and Junior Second Officer Arnott a series of relaxing and congenial crossings to and from New York.

The two-funnel, 27,000-ton *Britannic* had carried heroic numbers of Allied troops in the war, and she survived unharmed. *Georgic* wasn't so lucky. She was bombed and burned out at Suez Bay in 1941, but was beached and refitted, first as a troopship, then for service in the post-war emigrant boom from Britain to Australia. Because some steel sections of *Georgic* were still corrugated after the war-time fire, she was stuck with the nickname of 'The Iron Lung' until she was dismantled in 1957.

The Cunard-White Star Line became Cunard Line Limited in 1950, but the *Britannic* displayed, to the end of her life, the old White Star colours – buff funnels with black tops and a black hull broken by a yellow line with dark red boot-topping. On her final journey, we sailed her through The Minches to Inverkeithing in Scotland and gently ran her onto the beach there. Men from the Sheffield firm of Thomas Ward were waiting to cut *Britannic*'s fine steel platings into basic scrap for razor blades, but they didn't massacre the whole ship. At least one shred of treasure was saved: a rare old pewter ship's lamp now adorns the sitting-room of the Arnott home in Fleetwood. I rescued the lamp from a remote passageway in the dark depths of the liner, where it had swung since she had first sliced the water twenty-eight years earlier. My last glimpse of *Britannic* was as she lay forlornly on that sad Scottish beach. There was nothing I could do to help her, and I turned away, dejected, to head for Southampton and ships that were still alive.

My depression had vanished long before I reached the great south-coast port, even though I was due to stay aboard the *Ivernia* in Southampton docks over the Christmas holiday of 1960. I didn't sail with *Ivernia*, and around this time transferred, for one trip only, to the 22,000-ton *Carinthia* captained by Geoffrey Marr who later became Commodore of the Cunard Fleet.

Captain Marr was a great talker, words tumbling from his

lips at an amazing rate, and his gift for rhetoric was superbly demonstrated in his lecture presentation on the sinking of the *Bismarck*. Geoffrey had served in the Royal Navy Reserve on one of the ships that sent the German battleship to the bottom on 27 May 1941, so his graphic descriptions were wholly authentic.

Yet I remember him not so much for his oratory as for a remarkable piece of navigation that brought *Carinthia* safely to the Pier Head in Liverpool when the Mersey was cloaked completely in blinding black fog. We were anchored in the river waiting for the solid blanket to lift; even the ferry boats across the Mersey were unable to move. Suddenly Geoffrey's fine voice called: 'We're going in.' He talked our tugs to us over the VHF radio and, with visibility down to zero, took the huge 22,000-ton liner cleanly into the landing stage. Passengers, already resigned to another night at sea, cheered in relief and delight, and the crew, anxious to get home to loved ones, were equally elated. It was a magnificent achievement by the Captain, considering the quite elementary navigational aids of 1960 in comparison to today's sophistication. How did he do it? It's a matter of record that some Captains have a sixth sense in fog; they can 'see' things quite invisible to the eyes of ordinary humans, and have often made apparently inexplicable decisions which, within seconds, have saved ships and lives. Whether or not I have such a power is not for me to judge. In any case, Captains generally won't discuss the matter, and that includes the normally prolific talker, Commodore Geoffrey Marr.

When he retired, Geoffrey quickly became bored and generally disenchanted with life ashore. And after a Cunard career culminating in command of the great *Queens*, he signed on as second mate of a banana boat. His fellow officers on the West India freighter knew all about their second mate's illustrious past, and used to call him 'The Commodore'.

When Geoffrey left Cunard for his short-lived retirement, he found his wife had been taking a cordon bleu cookery course so that she could serve up meals as splendid as the exotic fare at the Captain's Table. Geoffrey ate up patiently for several weeks. Then he told his wife: 'I can't stand this any longer. Don't you realise I was already fed up with years of fancy dishes at sea when I retired. For goodness' sake, go out and get me some fish and chips.' Perhaps it was coincidence, but Geoffrey Marr left for sea again soon afterwards. But this time, as I've already mentioned, he chose a banana boat. There the food was whole-some, plentiful and decidedly plain.

My own career took a sharp turn upwards when I joined RMS *Media* for the second time. My appointment as chief officer on one of Cunard's passenger-carrying ships came when I was thirty-six, and it was a significant step towards the ultimate accolade of captaining a luxury liner. Commanding the *Media* at that time was Captain H. A. 'Stoney' Stonehouse, a pleasant but serious-minded individual. Years earlier, when we were both serving on the *Franconia*, I had had great difficulty convincing him that the latest printed, pre-calculated navigation tables were any use at all compared to the old methods, and now I found Stoney still reserved and, at time, rather diffident in his dealings with passengers. I'm sure he found it difficult to switch from the antiquated aloof system of command to the more informal, 'swinging' style already well under way in the early sixties.

Cunard ships have done their share over the years to build up the bloodlines which have produced today's multi-million-dollar racehorses. *Media*, for instance, regularly carried some of the best British breeding stock out to the United States to boost genetic strains at stud farms there.

But even with stabilisers, *Media* wasn't the ideal ship for carrying horses. We quartered our emigrant sires and dams in specially built wooden stables on the afterdeck, but in rough seas *Media* herself would rise and descend as sharply as a Grand National steeplechaser, immediately bringing on attacks of acute seasickness in our unfortunate horses. Once, a mid-Atlantic gale whipped the roofs off their stables, and I went inside the roofless stalls to comfort the anguished animals, while the ship's carpenters repaired the damage. And yet, in spite of all these traumas, Cunard never lost a horse through sickness. Like humans, the horses quickly cast off sorrows at sea the moment they stepped on dry land.

From veterinary ventures on the Atlantic, I returned to the Royal Naval Reserve and a month's winter exercises at sea on the coastal minesweeper HMS *Beachampton*. During one of the roughest months I've ever encountered in all my years afloat, many fellow officers and most of the crew were generally as sick each day in the Solent as our poor horses had been on the Atlantic. On one particularly vicious trip, when we were testing secret equipment, we had a young Yugoslav officer aboard, and the Captain ordered that the Yugoslav, normally a cheerful young fellow, should be kept away from the sensitive areas of the ship. The skipper needn't have worried. As we poked our bows out past the Dolphin to head for the Solent, our green-faced visitor pleaded, 'Please ask your captain to turn round and take me back,' but the British Navy couldn't do a U-turn because of seasickness. Our Slav friend spent the rest of the trip rolling around a bed in the sick bay. Our secrets were quite safe.

Although, at thirty-seven, I was getting a little elderly for the rigours of rugby, I played the occasional game for another year or so. Cricket was less likely to bring broken limbs and, until my mid-forties, I played at varied venues throughout the world. But none of these ships' matches gave me as much satisfaction as one of my increasingly rare appearances for Fleetwood Cricket Club, when I managed to fit in a game between voyages in July 1961. Our local *Fleetwood Chronicle* reported: 'Playing his first game for Fleetwood for eight years, Bob Arnott bowled the side to victory against Netherfield, taking seven wickets for twenty-eight runs in an unchanged spell of twelve overs.'

Around that time, I had also developed some sort of skill at badminton, and used to go along while on leave to the courts at Fleetwood Grammar School. Joan also played, and between games, while watching and chatting, pressed on with her knitting at the side of the court. One of her knitwear masterpieces was a thick woolly cardigan which I later wore gratefully on cold nights at sea. As she knitted away at the garment by the side of the badminton court, one of Joan's friends asked quite seriously, 'Is that blanket for you and Bob, or are you knitting it as a present for someone else?' Said Joan, 'It might do as a blanket for some fellows, but for Bob it's only a cardigan.'

Chapter 16

In August 1961 I returned to RMS *Caronia* and the gracious world of pleasure cruising. 'The Green Goddess' had circled the globe on a 31,000 mile, 95-day cruise earlier in the year as well as putting in several trips to the West Indies and to the Mediterranean countries. After navigating her on one or two short cruises around the Med, I charted a course for Casablanca, Tangier, Malta, Yalta and Odessa. This was my only visit to Yalta until I took the *QE2* there on the now-famous 1980 Soviet rendezvous.

Guides from Intourist – the Soviet Union's official travel organisation – showed *Caronia*'s tourists round the historic building at Yalta where Churchill, Roosevelt and Stalin held their 1945 conference. I was rather more interested in the high-speed, six-seater hydrofoil in which the Soviets skimmed some of *Caronia*'s officers around the Crimean coast. Our guide on the hydrofoil was a slimly attractive blonde girl in her late twenties. Her English was flawless, and I assumed, mistakenly as it turned out, that she was a British girl working in the Soviet Union. As the hydrofoil swept along the south-west coastline of the peninsula, the girl pointed out the port of Balaclava. 'Across there,' she told us, 'is where 600 British cavalry charged into the Russian guns. And, of course, 400 of the British were killed.'

'Oh yes,' I said pleasantly. 'We know all about the Charge of the Light Brigade. A great example of British courage, don't you think?'

'Well, it could also be viewed as an epic display of stupidity,' retorted the girl.

I smothered back anger and said, coldly, 'That's an unfortunate remark from an English girl.'

'Ah,' she replied, 'don't let my university accent fool you. I was taught your language by an Englishman, a Cambridge graduate, but I've never been out of Russia.' I was to recall that Crimean encounter a year or two later when the spy scandals involving diplomats who were former Cambridge men burst upon the world. Who, I wondered, was the girl's mysterious tutor?

From Yalta, *Caronia* crossed the Gulf of Karkinitsk to Odessa, where there were squads of uniformed guards patrolling the harbour area. Intourist officials who came on board mentioned that the guards had been ordered 'no fraternising with *Caronia*'s crew'. We stayed overnight in the great Ukrainian port, and the next morning, scores of our crew had head-in-hands hangovers from drinking vodka with the Russian patrolmen. The 'frat-ban', apparently, hadn't been too successful.

We left Soviet waters for the Romanian port of Constanta, where 400 passengers climbed into launches for the trip ashore. I went along for the ride, and was shown around the town's magnificent Opera House buildings that must have been a real cultural showpiece years earlier but, by 1961, the inside of the theatre was generally threadbare and didn't boast a single carpet. Soon we had more than theatre furnishings to worry about. It had been raining heavily as we went ashore, and now freshening winds blowing in from the Black Sea made it impossible to embark our passengers in the launches back to *Caronia*. They had brought only the clothes they wore and, as the chill darkness of an early November evening fell around Constanta, cheerful holiday chatter gave way to anxious queries of 'What's going to happen to us?'

Our Romanian hosts, friendlier than their Russian neighbours, were eager to help, but a major problem was that all the town's hotels had closed for the winter. I suggested to the chief guide that, if they ever wanted to see another British liner in Constanta, it might be a good idea to open up a hotel, and fast. They did, and our people at least had a roof over their heads for the night. But next morning the seas were even more turbulent, and returning to *Caronia* was, for the time being, impossible. And already, one of our passengers had become quite ill, moaning, 'I'll never see England again.' The poor fellow was a diabetic, and had left his insulin on the ship.

By noon, the weather was even more foul, and the storms had long since blown away the tattered remnants of Romania's romantic spell. Second Officer Cook saved the day, volunteering to take a launch through heaving seas to bring back supplies from the ship. Alerted by radio, *Caronia*'s doctor made up a parcel of insulin and syringes for our diabetic passenger and, as young Cook lurched his launch past the liner's bouncing accommodation ladder, a strong armed seaman threw aboard the medical supplies plus packets of toiletries for the other passengers. Fortunately, one of the ship's nurses had travelled with the shore party and was able to treat our diabetic gentleman when Cook returned. The weary passengers gave their second officer a hero's welcome, and later they bought him a silver lighter in appreciation of his feat of seamanship. After thirty-six hours, the rampaging Black Sea called a truce and we were able to transfer our tired tourists back to the ship. Our diabetic friend told me, 'I wouldn't have missed a moment of it. Now I've really got something to write home about.'

Some of our passengers spent their lives cruising the world. Mrs Helen Howard-Jones, an elderly wealthy Californian widow, never left *Caronia* except when the liner went into dry-dock for a yearly refit; then she moved into London's Grosvenor House Hotel for a month. Teams of attorneys and accountants flew over from the United States to confer with her there about her extensive interests in oil, real estate and cattle ranches. Back at sea, Mrs Howard-Jones confided to me, 'They tell me I have an empire of untold wealth, but since my husband died my only real interest in life is roaming the seas on the Goddess. I love her.'

Although she was in fine physical health, Mrs Howard-Jones was often forgetful. Some mornings, she showed up twice for breakfast, bidding a second cheerful 'Good morning' to the steward who had served her cereals, eggs and bacon only an hour earlier. Eventually, we suggested to the widow's advisers that she would enjoy her world cruising much more if she had a full-time travelling companion. One of *Caronia*'s nurses offered to do the job temporarily, and Mrs Howard-Jones liked the girl so much that she quickly became the widow's permanent companion. From working below decks on a ship, the girl – from Hull in Yorkshire – moved instantly into a fairytale world of fabulous wealth. A Cadillac was always waiting at the dockside whenever and wherever the pair were going ashore, and now the girl bought her outfits in London's exclusive West End fashion shops. But she added a new dimension of care and friendship to the wealthy old lady's world wanderings, and I reckoned the Yorkshire lass thoroughly deserved her good fortune.

Another celebrated *Caronia* traveller was Miss Macbeth. She was ninety and had lived aboard for fourteen years, rarely leaving the liner. When we reached Sydney on the 1962 South Pacific cruise, I asked, 'Aren't you going ashore here, Miss Macbeth?' 'Well no, Bob,' she replied. 'I saw the sights of Sydney in 1938, so today I'll stay aboard.' Despite her advanced age, Miss Macbeth always enjoyed the wonderful food sent by *Caronia*'s chef to her own special table, especially steaks washed down with champagne, and her only concession to age was that she allowed the steward who invariably looked after her to slice up the steak before he served it. No one ever saw Miss Macbeth out and about after nine at night; by then, she was sound asleep. But the next day, one of the first early-morning strollers working up an appetite for breakfast on the promenade deck would be the sprightly ninety-year-old spinster.

It was on that South Pacific cruise that I caught my first sighting of San Francisco from the sea. Bounded by the Pacific in the west, the waters of the Golden Gate to the north and San Francisco Bay in the east, to the approaching mariner the city looks like a many-sided diamond set in a cluster of rolling hills and finely cut peaks. But I was as much interested in Frisco's food as in her visual delights, and I made straight away for the sea succulents I had been told about at the waterfront emporia along Fisherman's Wharf. Looking out over the bay towards Alcatraz island, I feasted on abalone steaks, Pacific prawns and giant clams. Was it part of the punishment on that grim stone fortress, I wondered, for Capone and company to be separated from such gourmet gluttony by just a few miles of impassable tides?

After leaving one of earth's most splendid cities, *Caronia* headed out into the Pacific to a land of active volcanoes, colourful orchids, spectacular waterfalls and *aloha*. I had never seen the Hawaiian Islands before, and from a distance out at sea Diamond Head on Oahu looked to me as lovely and inviting as it must have appeared to Captain Cook when he discovered the islands in 1778.

During a brief visit ashore I took a bus along the waterfront to see the celebrated beach at Waikiki. I met throngs of aloha-shirted holidaymakers, but there wasn't a Polynesian grass skirt in sight. On the way back to the ship, I walked past ranks of glittering hotels fronted by carefully tended rainbow shower trees, and wondered what Cook would have now made of the extravagant, gorgeous lands he named the Sandwich Islands. Yet, my impressions of Hawaii then were by no means complete, as I found on later visits. The islands still hold a multitude of palm-lined silver beaches, coral reefs and lush, green tropical hide-aways, and the beauties of Lanai, Kauai and Kahoolawe islands were waiting for me on future voyages to the Hawaiian group. A native Hawaiian descended from the original Polynesians told me back in 1962, '*Aole oe i noho a ike ia Hawaii*' – 'Until you've seen all of Hawaii, you haven't lived.' My Hawaiian friend's immodest assertion was just about right.

From Honolulu I charted *Caronia*'s course over 2277 miles of blue Pacific to Pago Pago in the islands of American Samoa. This South Sea paradise had a large American naval force permanently based at its fine harbour, and the Polynesian natives began their sales pitches at their little market with gems such as 'Now hear this, old buddy,' and 'Betcha sweet life you're gonna look good in this . . .' But throughout the Pacific islands, the Polynesians were never too pushy in promoting their wares, taking the view that the important pastimes in life are fishing, eating and loving. As for selling things, for most of the time they just can't be bothered.

The Green Goddess sped away from Polynesia at an average speed of over 20 knots and in a couple of days docked at Auckland. I was surprised just how much the former capital of New Zealand had grown since I had been last there. Engineering and food-processing factories had grown up alongside the dock-lands, and the port no longer relied solely on its exports of lamb, butter and cheese. When I was at Auckland in 1978 with the *QE2*, Auckland had again almost doubled in size.

Five hundred miles further south, we called at the present capital. Wellington hadn't expanded with Auckland's fierce gusto, but the splendour of Port Nicholson harbour and the surrounding greenery of the hillsides were more vividly beautiful than I remembered. I took a brief drive along some of the city's thirty miles of waterfront roadway and, as we came upon rugged coves and quiet, sandy beaches, I thought how much the area resembled the Welsh coast around Aberdovey which I had grown to know well during my months at the Outward Bound sea school.

New Zealand faded into the far horizon as I stood on the bridge and pointed *Caronia* towards my homeland. A thousand miles and three days later, I was drinking a pint of creamy

Australian beer pulled by a glowing, young Australian lady in a Sydney bar. This was really home, I felt, even though Joan and the children were at the other side of the planet. I was hoping to travel round to Newcastle to see my relatives, but *Caronia*'s schedule didn't allow enough time; luckily my cousin Joyce Taylor from Manley, who I hadn't seen since 1948, came aboard the ship to say hello.

Caronia had been rather less than forty-eight hours in Sydney when, having taken on fuel, we set sail for Port Moresby in New Guinea. Another pint of cool, foaming Aussie beer served by another blonde and buxom Australian girl gave me the impression that the Papuan port was just a friendly extension of Sydney's docklands. We stayed only a day, then headed for Bali. I noted in my sea log that *Caronia* covered the 1962 miles to the island in four days, 13 hours and 18 minutes at an average speed of 17.95 knots. We cruised under shell-blue East Indian skies and across an ocean disturbed only by light westerly breezes. I recalled my frantic flight from the Japanese over those now-tranquil waters in my days as a Blue Funnel midshipman. Twenty-one years and many thousands of sea miles later, I was navigating *Caronia* through the Java Sea towards Singapore. There were lots of Japanese gentlemen around, but this time they were fare-paying passengers, and all very friendly.

A day in Singapore, and then off to the Thai capital of Bangkok. *Caronia* anchored out in the river delta and a large shore tender took 300 passengers up the colourful waterway to the city they call the 'Venice of the East', because it is built across the arteries of the delta. We saw Thai housewives shopping from their narrow punts at the floating, noisy markets, while others paddled up to the teak-built shops, many on stilts, that lined the banks of the River Menam Chao Phraya. Our stewards had brought along packed meals, because many Western palates don't much appreciate the very hot Thai food; however, I decided to give it a go. The small restaurant I popped into began my meal with soup for a starter, then a delicious local fish, and finally a curry, made from shredded and fried chicken. It was delicious, and to round it off I took a long, cool draught of *manow*, which is mostly crushed limes. Unfortunately, I then succumbed to the café owner's pleas to try out his Mekong – the Thai-distilled whisky. I wished I hadn't bothered. Johnny Walker would have wept at the concoction.

Hong Kong and its towering Victoria Peak came up over the dawn horizon some 1500 miles after Bangkok. Our passengers bought trinkets at the Chinese shops in Kowloon's narrow streets, and looked in admiration at the rich and fashion-conscious Chinese women wearing their tight-fitting cheong-sams – dresses with high mandarin collars and revealing side splits. Not so glamorous were the destitute Chinese who lay sleeping in some of Kowloon's shop doorways.

In Kobe in Japan, I bought a little blue pocket radio costing the equivalent of £5. It became my friendly companion on night watches across the Pacific, picking up stations all the way from Yokohama to Acapulco. As I listened, I scanned the blue-black Pacific sky and tried to spot the early satellites moving across a backcloth of familiar, shimmering stars. At that time the *Daily Telegraph* published a star map featuring the satellites' paths which I found an enormous help in my nightly searches. Now, of course, the skies are littered with so many chunks of metal that the excitement of those early post-Sputnik days has been blotted out by sheer weight of stellar scrap.

As The Green Goddess neared the end of her world travels, she put in at Acapulco on Mexico's Pacific coast. It was my first call at the sunny beach resort, and also the first time I came across the custom of tourists producing a few coins for the local boys to put on an impromptu show of diving into the sea. The lads pestered the passengers until they paid up, and then the brave youngsters plunged down a dangerous, rocky cliff face from a quite fearsome height. As we watched on that sunlit April afternoon, not one of the young divers was hurt as they hurtled from the cliff top at the precise moment that the waters swirling beneath appeared at their most benevolent. But some-times, we learned, the boys took chances. Then they might either strike the jagged rocks on the way down or drown as they hit the foaming Pacific. A series of deaths not long after brought official action, and now the diving displays are tightly controlled, but the new regulations came too late for the boys whose memories are marked by little shrines all the way down the cliff.

My friend Joe Divers, a retired Commodore of the Royal Naval Reserve, was captain of the *Caronia* on her world cruise. He was recovering from a serious spine operation, and used to spend a lot of time reading. As navigator, each noon I would take a chit with the previous day's mileage and other cruise data to the Captain's cabin. As I went in, he would put his book down and ask, 'What is it to be today, Bob?' In the best naval tradition, I invariably answered, 'Pink gin, please, sir.' One day the Angostura bitters had run out, and Joe suggested 'Why don't you drink plain gin and water, like me?' I tried it, and have stuck to the potion ever since – except when I'm drinking whisky and water.

A few weeks after leaving Joe Divers and *Caronia*, I was called to Portsmouth – the Royal Navy's Pompey – for naval training on the destroyer HMS *Caron*, and I spent a couple of months of 1963, during one of the worst winters of the century, working on the destroyer's open bridge. Navigators under training grumbled to me that their sextants misted up instantly, making proper sightings impossible. With a totally misplaced confidence, I said, 'I'll show you how to do it.' I tried keeping a sextant under my duffle coat to keep it dry until the last moment, but the split second I brought the instrument out, the mirrors streamed with water. Then I dodged behind a gun turret to get away from the chilling salt spray. Equally useless. I gave up trying, and my thoughts went out to those men who had served on destroyers' open bridges in the north Atlantic throughout the war. They had worked only thirty feet above the water – compared to the sixty-foot height of a cargo ship's bridge – and must have caught the ocean's cruel, daily beatings right in their faces.

Most days, *Caronia* sailed on navigational exercises out of Portsmouth. 'It's bad enough here in the Channel,' I said to the skipper, 'but at least we're lucky not to be patrolling the Atlantic.'

'Sorry, Bob,' he answered, 'I'm afraid our luck's just run out. We're off to the west of Ireland.'

Our mission there was to patrol the waters below while Her Majesty the Queen and Prince Philip flew overhead on their way to Australia and New Zealand. Other British warships were strung out on similar tasks across the world. We didn't catch sight of the royal plane, but we cheered in sheer relief when we heard by radio that it had flown safely over our patrol area. Soaked and shivering, we crashed the destroyer's bows through heaving grey rollers back towards the protection of Pompey. When I went ashore, a waiting letter helped to thaw me out: the Navy had decided to promote Lieutenant Arnott to Lieutenant Commander. I couldn't stay around to enjoy the benefits of my new rank, as RMS *Mauretania* and her considerable comforts were waiting to ferry me off to the gentler waters of the Tyrrhenian Sea and its principal port of Naples.

Cunard's Atlantic traffic had been slimmed down so alarmingly by the airline's incursions that the company decided to try its luck sailing out of Naples to Genoa, Nice and then New York. The gamble didn't pay off. Although Naples is one of Italy's major outlets for both passengers and commercial traffic, the Italians didn't intend to hand a chunk of the trade over to Britain without a struggle. They promoted their own shipping fiercely and, with a decisive home-ground advantage, the Italians didn't take long to win the match.

Meanwhile, *Mauretania* meandered around the Med picking up as many *signors* and *signoras* as Cunard could persuade to ignore the patriotic pleas of Italy's own shipping lines. The numbers, alas, were meagre, yet in the five months I was engaged in the unsuccessful Italian campaign, there was usually a laugh or two around during our visits to Naples for there was stationed Cunard's assistant manager, one Nick Anderson. He was what I can best describe as a 'character'. Often we sat in a little waterfront café sipping gin or coffee through the night as we swapped sea stories, for Nick was an accomplished yachtsman. One morning, as dawn lit up Naples harbour, Nick said suddenly, 'I'm off to walk up Vesuvius. Are you coming along?' Surprised but far from stupefied I quickly turned down the invitation. 'Sorry, Nick, I'm climbing into bed, not up a volcano.' Unperturbed, Nick set out alone for the smouldering summit.

Eventually Nick was appointed Cunard's manager in New York, the last Briton to occupy the post. A double for Prince Philip, Nick became a great friend of the then Mayor, John Lindsay, and moved easily around New York's social scene. I saw Nick once after he had left the United States to return to Britain and live in a houseboat on the Hamble River. I was taking the *QE2* down the Solent through the lines of warships massed for the Spithead Review when I spotted, through my binoculars, a small sailing yacht dressed with flags. I focused sharply on the peak-capped figure in the stern: it was Nick, pipe in one hand and a can of beer in the other. As the *QE2* passed the little boat, its Captain raised the beer can in a cheery salute, and I waved back to a truly singular sailor.

Chapter 17

My career with Cunard almost ended in the mid-1960s. Sometimes I felt I was missing irreplaceable moments in my family's growing-up years, and one day, while I was sitting in the *Sylvania*'s wardroom in Liverpool Docks, I received a phone call from our marine superintendent, Captain Angus Letty, to say that there was a vacancy coming up for an inspector in the Royal National Lifeboat Institution. I suddenly decided to apply. So did 300 other fellows. After several interviews at the offices of the RNLI in Grosvenor Gardens, London, I reached the shortlist of three. The Lifeboat Service was something for which I had always had the greatest admiration, and the job they were offering certainly carried more money than I was getting with Cunard. But by the time I was shortlisted, my urge to work ashore was well on the wane.

I talked the matter over with Joan. She said, 'The choice is yours, Bob, but do you think you'd really be happy going up and down the country like a commercial traveller?' When I heard that the future policy of RNLI was to change the districts of the inspectors every five years (which meant changing homes), my enthusiasm dropped to zero, so after the final interview the appointment was given to someone else. Looking back, I think Joan knew I would never have been really contented working ashore, but, as always, she left me to make up my own mind.

Once I had done this, I settled down to my career in a Cunard fleet that was being commercially annihilated by the faster and cheaper giant jets. I did one spell on the *Queen Mary* in 1965 and wrote to Joan from New York, 'It's like working in a ghost ship.' On that voyage there were fewer than 200 passengers in a first-class section designed to take 750 in sumptuous comfort across the Atlantic. I walked along the companionways where, a few years earlier, people would have been bumping into each other as they hurried from one party to another.

Now I met only memories. 'You know, sir,' I said to Captain Treasure-Jones, 'she's not sailing across the Atlantic, she's rattling across it like a great empty coffin.' Sadly, the skipper agreed.

But Cunard had been fighting commercial battles at sea for 120 years, and the company knew how to roll with the ocean swells and survive until the trade tides turned. Cruising, Cunard had decided, was the key to survival. *Saxonia* and *Invernia* were given a £3m transformation into luxury cruise liners, and re-named, respectively, *Carmania* and *Franconia*. And the most magnificent cruiser of them all, the *QE2*, was conceived on Cunard's Liverpool drawing boards.

On 4 July 1965 – American Independence Day – the first pre-fabricated section of the *QE2*'s keel was laid at Clydebank. The date was significant, for today eighty-five per cent of all passengers on the *QE2* are American, and the keel laying also marked the 125th anniversary of the maiden voyage of Samuel Cunard's *Britannia* in 1840. On 20 September 1967, Her Majesty Queen Elizabeth II sent the new wonder ship down the launch slipways, and just twenty-six days later I was appointed the *QE2*'s first ever chief officer. For more than a year, I stayed in Scotland to care for Cunard's fabulous fledgling while Upper Clyde Shipbuilders, formerly John Brown's, together with hundreds of outside companies, prepared the *QE2* for her maiden voyage.

I wish I could report that I was thrilled and delighted to be catching the train for Glasgow after a short home leave in Fleetwood, but for some reason my mood was one of despondency. Perhaps I wasn't looking forward to a winter in Scotland and a full year ashore. I changed a first-class rail warrant at Fleetwood station for an £8.11s return ticket to Glasgow and my gloom deepened at the thought that, when I arrived there, I would have to start looking round for somewhere to live. I wasn't, I'm afraid, accustomed to having to search for living quarters. That had all been taken care of ashore for me by my wife, and at sea by Blue Funnel, the Pacific Steam Navigation Company and then Cunard. Now, for the first time in my life I had to hunt for a home.

I booked in at the Boulevard Hotel on the Great Western Road not far from Clydebank. Each morning, afternoon and evening I searched Glasgow from north to south and from east to west. It was a cold, damp and dismal experience. The premises advertised in the Glasgow papers at prices I could afford were generally grey and cheerless, which wasn't surprising because my total weekly allowance for food and accommodation was just £12.10s. After eight days of walking, catching buses and trundling on trams I called off the quest.

I now took the commonsense step I should have thought of long before I even arrived in Scotland: I went along to the offices of the *QE2*'s builders, and asked for help. One of John Brown's administrative staff summed up the situation, telling me, not unkindly, 'Ye knaw all aboot sailin' a ship aroond the world, yet ye canna' find a flat in Glasgow.' That, I thought, was the last straw. The man must have read my face. He added, quickly, 'Dinna worry, ye've come to the right shop. We canna see the *QE2*'s chief officer out on the streets. We'll fix ya up wi' a fine flat tomorrow.' And they did.

John Brown's offered me the tenancy of one of their unfurnished, executive luxury flats at Whittingham Court, in the west of the city. The weekly rental, including electricity, came to £8.10s. My old friend Bil, Captain William Eldon Warwick, first Captain of the *QE2*, had a flat in the same block as mine, as did the ship's Chief Engineer Jack Marland. Bil Warwick spent most of his time working in London and usually came up to Glasgow only once a week. I was Cunard's 'man on the spot'.

Other people in the flats and the area around were obviously not lacking in the elegant extras of life. Across the road at Buckingham Court lived three Rolls Royces and their owners, while at Whittingham Court the garages attached to each flat housed Daimlers, Jaguars and one or two Rovers. My own garage was quite empty, and at first so was my flat. It had no carpets, curtains, linoleum, pots, pans or crockery, the sole furnishings comprising one former ship's bed plus a mattress. I borrowed some ship's bedclothes from the yard, hired a second-hand television set for £1 a week, and reckoned I'd made a fair start at setting up home. After a couple of weeks I travelled home to pick up the blue curtains Joan had made up to my telephoned measurements. Meanwhile, John Brown's sent me over a comfortable ship's leather armchair and some warm blue carpeting from a liner long gone. On a lunchtime reconnaissance from the shipyard, I bought a well-used, solid teak chest of drawers, and with the warm, comfortable lounge bar of the

Pond Hotel only forty yards from the front hallway of the flats, I began for the first time to feel pleasantly content in Glasgow.

It was just fifteen minutes' ride on a Corporation double-decker bus from my flat to the fitting out yard where the *QE2* lay. Sprawling across the basin and open to the skies, she seemed to my first sighting incredibly vast and strangely vulnerable. I got the feeling, from where I don't know, that the huge, half-finished vessel was already the victim of some alien antagonism. Maybe this arose from a sixth sense granted to the *QE2*'s future Captain. A few months later I came to realise that my intuition was right on target. The new *Queen* was being stolen by some of the local citizenry, piece by expensive piece.

But in the meantime, I could see hundreds of craftsmen swarming over her lower decks. Construction of these was well under way, but the ship had no superstructure and the public rooms were simply bare metal and open spaces. I went to the office I had been allocated at the Clydebank yard and began to study the ship's detailed planning data, together with her building schedules.

Cunard's chief naval architect, Dan Wallace, and Technical Director Tom Kameen, headed up the teams which had carried out the design and layout of the ship. Dan's work on the *QE2* really began in 1954, when Cunard were thinking about an 80,000-ton successor to the *Queen Mary*, to be known as 'Q3'. Although work on that project was abandoned, much of the experience acquired was put to profitable use on the *QE2*. Dan also designed the successful conversion to cruise ships of *Carmania* and *Franconia*. Like Captain Warwick, Dan came up to Glasgow once a week, and his Clydebank office was run by senior naval architect Joe Lunt. Joe was the first man I went to see when I arrived at the Upper Clydeside shipyard. He explained to me that the ship was being built on a modular system, in other words, that one section of the ship and its fittings were completed before the workforce moved onto the next. A computer kept a day-to-day check on just how much had been accomplished, although it didn't show the lorry loads of fine furnishings, bathroom fittings and electrical equipment that had been stripped from the defenceless *Queen* the previous night.

My job was to see that the actual construction of the ship matched up to the sheafs of specifications and plans I carried

141

around with me, and I gradually acquired a fair expertise in ship's carpentry, plumbing, steel fabrication and electrical contracting. Every pipe, every piece of cabinet work, every electric cable and light fitting had to slot into its appointed place. In the building of what was destined to be a floating holiday resort, to check that every part of the gargantuan jigsaw fitted flawlessly was truly a daunting task. I also examined every item and its role in the overall picture from the point of view of a master mariner. How was it all going to work out at sea?

With Captain Warwick and Cunard's departmental heads, I attended frequent management meetings to review progress. For a variety of reasons, including the wholesale larceny, our completion schedules were tending to drift off course. Every day's delay in the shipyard deferred the moment when the *QE2* would sail from Southampton with a full load of passengers and start to pay dividends on the near £30m which Cunard had invested in her.

There were no easy answers to the various problems which developed and it was always the bad news about the *QE2* that achieved international publicity. Yet I found tremendous dedication, goodwill and shipbuilding skills among most of the people I met in the year I spent at Clydebank. This was, after all, the most complex, ingenious and innovative project ever attempted in any of the world's shipyards. A brief rundown on what was involved was explained to me by Cunard's naval architects' team. Here are some of the main points.

The *QE2* was definitely not going to be an updated version of the *Queen Mary* and the *Queen Elizabeth*. She was conceived as a floating resort hotel, with the advantage over a land-based hotel complex that she could always follow the sun. At 65,863 tons gross, she was among the largest passenger liners, yet her 963-foot length, 32½-foot draught and 105-foot breadth would enable her to cross from the Atlantic to the Pacific through the Panama Canal and to use the Suez Canal. She had also been designed to take her passengers to many cruise ports that were out of bounds to her deeper-draughted forerunners. Her service speed would be 28½ knots.

Because of a revolutionary design approach, the *QE2*'s passengers would have fifty-two per cent more space each than those on the old *Queen Elizabeth*; the *QE2*'s tourists would have 72 square feet each, compared with 47.75 square feet each on the older *Elizabeth* – then the largest ship in the world. And the *QE2*'s 6000 square yards of deck space was to be the largest open area on any passenger ship. The crew–passenger ratio would be around one to two, with 900 Cunard personnel attending to the every need of 2025 passengers.

The new *Queen* would have drive-on/drive-off facilities for eighty cars. There would be two outdoor and two indoor swimming pools, and three main restaurants seating separately 100, 500 and 815 diners. She would have twenty-two lifts, thirteen decks, a plant turning seawater into freshwater at the rate of 1200 tons daily, and twin sets of stabilisers on each side to cut rolling to no more than three degrees. Non-inflammable materials were being used throughout and, for additional safety, a complete sprinkler system was also being fitted. The ship's ultimate depth in the water was to be significantly reduced by the use of lightweight metals in construction, including 1100 tons of aluminium.

Because of enormous technological advances since the days when the two other *Queens* were built, the *QE2* would now have only one engine-room instead of the previously usual two, and would consume half the normal fuel – 520 tons instead of 1100 tons a day. Her turbines would send 110,000-shaft-horsepower to her six-bladed twin screws.

The co-ordination of design work was being undertaken by James Gardner and Dennis Lennon. Mr Gardner's brief was to ensure that the shaping of the superstructure, the single mast and the funnel, blended into one aesthetic whole. Mr Lennon had charge of all internal design, and had a support team of Britain's most distinguished designers. Overall, they were producing a remarkably handsome, striking and effectively functional interior.

In standard accommodation, the *QE2* would have 687 rooms all with bath or shower, offering 1441 berths. There would be 291 de luxe rooms, and forty-six of these would be luxury suites. Passengers would travel from ship to shore in the six motor cruisers being fitted, which had big windows and enclosed coach-tops and carried up to eighty people at a time. There would also be twelve thirty-six-foot motor lifeboats and two water-jet-propelled emergency sea-boats, as well as sixty-two inflatable rafts, each capable of carrying twenty-five people.

The *QE2* was to have the first computer of its kind in a

merchant ship. Its sophisticated technical, commercial and operational functions at sea would include data logging, alarm scanning, machinery control, prediction of fresh water needs, weather implications and control of food stocks.

And among the *QE2*'s mammoth inventory would be twenty-five miles of wool carpet, two million square feet of Formica laminate, 115 vacuum cleaners, sixty-four carpet cleaners, eleven baggage and stores trucks, 1300 telephones and 7440 feet of mooring rope. To give everyone aboard the best possible views, there were to be 1350 portholes and 577 windows. *QE2* was to be supplied with 64,000 items of crockery, 51,000 items of glassware, 35,850 pieces of cutlery, 5864 tablecloths, 8600 blankets, 23,200 pairs of sheets, 26,200 pillow slips, 31,000 hand towels, 26,000 bath towels, 1500 deck rugs and 14,000 glass-towels.

If the *QE2*'s catalogues seem endless now, they appeared truly colossal to me at the time. There were to be nightclubs and discothèques, dog kennels, card-rooms, libraries, hairdressing and beauty salons, a print shop producing the *Daily Telegraph* at sea, a fully equipped hospital, a shopping arcade, a photographic studio and conference centres featuring simultaneous translation facilities. Today I see all these and hundreds of other floating facilities on the *QE2* working smoothly and effectively. Back in 1967 and 1968, my faith in the end result was severely tested more than once.

Apparently, stealing from ships being built is known on Clydebank as 'squirreling'. It didn't start with the *QE2* and I'm sure it didn't end there. The theory behind it all seemed to be, as was explained more than once, that the more you stole from a ship, the longer it took to finish it. That way you kept a well-paid job longer that also carried its own prolific perks.

To illustrate, when police searched the home of just one electrician who was working on the *QE2* in 1968 they found he had taken from the ship, within three months: thirty yards of carpet, two chests of drawers, a wall cabinet, three bookcases, three lounge stools, four settee backs, one toilet seat, five lamp shades, one bulkhead lamp, one shower valve, one drilling brace, three strip-lighting units, an electric radiator, eight electric bulbs, 180 feet of fibreglass, four wooden gratings, four curtain rails, five sheets of plastic, two buckets, eight gallons of paint, a roll of wire netting, six teacups and saucers, six side plates, six cereal plates, three cushions, five curtains, two sheets, a blanket, a canvas tarpaulin, five fluorescent tubes, 350 feet of electric cable, and 216 yards of Sellotape. The man's solicitor told the local court, 'There was in this ship a kind of atmosphere which tended to encourage this kind of conduct. It wasn't an ingenious crime. My client just walked off the ship with the stuff.'

The police reported that there was a thriving market around Glasgow for materials bearing the exclusive *QE2* design. The going rate for eight foot by four foot of Formica was ten shillings (50p), delivered to the door. The brilliant orange, green and red paint used in the engine-room and on the pipework on the ship cost £1 a gallon delivered. Light fittings and shades from the cabins were always available at five shillings (25p) a set, with extra bulbs a few coppers more.

One Monday, two new lifeboats were delivered to the *QE2*, and by the following day, they had been stripped of their compasses, sirens, torches, rope ladders and iron rations. Another time, after the citizens of nearby Greenock were invited aboard to inspect progress, scores of their children were playing in the streets the next morning with the *QE2*'s orange-coloured alarm whistles. Then, a welder working on the liner seemed to be clanking somewhat as he walked out through the shipyard gates. A search showed he was encased like a Dalek in copper-sheet armour tailored to fit closely to his body and bound with wire.

The Clydebank police, I was told, took a philosophical view of the thieving, feeling that, if they were called to the yard too often, it would cause far more trouble than the disappearance of the gear. One of the gates through which most of the stuff vanished was next door to the local police station. An officer said, 'They are stealing an ocean liner, and there's very little we can do about it.'

Security, of course, wasn't my affair, but Cunard's overall interests definitely were. I couldn't help feeling deeply worried about what was happening, yet it was something we all had to live with. A succession of family friends travelled up to Glasgow to see me and helped to take my mind off matters of grand larceny. Former shipbuilder and repairer Bill Newton came up from Fleetwood with my father, and Terry Windle, an old friend from Thornton Cleveleys, and Gilbert Ashton, head of a

Lancashire printing company, also showed up. I took them all along to the yard to see the state of the *QE2*'s progress – but didn't mention the 'squirreling' affair.

Then Joan and the children came up one weekend, driven to Clydeside by my chum Ken Gibson, our local Midland Bank manager. By now I had bought a bed-settee which we fixed up in the lounge for the youngsters. When I talked to Joan about my concern for the new *Queen*, she said, 'You know, Bob, you're getting upset over something you can do nothing about. It's all very sad, but even if you were Master of the ship right here and now, I don't think you could change the situation.' She was absolutely right.

As part of my preparation for sea service on the *QE2*, I left Glasgow occasionally for specialist studies. I travelled to Portsmouth to a management seminar at the Polytechnic College there, and went to Slough on a work-study course. Both exercises proved invaluable when I took command of the giants in Cunard's fleet.

I requested a voyage to New York aboard the first *Queen Elizabeth* to study various operational aspects of a large liner at first hand, including anchor fitting, mooring and baggage arrangements. To relieve me at the yard, while I went on that trip, came Harvey Smith, now staff captain of the *QE2* and one of my best friends. When I reached New York, the Gallic leviathan *France* was also docking, and this gave me a double viewing of the subjects I had come along to research.

Back in Glasgow, I went to a radar simulator course at the local technical school. The instructor simulated a collision course on the screen, as well as all types of marine obstacles and many other problems designed to keep a liner Captain on his bridge rather than presiding at his table over dinner. But probably my most realistic course was the fire-fighting exercise laid on by Leith Fire Brigade. They built a mock-up of a ship as big as a house and simply set it on fire. Looking like one of the first men on the moon in my asbestos suit and breathing apparatus, I attacked blazes all over the 'ship' with hosepipe, chemical foam and tremendous enthusiasm. Although awash with the foam and water that I had splattered on it so liberally, the mock-up, I felt, would have stayed afloat.

At Clydebank, the *QE2*'s bridge and superstructure began taking on the distinctive shape which is now familiar in the

146

great harbours of the world. For me, the addition of more decks meant a lot more tramping round on tours of inspection, and late at night, when the ship had a minimum of people around, we carried out inclining tests using the *QE2*'s trimming tanks and plumb lines to calculate her stability. Day or night, there just wasn't time to sit down. My feet began to feel as if they were running a daily marathon race, but fortunately my rugby training stood me in good stead. Often, John Rannie, managing director of the shipbuilders, invited me back to his home near Clydebank for a late-night drink on my way back to the flat. As I sank onto John's settee with a whisky and water, I reflected that, without the solid leg muscles I had built up over years of sport, each day would have been an even greater physical test.

Nevertheless, I decided I would have to curtail some of my weekend work on the *QE2*. One of my Cunard colleagues, Eldridge Parker, went home by train on Friday nights and lent me his VW 1500 for the weekends, and I used the little Beetle car to get away from Clydebank. In it, I discovered the wild beauty of the Trossachs, drove along the shores of Loch Lomond and ate a fine Sunday lunch in the George at Inveraray. At Oban, I hired a sailing dinghy and sent her scudding into the choppy waters of the Firth of Lorn, and just seventy-five miles from Glasgow, at St Michael's churchyard in Dumfries, I stood at the mausoleum of Scotland's national poet, and sighed at the thought that Robert Burns had been burned out, and all those wonderful talents terminated, long before he was forty.

These vistas of another Scotland, in sharp contrast to the gaunt profiles of Clydeside, helped to hurry the weeks along until 19 November 1968 when the *QE2*, her exteriors now completed, was due to leave her birthplace, at the tip of the tide's reach, and head out to the open seas.

His Royal Highness Prince Charles travelled up from London to sail downriver on the ship that proudly carried his mother's name. It is the only time he has been on the *QE2* and he was, in fact, her first passenger. The night before the big day a few of us who had worked together aboard the *QE2* over the previous year toasted the Prince in a quiet booze-up in the Pond Hotel across the road from my flat. 'Here's to Bonny Prince Charlie – the Second,' I proposed as we raised glasses well charged with Scotland's golden spirit.

Unfortunately, I didn't meet His Royal Highness, but by

way of consolation before I went aboard I talked to BBC Television's Richard Baker in John Brown's office. Richard was covering the trip downriver for millions of viewers, and he asked, 'Any interesting anecdotes you can tell me about the last few months here on Clydeside?' I shook my head. 'Nothing in particular.' No point in stirring up trouble, I thought. After all, we still had to get the liner off the premises.

By eight in the morning of Tuesday, 19 November, everyone who was sailing had already joined the ship. I noticed Cunard's chairman, Sir Basil Smallpeice, coming aboard, followed by his deputy Lord Mancroft, Operations Director Brian Cocup and Nautical Adviser Captain Jack Storey. The Prince was standing on the bridge with Captain Warwick. As the minutes ticked away towards zero hour at nine o'clock, excitement mounted both on the ship and on the crowded banks of the Clyde. Thousands of Glasgow schoolchildren and their parents took the morning off to cheer loudly all along the river as the new *Queen* moved out towards her rightful domain.

The *QE2*'s descent to her ocean kingdom carved a channel she would cut only once; she was leaving the waters of the Clyde, never to return. All sea and road traffic in the area stopped as the *QE2* started to make her move. A Scottish journalist wrote that day, 'Still, for a little while, she is Scotland's pride. And no matter what strange seas her forefoot furrows, beneath which distant peaks she passes, we shall remember it was the Clyde which gave her to the world.'

I had little time to appreciate such aesthetic aspects of the *Queen*'s exodus. I was intensely occupied in the aft of the vessel, controlling the letting-go of moorings, making fast to the tugs and then, as the enormous power of the *QE2*'s two engines began to throb through to the shafts, safely breaking away from tugs towards the unfettered freedom of the seas.

First, however, the *QE2* had to go into the King George V dry dock at Greenock, some ten miles downriver, and we cruised there gently at around 6 knots, exhilarated by the fresh northern breezes blowing in our faces. The liner stayed in dock five days, the first time she had been out of the water in over a year. On 24 November, with nether regions cleaned up and re-painted, the *QE2* left to take a measured-mile speed test. One or two engine problems developed, and she had to return to dock, and this time, with the vast basin filled with water, she stayed thirteen days. Our schedule was falling even further behind and a day's planned Press cruise was cancelled but, eventually, we were able to surge over the measured mile at full power speed of 31.87 knots. The young *Queen* handled with all the ease and delicacy of a thoroughbred racing yacht, although by this time she should have been sailing on her first money-earning cruise.

A feature of the *QE2* which had caused some controversy was her bulbous bow beneath the waterline. The idea behind this was to create as little turbulence as possible from the *Queen*'s bow wave, just as a bulb-headed whale cleaves through the water with hardly a ripple. The purists complained that a foaming white bow wave should be as much a part of the liner as the name of Cunard painted on her superstructure. The speed trials proved the traditionalists wrong. The underwater bulb guided water smoothly away from the ship, cutting down water resistance and increasing fuel economy, yet, I must admit, even today we don't ever get the same impression of speed that a V-wedge prow, cutting sharply into the waves, would produce. Ship designers are now taking the whale analogy a lot further. Our blubbery brethren have corrugated hides and the latest thinking is that ships should be equipped in similar fashion, with ridges below the waterline. Air bubbles would be released along the forward surfaces helping the ship to glide along, like a whale, on ripples of air. Using more orthodox progression, the *QE2* arrived in the Irish Sea at the end of December 1968, ready to make her belated voyage to Southampton.

A full crew hadn't been necessary on the *QE2*'s sea trials, but with the southbound trip imminent, two special trains brought nearly 1000 élite Cunard professionals up to Greenock. They took over quarters specially created by distinguished designer Jo Pattrick to provide a comfortable and colourful home-from-home at sea. Ratings found they had five recreation rooms and four crew restaurants while the officers were perhaps somewhat dazzled to discover that their spacious accommodation was finished in five varying and attractive colour schemes.

We brought the *QE2* south, along the western shore of the Isle of Man and round Land's End into the English Channel. It was a two-day voyage and all the time a floating workforce from Clydeside sweated away behind the ship's serene exterior, finishing off a whole catalogue of still incomplete tasks. Upper Clyde Shipbuilders had hired a ferry boat from Ulster to act

149

as a seaborne hotel for their merry band and it was moored immediately astern of the *QE2*.

I saw our new *Queen* safely tied up in Southampton and would normally have taken off immediately for the three weeks' leave I was to have during the final fitting out. However, my brother-in-law Alan Hardern and his wife Wendy had just returned to Zambia, and the little grey Austin A35 which they had used while on leave was now available. I bought it for the princely sum of £85 and had to collect it from Wendy's father, Sir Noel Ashbridge, a former chief engineer with the BBC, who lived in Sidcup, Kent. I went there, had a chat and a cup of tea with Sir Noel, then returned to the ship to collect my gear. By this time the winter skies were an ominous grey, and my friend John Hall, who is now the liner's relieving staff captain, put it quite plainly: 'If you set off up north, Bob, into that sky full of snow, you're quite mad.' I recalled someone in Fleetwood who would also be pretty mad if I didn't appear there fairly quickly, so I left Southampton at 6.00 p.m. as snowflakes as large as halfcrowns began to carpet the northbound roadways. The chunky A35 defied ever-thickening blizzards as I drove almost blindly through Romsey, Marlborough, Swindon and on to Cheltenham. In the Midlands, snow yielded to clearer skies and the roads became ribbons of ice. A car in front of me crumpled like a crushed snowball as it skidded into a totally unyielding telegraph pole. A few miles further on, a lorry I was following slid straight ahead at a roundabout and ended sitting on top of it like a decoration on a white iced cake. I pressed on, thinking that perhaps the little A35's registration mark of UCD 755 stood for 'U-Can-Do-it by 7.55 in the morning'. In fact, I reached our front door at 4 a.m. after a ten-hour drive. Tired but triumphant, I drank the hot Horlicks Joan had left for me in a flask, then I quietly climbed the stairs. I fell thankfully beside her into the warmest and most welcoming bed in the world.

Chapter 18

I had been back in Southampton only a few days from my leave when I heard that Cunard had decided to give the *QE2* what is known in the trade as a shakedown cruise. It was to be a sort of dress rehearsal for her maiden voyage, with company personnel and their families playing the roles of fare-paying passengers, giving all the ship's services a thorough testing. After the disquieting experiences Cunard had already faced with their new flagship, this was a shrewd exercise before the company officially accepted her from the shipbuilders.

I phoned Joan. 'How would you like to bring the children on the *QE2* for a cruise to West Africa?'

There was a moment's silence before she answered, 'Are you pulling my leg or have you come into some money I know nothing about?'

I explained it was a shakedown cruise and that Cunard were footing the bill. 'Oh, Bob, we'd love to come cruising with you. But do you remember when I was with the ATS in the Isle of Man, how sick I was crossing the Irish Sea? Will it matter if I'm sick on your new ship?' I assured Joan it wouldn't, and that anyway she'd probably be all right on the *QE2* because that ship was somewhat larger than the Isle of Man ferry.

It would have been asking too much of my little two-door Austin to take six of us from Fleetwood to Southampton, so I borrowed my father's much grander Rover saloon. An old school chum lent me his roof-rack, and with that and the car boot bursting with the Arnott clan's holiday trappings, we set course for Southampton.

Our eldest daughter Jan, then eighteen, had worked out her own hypothesis on seasickness. 'Look, mum,' she told Joan, 'it's all in the mind. If you don't allow your thoughts to dwell on being sick, and instead think about something entirely different, such as doing your gardening, then you'll be all right.' I don't know if Joan followed that advice, but she wasn't sick at any time on the cruise. Nor was Jan's twin brother Roger, nor fourteen-year-old Gill, nor even our youngest daughter Kate, who was just nine and a half. But the 'sickologist' herself, poor Jan, suffered punishing nausea almost every day of the voyage.

One of the more important objects of the trip was to give the ship's air-conditioning system a complete workout in tropical conditions, which we found off Dakar in Senegal. With an air temperature of around 90°F, we all stayed cool and comfortable. The *QE2* also pottered round the Canary Islands, but no one went ashore.

Suitably shaken down, the *QE2* returned to Southampton after covering 5478 miles at an average speed of 28.81 knots. She'd come through her stringent tests well enough to be taken over officially by Cunard from the builders on 18 April. Meanwhile, I took the family home and returned to Southampton in time for the visit to the *QE2* on 1 May of Her Majesty Queen Elizabeth II and her husband Prince Philip.

After inspecting the red-carpeted ocean passenger rail terminal, the royal couple came up the gangway of the *QE2*. I was standing at the head of it, and gave one of my best naval salutes as Her Majesty reached me. The Prince, who, as Lieutenant Mountbatten, had served on destroyers throughout the last war, returned my salute, and then went on with his wife to tour the ship under the masterly guidance of Captain Warwick and Staff Captain George Smith.

As soon as the royal party disappeared along the companionway, I doubled back to the officers' wardroom. I had just been appointed first President of the *QE2*'s wardroom mess, and I wanted to make sure that everything was shipshape when the Queen arrived to sign our visitors' book. My own name was already in there; I'd signed it as a passenger on our recent cruise. There was a moment of panic as Her Majesty and Prince Philip walked in. It seemed unlikely that their illustrious signatures would be going into our book because the wardroom steward had forgotten to lay out a pen. I rapidly searched my pockets and found a gold-coloured pen which I lay beside the book. Her Majesty inscribed her own distinctive signature on the page, then handed the lifesaving pen to the Prince. After the royal couple had gone ashore, Bil Warwick told me, 'Good thing you had that fine gold pen, Bob, for Her Majesty. Didn't do our image any harm at all.' 'True enough,' I replied modestly.

No point in marring a famous occasion by explaining that the 'gold' pen was merely gilt.

A fiesta mood danced along the normally staid Southampton Waters a couple of days later when, at precisely 11.30 p.m., the *QE2* left on her maiden voyage to New York. Bands played rousing maritime marches on the quayside where thousands of well-wishers were waving a massed 'God Speed' to Britain's new sovereign of the seas. As we reached open water, the decks of passing tankers, cargo boats, luxury yachts and humble tugs were crowded with fellow mariners shouting, cheering or blasting on ships' whistles their unmistakably joyous greetings. The departing *Queen* hooted over and over again her own traditional salute of three long blasts of her siren, acknowledging the hearty hailing of her subjects and also, I felt, celebrating the fact that at last she was out and about earning her keep as the supreme mercantile monarch.

Our welcome in New York was even more uproarious than our farewells from Southampton. The harbour was ablaze with bunting and echoed with whistle blasts from a reception flotilla of liners, freighters, tugboats, and dazzling white yachts. New York's fireboats hurled aloft a triumphal archway from their powerful hoses, while sightseeing helicopters thrashed about in friendly but dangerous proximity to the *QE2*'s 204-foot-high funnel. For me, one of the more impressive aspects of our arrival in the United States was the sudden near touchdown of a pair of RAF Harrier jets on the wings of our bridge. A 'jump jet' hovered at each extremity of the bridge as we entered the harbour, and gave the whole memorable affair an additional dimension of a gigantic sea and air display of twin triumphs in British design, advanced technology and engineering skills. It was just unfortunate that the ferocious blast from the jets' Rolls-Royce engines blew away, like petals in the wind, the white linen tablecloths – and their goodies – from the packed picnic tables laid out in bright sunshine on the decks of scores of launches and yachts escorting us into New York harbour.

That night we held open house on the *QE2* for more than 2000 of New York's top socialites. Glancing through the guest list for that glittering evening of 8 May 1969, I can see the names of the cream of New York society, plus a fair sprinkling of British blue bloods. In the ship's showpiece Double Room – the largest public arena in any ship afloat – the George Haley

Orchestra played for dancing. Youngsters flocked to the Theatre Bar to rock to the music of the Applejacks and the Anna Dell trio, while in the glamorous Queens Room the Canadian star Edmund Hockridge sang some of his show hits to the music of the Basil Stutely Orchestra. In the Q4 Room, the Dougie Ward trio jumped around offering up folk music and pop. In the Midships Bar, George Feyer, from New York's Stanhope Hotel, featured his own exclusive style of piano artistry. And so it went on. It was a splendid evening of on-the-house entertainment for our guests, followed by a sumptuous supper feast served in the Britannia and Columbia restaurants.

When our distinguished guests went ashore after their evening of lavish hospitality, so did hundreds of salt and pepper sets, presumably wrapped in the multitudes of linen table napkins which also vanished. Each of the silver-plated, cylindrical condiment sets was embossed with the Cunard motif, and had been specially designed for the *QE2*. Perhaps that's where we made our mistake; maybe we should have supplied something like the Woolworth's salt and pepper sets we had to send out for the next day for the return trip across the Atlantic. These stayed intact for months until our next delivery of customised condiment containers arrived from the manufacturers.

As chief officer, one of my responsibilities was to ensure the ship's constant stability, no matter what conditions she faced. The appropriate trim is largely achieved by varying the disposition of oil and water in the ship's tanks, and on the *QE2*, once I had worked out this calculation, the necessary transfers were carried out from the safety control room at the touch of a button. This may seem relatively uninteresting to many folk, but it was a matter of intense curiosity to His Royal Highness the Duke of Edinburgh when he paid a brief visit – alone – to the *QE2* on 29 May 1969, when it was my privilege to explain to him the workings of the safety control room.

'You know, Arnott, some of my naval ships steamed much better with their heads slightly down,' said the Duke. 'Is it the same with the *QE2?*'

I told His Royal Highness it didn't really matter with the *QE2*, but usually we kept her on a pretty even keel except when entering shallow water; then we ran her with the stern slightly up.

'Ah well,' insisted the Duke, 'in my experience they run that much better with their heads down into the water. Don't you think you should at least try it?'

'Well sir,' I said diplomatically, 'I'll put it to the Captain.'

'All right then,' replied the Duke, disappointed. 'But I'm speaking from years of experience, you know.' I felt I hadn't convinced Prince Philip – a fine seaman – that the *QE2* didn't need to dig her bulbous bow into the depths to achieve the most efficient and comfortable progress, but I was equally sure the Prince's head-down system had worked a treat on the destroyers he had commanded some twenty years earlier.

The Prince's uncle, Admiral of the Fleet Earl Mountbatten of Burma, took as keen an interest in the fortunes of the *QE2* as his nephew. He had been an honoured guest at the maiden voyage supper dance in New York, and on the voyage back to Southampton, after a tour of the ship, he joined other officers and myself for drinks in the wardroom. A few days later, Lord Louis wrote to me from his home at Broadlands, Romsey. 'My dear Arnott,' he wrote, 'I am writing to thank you and the members of your Mess for your kindness and hospitality to me. I must say your Wardroom Mess is one of the finest layouts I have ever seen in any ship. I understand you would like a signed photograph to replace the one on the old *Queen Elizabeth*, and I enclose one with my very best wishes. Yours sincerely, Mountbatten of Burma.' That letter was dated 14 May 1969, and the photograph which the great sealord sent me now hangs in a position of poignant honour in the wardroom where he was so much at home.

A month or two after my discussion with the Duke, I was sitting on the luxurious, green velvet upholstery of the Midships Bar, sipping a quiet mid-Atlantic, after-dinner whisky and water, when Natalie Wood and her then estranged husband Robert Wagner came in and walked over to me. I had exchanged polite early morning chat with the San Francisco-born actress earlier in the voyage as she strolled around the promenade deck, but hadn't come across her handsome young husband before, except on screen in such films as *The Longest Day* and *All the Fine Young Cannibals*.

'What do you think, Bob [they all called me Bob by this time],' said the darkly beautiful Natalie, 'about our getting together again? We're considering giving our marriage another go. Do you think we should?'

155

I looked apprehensively at the deceptively nonchalant expression of Mr Wagner. It was the sort of question that could get a fellow a punch on the nose if he gave the wrong answer. Yet young Wagner was nodding in quiet assent to Natalie's query, as if inviting a spot of homely advice. 'Well, you've got a lot going for you,' I said, reflectively. 'I'd say from the way you're holding hands and adoring each other with your eyes that it would be sheer cruelty to keep you apart. Yes, of course I'd have another go.'

'Oh, thanks, Bob,' said Natalie, smiling. 'I was hoping you'd say something like that.'

Robert Wagner shook my hand. 'You're obviously all in favour of love and marriage,' he said.

It was my turn to smile. Any danger of a Wagnerian left hook had obviously passed. 'Why, yes,' I replied. 'If two people are meant for each other, there's no other way to live.' In the best Hollywood tradition, Robert and Natalie walked off, hand in hand, towards the Atlantic moonlight. And I was glad to hear afterwards that they had achieved a long-lasting, romantic repair job on their marriage, cut short only by Natalie's tragic drowning in 1981.

It was, undoubtedly, a splendid sort of life on the *QE2*. I had been with her since her traumatic gestation and could easily handle every aspect of the chief officer's shipboard portfolio. But I wanted more. I still hadn't had the prefix 'Captain' before my name and, at forty-six, felt it was time I should. I talked the situation over with Captain Warwick and he agreed with me that it would be better for me to leave the *Queen* to take up promotion on another Cunarder. On 14 March 1970, I put four gold bands on my tunic sleeves, a cluster of gold oak leaves – otherwise known as scrambled egg – on my peaked cap, and joined the cruise liner *Franconia* in New York as the proud and elated Staff Captain Robert Arnott RNR.

Becoming a staff captain and returning to the congenial world of weekly cruising amounted, I reckoned, to being served up with a double helping of life's pleasures. For RMS *Franconia* was Cunard's Bermuda ship. Once a week, she left New York for the balmy airs of the world's most northerly group of coral islands, and because of the shiploads of high-spending tourists she regularly deposited there, RMS *Franconia* was held in special esteem by the Government of Bermuda, guaranteeing that her

CAPTAIN
OF THE
QUEEN

Above: Robert Arnott (back row, fourth left) during schooldays at Fleetwood Grammar School: at 14, already an established all-rounder at cricket, rugby, hockey and tennis.

Left: The newest midshipman in the Blue Funnel fleet: Robert Arnott at 17, pictured just before joining *S.S. Antilochus* in Liverpool.

Right: Joan Hardern at 17 — 'a fine young sportswoman, playing a graceful but devastating flow of tennis shots' — and now, 40 years later, grandmother, diarist and my constant companion on the *QE2*'s world cruises.

Below: On leave in the Lake District — with Dad's treasured Triumph Gloria.

SS *Antilochus,* the first ship I ever sailed in, moored in Sydney during an early wartime round-the-world voyage.

'My days in the halfdeck were over when I was posted to Glasgow as Fourth Officer in the motor vessel *Ajax,* in January 1944.' Here, MV *Ajax* is under way in the Mersey.

MV *Santander.* 'I tramped round Liverpool's shipping offices until I heard on the grapevine that the Pacific Steam Navigation had a job waiting for a young officer on their motor ship *Santander.*'

RMS *Queen Elizabeth*. 'I joined her on 28 August 1950 at Southampton as Junior Third Officer for just £45 a month.'

RMS *Caronia,* 'The Green Goddess'.

RMS *Queen Mary,* pictured here at her permanent resting place at Long Beach, California.

RMS *Parthia.* 'I was Second Officer in 1953 and handled the 4 a.m. to 8 a.m. watch with the Chief Officer.'

Lieutenant Robert Arnott (back row, fourth from right), on Royal Naval Reserve service, Course P10, at Portsmouth, 1953.

RMS *Franconia.* 'I practised for an hour until I could guide the canoe round the lake almost as smoothly as I could bring *Franconia* into the St Lawrence estuary.'

The sloop HMS *Fleetwood* — Fleet Pennant Number 47, the same number as my house. I sailed with her from Portsmouth as Mess Secretary and officer in charge of her confidential documents during my first long spell of service with the Royal Naval Reserve

The picture Joan Crawford gave me soon after she joined *Mauretania* in Barbados. She wrote: 'Hello to Senior Second Officer Arnott — from Joan Crawford.' When I showed it to my own Joan, she said, 'That will be a big help in bringing up the children.'

This fine picture of the old RMS *Mauretania* hangs in the *QE2*'s Quiet Room.

MV *Andria* pictured in the Channel off Dover Castle: 'the only two-funnelled collier on the North Atlantic.'

RMS *Sylvania.* 'She was just a year old when I joined her as Junior First Officer.'

Right: MV *Britannic.* 'My last glimpse of *Britannic* was as she lay forlornly on that sad Scottish beach.'

Below: RMS *Carinthia.* 'I transferred, for one trip only, to the 22,000-ton *Carinthia* captained by Geoffrey Marr.'

Her Majesty the Queen and His Royal Highness the Duke of Edinburgh arriving at Clydebank for the launching ceremony of the *QE2*. PHOTO: JOHN BROWN SHIPBUILDERS

Moments after Her Majesty has cracked the traditional champagne over her, the *QE2* surges down the Clydebank slipway to the cheers of the thousands of packed spectators. PHOTO: JOHN BROWN SHIPBUILDERS

Right: The *QE2* arriving in New York Harbour on her maiden voyage in May 1969.

I explain to HRH the Duke of Edinburgh the intricacies of the *QE2*'s safety control room. PHOTO: SOUTHERN PHOTOGRAPHIC STUDIOS

My first command, RMS *Carmania*, pictured from HMS *Ark Royal* in Grand Harbour, Malta.

Below: Cunard Ambassador leaving Rotterdam on her maiden voyage.

Cunard Ambassador and *Cunard Adventurer* berthed together at Grenada.

he bridge
unard
enturer,
ring St
nas
our in the
n Islands.

CUNARD ADVENTURER. Caribbean Cruise 1974.

ng with
1 and my
ts at the
tain's
le of
ard
enturer on
of her
4
ibbean
es.

The Captain
and his Lady.
Aboard
Cunard
Adventurer on
a 1974
Caribbean
cruise.

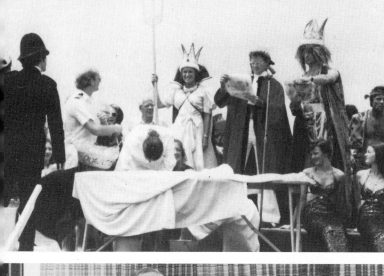

King Neptu
holds court
the *QE2*
crosses the
Line on 24
January 197

Miss Nagas
presents me
with a
beautiful
encased
Japanese do
during the
QE2's first
visit to the
atom-bombe
city in Marc
1977.

The day bef
Her Majesty
the Queen
reviewed her
fleet in the
Solent, the
QE2 makes
own majesti
way through
the arrayed
warships.
PHOTO:
SOUTHERN
NEWSPAPERS
LIMITED

The QE2 cruising in Milford Sound, off New Zealand, on her Great Pacific Cruise, 1978.

View from the QE2, arriving in Sydney Harbour with an escort fleet of hundreds of small boats for her 1978 visit to Australia.

To introduce the Sultan of Kelantan, Malaysia's Supreme Head of State, and his wife to the ship's officers and cruise staff off Singapore during the Great Pacific Cruise of the QE2 in 1978.

Taking a sighting on the *QE2*'s anti-collision radar equipment, fitted by Decca in 1976.
PHOTO: DECCA RADAR LIMITED

At Buckingha Palace wit daughter I and Joan, Her Majes garden pa on 20 July 1978.

I take in a bird's-eye view of the Suez Canal from the *QE2*'s bridge 'wing', during the ship's first-ever transit of the Canal.

The *QE2* entering Yokohama Harbour, Japan, during her 1980 voyages through the Far East.

A friendly gesture in the Friendly Isles. I'm presented with a plaque by Russell Mariott, the Kingdom of Tonga's Government Tourist Officer (left) and His Excellency Bernard Coleman, British High Commissioner (right), to mark the first visit of the *QE2* to Nuku'alofa Harbour, on 11 February 1981.

The *QE2* arriving in Sydney Harbour and sailing past the famous Opera House on her 1981 world cruise.

A night out in Hong Kong during the *QE2*'s 1981 world cruise as guests of Ann Brooks (third left) at the Mandarin Hotel. Left to right: Joan, myself, Ann, Dr Peter Oliver, Frances Franklin and 'Happy' Franklin.

own berth was always available whenever she arrived with the cargoes that formed a significant contribution to the island economy.

I quickly decided Bermuda wasn't just for the tourists to enjoy. Playing golf, cricket and squash, wining and dining in some of the gorgeous homes scattered liberally around the island, and taking sightseeing tours on a hired moped, soon became part of my way of life. My squash career, I had thought, was at an end, but not so. Local magistrate Richmond Smith was a fine player, and our weekly ding-dong battles sharpened the edge on my game. I revived the *Franconia*'s cricket team, too, and our first match was against the Bermudian Police first eleven in the National Stadium. We lost the four-hour fixture, but some of the *Franconia* lads – who turned out as the Gold Braid Brigade – gave the crack police team a fine tussle.

When I went out to dinner in Bermudian high society, I came across, for the first time, their fashion of wearing black shorts and black stockings as part of the dinner suit. It was a bit too much for me, and I wore shorts only during the daytime. Usually I drove around the island on a moped that I hired from Astwoods Hire Company, right across the street from where *Franconia* docked, but mopedding was a risky business. Tourists roared round the island roads as if they were competing in the Isle of Man TT races, and head-on, bloody-nosed crashes were frequent, particularly at night. When Captain Bill Law and I were invited to an evening naval cocktail party on board HMS *Malabar*, at Somerset on the west of the island, we took no chances and hired a taxi to take us there and back. Cars on the island are restricted to one per family – in the interests of cleaner roads – but cab charges, we found, were surprisingly reasonable.

A pleasant and satisfying part of my job as staff captain was to foster friendly public relations with the island folk. They were never hesitant in their response, and firm friendships were quickly established on that enchanting atoll. My Bermudian buddies included Dr and Mrs Bill Armstrong, Colonel Brownlow Tucker who has just retired as an MP for Bermuda's Upper House, Colonel Frank Vanwyke-Mason of Hamilton Head, harbourmaster Clive Bennett and his assistant Russell Southern – a former watchmate of mine – and my golfing partners Mike Cheadle from BOAC and Ian Morris of Qantas.

We usually played at the famous Castle Harbour course, where Gary Player was non-resident professional.

Occasionally I had a round at the Riddles Bay Club with Bill Brewer, president of our agents' company. One sultry summer's day, Bill and I were looking forward to cooling our parched throats with a chilled beer from the ice box kept in a tree-shaded hut half way round the course. Said Bill, 'There'll be some chicken sandwiches, too. It's all very safe because the cold cupboard has a combination lock.' But when we got to the thirst-slaking oasis, Bill had forgotten the combination numbers and had to phone the clubhouse for the vital sequence. As we sipped cooling lager, Bill said, 'That's the last time I'll trust my memory. Lend me a pen, Bob, and I'll write those damned numbers down.' I handed him my trusty golden special.

I was becoming almost as familiar a part of the Bermuda scene as the screeching gulls and terns that hunt for their fresh fish suppers in Hamilton's ample harbour waters. Yet there were lots of places and faces I still hadn't seen on my weekend explorations when, in the early autumn of 1970, I was appointed staff captain of the *Carmania*. I said only a temporary goodbye to the islands first visited in 1515 by the Spaniard Juan de Bermudez, and dusted off my charts of the super-salinated waters of the Mediterranean.

Comedian Frankie Howerd was one of the first people I met on my first *Carmania* cruise. One of the busiest people in showbiz, Frankie was taking an ocean furlough for a couple of weeks. 'You know, Bob,' he said, 'it's a great relief that, out at sea, people don't expect me to be funny the whole time. I'm quite a serious sort of bloke, and it's a treat to relax, all solemn and staid.' I'm afraid we interrupted Frankie's repose by asking him to do a spot on one of the ship's shows in aid of a children's charity. Frankie instantly said, ' 'Course I will,' and, as expected, he had his fellow cruisers rolling around in their seats. We had a drink after the show. 'I enjoyed that,' said the Yorkshire comic. 'I'm always as happy on the stage, if I tell the truth, as I suppose you are on the bridge of a ship.' I knew exactly what Frankie meant.

In *Carmania*'s archives, I unearthed a yellowing book which gave a graphic account of how a much earlier Cunard *Carmania* fought and sank the German armed liner *Cap Trafalgar* off Trinidad in September 1914. The story began: 'Here is a tale

158

to thrill the blood of every Briton, a tale for which no parallel could be found since the days of the American War. Armed merchantmen in action and fighting to the death!' It sounded better than anything in *Chums*, *The Magnet* or in the ship's latest delivery of paperbacks. As our 1971 *Carmania* cruised south from Naples into the Med, I could almost hear the crash of the 4.7-inch guns mounted on her namesake in that legendary victory of more than half a century earlier.

Completed in 1905, the *Carmania* was a triple-screw, turbine-driven vessel of 20,000 gross tons. Her length was 675 feet overall, and her 21,000-horsepower engines gave her a sea speed of 18 knots. Captain Noel Grant RN was given war-time command, and *Carmania*'s peace-time Captain, J. C. Barr, was appointed navigator with the rank of Commander Royal Naval Reserve, when in August 1914, and within a week of arriving in Liverpool from an Atlantic crossing, the ship was stripped and fully converted for war. A month later, *Carmania* arrived off Trinidad – not the island in the West Indies, but an uninhabited, isolated peak jutting out from the Atlantic some 500 miles off the South American coast. The island had a good anchorage, and was a favourite spot for secret re-fuelling by German vessels. The *Cap Trafalgar* – newer, faster and with longer range guns – was spotted by Commander Barr lurking at the other side of the one-and-a-half-mile wide island.

Cap Trafalgar didn't run. She closed with *Carmania*. Captain Grant cried, 'Let him have it!' The two armed merchantmen hurled shells at each other from a one-and-a-half-mile range – point blank in naval terms. *Carmania* caught fire, had her bridge put out of action and her main rigging and wireless aerials were shot away. Still she poured her shells at the *Cap Trafalgar*, the pride of the Hamburg–Sud-Amerika Line. The German caught fire, began to list and suddenly thrust her stern high in the air, plunging vertically into the cold Atlantic depths. In an action lasting an hour and forty minutes, *Carmania* had been hit seventy-nine times and was holed in 304 places; nine sailors were killed and twenty-six wounded.

In 1919 the Navy League presented *Carmania*, now back in peace-time service, with a piece of Nelson's silver plate to commemorate the South Atlantic fight. Admiral the Hon. E. R. Freemantle declared at the presentation luncheon, 'There never was a single ship action which reflected greater credit on the

159

Royal Navy, on the Mercantile Marine and more especially on the Royal Naval Reserve.'

As I put down the book, I reflected that its fading pages contained far more than a simple adventure yarn. They brought to life again a golden chapter in the history of Cunard seamen who turned their hand to war. And a stirring feature for me was that the gallant *Carmania* battled under the colours of the Royal Naval Reserve, with which I was so deeply involved. A few months later, on 23 April 1971 – St George's Day – I remembered again with humble pride the glorious combat role of the long-deceased Cunarder when I became Master of her direct descendant, the glamorous cruise liner RMS *Carmania*.

Chapter 19

Each Captain on a Cunard liner has his own personal steward, who's known as his 'tiger'. My first one was Barry Rowlands, who is now a bar-keeper on the Cunard *Countess*. Barry moved the old leather trunk, bought by my parents many years earlier, into *Carmania*'s Master's quarters right below the bridge. That trunk and I had crossed the oceans of the world for over three decades before we finally dropped anchor in the marine penthouse known as the Captain's cabin.

Carmania made a bumpy passage out into the Atlantic, then swung southwards to the Azores. I hadn't been to the islands since my days with HMS *Fleetwood* and somehow the atmosphere of Ponta Delgrada, chief town of the group, seemed rather more salubrious the second time around. We only stopped for a few hours, then I watched the peaks of San Miguel Island fade over *Carmania*'s wake as my officers set course for Madeira, 532 miles distant. Cliff Nicholson, was my staff captain on that voyage, and the chief officer was Peter Bingley. Poor Peter eventually returned to cargo ships, and was lost overboard off Cape Town.

From Madeira, we cruised overnight the 258 miles to the snow-capped volcanic island of Tenerife, then on to the Canaries' capital of Las Palmas. My lunch partner there was the redoubtable Eugene Pavillard, who was involved in a bizarre plot in 1936 to get the Canaries' garrison commander, General Franco, back into Spain. A Spanish general had been shot in Las Palmas, and Eugene was suspected by the authorities of trying to get Franco into Spain by sending him to the funeral. It didn't work, the government only allowing the future dictator to see the burial from a launch moored offshore.

For generations, Eugene and his family have been shipping agents both for Cunard and the Union Castle lines, working at ornate, carved mahogany desks in an office packed with the Spanish equivalent of Victoriana. But there's nothing out of

161

date about Eugene. He's large, balding, jolly and shrewd, and his wife speaks more than a dozen languages.

I took *Carmania* from Las Palmas to Casablanca, then across on a star-lit passage to Cadiz on Spain's southern shore. There my mid-day good fortune held out, and I ate lunch with our agent, Marcus Domecq, scion of the famous sherry family, who took me out to the bodega where his renowned Dry Sack brand was made. Since the early 1800s, all the Domecq sons have been born on the Cadiz estate, and like so many of my overseas friends, Marcus was proud to have been educated in England. 'At Jerez, we have the finest vineyards in the world,' he declared, 'but there are no schools anywhere like those in your country. Now, will you try our golden oloroso?'

A pleasant new dimension was added to my ocean wanderings in August 1971 when my wife Joan sailed with me for the first time. Since then, she's explored the world with the dedicated enthusiasm of a latter-day Captain Cook and knows the cruise-ways of the Caribbean, Mediterranean and South Atlantic as well as most Cunard veterans. Apart from the fact that, after thirty years of marriage, I still love to have her around, Joan takes a great workload from my shoulders in the shipboard social scene by acting as hostess at my parties and generally making every passenger she meets feel welcome and wanted. The list of friends she's made everywhere from New York to the New Hebrides can only be slightly shorter than that of Father Christmas.

But on that hot August morning when Joan first stepped aboard *Carmania*, her normally cheerful features were slightly overcast. 'Oh, Bob,' she said anxiously, 'I've been so looking forward to sailing to the Med as the Captain's lady. I do hope I'm not going to be sick.' But she was. I asked the doc to give Joan an anti-seasick injection after her first twenty-four unhappy hours at sea. That did the trick, and we both began to realise that we were right on course for some of the best years of our lives – because the times of long separation had gone forever.

Joan had chosen a Mediterranean cruise for her debut as Captain's mate. The way her days went along are vividly described in the diaries she has always kept from the day she first walked up the gangplank of the *Carmania* right up to the present, when she cruises the world as First Lady of the *QE2*. Here are one or two of Joan's early diary extracts.

1 August 1971, Southampton
Went up on bridge at 11 p.m. to watch cast-off. *New Amsterdam* (34,000 tons) taking on passengers nearby. We had three tugs instead of usual two because of bad weather forecast. Left bridge about half past midnight and had a bath. Ship moving quite a bit up and down. Bob down from bridge around 1 a.m.

2 August, at sea
Didn't feel very well after breakfast, so lay on bed. Bob decided an inoculation called for, had one, then to sleep. Finally woke up 5.30 p.m. Weather stormy. Bob says should get into calmer weather rapidly. Hope so, as I hate this swaying floor.

3 August, at sea, off Gibraltar
Feel better. Went to talk on the Rock by Brian Price. Lots of colour slides. Attended Lonely Hearts cocktail party, then to talk on 'Ramblings of a Rose Grower' by famous rose man Harry Wheatcroft. Very entertaining. Bob's table guests at dinner included TV man John Junkin – hilarious character – Mr and Mrs Hewitt, Senator and Mrs Lewis, and Mr Purches – a really witty and happy table. Went to Nantucket Room after dinner, danced till one and then, after bath and glass of milk, to bed.

4 August, Gibraltar
Up 8.30. Did sewing, then sunbathing after grapefruit and coffee. 12.15 had lunch, then by car round Rock, St Michael's Cave, Apes' Den, Moorish Castle, Spanish border. Walked back to ship, a mistake. On bridge to see Gib leavetaking. Beautiful night, stars like fairyland.

6 August, off Palermo
Sunbathed on Monkey Island (sundeck). The Wheatcrofts, the Bass's, etc. came to Captain's party. Dinner in ship's Tivoli restaurant, watched cabaret then to bed, as we arrive in Sicily some unearthly hour.

7 August, Palermo
Bob woke at six, but I fell asleep again. Went on bridge at 7 a.m. Already 78 degrees, sea golden liquid in sun. Signor Taggliavia, our agent, and his wife, drove us round Palermo. Visited fine cathedral at Monreale. Hotel Torre Normanna for lunch; it's a

fabulous spot at Altavilla Milicia 20 miles out. Back to ship via Palermo shops, bought roses in street and postcards. On board 7 p.m., had to scamper to make dinner. Sicilian folk dancers came on board to give show. Full moon, sea like molten silver.

9 August, Palma, Majorca
Felt better. With agent by taxi to visit Gothic cathedral and Bellver Castle. Cathedral too dark, castle too hot. Went out to Santa Ponza beach for swim. Like Blackpool on Bank Holiday. Returned to comfort of ship. Hair like rats' tails, washed and set it once more. Evening, to Les Rotes farm by coach for barbecue and riding display on Andalusian horses trained for Spanish riding school. Then, salad, baked potatoes, chicken, pork, ice cream and both red and white wine. Bob and I left after midnight. Went on bridge for sailing. Harbour beautiful in moonlight.

11 August, Cadiz
Up about 9. Bob out by 6 for docking. Cadiz is lovely shopping centre. Back on board, met Marcus Domecq. Handsome and entertaining. Took us to best fish restaurant in Cadiz, had grilled prawns and huge sole. Superb. Apparently last time here Bob sailed without tugs or pilot. They were late, and he wouldn't wait. Marcus says locals still talking in admiration about that. Night, watched ladies' headdress competition, then stroll on promenade deck, lights of Tangier on portside. Bed, 12.30. a.m.

Joan, of course, wasn't always with me at sea, as we still had a fairly young family back in Fleetwood, but as they grew older she was able to come with me more often.

A month after Joan had flown home from Nice, company officials came aboard *Carmania* with the news that Cunard was slimming down on staff. When I was with the *QE2* on Clydebank I was one of a number of people asked by our nautical adviser Jack Storey to prepare a list of people for redundancy. I refused. 'What I will do,' I told Jack, 'is to choose the ones I'd like to stay with Cunard.' That was as far as I would go. I certainly wasn't going to recommend any of my old shipmates for the sack. Nevertheless, the redundancies went ahead and many familiar, faithful faces left the line to which, in many cases, they had devoted their entire working lives.

In the autumn of that year I came home for the event of the year in our family. Friday, 15 October was my parents' golden wedding anniversary and Sunday the 17th was Jan and Roger's twenty-first birthday. So on the Saturday between we had a combined party at our local golf club. The young joined their elders in ballroom dancing and the older guests thoroughly enjoyed the disco – there was certainly no generation gap that night. Joan made two magnificent cakes (there's no limit to that girl's talents) and our school-teacher friends from across the road, Edna and Hilda Wilkinson, paper-sculpted a wonderful 'gold clock' which my parents still treasure. All of our friends were there, including some of those who kept an eye on the Arnott premises when we were away at sea. David Jolly, one of our next door neighbours, digs the garden and trims the lawn, while Jack Turner on the other side watches it closer than a pack of Dobermans. Jim Westhead, the chum I used to shoot rats with as a boy on his father's farm, was there with his wife Emmy. Nowadays they live just across the way and I buy my cars from Jim at Fleetwood's Lighthouse Garage. That night I produced one of my standard slim-line speeches. I never could waffle on like some ships' Masters I've had to listen to over the years. There's nothing like standing up, coming straight to the point, then shutting up and sitting down – I leave comic patter to the comedians.

My return to *Carmania* was a sad mission. She had made her last voyage under the Cunard pennant and was laid up with the *Franconia* to await a buyer. I stayed with the forlorn pair, berthed opposite each other at Southampton, on stand-by duties until 25 February 1972, when I flew to New York to join the *QE2* as her staff captain.

As I packed my gear ready to return to the Cunard flagship, I heard from the Admiralty that I had been promoted to Captain, Royal Naval Reserve. That's as far as a reserve officer can get, and I had apparently achieved the rank in the shortest possible time permissible. Almost immediately, one of Cunard's chiefs applied for a 'job'. Brian Cocup, operations director, wrote: 'Dear Captain Arnott, I have been informed by the Admiral Commanding Reserves of your promotion to Captain, Royal Naval Reserve. If ever there was another emergency which found us both back in uniform, I hope you would find room as a watch-keeper in your ship for a junior Lieutenant Commander, RN!

Many congratulations and every good wish for continued success in your RNR activities.' I told Brian I would keep his 'application' right at the top of my filing cabinet to be brought out immediately in case of war. Happily, it's still in the cabinet.

By the time I returned to service on the *QE2*, Cunard had been taken over by the Trafalgar House Group, and already Trafalgar Chairman Victor Matthews had been able to report the transformation of a £2m loss in the last year of Cunard's ownership into a healthy £487,000 interim profit. I thought that 'Trafalgar' was at least the right name to run a shipping operation, but I was even more pleased to hear Victor Matthews say, 'We are going to market the *QE2* aggressively in every possible way.' I didn't want to see the new *Queen* going the way of the old ones. A superb ship deserved the finest possible management, and now, it seemed, the *QE2* had got it. Within weeks of taking over, Victor Matthews wrote a personal letter to hundreds of eminent and wealthy people inviting them to buy a trip on the *QE2*. Many of them did, and during the winter of 1971 fifty per cent more people travelled on the *QE2* than in the similar period of 1970. Westbound at 30,000 feet over the Atlantic on my way to join the *QE2* in New York, I got the feeling that at last the cash tides were flowing favourably again for the illustrious House of Cunard.

All winter the *QE2* had been roaming the Caribbean tourist territories. Now, for the summer, she was returning to her Atlantic domain. We sailed from New York on 16 April 1972, bound for Southampton, and after only twenty-four hours at sea ran into a frenzied storm that battered the *Queen* and her 1800 passengers to a standstill. Whipped to foaming fury by winds of more than one hundred miles an hour, heaving Atlantic spumes smashed right over the *QE2*'s towering superstructure, forcing us to lie hove-to for 21½ hours.

Heaving to means staying put. This was achieved by keeping the seas on the bow and using the engines to maintain steerage way. Yet, at times, the merciless North Atlantic heaved the *QE2* and her 65,863 tons skywards as if she were a mere toy. That evening as I was entering the Columbia Restaurant to take my place at the Captain's Table, she took a terrific lurch to port, and dozens of diners were hurled from their chairs, and crockery and food were everywhere. When she settled down, I proceeded to my table (although my natural instinct was to go to the bridge to see what was going on), picking up prone passengers as I went. Mortimer Hehir, the Master, who was on the bridge conning the ship through the storm, said afterwards, 'If Bob Arnott had turned in that doorway and retreated, there would have been instant panic and uproar.'

As the storm abated, the *QE2* counted her contusions, then scudded eastwards on a course, south of our original line, onto which she had been blown while hove-to. We issued all the passengers with a special storm certificate, commending them for 'sharing this unique experience with great cheerfulness and calm'. As the *QE2*'s black bows carved a path into the waters of her home haven at Southampton, none of us realised that, within weeks, she would be facing an even fiercer hullabaloo in mid-Atlantic.

Chapter 20

Late at night on 17 May 1972, a coded dispatch reached the radio-room of the *QE2* from Cunard's London office in Lower Regent Street. We were two days out into the Atlantic eastbound to Southampton. The message was de-coded and handed immediately to Captain Bill Law and myself. It said: 'THREAT OF EXPLOSION TO DESTROY SHIP UNLESS DEMAND CASH PAYMENT MET. EXPLOSIVES SET ON SIX SEPARATE DECKS. AUTHORITIES ADVISE TAKE ALL NECESSARY PRECAUTIONS. TWO ACCOMPLICES MAY BE ON BOARD. MONITOR ALL CABLES, TELEPHONE MESSAGES.'

A few hours earlier, the switchboard girl at Cunard's New York headquarters had taken a bizarre call from a would-be extortionist. Put through to Cunard's administrative and finance vice-president Charles S. Dickson, the mystery caller demanded: 'Pay me $350,000 or the *QE2* will be blasted out of the sea.' Speaking with what was described as a New York accent – but not with the Brooklyn intonation – the man said he had two accomplices on the ship. One was an ex-con and the other a terminal cancer victim. Both men, he claimed, were ready to die with the ship if the ransom wasn't paid. The caller added that six armed explosive devices were hidden in bulkheads well beyond the reach of searches. The bombs would be disarmed only if the cash – made up of ten and twenty dollar bills – was handed over. Instructions where and when to make payment would follow.

As soon as Mr Dickson put his phone down, he told his boss, Richard B. Patton, what had happened. They decided to call in the FBI, and also contacted Cunard's managing director, Norman Thompson, in London, who in turn at once called in his chairman. Victor – now Lord – Matthews. Within minutes Scotland Yard and the British Ministry of Defence were also brought into action, and the Ministry decided to send out four bomb-disposal experts to drop by parachute into the Atlantic as closely as possible to the *QE2*.

It was time, we decided, to take the passengers into our confidence. Captain Law put out a brief broadcast over the ship's loudspeaker system, the bustling, noisy shipboard routine suddenly hushing as he announced: 'Ladies and gentlemen, we have received information concerning the threat of a bomb explosion on board this ship sometime during this voyage. We have received such threats in the past, which have always turned out to be hoaxes. However, we always take them seriously and take every possible precaution. This time we are being assisted by the British government who are sending out bomb-disposal experts. They will be parachuted into the sea, picked up by boat and brought on board.'

Captain Law added: 'Cunard are taking every precaution ashore and on board. If there is any question of it being necessary to pay money over to the extortionist, this will be done in New York. I can only now ask you to remain calm. On these occasions a lot of rumours circulate. Take notice only of information that comes from me or my officers.'

As soon as the first alert had come in, we had started standard search procedures. In spite of the threat that the bombs wouldn't be found, our search routines are so thorough that it was unlikely that there were any hiding places on the *QE2* beyond the reach of our men, specially trained to comb every inch of the vast vessel. And their first intensive inspections from the *QE2*'s masthead to her keel-base discovered absolutely nothing.

But we could take no chances. A coded message from Cunard in London gave us secret and precise instructions for the ocean rendezvous with the parachutists. The company also asked us to check if any passengers matched up to the ex-con and cancer victim descriptions. So far as we could tell, they didn't. In replying to the instructions, we were asked to refer to the military men as 'friends', and the alleged shipboard gang of extortionists as 'special passengers'. Those must have been the euphemisms of the year.

By this time, an RAF Nimrod jet reconnaissance aircraft had taken off from St Mawgan in Cornwall. Its task was to advise on sea and weather conditions for the air drop, and also to act as a communications centre between Britain and the threatened liner. The aircraft located our position, 45.47 north, 35.05 west, 740 miles east of Cape Race, Newfoundland, and circled over-head. An hour and a half later, there were cheers from our passengers packing the upper decks as an RAF Hercules swept out of the low cloud cover right on target after its 1380-mile flight from Lyneham in Wiltshire.

Suddenly, the huge Hercules climbed back into the dense clouds which were spilling incessant rain onto the grey Atlantic only 400 feet below. Seconds later two parachutes came swinging seawards from the clouds. Then another pair of chutes followed. The Hercules had gone up to around 800 feet before its four bomb-disposal specialists could jump. Our launch was waiting for them as they hit the water only 200 yards ahead of our bows. Within minutes we were helping the servicemen, their black frogmen's suits glistening with salt, onto the *QE2*.

I wondered just what was happening when I saw dollars and sterling notes changing hands among the passengers. They had become remarkably relaxed and cheerful as soon as the parachutists were seen in the sky, and later I learned that they had been making bets between themselves as to the exact time the army men would hit the sea. Two of our passengers that I didn't see on deck were the ninety-year-old conductor Leopold Stokowski and George Kelly of Philadelphia, uncle of Princess Grace of Monaco. For them and the remainder of the folks who hadn't watched the jump, I put out a broadcast saying that the four parachutists had been safely picked up and were all fit and well. The team was led by Captain Robert Williams, of the Royal Ordnance Corps, with Lieutenant Richard Clifford, Staff Sergeant Clifford Oliver and Corporal Thomas Jones, all of the Special Boat Service and experts in marine explosions.

In mid-afternoon on Thursday, 18 May, a handwritten, special-delivery letter arrived at the Cunard offices in New York – postage due 28 cents – addressed to Mr Dickson. In a weird, hieroglyphic style of hand printing, the extortionist ordered Mr Dickson to take the $350,000 to a designated phone booth.

Mr Dickson and the cash set out by car to the location. When he got inside the booth, the phone rang. He recognised the voice as that of the extortionist. 'Why have you brought the police in?' asked the man. Mr Dickson answered that, if the police hadn't been notified, there would have been no money forthcoming from Cunard. The caller then ordered our emissary to go to the washroom of a nearby café where there would be a further message taped under the edge of the washbasin. Two guns, snarled the voice, would be trained on Mr Dickson the whole time.

Our brave envoy set out again and soon located the next message. This instructed him to drive over Bear Mountain Bridge to the town of Beacon. An attached diagram showed an out-of-town parking lot. There Charles Dickson spotted the marker where the ransom was to be left. FBI men kept a discreet and distant stake-out, but no one collected the bag of cash. Next day it was picked up and returned to Cunard.

Out in the Atlantic, the pay-up-or-else deadline set by the extortionist had passed. We opened up our public radio communications again which had been blacked out for security reasons during the emergency. Questions poured in from the world's Press, TV and radio reporters, and our passengers rushed to their phones to tell anxious relatives ashore that they were OK. And in the wardroom our four doughty parachutists were treated for their saltwater soaking with the traditional remedy of naval grog. From the moment that we had hoisted them inboard, our explosives experts had scoured the ship. They often blew up vessels – quite legally – and on the *QE2* they searched in the hidden recesses where they themselves would have planted explosives to cause the most devastation.

'I'd like to propose a toast to you fellows,' I said, 'for sheer bravery in jumping into the ocean when you couldn't even see through the clouds.'

'Well, Bob,' replied Captain Williams – who had never jumped before – 'I've always wanted to sail on this marvellous ship, but what a heck of a way this was to get onto the passenger list.' Cunard immediately put that right, and invited each of the servicemen to take a free trip on the *QE2*. So far, I believe, two of them have taken up the offer.

As the ship neared Cherbourg, Cunard's American chief, Richard Patton, decided that the time was right to issue congratulations all round. He accorded an ovation to the FBI, the police, his switchboard staff and especially to Charles Dickson. 'He was at times in great personal danger,' said Mr Patton, 'but when I asked him how he felt at the worst moments, his only complaint was that his mouth was dry. I'm proud to have such a man working for Cunard.'

For us, that was the end of the incident. Not so for the FBI.

A few months later they arrested and charged an upstate New York shoe worker with extortion; he was convicted and sentenced to a hefty spell in the penitentiary. We never uncovered his supposed accomplices on the *QE2*, and I doubt if they existed outside his cunning inventiveness.

As the FBI were closing in on their quarry, the *QE2* left the Atlantic for the sunny blue waters of the Caribbean, Joan joining me in Southampton. Then, it was across to New York where we were picking up American, Bermuda-bound sunseekers. Among the fortunate Britons making the round trip from Southampton was the skinny super-model Twiggy.

Twiggy was shown on our passenger list as Miss Leslie Hornby. I should think her trunks and cases tipped the scales at considerably more than she did; I would have been surprised if she weighed anything like 100 lb. Being a fairly tall girl, Twiggy showed up against a vast ocean backcloth only as an elfin and ephemeral outline. Yet that frail front was obviously deceptive. A male member of her entourage told me, 'When that young lady was modelling in the States recently, she was pulling in around $300 an hour. You don't get that sort of loot just for sitting there and looking pretty. The girl's a real grafter.' On the *QE2*, Twiggy took it easy. She hosted one or two champagne parties for her friends, but during most of the trip she seemed becalmed in a mood of relaxed tranquillity.

A cannon fired from St Catherine's Point on the northern tip of the Bermudas marked our arrival there on 29 May. The crash startled Joan, who had come up on the bridge at 6 a.m. to see our approach to the cluster of coral gems, but she recovered her poise in time to take the 9.30 a.m. shore tender for a swimming expedition to the Coral Beach Club, returning in ample time for Captain Mortimer Hehir's pre-dinner cocktail party. Her verdict on Bermuda: 'Just about as near paradise as you can get – but I think its sun has caught me.' I told Joan that the Bermudas are on the same latitude as Savannah, in America's Deep South, and moreover they're warmed by the waters of the Gulf Stream. 'Oh dear, I wish you'd told me all that before I went off swimming,' she said. 'I'll just have to wear an on-the-shoulder dress for the cocktail party to cover up my flaming skin.' My simple life at sea, I thought, was taking on new complexities.

When the *QE2* tied up at Southampton after returning from

her calypso carousel, I drove home with Joan in the white Bond Equipe I had bought a couple of years earlier to celebrate my first command on *Carmania*. I spent a couple of pleasant weeks at home with the family in Fleetwood, and then I was driving south again to show prospective buyers round the ship that I still held in deep affection – *Carmania*, moored with *Franconia* in the River Fal, just south of Truro in Cornwall.

As I went aboard I saw that the stand-by crews on each ship had slung a fine mesh net between the two silent sterns. 'What on earth is that hanging over there for?' I asked a seaman as I went aboard my old ship. 'It looks as if you're taking in washing to pass away the time.'

'Not washing, sir, fishing,' explained the man. 'Some grand cod, skate, whiting and bass get up the river here. Cheers up the men, sir, to have fresh fish for supper.' I felt that an old fishing net draped between two luxury liners wasn't really the best adornment to entice prospective buyers, but then neither was standing by a mothballed vessel the most exciting job for our crewmen. I didn't interfere with their fishing fun, and eventually the two ships were sold to the Panamanian subsidiary of a New York shipping group.

As well as selling ships in Britain's West Country, I travelled to Rotterdam from my Southampton office at least once a week during the late summer of 1972. *Cunard Ambassador*, a custom-built Caribbean cruise liner, was nearing completion in the Rotterdam shipbuilding yard of P. Smit, Jnr. I was to be her first staff captain, and with her Master-designate, Captain Victor Arbuckle, I went to progress meetings at the Dutch shipyard – much as I had done on the *QE2*.

There were no disastrous delays in Holland, and on 21 October, Joyce Matthews, wife of Victor Matthews, named the splendid new liner in a champagne ceremony at the Wilhelmina Quay. The Dutch style is to name the ship shortly before she is due to sail, rather than the British way of having an elaborate launching months before she is completed, so a few days after Mrs Matthews swung the champagne bottle at the creamy white new Cunarder, we set out from Rotterdam bound for Las Palmas in the Canaries, then across the Atlantic to the Caribbean cruising grounds.

Cunard's lovely new cruiser weighed in at 15,000 tons and carried 650 passengers in superb, air-conditioned comfort. Her staterooms were set into four luxurious decks, named after the famous Cunarders *Mauretania*, *Aquitania*, *Britannia* and *Carmania*. There was an open-air swimming pool, a lido and a sauna. *Ambassador*'s main restaurant, also called after the *Mauretania*, was set high in the superstructure, giving panoramic sea views, and for rainy days at sea the ship had a 100-seater theatre, three cocktail bars and both hairdressing and beauty salons. She was also the first ship I had navigated that had direct push-button control from the bridge to the variable pitch propellers and bow thrusters, making *Ambassador* as easy to 'drive' as a modern Cadillac or Rolls Royce.

As I took *Ambassador* on her serene, stabilised progress through white-crested Atlantic rollers off Portugal's northern coast, I didn't dream that the deities who dish out ships' destinies had decided to condemn this comely Cunarder, not many months hence, to the fate of carrying sheep around the South American coast. The *Ambassador* was to catch fire off Key West in Florida, and so badly gutted was she that Cunard sold her off to become the Pacific's first lamb liner. Fortunately, there were no passengers on board when the blaze broke out.

That awful day for the new liner was still an unborn nightmare as I took her into the Tagus estuary off Lisbon where we were picking up our second shipment of passengers, most of whom were flying in from Britain. Our first payload of passengers had joined us at the Holland–America Line terminal at Rotterdam, and there was no mistaking the way they earned their living. Brand-new cars were scattered across our decks with windscreens bedecked with banners proclaiming that Bristol Street Motors of Birmingham were taking to the waves. The cars, including a Rolls, a Fiat 132 and a Ford Cortina GXL, were prizes for competitions being run among the 250 Bristol Street staff and guests, who had all been led aboard by company chief Harry Cressman and his wife Barbara.

At Lisbon, another 180 sun-hungry Britons joined us, including my father's usual travelling chum Harry Hayes, a retired businessman who lives in a delightful 'olde worlde' cottage in the Lancashire village of Preesall. Soon after *Ambassador* left Las Palmas, where I had lunched again with Eugene Pavillard, Harry called me to say, 'It's not good enough, Bob. No afternoon tea aboard a British ship. Whatever next?' It was true. Our tea stocks were exhausted. Someone had slipped up in Rotterdam when provender for the cruise was being taken into our storerooms, and now the tea cupboards were bare.

On a British vessel with an all-British passenger complement, running out of tea in mid-ocean was a bitter blow. Vic Arbuckle and I talked about organising a parachute drop of tea chests into the sea, and a young officer who fancied he had a flair for public relations suggested we should book the famous British tea-commercial TV chimps to make the jump. On that note of ridicule we dropped the whole idea, and instead asked the bedroom stewards, who normally keep a private stock of tea for serving their own particular passengers, to come clean and donate their supplies to the common teapot.

By strictly rationing the meagre poundages that emerged, and serving up the precious liquid at only five per cent of proof, we managed to reach Barbados just as the last tea-dregs were disappearing down *Ambassador*'s drains. Stewards and passengers alike rushed ashore at Bridgetown, first to indulge in an orgy of tea drinking, and then to load up the bushels of teabags for the rest of the cruise. Happily the shopkeepers of Barbados – traditionally as British as cricket – kept ample stocks of the refreshing leaf.

Now oozing with tea, we cruised gently around the Windward Islands, calling at St Lucia, Martinique and St Thomas, before going on to *Ambassador*'s future base port of San Juan in Puerto Rico. When a top government delegation came on board to welcome the new ship, we made sure that the flags of the United States and Puerto Rico were flying at equal heights at opposite sides of the yardarm. Since 1898 and the Spanish-American War, the island has been under the American flag, and Puerto Ricans have been citizens of the United States since 1917 and have enjoyed self-rule from 1952. They're rightly proud of their flag, which is red, white and blue bisected by a V, hence our care in making sure that the island's national colours weren't outshone by the Stars and Stripes.

Our local adviser on such matters was Cunard's agent, Colonel Pepe Oller, a dentist by profession, who also runs his family business, the Caribe Shipping Company. Pepe is a member of several island golf clubs, including the magnificent Dorado Beach complex, which has two eighteen-hole courses starting from a mutual centre. He and I used to play quite a few sun-splashed Saturday rounds there as *Ambassador* was loading up for the following week's cruise.

Occasionally, American organisations chartered the whole ship, and I had just taken over as Master of *Ambassador* when we had a memorable booking of men from Michigan. Standing on the bridge of the ship in the harbour of Frederiksted, St Croix, I awaited the arrival of 600 members of the Greater Detroit Chamber of Commerce at Alexander Hamilton airport, just along the island's coral coast. I've rarely come across a bunch of blokes – it was an all-male extravaganza – with such a determined zest for lavishing hospitality on themselves and everyone else in sight.

Highfliers from Detroit's banks, real-estate firms, super-market groups and a hundred and one other commercial go-getters slurped their way around the Caribbean with such enthusiasm that they needed the ministrations of a special Eye Opener Club before they could face each new day. Many of the larger cabins had their beds removed so that they could be used as hospitality suites, and the earliest of these to sling open its pie-eyed portals was the Eye Opener. From 7.30 each morning club 'officials' served liquid breakfasts – large tumblers of neat bourbon topped with ice cream. I tried just one of these depth charges, and then suggested to the club's amiable officials that Eye *Closer* might be a more appropriate appellation. I still have the goblet, inscribed with the motif of the Chamber of Commerce, which the members of that bizarre club presented to me.

I took the revellers from Detroit along the seaway followed by Columbus in 1493 when he discovered the territories he named the Virgin Islands after the legendary St Ursula and her 11,000 virgin martyrs. Not surprisingly, the Michigan men didn't always make it back to the ship when they had been ashore. At Charlotte Amalie, capital of St Thomas, fifty adventurous souls hired half the island's fishing fleet and headed out to sea with rather more bottles than bait. I was due to sail at six in the evening, but the fisherfolk hadn't returned. Holding up a liner is an expensive business, but I gave them another half hour. Thirty or so came back on board, but I had to leave the rest to make their own way to our next island port of call. I never learned how they spent the next twenty-four hours, but there were no complaints when they returned. 'We had a marvellous time,' said one glassy-eyed hero. 'Those crafty old pirates certainly knew what they were about when they came to the Caribbean.'

Later that summer, it was decided to sail *Ambassador* between New York and Bermuda, calling at Boston on the way. I was always delighted to pop into Boston for two reasons. The first was that Jimmy's seafood restaurant, just walking distance from our berth, served fantastic oysters, which I usually followed up with grey sole grilled on the bone and eaten without any sort of sauce. I used to eat at Jimmy's while looking out over Boston Harbour and watching the colourful fishing boats landing their catches. And, of course, out of the corner of my eye I could watch what was happening on *Ambassador*.

The second reason I liked calling at Boston was that it was quite a thrill to watch a real salesman of the sea in action. David Paresky, president of Boston's Crimson Travel Service, never missed a trick in packing his clients aboard our ship. Almost to the moment we were sailing from the historic port, Dave was haranguing the local populace on the radio telling them, 'Pack your bags now, folks, there are just one or two berths left on *Cunard Ambassador*. Leave your worries behind in Boston and head for the carefree Caribbean.' On our return, when we docked in Boston, Dave was likely to be there again, he and his assistant Annette Toscano interviewing returning passengers and recording their comments on tape for future publicity. I know Dave was bitterly disappointed when the *QE2* pulled out of his port, but maybe one day I'll take her back in there and meet up again with that salesman supreme.

Chapter 21

Towards the end of the summer of 1973, I took command of *Ambassador*'s sister ship, the *Cunard Adventurer*. Her departing captain was Peter Jackson, the man I had hauled in from the sea thirty years earlier after his ship had been sent to the bottom by a U-boat. I signed the official forms certifying that I had taken over *Adventurer*'s navigation instruments, charts, books and her general inventory, then I invited Captain Jackson back to the quarters he had just vacated. 'Here's to you, Bob,' said Peter as our glasses of gin and water clinked together. 'I never thought, when you fished me out of the drink not too far from here, that we'd both end up as Cunard captains. Did you?'

'Hardly,' I answered. 'We were lucky even to get through the war. Let's drink to the memory of all those Blue Funnel chaps who didn't make it. Here's to our old shipmates.' On that nostalgic note, Peter left to join the *QE2* as relieving Master, and subsequently he was appointed the first Master of *Cunard Countess*. A year later, Peter became Master of Cunard's newest Caribbean luxury cruiser, the *Cunard Princess*. Appropriately, his new command was invested with her title by Princess Grace of Monaco in a royal champagne launching in New York.

Like her sister ships, the elegant *Adventurer* roamed the blue waters of the Caribbean clothed in creamy white livery. She carried 750 passengers – mostly Americans – around the sub-tropical ·paradise islands of the West Indies and the Dutch Antilles, which contain that sliver of old Holland known as Curaçao. Since my time in Rotterdam during the building of *Ambassador*, I had developed quite a liking for the piquant salted herrings prepared by a company of piscatorial alchemists based near the Smit shipyard, who always consigned the first barrel of each new season's salted herrings to the then queen, Juliana, but sent the second cask across the Atlantic to the offices of the Curaçao Dry Dock company. Devotees of the fishy delicacy swallow the shining herrings whole, not the most hygienic practice. Bare hands, including mine, dipped into the Curaçao barrel, at the invitation of the dry dock company, and out came the silver morsels. My throat has generally enjoyed a fair reputation for its swallowing capabilities, but I couldn't manage a whole herring, so I split the salty, sticky and scrumptious fish in two with my fingers.

A century or two ago, the lush Caribbean islands sheltered the colourful sailing ships of assorted rogues and pirates. Their modern heirs are the intrepid smugglers of the Antilles who hurtle their liquor-laden launches between the islands and the mainland of Venezuela, whose prosperous local citizenry happily hand over fat cash bundles for the fine quality, contraband whiskies, gins, rums and vodkas. I would watch the skippers of the floating missiles loading up crates of hooch and stacking them on deck among forty-gallon drums of petrol for the three enormous Mercury outboards fitted across the transom of each launch. These ferocious power packs send the craft zooming across the deep coastal waters at speed well beyond the reach of any pursuing customs craft.

'You wanna come along for the ride, massa?' asked a swarthy smuggler in Aruba, all loaded and ready to go. I looked at his twenty-five-footer piled high with an indiscriminate mixture of petrol and spirits powerful enough to fly an aeroplane, and shook my head. 'No thanks, old chap, some other day. Bon voyage.' As he kicked the starter, I wondered if he would move forwards or ascend swiftly to the heavens. Fortunately for everyone on the island, he made it to the open seas.

To the north-east on *Adventurer*'s Caribbean tourist track lie the American Virgin Islands of St Thomas, St John and St Croix. There, American citizens are allowed a full gallon of duty-free spirits, which they order ashore and then legal liquor launches bring them out to the ship. The skippers of these prosperous little craft aren't renowned for their punctuality and, more than once, after waiting beyond sailing time, I've threatened to up-anchor and leave the booze boat behind. But one well-known Cunard skipper who did that found he had a near mutiny on his hands from his passengers before he was clear of the anchorage. They had paid for their spirits, they said, they wanted them and to hell with sailing schedules. Tactfully, the skipper backed down and waited. There are no such problems with British passengers in the American Virgins.

179

They're allowed only one duty-free litre each, which hardly calls for chartering liquor launches.

On 10 August 1973, my twin daughter Jan was married at Warrington in Cheshire but, not surprisingly, I was thousands of miles away on the island of St Thomas. On my next leave, Joan and I took Jan and her new husband, a sociology lecturer, out to a celebration lunch at the Bells of Peover Hotel near Knutsford, the Cheshire market town where novelist Elizabeth Gaskell was brought up. A few months later, Joan flew out to join me in Puerto Rico.

Joan had been hoping to take a coach tour from Venezuela's port of La Guaira up to the capital, Caracas, a seven-hour round trip, but as I approached the Venezuelan coastline I heard that all the country's northern ports were strikebound. *Adventurer* crossed the wakes of three cruise liners heading away from La Guaira, but I decided to go in and take a look anyway. A few hours later, the strike was settled and Joan was able to stroll round the dilapidated shops of the harbour area as some sort of consolation for missing the lofty opulence of Caracas.

The next day *Adventurer* arrived at Grenada, but our agents advised, 'Don't go ashore. Strikers could cause trouble.' Things weren't working out too well for Joan's holiday, so I decided to take her for a sail around the palm-fringed Grenada beaches on the commercial trimaran *Wanderer*, still unaffected by the on-shore strike. A few other passengers came along, and when we reached a deserted bay on the leeward side of the island, we anchored the white-sailed yacht and swam ashore onto the hot, silver sands. I had brought along snorkels, and the exotic fish population of that lonely cove must have wondered what brand of splashing, gurgling, laughing creatures had suddenly invaded their pellucid parish.

Cool rum punches awaited us back on the yacht, where the unanimous vote was that we should thank the strikers for steering us into an afternoon of remote rapture. That evening Joan and I went to the birthday party for Jackie Lynn, one of our shipboard songsters. After we'd sung 'Happy Birthday', Joan sighed deeply. 'What's the matter, dear?' I asked.

'Why, nothing, Bob,' she replied. 'It's just that I lived through so many lonely moments without you. But today, I felt I was the luckiest wife in the world.'

Lucky or not, Joan hit another strike the following day when I headed *Adventurer* through the early morning haze into Castries, island capital of St Lucia. All the organised tours for passengers were off, but our agent turned up at the ship and volunteered to drive Joan and a couple of her friends across the island to Soufriere for lunch, followed by a walk round one of the Geest Corporation's enormous banana plantations. That, I felt, would appeal to Joan's keen horticultural interest. 'How did you like it?' I asked when she returned.

'It was fascinating on the plantation, but I couldn't get used to the idea of all the bananas growing in blue plastic bags to protect them from chemicals sprayed onto the trees. Somehow, it spoiled the whole effect.'

'Ah well,' I said, remembering our idyllic swimming safari, 'you can't win all the time.'

Our call at Charlotte Amalie on the Virgin island of St Thomas next day was strike-free, and Joan left the ship for lunch at the lovely Harbour View Hotel with one of our elderly regular passengers, Chandler Ross. Pleasantly sated with gazpacho, West Indian pie and rum punches, Joan arrived back in time to take an afternoon tour of the island with harbour pilot Dick Griffin and myself. Dick drove his truck at a leisurely pace, for around every other corner were a couple of native motorists who had stopped their cars for a chat in the middle of the road.

'That's about the most dangerous thing that's likely to happen here,' said Dick, 'unlike the lunacy on the other island.' I knew what he meant. A couple of years earlier, on nearby St Croix, five young black islanders shot and killed four visitors from Miami together with four workers from the island's luxurious Fountain Valley Golf Club. Ironically, the auto licence plates on St Croix all bear the legend 'American Paradise'. For many months after the killings, tourism plunged there and paradise was certainly lost. But now, as Joan and I watched a throbbing steel band wend its cheerful way along the dusty St Thomas road, I got the feeling that perhaps, at last, paradise had been totally regained.

The end of Joan's first week's cruising came as *Adventurer* tied up in San Juan. Between her tours around the islands, she had found time to write forty postcards to friends in Britain, and she popped ashore in the Puerto Rican capital to drop them into a letterbox. That afternoon she complained, 'I've got a headache, Bob. Think I'll take a couple of soluble asprins.'

'Good idea,' I said. 'Should put you right.' A couple of hours later, I went to our stateroom to see how the headache was faring. Joan was fast asleep, and stayed that way until we were out at sea well on the way to Aruba next day. We found later that, instead of aspirin, she had mistakenly swallowed a couple of Mogadon sleeping tablets. I consoled her by saying that the rest would do her a world of good before she tackled her next hectic island roundabout.

In Aruba once more, Joan and I went to see my friend Theo Blok, Oranjestad manager for New York jewellers Spitzer and Furhman, who was leaving to start a new life in Canada and wanted me to meet his successor John Wise. Joan couldn't resist trying on a huge green emerald ring priced at $40,000, which Theo had produced for us from his glittering stock. A dozen of *Adventurer*'s passengers who had been watching us through the shop window rushed inside. 'Oh, do buy it for her, Captain Bob,' they clamoured.

'Now look,' I began, 'I don't actually own the *Adventurer*, you know. . .'

Joan interrupted: 'No, I don't think the emerald is really me. Such a pity.'

Theo invited us into his private office, and over a glass of curaçao presented Joan with a gold chain and locket embossed with a picture of Aruba and one of its famous divi-divi trees. That, I felt, suited her much better than the emerald.

'Good thing you weren't too keen on that ring, Joan,' I said when we were safely back on board ship. 'I'd have had to mortgage our house to buy it.'

'Bob dear,' she said rather sadly, 'I sometimes think you don't know anything about women. I loved that emerald. It was fabulous. But just because I live like a queen on your ship, I don't imagine for a moment that you can spend like a king.' I decided we'd better talk about Joan's trip to Caracas next day.

With La Guaira's strike settlement still holding, our coach party was safely on its way to the Venezuelan capital soon after breakfast. Caracas is only ten miles from the coast but stands on an elevation of more than 3000 feet above sea level. For once I was able to go ashore, this time with Mr and Mrs Stritchfield, owners of the Rest and Be Thankful pub at the edge of wild

Exmoor. Eight hours later, over dinner, we chatted about our day's adventures. We had been on a cable-car ride over dense jungle to the 7000-feet high peak of Mount Avila, toured the house where Simón Bolívar was born, and eaten a fine cold lunch at the edge of the swimming pool at the magnificent Tamanaco Hotel. However, as I took *Adventurer* out into the starlit Caribbean later that evening, Joan was suddenly stricken with seasickness. It was forty-eight hours later, in St Lucia, before she began to feel really well again. When we reached St Thomas, she went ashore to buy her usual crate of presents for everyone back home, and, after an overnight sail to Puerto Rico, Joan's Caribbean interlude was at an end. I saw her off at the airport, then prepared to welcome aboard *Adventurer* the stars of Aston Villa, one of Britain's most historic and illustrious soccer clubs.

Villa were celebrating their promotion to the Football League's First Division by taking a pre-season Caribbean cruise. Club chairman Doug Ellis jokingly tried to persuade me to play a spell in goal at an exhibition game Villa had lined up in Barbados. When I saw the strenuous limbering-up exercises that such lads as Frank Carrodus, Jim Cumbes, Roy Maclaren and Ray Graydon were put through each morning by club manager Ron Saunders, for what was described to me as 'just a friendly game', I felt that I would be far more use to these supremely fit professionals by cheering them on from the stands. As it turned out, I wasn't able to cheer or play. *Adventurer*'s engine-room caught fire late one night. I had to switch off the engines while our fire crews fought the blaze, and for several hours we were adrift in the Caribbean. It was almost first light when the fire was finally put out and, although we were mobile again, that was the end of the cruise.

Our footballers chartered an aircraft to fulfil their fixture in Barbados, where, I'm told, they easily beat a local eleven. Remarkably, the fire had broken out in almost the identical spot between La Guaira and Grenada where we had a smaller fire in the generator room the previous year. Each time, our fire crews fought and mastered the blaze in the depths of the ship while carefree passengers above dined or watched a cabaret, largely unaware of the white-hot drama being played below.

Adventurer was out of action for a few weeks while her power-house was put right at Curaçao, then we were out and about again on our Caribbean milk round. 'Isn't it boring, and don't you get tired of trailing round the same ports, however exotic?' was a question journalists often used to put to me in their interviews for various island newspapers and local radio stations. My stock answer was: 'Definitely not. First of all, I'm never tired of the splendours of your islands, and secondly, every cruise party that steps aboard brings us a new sort of adventure.'

Take the case of New York's New School charter cruise. As the hundreds of students came aboard, I remarked to my staff captain that they would never see youthful schooldays again. This was an academy strictly for adults, directed by Dr John and Mrs Everett. As adults, I suppose they were quite entitled to run classes in sex education in *Adventurer*'s theatre, but the erotic erudition caused us one or two problems. The trouble was that the school's sophomores in yoga reckoned that, in the hours before noon, territorial rights in the theatre rested with them, when they wished to contort themselves under the guidance of shapely Swedish instructress Solvig Eskeadhal. The sex-study devotees claimed that, because their chosen topic was more popular than yoga, they should have first call on the theatre.

I handed that one over to our cruise director, Brian Price, who solved the problem, but not to Solvig's satisfaction. Brian had to admit the sex students had a point about their subject's universal appeal which perhaps the yoga students didn't, so he advanced the yoga classes to 7.30 in the morning. Brian told me afterwards he'd never realised that the Swedish language contained so many swear words.

Of course, most of the school's scholastic sessions were rather more ordinary, although some of their tutors definitely weren't. Ex-Senator Eugene McCarthy, for instance, took classes in poetry. The doughty Democrat was given to roaming the decks reciting *The Eve of St Agnes*, or surprising my crew by alleging, 'Spanish waters, Spanish waters, you are ringing in my ears . . .'

By way of contrast, we then had some very different groups on board over a short period: the Frigidaire Group headed by General Motors vice-president Wally Wilson; ship enthusiasts including Dr Melvin Jackson, curator of the Smithsonian Institution's marine transportation division, Herbert Frank, New York editor of the magazine *Steamboat Bill*, and Frank Corrigan, president of the Ship Craft Guild; stamp collectors, with Mr and Mrs Jacques Minkus of the famous New York stamp company, plus executives of the equally famous British Stanley Gibbons company; ornithologists; and the Cincinatti Reds baseball team.

It was always a delight, when *Adventurer*'s itinerary included St Lucia, to row across the harbour at Castries for a drink with former Royal Navy Engineer Commander Jim Griffin. Jim's single-masted, white yacht *Northern Light* was moored in what was then quite a small, enclosed and singularly beautiful harbour; in fact, when *Adventurer* and a Geest banana boat arrived in St Lucia together, there was no room for any other large vessel. But as the island's tourist trade prospered, the harbour was dredged and a new pier built exclusively for Geest ships.

In July 1975, Commander Griffin invited me over to lunch on his sturdy, six-berth sloop. He had been around the island for a year, eking out his small naval pension by giving lectures in St Lucia on maritime affairs, plus doing the occasional yacht survey. Jim Griffin's crew comprised his wife, three daughters and a bevy of cats. The girls had grown up on their father's mahogany yacht as he sailed it around the world, stopping at ports here and there to earn money for provisions for the next stage of an apparently endless voyage.

As we sipped our gin and water, I asked the Commander which seas his white sails would be scudding across next. He considered for a moment. 'Well Bob, I think I'll go through the Canal and head out into the Pacific. But I'll have to consult the crew about which islands they'd like to call at in the South Seas.' I knew Griffin was serious about talking to his 'crew'; he kept his ship's articles right up to date, and signed on his wife and daughters as ordinary seamen whenever they came on board. Once he explained to me why he did this. 'It means they're proper Merchant Navy personnel, and we get all the mercantile perks going at whichever port we reach,' he said, 'and that even includes concessionary rates on aircraft.'

On our next call at St Lucia a couple of weeks later, Commander Griffin asked if we could let him have some paperbacks from our huge stock on *Adventurer*. I set out for the yacht with my staff captain, Don Lee, and as many paperbacks as we could carry. Griffin met us at the quayside and took us out to *Northern Light* in his ship's tender – an eight-foot dinghy. Like me, Don Lee weighs around 16 stone, and I could see the watch officers on *Adventurer*'s bridge laughing at our dinghy's almost upright progress across the deep blue waters of Castries harbour. No doubt, I thought, those so-and-so's were envisaging some very swift promotion as their two senior officers squatted, crushed together, in the dinghy's stern, but Griffin knew how to handle the little rowboat as well as his yacht and we reached *Northern Light* with nothing worse than cramp in our knees. On the return trip the Commander asked one of his crew to help him out, and he stationed his wife in the bows of the dinghy, giving it a much better trim. A year or two later, I heard that Commander Griffin had safely negotiated the Pacific and that two of his daughters had married naval officers, one in Malta and the other in Hong Kong. I wonder whether, with a depleted crew, the good Commander is still roaming the world's oceans.

The harbour at San Juan is much larger than that of Castries and is far, far busier. The comings and goings of cruise liners make this beautiful bay probably the most bustling stretch of water in the whole of the Antilles. For *Adventurer*, with her bridge control, getting in and out of harbour was usually a fairly uneventful exercise. But not always. One Saturday as I was approaching the berth, I moved the controls to 'stop', but the ship seemed to accelerate, so I rang 'full astern'. She still went ahead as if determined to climb right onto the solid stone wall at the end of the quay. I realised the port engine was still going ahead so I stopped it with the emergency stop button, but the ship was, by now, swinging to starboard. Unhappily, the Italian Costa Line cruise liner *Carla C* was making her docking approach some three ship-lengths away. Our bows brushed her amidships and there was a crash of breaking glass as about five of the big windows on her promenade deck disintegrated. With some sort of control restored, I backed *Adventurer* off the startled Italian liner and, as we retreated, I saw that our nose was bent to about the same angle as that of Concorde. Impaled on it were cases and trunks which had been stacked on *Carla*'s deck ready for taking ashore.

Investigation showed that a pin on *Adventurer*'s control mechanism had sheered. Fortunately, no one was hurt and there was no underwater damage to either ship, but until her next refit, *Adventurer* sailed the Caribbean sporting her bloodied nose. Then she was given a completely new upper bow in the

Curaçao Dry Dock, and emerged in creamy pristine glory. Accidents are popularly supposed to run in a series, and certainly another one quickly followed *Adventurer*'s joust in San Juan harbour, but this time the venue was thousands of miles from that minor Caribbean calamity. In Britain's lovely Lake District, Joan fell down a hillside and shattered her leg.

As ever, I was an ocean away, but our daughter Gill was with her and was able to take care of her. A few days later Joan spoke to me on the phone to Barbados (I used to call home from there most Wednesdays). Joan told me that she'd been in the Lakes on an outing from Chaucer School, Fleetwood, when she suddenly slipped on a stretch of treacherous turf.

'I blacked out immediately,' she said. 'That wasn't surprising because somehow I'd sustained a compound fracture of the right leg. I could have wept, because I'd gone out wearing all the right gear – mountain boots, weatherproof anorak and all that sort of thing.' When she came round, added Joan, she found she had been taken by the Lakeland Mountain Rescue team to Kendal Hospital.

For three months after the accident, Joan's leg, shored up with steel pins, stayed in plaster, and she could walk only with a stick for several weeks after that. Only once did she complain. On leave, I took her to dinner at London's Ritz Hotel. As she clumped from the taxi into the hotel foyer, Joan grumbled, 'Oh dear, Bob, this is worse than being seasick.' The broken leg is good as new now, but Joan's occasional acute discomfort afloat still hasn't mended.

Chapter 22

The evening breezes rippling the azure waters of Charlotte Amalie's harbour were still pleasantly warm as I went out onto *Adventurer*'s spacious open bridge to join her officers and crew. Don Lee, our stalwart staff captain, poured me a generous measure of gin and topped it up with chilled water.

'Well, sir,' said Don, 'it's been marvellous serving with you on *Adventurer*, and all of us here are sorry you're moving on. But we'd like to offer our congratulations on your taking command of Cunard's fleet flagship.' Don raised his glass. 'Gentlemen,' he said, 'I'd like you to join me in drinking the health of Captain Bob Arnott, the next Master of the *QE2*.'

This amiable assembly of white-uniformed comrades was, in fact, my farewell party. *Adventurer* was about to sail to Curaçao for her annual refit and after I had delivered her to the Dry Dock Company there, I was booked to join the *QE2* at Port Everglades. Meanwhile, a languid Caribbean dusk rolled gently across the bay as *Adventurer*'s men of the sea chatted over their gins, whiskies, cold beers and rum punches.

That night of 30 April 1976, marked the end for me of another era of enchantment spent cruising the West Indian islands. Forty-eight hours later, I was on a Miami bound jet. I picked up a car at the airport and drove along the steamy roadway to Port Everglades. As I swung into the docklands, I saw her in the distance,.waiting quietly for me. The *QE2* was markedly hushed, I thought, as I went aboard. Maybe she was simply resting up after her lengthy 'Cradle of Civilisation' cruise. A friendly, familiar voice interrupted my musings. 'Welcome back, Bob,' said Captain Mortimer Hehir.

I had been away from the first lady of the seas for nearly four years, and Cunard had suggested that, before I took command, I should do a short spell as staff captain. That didn't appeal to me so I suggested that one trip as a passenger would be enough for me to pick up the ropes again. Cunard agreed, and on the crossing from Everglades to Southampton, I sat, relaxed and contented as a transient movie star, at the Captain's Table in the *QE2*'s Columbia Restaurant. During the voyage I roamed the ship – dressed like any other passenger – to rediscover the inner workings of the *Queen* which a Master needs to know, and by the time we reached Southampton I was ready to take command.

After three leisurely weeks of leave in Fleetwood, I was back aboard. The date was 22 May 1976, and I was in command, as relief Master, of Britain's Queen of the Oceans. I stood astride the great liner's sky-reaching bridge as we moved through the crowded waters of the English Channel, and silently and gratefully pronounced myself the happiest and most fortunate of men. I remembered the morning thirty-six years earlier when my father saw me off at the station to join my first ship, and I wished he could have been standing beside me to share my unforgettable moment of pride.

But with 1500 passengers and 1000 crew to be delivered safely to the other side of the Atlantic, there was little time for extravagant emotions. My first voyage as Master of the *QE2* was, I reckoned, a fairly straightforward affair with an eleven-day round trip to and from New York. However, I quickly found that being absolute ruler of a floating empire as immensely comprehensive as our latest *Queen Elizabeth* demands, as well as a lifetime's skills in seamanship, doctors' degrees in diplomacy, joke appreciation, advice to lovers, drinking, table talk, speech spouting, handshaking and 1000 other skills I'm still researching.

As always, we had on board a broad selection of people who had achieved excellence and international recognition in their chosen callings. On the way out to New York, I had as guests in my cabin the industrialist Sir James Lyons and his wife, financier Harry Danziger, Bob and Janette Martin – composers of the Eurovision Song Contest winner 'Puppet on a String' and Cliff Richard's 'Congratulations' – and Tunbridge Wells travel tycoons Tom and Phyllis Botting. On the return trip to Britain my guests included Princess Lucie Shirazee, US actress Maureen Stapleton, and my long-standing friend British comedian Dickie Henderson and his wife Gwyneth.

Princess Shirazee, a personable and popular member of New York's opulent circle of socialites, was in a small but regal way in competition with the *QE2*: she owned the superb barquentine yacht *Barba Negra* and chartered or lent it out for scientific, social and charitable projects. The Princess's Atlantic travelling companions were her two snow-white pet doves. Somewhere, I felt, there was a company order forbidding the presence of such pigeon-like personages in the *QE2*'s most expensive deck suite, but I didn't delve too deeply in the book of 'Queen's Regulations' to find it.

In New York, I had been welcomed by Cunard's new managing director in the States, Ralph Bahna, who is now also president of our company in America. Ralph took me to lunch at the exclusive Metropolitan Club near Central Park. Said Ralph, 'I've invited Charlie Dickson to join us. Remember him? He was very much concerned, like yourself, in the bomb episode on the *QE2*.' I shook the hand of the man who had played the leading role in America during our extortion drama, and told him how much everyone at sea during the bomb alert had appreciated the cool fashion in which he had tackled his awesome task, particularly when his head could have been blown off at any moment.

'I didn't have time to be scared, Bob,' said Charlie. 'I was too busy following that vulture's orders. I guess I was more worried in case there really were bombs on the ship. Mine was just one life. There were a couple of thousand innocent folks out there on the Atlantic. Thank God, the law caught up with the bastard who thought it all up.'

On the next couple of trips I had on board playwright Tennessee Williams, singer Mel Torme and his wife, and Mr and Mrs Lauder of Estée Lauder perfumery fame. Mr Williams I found in melancholy mood; shipboard parties, apparently, weren't for him. When I talked to him briefly – I was generally fogbound on the bridge during his trip – the famous dramatist remarked only on the prospects of reaching port, or otherwise, through the swirling mists that were chasing the *QE2* across the Atlantic. I assured him cheerfully we would make it, which brought the sardonic reply: 'Ah'd be surprised if you told me we wouldn't.'

Mel Torme and his wife were comfortable travelling companions. At my party, Mel told me, 'These days, I enjoy writing as much as singing. I'd like to become a best-selling author.' I wished him lots of luck, and was delighted to read somewhere not long afterwards that Mel's book on Judy Garland, *The Other Side of the Rainbow*, had hit the bestseller lists.

Mr and Mrs Lauder kept their word to send Joan a parcel of their exotic perfumes, but our daughter Jan collared most of the fragrant potions. 'They suit me, mum, far more than they do you,' she claimed. 'These perfumes are blended more for a younger person.' There was little point, Joan felt, in arguing against that.

Dr Magnus Pyke, the British scientist and television personality whose trademark is waving his arms around like a windmill as he elaborates on his subject, was invited to the officers wardroom one lunchtime by our Chief Radio Officer Don Butterworth who was president of the mess. We found Magnus reasonably businesslike. 'Now, lads,' he said, treating us to a sample handsweep, 'I'm here for a lunchtime drink and I'm quite prepared to earn it. Do you want me to talk to you for five, ten, fifteen or twenty minutes?'

I laughed with my officers at what I imagined was the doctor's joke. A hand touched my arm, and Mrs Pyke whispered, 'Don't laugh, Captain. He's quite serious. My husband weighs up everything in scientific terms, and believes in giving exact value for money.' I don't know what Don then said to our guest, but we weren't treated to a popular science programme that lunchtime, which was a pity because I always enjoy Pyke's antics on television.

Towards the end of July 1976, I came home on leave, but while I was away from the *QE2* she caught fire heading out into the Atlantic near Bishop's Rock lighthouse. Although damage was limited to the boiler-room, the ship was in no state to carry on to New York, and Mortimer Hehir brought her back to Southampton. I rejoined her early in August when she had passed her fire repairs sea trials, and took my daughter Kate with me on the round trip to New York, who, at eighteen had just left school. I reckoned a fine going-away present to mark her departure from Fleetwood Grammar School would be a there-and-back voyage to the United States. Katy didn't argue. Her bags were packed a couple of days before we were due to leave for Southampton. My friends at the Port Authority of New York helped me to make her first visit to the United States an occasion she would always remember, by laying on one of their bright yellow helicopters for a sightseeing tour for Kate and myself.

'Oh look, Dad, there's the Statue of Liberty,' said Kate excitedly as we flipped along the river past Liberty Island. Kate had done her homework on New York's topography the previous night. 'Look, Dad, that's the World Trade Center – the tallest double skyscraper on earth.' She pointed to the Center proudly as our pilot skirted the Hudson River. I think I was as thrilled as my daughter at skimming over the rooftops of famous buildings I had seen a hundred times only from the ground – the Empire State Building, the towers of the Rockefeller Center and the United Nations Building all soaring skywards towards our tiny bubble. Then we were out again over the East River.

Kate's sharp young eyes spotted the *QE2* in her berth long before I did. 'Why are all the crew out on deck, Dad?' she asked with some concern.

I peered downwards. 'Only boat drill,' I assured her. 'Keeps everyone on their toes.'

That afternoon I took my still wide-eyed daughter on a somewhat slower tour of Wall Street, Broadway and Battery Park. We caught the subway to Thirty-Fourth Street and walked up Fifth Avenue, looked in at Gimbel's, Macy's and Tiffany's, toured the Rockefeller Center and Radio City, then caught the crosstown bus back to the ship. 'Wow, Dad,' said Kate, 'we certainly packed a lot into one day, didn't we?'

'We did,' I replied. 'I think I've seen more of New York today than in all the other years I've been coming here.'

Just a few days earlier, Janet Armstrong, wife of the first man on the moon, cracked a bottle of champagne over the brand-new *Cunard Countess* in a ceremony both to launch the ship and to honour the Bicentennial year of the United States. For Cunard, this was a complete break with tradition. Queen Mary had launched the ship that bore her name, Queen Elizabeth the Queen Mother had named the first *Queen Elizabeth* and, of course, Her Majesty Queen Elizabeth II had broken a bottle of champagne over the bows of the *QE2*. It was reported at the time that Cunard asked Mrs Armstrong to name the *Countess* 'because of the astro-theme featured in the new custom-built cruiser'.

I felt that the head of Cunard's sea-going royal family, the *QE2*, should not be left out of the celebrations so, as the *QE2* sped eastwards across the Atlantic, I sent the *Countess*'s Master, Captain Peter Jackson, a special signal: 'Welcome to the Court. Wishing you and everyone on *Countess* all the best for the future, from Bob Arnott and all your friends on the *QE2*.'

Captain Jackson replied: 'Received, and many thanks. New ship handles well as befits a true countess. Your first Lady in Waiting has joined the royal family. Our greetings to all friends on the *QE2*.'

The start of the *Countess*'s cruising career was marked by a skirmish with the Russians who wanted to take their cruise liner *Odessa* on regular calls into Hamilton, Bermuda. The Bermudan government turned down the Russian request and awarded the Hamilton berth to the *Countess*.

One group of noble passengers that crossed the Atlantic to New York around that time included a Mr Dodge born in 1914, a Mr Franklin born in 1910, a Mr T. Ford born in 1911 and a Mr D. E. T. Abbott, who first saw the light in 1912. They were, of course, vintage cars, accompanied by their adoring owners, who were re-enacting the final stages of the famous 1908 New York-to-Paris Westward car race. In that year a nearly new Thomas Flyer crossed the Paris finishing line on 30 July to win the event. The 1976 entrants were racing over a curtailed course through Turkey, Bulgaria, Yugoslavia, Hungary, Italy, Switzerland, West Germany, Belgium and England, then across the Atlantic on the *QE2* before going on through twelve American states and finishing up in San Francisco.

I talked to auto dealer Eddie Schuler, of Morrison, Illinois, who reckoned that his participation in the event with his 1914 Dodge had cost him $25,000. Eddie, travelling with his son Mark, told me, 'In a way, I'm doing the same sort of thing as yourself, shaking hands with new-found friends all over the world. You have the *QE2*, and I have the old Dodge.' The current race, Eddie informed me, was sponsored by the World Auto Race Committee in Cleveland, Ohio. I never did hear who won the event, but I guessed that Eddie, sporting Number 13, wouldn't be too far from the chequered flag in his immaculate, sixty-two-year-old Dodge tourer.

I hadn't been back to Scotland since the *QE2* had left Clydeside in 1969, but towards the end of the summer of 1976, Joan and I took to the Scottish isles. I drove our Triumph Dolomite across the Scottish border and around a maze of lochs and firths to the tiny port of Oban, but somehow I lost my bearings in the diminutive dockland and we reached the last ferry boat of the day only minutes before it chugged its way to the Isle of Mull. I leaned over the deck rail and looked into the fading daylight of the Atlantic approaches; Joan joined me. 'Come away, Bob,' she said gently. 'It's someone else's turn tonight.'

We docked at Craignure, on Mull's eastern shore where Joan's brother Alan and his wife, who had travelled up from Wiltshire, met us at the seafront Craignure Inn. The four of us tucked into a delicious steak and kidney pudding supper which was just a sample of the marvellous table laid on throughout our week's holiday by the landlord, Jim Smith, who had been head chef of a nearby four-star hotel before he moved to the Craignure. Jim took a delight in preparing individual dishes specially requested by his guests, and I tested him out by asking for devilled seafood pancakes. The Craignure presentation of the dish, packed with shrimps, crab and lobster, was at least the equal of our Cunard version. We had been across to Iona that day and had worked up enormous appetites walking around the remote monastic island.

All too soon our holiday came to an end and I returned to Southampton. Captain Mortimer Hehir had retired on 5 October, and I was now full Master of the *Queen Elizabeth II*. On this voyage I found myself shaking hands again with the man who has, I believe, crossed the Atlantic on the *QE2* more times than any other passenger. Retired gold miner Walter Gostyla, from Connecticut, had by then made ninety crossings – on the strength of an income from lifelong investments in oil stocks. I always enjoy having Walter at my table in the Tables of the World restaurant on the *QE2*. He has fascinating tales to tell of Alaskan gold mining, and big-game hunting in Africa, America's far north and up the Amazon. Each summer, Walter used to climb into his car and drive the 10,500-mile round trip to Alaska. There, he told me, he has so many claims that there are some he hasn't even started to open up yet. The mines he has exploited plus the income from a petrol business gave him the capital for his oil investments. 'Years ago,' said Walter, 'I figured energy was going to be the world's big need. My investments in oil have turned into a gold mine in their own right.'

He has travelled the world on ships of many lines, but believes that the *QE2* is the queen of them all. 'I give her top marks for on-board entertainment, fabulous cuisine and cracking comforts,' he says. He loves our menus, but won't eat after mid-day, and one day, when I persuaded him to give a talk on his travels at a party I had arranged for him in my cabin, he explained his noon curfew on food: 'I don't live to eat, I eat to live. I have a huge lunch, then give myself the rest of the day for it to wear off. This helps me to stay in shape for all my travelling. I can still comfortably get into the trousers I wore in the army in 1941.' A bachelor, Walter Gostyla knows most of my crew by their first names. They are, he says, 'my floating family'. I expect that, one of these days, I'll hear that Walter has scored his century of Atlantic crossings.

Soon after I had said my ninetieth goodbye to Mr Gostyla, I welcomed aboard another muscular, much travelled gentleman. My father was making the round trip to New York with his chum Harry Hayes, last seen buying teabags in Barbados. It was my father's first voyage to the States, and he covered an amazing amount of New York terrain with his pal Harry during the *QE2*'s turn-around day. I did a personal check to make sure they were well supplied with tea – and other beverages – on both legs of the voyage.

Of tea, we had plenty, but kennels, on the other hand, were in short supply. A Mrs Nagle and a Mrs Ellis were hauled up the gangplank at Southampton by their pets, a pack of eight donkey-sized Irish wolfhounds. 'Where,' I asked, 'do you think you are taking those fellows?'

'Why, to New York,' came the reply. I shook my head, and tears welled up into the eyes of the two ladies. They couldn't possibly leave their pets behind, they pleaded. I pointed out that our kennels were built for nothing larger than an average Alsatian, but I could see that I was wasting my breath.

With only half an hour before sailing, I had to ask the *QE2*'s carpenters to knock up eight shipboard mansions for the wolf-hounds. We sited the structures in the former crew cinema, and there the immense Irishmen struck up an immediate friendship with our two kennelmaids. The girls were truly sorry when Sean, Michael, Brendan, Patrick, Seamus, Cathal, Casey and Kerry Wolfhound wagged their shaggy tails for the last time on the *QE2* before towing their lady owners ashore.

Travelling on the same voyage as our Irish friends were Lord Porritt, Governor General of New Zealand, and Lady Porritt. Over lunchtime drinks in my cabin, I talked to His Lordship about our mutual lifelong interest in sport. He thrilled me by describing how he had won his heats to reach the final of the

1924 Olympic 100 metres in Paris, and talked, too, of meeting Hitler when he managed the New Zealand Olympic athletes at the 1936 Berlin Games. Lord Porritt also recalled that, at Oxford, he had broken the 100- and 220-yard hurdles records. All that, I thought, before going on to a distinguished medical career during which he was surgeon to both the royal households of King George VI and his daughter, Her Majesty Queen Elizabeth II.

From sport and medicine, our gossip switched to motoring. 'I've been driving for sixty years, Captain,' said Lord Porritt, 'but now I'm seventy-seven my wife thinks I should be getting off the road, even though I'm president of the Veteran Motorists' Club. What do you recommend?'

'My Dad is on board. He wouldn't dream of giving up driving, and he's a year older than you. Does that strengthen your case?'

Lord Porritt grinned. 'It does indeed. Did you hear that, Kath?'

Lady Porritt smiled, to. 'Now you don't expect me to take on the two of you, do you? she asked. 'How did you find New Zealand on your last visit, Captain?'

My father and his friend Harry also came to one of my lunchtime parties, where my other guests included Danny La Rue, Sir Michael Redgrave and Caribbean industrialist Jack Hanson. The likely lads from Lancashire weren't at all overawed. 'Grand bunch of chaps,' was my father's verdict on his fellow guests. He especially liked meeting Sir Michael, one of his favourites over many years of theatre and filmgoing. 'Clever lad, when you get talking to him,' said Dad.

'Yes, you could say that,' I agreed. 'Comes from being a Cambridge graduate before he took up acting.'

'Of course,' chimed in Harry. 'We knew that all the time.'

Early in December 1976, the *QE2* ran into a really foul night of Atlantic weather, and the next morning we found a 12½-ton anchor had decided to leave us and had punched a hole in the bulbous bow on its way into the sea. Constant pumping evicted the unwelcome Atlantic, and the *QE2* made it to Boston to pick up a Crimson Travel cruise party. When we arrived at the New England port, ship repairers fitted metal patches inside and out, and we left behind 20 degrees of frost to head for the Caribbean sunshine.

Over Christmas that year we were again out and about in the West Indies. From a shivering New York, I pointed the bow towards Port Everglades where more escapees from winter came on board. We spent a far from white Christmas being caressed by the warm breezes fanning the coasts of Haiti, Curaçao, Barbados, Martinique and the Virgins. On 23 December, I sent a telex message of loyal Christmas greetings to Her Majesty at Windsor Castle. On Christmas Eve, Queen Elizabeth replied: 'I warmly thank you and the ship's company of RMS *Queen Elizabeth II* for your kind message of Christmas greetings that you sent to me and my family. I very much appreciate your kind thoughts, and warmly reciprocate your good wishes.'

Christmas parties roared on merrily for days in every quarter of the ship until, on New Year's Eve, the ship's bell was carried by four hefty crewmen into the *QE2*'s Double Room, already crowded with Hogmanay revellers. At midnight, the youngest member of the ship's company, a lad of sixteen, struck sixteen strokes on the bell, eight for the old year and eight for the new, and the strains of 'Auld Lang Syne' from 1000 voices welcomed 1977. I brought the *QE2* back into New York two days later. She was bound for dry dock, and I caught a plane home.

After only four days with my family in Fleetwood, I returned to New York followed a day later by Joan who was accompanying me on my next assignment on the super-ship – a three-month long, 40,000-mile voyage around the world.

Chapter 23

Blinding blizzards were thickening the carpet of snow already covering New York as I eased the *QE2* away from her berth on the evening of 15 January 1977. Almost buried in their heavy coats, people were strung out along the quayside waving good-bye and shuddering in the grip of winter's deepest frost. For the fortunate folks on the *QE2*, the ice age was over. We were destined for the sun-drenched harbours of Bahia, Rio, Capetown, Bombay, Yokohama and Honolulu.

For the luxury and privilege of sailing round the world in the *QE2*'s top penthouse suites, the Queen Anne and the Trafalgar, two of our passengers were each paying £62,000 ($120,000). Was it worth that sort of cash to spend ninety days on the finest ship afloat? Our penthouse plutocrats, a Mrs Blessman and Austrian pop singer Freddy Quinn, obviously thought so. Most of our other 1000 world travellers were paying rates that ranged sharply upwards from a basic £4000, and there were also lots of people taking only varied slices of the whole trip – such as actor Lloyd Nolan and his wife – a convenient and economic cruise custom that's become very popular over the last few years.

Our holds were packed with the provender we would need for a three-month odyssey. Taking a densely populated floating city around the globe presented problems similar but far vaster in scale to those *Britannia* faced on the Atlantic in the 1840s. Charles Dickens had sailed to America on Cunard's first flagship in 1842, and he wrote, 'Men were filling the ship's icehouses to the very throats with fresh provisions, with butchers' meat and garden stuff, with pale suckling pigs, calves' heads in scores, beef, veal, and pork and poultry out of all proportion.' Dickens also stole a sympathetic look at the ship's cow as she went on board, but her milk was restricted to the women and children sailing on the sturdy wooden paddle steamer.

On the *QE2*, everyone gets milk. Crossing the Atlantic, we use up 12,000 gallons, and on the world trip we needed twenty times as much. Our storerooms were also crammed with tens of tons of beef, lamb, mutton, pork, poultry, veal, fish and game, and at ports all around the world, our hotel managers would be buying up the finest seafoods, vegetables and fresh fruits to enhance the hundreds of superb and varied dishes on daily offer on the *QE2*'s cruise menus.

Although, traditionally, such splendid fare as caviar and champagne has always featured in Cunard restaurants, I've noticed over the years that, generally, the wealthier or more famous a passenger happens to be, the more likely it is that he or she will go for simple and homely dishes. The favourite shipboard banquet of Richard Burton and Elizabeth Taylor was English steak and kidney pie, while Noël Coward often frustrated our imaginative chefs by ordering the Cockney stand-by of bangers and mash (sausages and mashed potatoes). When she travelled with her husband Rex Harrison, the lovely late Kay Kendall preferred the humble delights of cottage pie to any of our exotic specialities. However, the heavyweight championship for gargantuan plain-eating at sea must go to hefty he-man Victor Mature, who often sailed on the *Queen Mary* and first *Queen Elizabeth*. The screen Samson loved roast turkey and could demolish a whole twelve-pound bird at one sitting. Victor once autographed a menu for one of our chefs: 'Cunard cooking is as great as sex – almost.'

Not only foodstuffs were jamming every available corner of the *QE2*'s storage space as we headed southwards towards Port Everglades. The huge car deck which can hold eighty limousines on transatlantic crossings was now packed with more mundane items such as a quarter of a million toilet rolls, 10,000 spare light bulbs, thousands of replacement carpet lengths and hundreds of gallons of methylated spirit for our food warmers and flambé equipment. In most parts of the world outside Britain and the United States, it's impossible to buy such stocks in the huge quantities the *QE2* needs.

Our course was plotted so that we would travel around the globe eastwards. First-time passengers didn't realise that they were about to embark on a crash course on how to lose sleep at the rate of one hour each night, as we were sailing against the clock, which meant a nightly forward adjustment of all time-pieces on board. That took care of the mathematical side of the situation, but didn't improve the tempers of either passengers or staff who couldn't accustom themselves to regular nocturnal havoc. Luckily, from my earliest days at sea, I have always had the knack of being able to wake at any particular moment I set my mind to at any time of day or night. On the *QE2*, it is hardly ever necessary for anyone to call me, although I do have a talk-back set at the side of my bed. Assuming I am due on the bridge at 6 a.m., as on most days, I usually come right out of a deep sleep at about 5.30, and call the bridge immediately to say simply 'I am awake.' Waking up to order is a gift I've been grateful for all my seagoing life. Many sailors just don't have it, and it can make life difficult for them when they're due on duty in the early hours.

Joan had flown to New York to join me for her first world cruise, and as she came on board, some lunatic was phoning the police to say there were 400 lb of dynamite hidden in the baggage loading area. It was a hoax, but the inevitable search meant that we were hours late in arriving at Port Everglades. There, the local folks turned out in their thousands to welcome the *QE2*, cars lining the waterfront with horns blaring, and red, white and blue streamers fluttering from the tall blocks of flats and houses lining the channel. The fine folk of the Florida port welcome dozens of cruise ships, but they always have a special affection for the *Queen*.

The remainder of our passenger complement had joined us at Port Everglades, and as the *QE2* glided southwards through the Caribbean warmth I met a titled British woman I had seen a hundred times on the television panel game, *What's My Line?* Lady Isobel Barnett was travelling as far as Cape Town, and I chatted to her over a lunchtime drink in the wardroom.

'I'm glad Cunard invited me along to lecture to your passengers,' said Lady Barnett. 'It brings back to me all the wonderful times we used to have at the studio in the Sixties. Life's seemed rather flat since *What's My Line?* ended.' I doubted that this lively, attractive woman – a qualified doctor – could ever find life uninteresting, and I gently told her so. 'I'm afraid it is, at times,' she insisted. 'Of course, I give talks about my TV appearances to luncheon clubs and so on, but the real zing has vanished.'

'Well, your ladyship,' I said, 'I'm sure something will come along to drum up the old excitement.'

'Let us hope so,' came the quiet reply. Unhappily, it did: soon after being convicted of shoplifting, widowed Lady Barnett was found dead at the splendid home she once shared with her wealthy husband. I was at sea when I heard of the tragedy. What an awful end, I thought, to the life of such a gracious lady who had given so much happiness to millions of people.

The actress Joan Bennett brought her husband along to one of my lunch parties, and we sipped whisky and water as the *QE2* drew near to the colourful coastline of Curaçao. 'I'll always remember your performance in *The Macomber Affair*,' I said, by way of small talk, to the still alluring Joan.

'My film days, dear Bob, have gone for ever, I should think. Now they call me the Queen of the TV soap operas, and I love it. I don't hunger for the old Hollywood one bit.'

And then there was Gladys. Everyone on the *QE2* had heard about Mrs Gladys Whitfield-Solomon. She didn't have just one of our more expensive suites – she had two. Gladys was cruising the world in one of them, and her wardrobe was accompanying her in the rooms next door.

'I can't stand to wear the same thing twice, Bob,' said Gladys. 'I want to come out every day looking as beautiful as your gorgeous ship. I can't do that in something I've already worn, can I?' I tactfully agreed, and hoped that Joan wasn't around listening to such financial heresy. Gladys' second suite was a treasure chest of high fashion. Adolfo, her own personal designer in New York, had run up several outfits for each of the ninety days of the cruise. 'You can see why I really need the extra accommodation,' explained Gladys. 'It's not in any way an extravagance.'

New York industrialist Mr Whitfield-Solomon wasn't making the full cruise with his wife, but was due to join her at Los Angeles for the last section through the Panama Canal; no doubt he would admire the $30,000 ring which Gladys had bought on a quick shopping spree in Hong Kong. It was Mrs Whitfield-Solomon's second world cruise. 'Where else in the whole world could anyone enjoy themselves as much as I do on the *QE2*?' she asked.

'Where indeed, Gladys,' I replied, 'where indeed?'

Not all the limelight fell on Gladys. Marjorie Tomayo, widow of a Venezuelan millionaire, came on board with a collection of jewels that could almost have matched the one in the Tower of London. She had left behind in Caracas the Chinese porcelain which is reputed to be the finest assembly of specimens anywhere outside China. 'Your ship is about the only place where I can wear my lovely jewels in safety,' said Marjorie. Marjorie's remark about the *QE2*'s safety is one I often hear from passengers in every corner of the world.

On this cruise Joan met, for the first time, Louise ('Lulu') Edwards, a relative of the Camel cigarette family. Lulu goes on every world cruise of the *QE2*, and as well as being one of our more lavish hostesses, both on board and at ports around the globe, she's also one of our most regular church attenders, usually sitting next to Joan at my services. Like many of our regular cruisers, Lulu always likes to have the same cabin, and Stateroom number 1030, with panoramic sea views, is the round-the-world residence of Mrs Louise Edwards.

However, many of the passengers flocking ashore at our next port, La Guaira, were thrifty, ordinary men and women who had saved up for years to take the holiday of a lifetime. Librarian Audrey Parsons was sailing on the New York–Hong Kong sector – the exact distance she could afford before having to fly back home to the States. From my home town of Fleetwood, nursing sister Ruby Jones had decided to celebrate her early retirement by splashing out on a world cruise, and hundreds of our carefree travellers had similar stories to tell.

For one lady, the voyage ended at La Guaira. The night before we docked there, she treated the diners in the Columbia Restaurant – one of the world's most exclusive eating spots – to a fandango danced on a table with her skirts flung high above her head, and she climaxed her act by offering $1000 to any man who would take her to bed. There were no offers. For her own protection I had her put ashore next morning – rich and beautiful wives can be just as dangerous as anyone else when jealous passions are aroused.

From the Caribbean coastline of South America, I turned the *QE2* into the broad Atlantic rollers and set course for Bahia. Anchored in the hazy Brazilian heat of Salvador harbour, I focused my binoculars on giant sacks being loaded into the holds of an elderly freighter. 'They're cocoa beans,' our agent told me. 'Everyone knows, of course, that Brazil grows coffee, but I bet you didn't know that in this province we also produce a fair slice of the world's cocoa.' I had to admit that particular gem of erudition had eluded me.

202

With the geography lesson over, I saw Joan off on the shore tender with our friends Bernard and Lorna Crisp. Bernard is sales and marketing director of the Cunard Line. The shore party went to see a remarkable fight-ballet at Bahia's Portuguese club. Apparently the dance originated in the old slaving days when Africans that had been sold into the plantations could be whipped for fighting; so that their martial skills wouldn't be totally lost, the slaves evolved the fight-dance. 'Amazingly realistic,' said Joan on her return. 'The beat of the war drums came right out of the depths of an African jungle, and the fighting was ferocious.'

On a more peaceful note, a tropical rainstorm had obligingly washed down the famous beaches of Ipanema, Gavea and Copacabana on the morning I took the *QE2* through the two great headlands guarding the approach to the magnificent harbour of Rio de Janeiro. Many of our passengers spent the day lazing around on the beaches they had previously heard about only in songs, while others took off for the hills to see at close range the enormous statue of Christ reaching out over Rio from the lofty peak of Corcovada.

Crossing the South Atlantic between America and Africa, my navigator pointed out to me at 11.20 on the morning of 31 January that the *QE2* had reached a mid-ocean point 28 degrees 32 minutes south and 28 degrees 32 minutes west – a navigational coincidence I've never run across before or since.

A howling gale greeted our arrival in Cape Town, and the pilot, Willy Rowe, and the South African customs men had to be winched down to the *QE2* by helicopter as we approached Table Bay with 30-knot winds whipping up the waters around us. For a short time, the gale relented and we were able to manoeuvre into the main harbour, but as soon as we were inside the dock, the south-westerly struck again and our wind-speed recorders showed readings of 45 knots.

That night, the strong winds continued, but the next afternoon a shore trip to the Milnerton race meeting overshadowed weather worries for a time, particularly when we got a winning tip for the big race. Quite as delighted by our small win as if it had been a fortune, Joan and I returned back on board in time to welcome Moira Anderson, the Scottish girl with a voice as enchanting as her smile. Moira was travelling with her husband, Dr Stuart McDonald, and was due to entertain our passengers on the next stage of the cruise. It was the first time I had met Moira, but now she and Stuart are old friends. I've often told her, 'You could have been as big a success in comedy as you are as a singer' – she's one of the most hilarious guests I've ever had at my parties.

The gale – Force 7 – was still blowing when we were due to leave Cape Town, and it was well after three in the morning – eight hours behind schedule – when the wind abated sufficiently for us to sail and head up the coastline towards Durban. Although 'sunny South Africa' wasn't living up to its promotional blurb, our cruise customers had a wealth of sheltered shipboard diversions. There were shows featuring the lovely Moira. as well as Ron Moody, the multi-talented star of the film musical *Oliver*, and the romantic Italian tenor Roberto Cardinale. Dancers could swing along to the melodies of Joe Loss or Ray Ellington and, on the cultural front, the lectures of American writers Cleveland Amory and Helen MacInnes offered an inexpensive contrast to some of the more costly mathematical problems posed in the casino.

The sun didn't break through the cloudy African skies until our second day in Durban. Abraham Rijkstra, one of our agents, and his wife Lynette took Joan and me out to the Valley of a Thousand Hills to see a Zulu *kraal*, where the ebony residents put on a lively and aggressive dancing display which reminded Joan of the bellicose spectacle she had watched in Bahia. The Zulus I saw pulling their traditional chariots along the Durban seafront were in a much more peaceable mood.

Clipping across the familiar and friendly warmth of the Indian Ocean, I talked with American financier Joseph Hirshhorn at one of my parties, who told me he had handed over his art collection to the US Government eleven years earlier. Envisaging just a few paintings, I commented, 'That was a very nice gesture.'

'Nice and expensive,' said Joe Hirshhorn. 'Even then it was worth around a hundred million dollars. They've had to build what they call the Hirshhorn Museum at the Smithsonian Institution to hold everything.'

It's not often I'm at a loss for words, but all I could say was 'Wow'. 'Yeah,' said Joe, 'the States has been very good to me since I came over from Latvia, so the art collection was a sort of thank-you gift to Washington.'

When we anchored at Mahé, the gift I handed over to Stanley Hinton, Acting High Commissioner of the Seychelles to mark the *QE2*'s first visit to the island group was rather less ambitious but still quite fascinating in its antecedents. Stanley Hinton and his Seychellian wife came out to the ship, and in my cabin I presented to him a fountain pen made by the Parker Pen Company from some of the brass fittings of Cunard's first *Queen Elizabeth*. I told the gathering, which included the US chargé d'affaires, that after being bought by the Chinese shipping magnate C. Y. Tung for conversion to a floating university, the *Queen Elizabeth* had caught fire in Hong Kong harbour and was virtually destroyed. The Parker Pen Company of America then acquired 315 kg of brass from the *Queen*'s portholes, and used this metal to make a limited number of pens with brass barrels and caps, some of which the company had given to me to present to dignitaries that I met on my world travels.

The tips of Seychelles' mountain peaks were disappearing beyond the far westerly seas as I chatted with a group of West German voyagers at my pre-dinner cocktail party. 'A far more pleasant way of crossing the oceans than either of us was used to in war-time, *Herr Kapitan*,' said one of my guests, who had been introduced to me as Herr Dankworth, navigator of the pocket battleship *Scharnhorst*, sunk in 1943.

'Why yes, it certainly is more agreeable,' I replied, 'and I'm not expecting anyone to fire a torpedo at us tonight.'

Herr Dankworth laughed. 'It's good when you can joke about those war years. Did you enjoy them?'

'As a matter of fact, I did,' I answered. 'I was lucky never to have been torpedoed, and at the end of it all, our side won.' More laughter from my German friends. And I wasn't really joking.

War-time memories were stirred again when I reached Bombay. I reckoned that there were more warships in the harbour on that day than I had ever seen there since the 1940s. A Russian-built submarine slid smoothly out towards the open sea as I took the *QE2* gently alongside her designated berth. The next day, Joan and I were up at 3.30 in the morning to fly to Agra. I marvelled at the cool glory of the ageless Taj Mahal, and was photographed with Joan on the seat fronting the great white monument. Some of our party were somewhat shaken to hear that, at the nearby exquisite Red Fort where hundreds of the reigning prince's harem once lived, adulterers, thieves and murderers were summarily trampled to death by an elephant executioner. There were more 'oohs' at Fatehpur when we came across a huge monument to one of these giant grey Pierrepoints.

The *QE2* cruised across the Gulf of Mannar under black velvet Indian skies to reach Colombo in Sri Lanka soon after dawn. Others had also been out and about before first light, for a gaily uniformed, smiling Sinhalese band was playing on the quay as I took the *QE2* alongside. Later in the day Joan and the ship's eager army of shore shoppers descended on the Pettah bazaar, where they bargained with amiable stallholders for delicate Kandy silverware, Kalatura lace and Galle tortoiseshell, all beautifully made in the island's cottage workshops. Meanwhile, the tourists who had ventured by coach as far as Kandy, some seventy-five miles from Colombo, were surprised when their driver headed right into, and through the enormous girth of a banyan tree straddling the dusty roadway. A torrential storm burst over the island that afternoon, delaying their return over roads now awash with red mud and, after their return, my thickest sea-mac couldn't save me from a drenching right through to the skin as I stood on the bridge to take the *QE2* out of Sri Lankan waters and into the broad reaches of the Indian Ocean towards Singapore.

Tall, yellow-blossomed angansana trees reached out across the broad highway as Joan and I drove out to the Raffles Hotel for afternoon tea. The venerable establishment, with its air of faded Victorian gentility, was about to be totally modernised. A little sadly, we drank our tiffin in the well-worn lounge of that Far Eastern Ritz, then walked out to watch a Chinese street opera celebrating the New Year of the Snake. 'In Chinese, it's called *kong hee fatt choy*, which means prosperity,' explained one of the open-air troupers. Having just paid £1 each for the few biscuits we had eaten at the Raffles Hotel, I could understand why.

That evening we took a stroll along one of Singapore's more illustrious streets of sin. When we arrived there, it seemed that at least half of the *QE2*'s passengers had come up with a similar sightseeing notion; they thronged the bustling Bugis Street, heavy with the aromas of Oriental cooking and sweetly scented perfumes. At pavement café tables, bevies of beautiful 'girls', in slit skirts and glossy hairstyles, unashamedly bartered their bodies in closely whispered sessions with wealthy, perverted patrons. Joan and I took a seat at an empty streetside table to watch the show and, with his £1-a-bottle beer, our waiter threw in a free commentary on the street's strange commerce.

'All those, how do you say it, "gorgeous dolly birds",' he said, 'are really boys of sixteen, seventeen or eighteen. From the time they were small babies, they were sent by fathers and mothers for ancient herbal and, these days, hormone treatments to grow boobs and build up curved bottoms. And they're brought up as girls, not boys. They reach teens, and earn here in street plenty of money for parents. You like more beer?'

'No thank you,' I said, 'but thanks for the little lecture.' I led Joan out of that remarkable thoroughfare back to the saner sensualities that flourish on board ship. When we returned to Singapore a couple of years later, Bugis Street had vanished under the blades of city clearance bulldozers. Had they also managed to flatten the trade operated by the glamorous 'girls'? I doubted it.

Trafalgar House Group chairman Nigel Broackes had come aboard with his wife for the next sector of our voyage, along with 200 or so affluent Chinese gentlemen and their ladies. When we anchored off Bali, a curious shark swam around the ship and then lay in wait on the seabed for unsuspecting members of the ship's sub-aqua club. A face-to-face meeting with Jaws of Asia hadn't been mentioned on the morning's programme, and our swimmers surfaced like a salvo of Polaris missiles. This manoeuvre outwitted the shark who presumably had to look for his Balinese breakfast elsewhere.

Our call in Bali coincided with Joan's birthday. Her friend Lulu Edwards laid on a giant celebration cake and, a couple of days later, Ann Brooks, a Beverly Hills society hostess and another of our regulars, took over half the ship's Q4 nightclub for a party in Joan's honour. The canapés were fantastic, and I tucked into my own special favourites – hot chicken livers wrapped in bacon. Delicious!

Our next port, Kota Kinabalu in Sabah, formerly North Borneo, hadn't welcomed the *QE2* before, and to Encik Yap Loong, Sabah's Minister of Manpower, I gave a set of goblets inscribed with a *QE2* motif. In return, Chief Minister Harris bin Mohd presented me with a plaque made from Malaysian pewter and bearing Sabah's emblem and flag. From the bridge I looked out across Gaya Bay at the dense Malaysian jungle where, more than thirty years earlier, Japanese troops had fled the onslaught of American bombers. Now, children played peacefully around houses built on stilts at the seafront fringe of the jungle.

From Sabah, I took the *QE2* across the South China Sea to Hong Kong. Television and radio teams came on board to talk to me, and afterwards I took Joan through the New Territories to the Chinese border. We drove past fish and duck farms, watched water buffalo grazing near the walled village of Kamtin and, returning from the Shumchin River which marks the border, Joan spotted a huge rock resembling a woman carrying a baby. Villagers told us that, thousands of years ago, a woman looked out there every day for her husband lost at sea. The gods took pity on her, killed her and her baby by lightning, and sent their spirits off to join that of the drowned husband. The bodies of the mother and child were turned to stone, and remained as a tangible memento of the gods' generosity.

That spooky story didn't in any way put me off my shark's fin soup, followed by sweet and sour pork, at the New Paris seafood restaurant. We walked back to the ship along the waterfront of the 'Fragrant Harbour' (the meaning of Hong Kong's name) in time to welcome aboard British TV conjuror David Nixon and his wife, my value-for-money friends Magnus and Mrs Pyke, and TV pundit Ludovic Kennedy with his lovely ex-ballerina wife Moira Shearer.

Nagasaki was another 'first' for both the ship and me. I entertained a host of Japanese dignitaries headed by Kan Kubo, the governor, and the mayor, Yoshitake Morotani, at a luncheon reception in the *QE2*'s Queen's Room. In my speech, recorded and later dubbed for Japanese TV, I said that, like most other people, I had believed that everything in Nagasaki had been flattened by the atomic blast but, that morning, I had added to my education by learning that several historic buildings had survived, and were now legally protected. At lunchtime, Joan and I went to an official party at the Kagetsu (Flower Moon) Restaurant, where giant golden carp looked at us open-mouthed from lily ponds hidden under the shadow of bonsai trees. Sitting on cushions on the floor, which isn't easy with the length of my legs, we ate raw fish, lobster, beefsteak, raw cabbage and radishes, with strawberries to follow and all washed down generously by cold beer and sake. After a quick look at the house said to be the original setting for *Madama Butterfly*, we were on our way to Yokohama. There, during our two-day stay, half a million Japanese sightseers filed past the ship. David Nixon, now sadly departed, commented: 'If I'd known we were going to draw an audience this size, I'd have been down there on the waterfront selling tickets.'

When we were in mid-Pacific on the way to Honolulu, the ocean certainly didn't live up to its name. A heavy swell thoroughly tested our stabilisers, and like so many trans-Pacific voyagers before us, we were very glad to reach the island of Oahu and the sheltering warmth of Honolulu harbour. Van Johnson came aboard to sail with us back to the States, and I chatted with him about some of the films he had starred in over the years. 'I really enjoyed your performance in *The Caine Mutiny*,' I remarked to him at my party the first night out after Honolulu.

'Well, as a master mariner you would,' he said, 'but I guess like many on that set I was a little overwhelmed by Bogey.'

'You mean Humphrey Bogart?'

'I do indeed,' said the tall, greying actor. 'D'ya know he learned his seamanship from Katie Hepburn in *The African Queen*?' I smiled, and Johnson went on: 'Don't get me wrong, Captain. Bogey was only half your size, but he sure as hell showed us who was Master, and a mad one at that, on the *Caine* set.'

Lillian Gish joined the ship in Los Angeles. The superstar of the early days of film was lecturing on her career from the time of *The Birth of a Nation*, which she made in 1913–14, to *The Night of the Hunter* of 1955. Lillian, a lively and loquacious lady, has made many similar talk-trips on my ships, and I'm always fascinated by her anecdotes. Also making the American sector of our voyage was the operatic soprano Anna Maria Alberghetti. She's not, I'm afraid, my style of entertainer, but Anna Maria scored an enormous success with our American passengers in the *QE2*'s Queen's Room. They loved her songs from the shows, particularly from the Broadway musical *Carnival* which, I was told, earned her a 'Tony'.

The *QE2* sailed north-west through the Canal and on to New York, the last stop for most of our passengers. Then I brought the two ladies I had accompanied around the world – Joan and the *QE2* – across the Atlantic, back to Southampton, docking at 4.48 a.m. on 12 April. That night Joan and I stayed at the home of our son Roger, who is a service engineer and lives on the outskirts of Southampton. He had been looking after my car while we were at sea, and the next day I pointed the Triumph Dolomite's bonnet northwards. There's a popular song that says 'It's nice to go sailing, but it's oh so nice to come home,' and that summed up our feelings as Joan and I walked a little wearily through the front door of our house in Rossall Grange Lane, Fleetwood. It had been without its devoted owners for just ninety-two days.

Chapter 24

From her role of world explorer, the *QE2* returned to regular, but far from routine, crossings of the North Atlantic between Southampton, Cherbourg and New York. Our aim is always to make these shorter voyages as enjoyable to passengers as any of the longer cruises and, for around £500, spent on sailing in the *QE2* one way and flying back on the return trip, the Atlantic crossing is transformed into an exciting holiday experience.

A typical mid-ocean day starts straight after breakfast with a family quiz on music, inventions, geography or a dozen other fairly simple topics. Hangovers or mid-morning blues can be chased away in a jogging session around the boat deck led by our resident physical culture expert Eric Mason. A little later, there's a 'grandmothers' get-together' in the theatre bar, run by social director Judie Abbott, where grannies swap stories and show off pictures of the youngsters. Meanwhile, for the ladies who haven't yet reached grannie status, there are beauty and hair-styling demonstrations, or talks on how to play bridge.

Elsewhere, author and doctor Robert Atkins is giving a lecture on 'How to eat your way across the Atlantic, lose weight and gain energy'. With the *QE2*'s lavish choice of menus, the doctor has a fight on his hands. Meanwhile, golf pro Bill Hunter attracts a dedicated gallery of enthusiasts to his coaching sessions at the One Deck Lido, and Eric Mason has now swapped his running vest for swimming trunks to show beginners how to pull a few strokes in the luxury pool on Seven Deck. Just before lunch, the Tote starts taking bets on how many miles the ship covered the previous day, then it's cocktails all round to sharpen appetites for mid-day feasting.

For the innocents abroad who have never heard the cry '*Faites vos jeux,*' there's a talk entitled 'Introduction to Gaming' in the Sportsman Club casino after lunch, while in the theatre, racing driver Jackie Stewart is presenting the film *Monaco 1977*. In various centres there are card parties, trap shooting, arts classes, yoga sessions, table tennis and children's fancy-dress parades.

As dusk envelops the North Atlantic, the *QE2*'s restaurants, bars and entertainment centres flash out a scintillating sparkle of lights over the darkening ocean. Honeymooners sway to the rhythm of the Ronnie Caryl orchestra, and there's applause for the dazzling dance routines of our Sweet Elegance girls. The ship's late-evening showtime features the songs of Judie Abbott, Bob Arno and Akiko, and the hypnotic skills of Tony Sands.

In a summer season of Atlantic sailings, there are, of course, a multitude of variations in our range of passenger programmes, and shipboard entertainment is largely immune from the dense warm weather mists that have haunted the Atlantic in recent years. The Captain's job isn't. When fog rolls across the waters, my first concern is the ship's safety, and sometimes that means staying on the bridge for days. Guests I've invited to dine at my table, or to attend one of my cocktail parties, just have to get along without me. On one of the crossings in the early summer of 1977, I missed meeting, because of fog, Orson Welles and his wife and daughter, the Sheikh of Bahrain and his entourage, a family group of Rockefellers, and schoolteacher Pat Draper from Boston, who travels with us at least once a year. And there were scores of others.

Another voyage which eventually ran into mid-Atlantic mist started out in bright sunshine on 27 June, the day before Her Majesty's Silver Jubilee Review of the Fleet. As I took the *QE2* past Cowes out into the Solent, 180 of the world's finest fighting ships were stretched out all the way to Spithead in a full-scale rehearsal for the historical royal naval event. Practically every one of our 2000 passengers and a hefty proportion of the crew crowded deckrail vantage points as we went past the arrayed aircraft carriers, cruisers, submarines, frigates, and mine sweepers. One or two of our American passengers didn't realise that it was Dress Rehearsal Day, and probably still believe that the warships from Britain and a dozen other nations were on parade solely in honour of the *Queen* of Britain's maritime fleet.

Perhaps the playing of 'Rule Britannia' and 'Land of Hope and Glory' over our ship's loudspeakers fostered their belief. The occasion, I felt, certainly called for us to fly a patriotic flag signal, but that presented problems. Any effusions we hoisted onto the yardarm were somewhat limited by its compact length, and by the number of 'letters' we carried in the flag locker. Nevertheless, we managed to put aloft the flag-signal: 'Well done the Royal Navy.' Our Blue Ensign dipped in frequent salute as I took the *QE2* through the ranks of the assembled fleet, and the warships responded immediately, often six at a time. With twelve admirals and 30,000 sailors aboard the naval vessels, that sort of alacrity seemed only fitting.

We received rapid ripostes from the American nuclear submarine USS *Billfish*, and from Britain's own first nuclear-powered sub HMS *Dreadnought*. A sleek visitor from the French Navy, FS *Duquesne*, flashed out her greetings to us, and I was delighted to offer our salute to a visitor from my homeland, HMAS *Melbourne*. She was the largest – and oldest – visiting warship on view, having been completed at Barrow-in-Furness in 1945. I spotted a lethal-looking destroyer riding at anchor nearby, the latest bearer of the name of HMS *Sheffield*, and near her was the only nuclear-powered surface ship on parade, the 10,000-ton cruiser USS *California*. Her colourful United States naval ensign waved briskly in the freshening breezes, contrasting with the white naval pennants flown proudly a little further along the line by the guided-missile destroyer HMS *Kent* and her companions HMS *Diomede* and HMS *Arrow*. The fastest ship I spotted was the 57-knot missile attack craft built for the Royal Brunei Malay Regiment, and the newest was the Greek Navy's missile launcher *Lieutenant Troupakis*.

Our cruise staff, helped by naval briefings, put out an action commentary over the loudspeakers, and I heard our broadcaster report that fifteen overseas navies were represented, including those of Australia, Belgium, Canada, Denmark, Greece, India, Italy, the Netherlands, New Zealand, Norway, Portugal and the United States. Britain, declared our man, was still possessor of the world's third largest navy, both in numbers of ships and fire power. But, he added, four notable absentees from the Review were the Polaris subs *Resolution, Revenge, Renown* and *Impulse*, which were deployed at sea, each carrying missiles with a fire power greater than all the bombs dropped by both sides during World War II.

Our passengers were still considering that awesome statistic from the *QE2*'s commentator when we cruised alongside the Fleet flagship, HMS *Ark Royal*. A great emotional roar went up from our packed decks at the sight and sound of the *Ark*'s immaculately uniformed Royal Marine band marching and countermarching along the broad sweep of her flight deck. As I exchanged salutes with Admiral Sir Henry Leach, Commander-in-Chief of the Home Fleet, I noticed that his flagship was swinging on the tide towards the Canadian warship HMCS *Huron*, drastically narrowing the gap which the bows of the *QE2* were about to enter, but an Admiralty tug, patrolling near the huge aircraft carrier in case of such an eventuality, also saw the danger and opened up our path by giving *Huron* a gentle push.

As we drew away from the eastern flanks of the great assemblage, five helicopters, packed with reporters and photographers, which had hovered over us right along the Review line turned back towards the Royal Naval Air Station at Lee-on-Solent. Next day the banner headlines over two of their stories proclaimed '*Queen Elizabeth II* rules the Waves OK', and '*QE2* Stands in for *Britannia*'. We had, I felt, accomplished a fair performance as understudy to the Royal yacht, due to take Her Majesty and Prince Philip over a zig-zag version of the *QE2*'s Cowes-to-Spithead review course twenty-four hours later.

At dinner that evening, an elderly lady from Atlanta confided to me, 'That was a memorable sight today, Captain. Imagine all those warships turning up to pay tribute to our ship. Wasn't that something?'

'Yes, wasn't it just,' I answered. 'Something to tell your grandchildren about back home, and don't forget Her Majesty is inspecting those same ships tomorrow.'

'No, I won't, Captain,' said the dowager seriously. 'But we saw them first, didn't we?'

Another massive but infinitely less belligerent assembly of ships awaited our arrival in the United States. We reached New York just at the start of the city's Harbour Festival '77. For two days, the broad mid-town reaches of the Hudson River were bustling with liners, tug boats, harbour launches and a fantastic sailing flotilla of more than fifty schooners, barquentines, brigantines, sloops and naval yawls. It was like turning back the pages of harbour history some fifty years.

Berthed alongside us at the Steamship Passenger Terminal, I saw the fluttering dress flags of the cruise liners *Statendam* from Holland, the Panamanian *Oceanic* and her sister ship *Doric*, our own *Cunard Princess*, the *Rotterdam* from the Netherlands Antilles, and the Russian *Kazakhstan*. That afternoon, while we embarked for the return Atlantic trip, our six Caribbean-bound companions set out in procession downriver, past the Manhattan and New Jersey shorelines, and the Battery Park, Brooklyn Heights and Shore Parkway promenades, in a nostalgic pageant that marked the opening of the Festival. Before the liners sailed, I talked to New York's Mayor Beame at a reception laid on by the Festival organisers and the Port Authority in a huge glass-walled conference chamber in the Passenger Terminal building at Pier 90. 'Great ship, the *QE2*,' said the blue-suited mayor. 'I once used her myself for a function to raise funds after an election campaign.'

However, after the ebullient civic leader had handed me a certificate of appreciation for taking part in the festival, a journalist covering the event whispered to me that Mayor Beame's booking of a suite in the *QE2* for his cash-raising party in 1974 had caused a hostile backlash from the city's hotel industry, who felt that Citizen Abraham Beame's festivities should have been accommodated on dry land in one of New York's myriad hotels. Happily, that episode had receded into ancient political history on that sunny afternoon as I enjoyed a drink with my white-uniformed fellow liner Masters. We totted up our respective passenger lists and found they totalled over 11,000 people. 'Something like the good old days for the great liners and for your port,' I told Mayor Beame. 'What a shame it can't happen more often.'

'It sure is,' said the diminutive mayor. 'Look out there at the way our New Yorkers have got themselves all excited over the big ships.' Through the windows of the Passenger Terminal, I could see thousands of people milling around. Guests who showed up late at the reception said there were dense traffic jams in and around the West Side Highway, and police were diverting traffic all the way back to Fifty-Ninth Street. Street vendors were out and about in the streets near the terminal, selling hot dogs, flags, and programmes headed 'The Great Ships – '77'. Standing under a sign proclaiming 'No selling here', a quayside capitalist in white smock and straw boater was serving Danish pastries and paper cups of coffee with his right hand, while his left hand was busily selling souvenir brochures. 'Fine day for business, too,' said the mayor.

As I watched the six liners sail sedately down the Hudson

215

from my vantage point on the bridge of the *QE2*, I remembered some of the ocean leviathans I used to meet in New York that had been blasted from the seas by the roaring jets. I thought of America's own Blue Riband winner, the *United States*, of the French liner *France*, and of Italy's super-liners *Michelangelo* and *Raffaello*. With our own two earlier *Queens*, they had all been among the last of the legendary line of Atlantic giants that carried more than one million passengers a year between Europe and America. Amid all the cheerful Saturday afternoon port festivities, it was a chilling reflection that the number of people sailing the Atlantic in 1977 might only just reach 45,000.

On my next crossing to New York, I had the pleasure of entertaining at my party a group of fine folks who preferred to travel the leisurely liner way. My guests included Britain's ex-Ambassador to Mexico Sir John and Lady Galsworthy, Sir John and Lady Galvin and their daughter, Princess de la Tour Dauvergne, BBC Outside Broadcast Chief Peter Dimmock and his wife Polly Elwes, University of Chicago economist Professor Milton Friedman and sculptress Edwina Sandys.

Shortly before the trip, our shore management had contacted me on Miss Sandys' behalf with the request that I should marry her to her boyfriend on the forthcoming transatlantic crossing. When she came aboard, I told her it couldn't be done, but she pleaded, 'Make an exception – just once.'

I knew Edwina was the daughter of the eminent politician Duncan Sandys and I really would have liked to have accommodated her if at all possible. I rang Joan and asked her to consult our local vicar, but an hour later she called back, saying 'No luck, Bob. British law demands the presence of an official Registrar of Births, Marriages and Deaths to legalise any wedding. That's what the vicar says and he should know.' In spite of her disappointment, Miss Sandys enjoyed her trip and the exhibition of her work on the *QE2* was greatly appreciated.

When we reached New York, the scene reminded me of war-time Britain: it was the 'Big Blackout'. There had been a total power failure and the city's illumination came only from headlights, hand torches and starshine. Thousands of people were stranded in their high-rise flats when the lifts joined the electrical mutiny, and passengers joining the ship spoke of having to descend hundreds of stairs to reach ground level from skyscraper offices and dwellings. But it wasn't all bad news. A

216

few months later I read that New York's birth statistics were about to take a giant leap upwards as a result of couples having to supply their own central heating and light entertainment on that night of starry seclusion.

Former world Grand Prix champion Jackie Stewart and his wife Helen travelled to the States with me on my next crossing. 'Do you miss the thrills of the track?' I asked him.

'Not as much as I thought I would,' he replied. 'And with a world-record total of twenty-seven Grand Prix wins, I reckon I did my whack.' The likeable Scot added that, in any case, he was never far away from the Grand Prix circuit because he was already building up a second career as a TV auto-race commentator. I asked him what he had been driving since his retirement. 'Same as ever, a Ford,' he told me. 'We're a three-car family, and they're all production Fords. The company has the long experience, the money for research, and its models have the absolute reliability that you need to feel safe behind the wheel on today's roads.' How much, I wondered, would such an unsolicited commercial have been worth to Henry Ford II? Apart from that, I was pleased to hear Jackie's comments, because, by coincidence, I had just ordered my first Ford Escort. All my family are Ford enthusiasts and echo Jackie's sentiments, and I am now the proud possessor of an XR3, a wonderful little car for driving when I'm on leave.

I returned to Britain in time to give my daughter Gill away when she was married at Fleetwood Parish Church on 6 August 1977 to a chemist with ICI. After the wedding we adjourned to the restaurant of the former manor house at Ryecroft Hall, Hambleton, for the reception. Gill, a teacher, had met her husband-to-be when he was working in Harrogate in Yorkshire and she was studying at college in York.

At the time that leave seemed to be quite normal and I suspected nothing, but with hindsight I realised that some odd things did happen. At home, Joan answered the phone to an inordinate list of callers who were, she said, 'wrong numbers'. Tinkering with the car one day, I remembered something I had forgotten to tell my parents, whose house adjoins our back garden. Up to my elbows in oil, I popped my head round their open doorway, only to find that Joan was there, trying to make a secret telephone call, as she later told me. 'Can't you leave her alone for five minutes?' said my mother in exasperation.

A couple of weeks later the whisperings, wrong numbers and furtive secrecy all slotted into place, but before all was revealed, I did another couple of voyages to the States. I took to New York His Royal Highness Prince Amir Fahd bin Abul Aziz, Crown Prince of Saudi Arabia, Mrs Gimbel of department store fame, and my old friends Lord and Lady Robens. His Lordship delights in his nickname 'Old King Coal', which he acquired as chairman of Britain's National Coal Board, and I can vouch for the fact that he is, at least on board ship, a 'merry old soul'.

Returning to Britain, I chatted to balloonist Dr Will Hayes, who was travelling with his wife to take part in a balloon-flying event in Yorkshire. 'Fancy coming along, Captain?' asked the doctor. 'I could teach you how to navigate a balloon in no time,' he assured me. 'With your experience it would be as easy as . . .'

'Falling out of a gondola?' I suggested.

'Heck no,' said Dr Hayes. 'You just show up on the Yorkshire moors and I'll have you flying as easily as you handle this lil' old ship.' It would be healthier, I reasoned, to stick to the sea, so I declined with thanks Doc Hayes' offer. 'Well, if you change your mind, it's all in here,' said balloning's persistent advocate, as he handed me a copy of his new book. So far, it hasn't persuaded me to take to the hot air.

A latter-day Phineas Fogg travelled with me on my next New York–Southampton crossing. French journalist Claude Mossé was in the late stages of his quest to emulate the feat of the legendary Phineas in travelling around the world in eighty days. In his careful, precise English, Claude told me that many attempts had been made to get around the globe by surface transport in the eighty days accomplished by Jules Verne's hero, but so far none had succeeded. 'I'll do it,' said Claude, modestly. 'A Scotch liquor firm has bet me my weight in whisky that I won't, but I intend to win where everyone else failed – except, of course, Monsieur Fogg.'

Claude told me that he had come through a typhoon as he crossed the Pacific by boat. He had landed at San Francisco, and caught the Zephyr express, and flu, on the way to Chicago, but the train was four hours late starting, and then had to stop altogether because there was a wreck on the line ahead. Claude, in true David Niven fashion, hopped off the train and took a cab from Downers Grove for the rest of the way in to Chicago.

Recalling the Mike Todd film, I asked Claude if he had

travelled by balloon on his world circuit. He lapsed into a Maurice Chevalier accent in indignation. '*Mais non*,' he answered, 'zat was not in ze book. Surface transport only – zat's why ah'm on your sheep.' I assured Claude we would keep a wary eye out from the bridge for any wrecks out front, and wished him all the luck in the world. I felt that a Frenchman used to drinking the wine of his country would be needing a little luck if he suddenly came into a windfall of around 180 lb of strong malt Scotch liquor.

As we reached Cherbourg, the last stop before Southampton, a strange sequence of secrecy, deceptions, disguises and smuggled cargoes aboard the *QE2* was about to enmesh its unsuspecting Master. I had fallen victim to a brilliantly conceived plot.

Chapter 25

Seven hundred passengers had eagerly volunteered for unpaid service as the audience in a television variety spectacular to be recorded in the *QE2*'s Queen's Room during our crossing from Cherbourg to Southampton. After a spell of heavy weather in the Atlantic, we were late in docking at the French port, and now there was further delay caused by getting heavy TV trucks and cameras aboard, which I needed about as much as I needed a hole in the *QE2*'s bulbous bow.

When Cruise Director Mike Constance asked me to introduce the show, I refused point-blank. 'Let the staff captain do it,' I said irritably. 'My job is here on the bridge, not hamming it up below while the ship's crossing crowded shipping lanes.'

But I was already written into the script, grumbled Mike, and an international 'mystery star' would be topping the bill and I was scheduled to introduce 'her'. It would be marvellous publicity for the ship, for Cunard and, it seemed, for everyone this side of the Iron Curtain.

'Oh, all right then, I'll do it, under protest,' I said, 'but if we hit fog in the Channel, I'm straight back onto the bridge.'

Mike's face broke into a relieved smile. 'Thank you very much, Captain. You've no idea how happy this will make everyone from the TV company.'

An hour later, I walked out under the hot glare of television cameras into the centre of the packed Queen's Room. I glanced at the script that had just been thrust into my hand. It didn't say who the mysterious top-of-the-bill would be. Either Shirley Bassey or Moira Anderson, I had heard someone say.

I picked up the microphone. 'And now . . .' My words were drowned in an explosion of applause. Perhaps I was more popular than I had imagined. I beamed, and waited for the clapping to subside. It didn't, and a large red album was thrust in front of me by a huge fist that materialised from behind my back. The fist's owner declared in an Irish brogue, 'Captain

Robert Arnott, Master of the *QE2*, this is your life.' The ecstatic audience, I immediately realised, had recognised Eamonn Andrews creeping up on me. Oh well.

The spadework that led to my being press-ganged into the hot seat of *This Is Your Life* had begun some three months earlier, when a cloak-and-dagger man from Thames Television arrived in Fleetwood and headed for the Arnott abode. Eventually he emerged with notebooks bulging with details such as how much I weighed at birth, blow-by-blow descriptions of my schooldays and my career at sea, plus lists of chums and shipmates scattered around the world. Joan, my mother and father, our children, and dozens of family friends were sworn to secrecy as they searched their memories at the behest of the television researchers. A mutual vow to 'Keep it all from Bob' explained the strange glances, the whisperings, and the hurriedly terminated telephone calls that had bedevilled me for weeks.

More machinations were in hand as I brought the *QE2* into Cherbourg from New York. A tall, slim, red-head, her face eclipsed by dark glasses, came aboard just ahead of a burly, bruiser of a man whose craggy features were half hidden by gold-rim spectacles and an Edwardian moustache. The disguised duo were, of course, Joan, complete with theatrical Titian topping, and Eamonn himself. My son Roger also walked shamelessly up the gangplank sporting an alien hairstyle and a stick-on moustache, and his sisters too were camouflaged in way-out wigs and exotic plumage. Even my parents had joined the fancy-dress parade. French customs finally officially approved the plot by stamping a false Cunard-prepared passenger list to cover the *QE2*'s short-haul stowaways.

Few of my crew were in on the secret, and Staff Captain John Hall was the chief 'mutineer', his job being to keep me busy while the Arnott family cast was being smuggled on board. John knew that one of my favourite ploys is to set off on a walkabout around the ship without warning, and there is no doubt that I would have recognised Joan in a head-on collision in a companionway, wig or no wig. To avoid such a meeting my staff captain raised an incessant stream of what I considered to be remarkably inane queries on the state of Channel shipping – designed to confine me to the bridge.

The TV people were lucky inasmuch as I wouldn't have gone to the theatre at any price if there had been fog about. But the

Channel's early autumn skies were crystal clear and the TV trap was sprung on me exactly as planned. It was a pleasant enough ordeal. Eamonn brought on old school chums, introduced filmed interviews with friends and shipmates from all over the world, including Captain Mortimer Hehir and Captain Peter Jackson. And then, of course, there was the whole Arnott clan. Dad told the remarkable story of meeting me by pure chance in a war-time Calcutta street, and Mum talked of our early days in Australia. Show-biz friends, including Joe Loss and Moira Anderson, added their anecdotes, and finally Eamonn handed me the red, leather-bound book he had been reading from. As soon as the cameras stopped filming, he asked me for it back. It then contained only typewritten script, but a couple of weeks later I received from Thames TV the completed volume, packed with photographs, titled '*Captain Robert Arnott*, RD, RNR, *This Is your Life.*'

The celebration party in my cabin after the recording continued until six in the morning, and I got very little sleep that night. At Southampton, Joan and her fellow conspirators went ashore looking exactly like themselves, Thames TV's make-up department having re-possessed the wigs, false moustaches, ostrich feathers and assorted pairs of dark glasses. Our managing director, John Mitchell, came aboard soon after we docked to present clocks or watches to lots of crew and hotel staff with twenty-five years' service, and then we sailed the following day to New York.

West-bound on the Atlantic once more, I glanced around my cocktail party guests and considered the wealth of material that they could provide for *This Is Your Life* programmes. The career of film director Robert Wise, quietly sipping martinis with his wife, would have been a fine excuse to parade before the TV cameras the stars of his productions such as *West Side Story*, *Run Silent Run Deep*, *The Haunting*, *The Sound of Music* and *The Andromeda Strain*.

As Robert happily described to me how he worked with our own Julie Andrews, I could picture the *This Is Your Life* scene. With her recorded voice-over singing 'The hills are alive . . .', Julie would be brought on stage by an American TV Eamonn. 'And here, Bob Wise, is a young lady we've flown all the way from Walton-on-Thames, England. You last saw her escaping across the Alps, but tonight . . .'

'And then, of course, there was Natalie in *West Side Story*.' Bob Wise's voice speaking about Miss Wood reminded me of the time I had acted as her marriage guidance counsellor, and brought me back to shipboard reality. Maybe being a TV star for a night had sharpened my imagination, but I was convinced that my party would have been a happy hunting ground for the biographical scouts of television.

The colourful Peter Cadbury, then a British television company director, was there too with his wife. My guest Mr Waddilove told me he had been private secretary to the Duke of Windsor; I should have remembered him travelling on the old *Queens* with the Duke, but I didn't. From the upper echelons of British industry, there was Sir Dan Mason, chairman of the Reckitt and Colman group, and from my own part of Britain I had the considerable pleasure of entertaining Sir Bernard and Lady Lovell.

The starry night skies had fascinated me as a boy, long before I knew anything about celestial navigation. Sir Bernard had been involved in his own highly sophisticated type of star-gazing since 1951, the year he was appointed Professor of Radio Astronomy at the University of Manchester and Director of the University's Jodrell Bank radio-telescope experimental station. While I was at sea searching the skies with binoculars for the early Soviet and American satellites, Sir Bernard was also satellite-spotting on land – with his 250-foot reflector giant steerable radio-telescope. He invited me along to his Cheshire observatory to see something of his work before his retirement, due shortly afterwards, but because of the busy sailing schedules I couldn't make it.

In November, the *QE2* went into the Scotch whisky business. Of course, we had always dispensed the finest old blends on board, but now it was decided that the prestige and selling power inherent in the *QE2*'s name should be distilled into promoting 'the world's most exclusive Scotch'. At eighty-five per cent proof, $25.00 a bottle, and guaranteed to be at least twelve years old, it had a fair claim to that title. But there was more to it than price and potency. The Duke of Argyll owned the Inveraray Distillery where our precious liquid was prepared, and His Grace had decided it would be a good idea for him to promote his product by travelling to New York and presenting to me, at a special shipboard reception, the very first flagon of

'*QE2* Scotch'. Memos, telex messages and cablegrams began flooding into my cabin from both sides of the Atlantic. Were any special glasses needed for a Scotch tasting session? Had we adequate supplies of the new concoction for the gentlemen of the Press. Could our Executive Chef Bainbridge whip up some buffet recipes utilising the new whisky. The answers to each of these anxious queries was an immediate 'Yes'.

John Bainbridge came up with an exotic *QE2* coffee, featuring freshly brewed coffee with whipped cream, brown sugar, crème de cocoa and 1/12 ounce of the Scotch per person. He also treated the VIP gathering to Shrimp Clan Campbell, in honour of the Duke who is head of the clan. This delightful dish combined freshly shelled shrimps marinated in the Scotch, white wine, thyme, shallots, tomatoes, parsley and fresh cream. I don't know how the Press felt about that one, but I certainly enjoyed it. All the special liquor-laced dishes served up at the whisky inaugural in the Midships Bar had been dreamed up, prepared and tried out on willing *QE2* volunteers within a couple of days of the first cablegrams reaching the ship. I thought Chef Bainbridge came up with a minor masterpiece in his Crème Inveraray sweet, containing chocolate-tipped sponge fingers, lemon jelly, sliced peaches and lashings of *QE2* Scotch.

The twelfth Duke, Admiral of the Western Coast and Isles, Keeper of the Great Seal of Scotland, and Hereditary Master of the Royal Household in Scotland, asked for his personal standard to be flown from our masthead while he was on board. The Argyll pennant fluttered proudly in lively autumn breezes rippling across the Hudson, as the Duke, resplendent in the green tartan kilt of the Clan Campbell, handed me the first, elegantly boxed flagon. We had hoped to present a similar tartan-wrapped pitcher of the golden elixir to each of the newspapermen covering our liquor launch, but in their wisdom the United States customs officers decreed that we couldn't. It was a point of honour, therefore, for the gentlemen of the Press to go ashore liberally tanked up with the splendid single malt spirit and, to a man, they did. They also gave us excellent coverage in their varied publications, and sales of *QE2* have since amply repaid the effort everyone put into the ducal junket in New York harbour.

At a private party in my cabin after the Pressmen had rolled ashore, my guests included the Duke and Duchess of Argyll, their American managing director, Ken Short, the Duchess of Marlborough, and Professor Rushdi, adviser to President Sadat, and Mrs Rushdi. It seemed a shame to switch drinks at that stage, so most of us stuck with the lovely libation from Inveraray.

'To magnificent ships and wonderful whisky, two world-beating Scottish exports,' said Ken Short.

'I'll drink to that,' said the Master of Inveraray Castle.

'And so will I,' said the Master of the *QE2*.

The next day we were off to Boston to pick up a Crimson Travel cruise group bound for the Caribbean and, as they were coming aboard, I walked along the waterfront for my usual Bostonian seafood feast at Jimmy's restaurant. Stuffed to the ears with oysters, I returned to the ship in time to greet 'Lulu' Edwards, escaping from America's plunging temperatures, and the Hon. Bernard St John, QC, Deputy Prime Minister of Barbados, who was returning to the island with his wife.

Sailing on our pleasant pageant of the islands around St Thomas, Grenada, Antigua, Curaçao and Haiti was one of my all-time screen favourites. Greer Garson appeared on our passenger list under her married name as the wife of Texan Colonel E. E. Fogelson – but even the teenage crew hands on the *QE2* recognised 'Mrs Miniver'.

'I think I've seen all your films, right from *Pride and Prejudice* onwards,' I told the elegant lady. 'I even have a beautiful rose bush in my garden of a variety called "Mrs Miniver". When my wife shows it off to people, they often get to talking about your unforgettable role in the film.'

A rather gallant gambit, I thought, but Miss Garson led me on with 'Oh, how nice of you to say that, Captain Bob. Did I remind you, then, of an English rose in my early films?'

'Why, yes. And most of your other fans took the same view, I should imagine, particularly in *Goodbye, Mr Chips*.'

'Well, young man, you were all somewhat mistaken,' said Miss Garson, with eyes twinkling. 'You see, Captain Bob, I'm as Irish as that lovely black porter you sell in your bars.' I said I was surprised. 'So are most people,' said the actress. 'I was born in County Down, where the Mountains of Mourne sweep down to the sea. As a navigator you'll know all about them. I admit I've never been a professional Hollywood Irishwoman, unlike some others we won't even discuss.'

I made a sentimental note to tell Joan that Mrs Miniver, Mrs

Chips and Miss Elizabeth Bennett weren't really English at all, and had been played by a rose of old Ireland, no less. Those red ringlets flourished by Greer Garson in her first colour films should, I reflected, have given me a clue.

On our returning voyage to Britain, I spoke by radio telephone from mid-Atlantic to the mayor of the port to mark the opening of the Southampton Boat Show. Our conversation reached the Post Offices Maritime Services stand at the show through Portishead Radio, and was broadcast over loudspeakers to publicise both the show itself and the work of the British Post Office's Maritime Radio Services Division. I've also spoken more than once from mid-ocean to the Earls Court, London, and the Birmingham Boat Shows. I'm told by the show organisers that there's always a certain measure of disbelief among the public that someone can actually speak to a liner moving at 28 knots some thousands of miles away. Thanks to the fine communications equipment on the *QE2*, plus the expertise of her radio officers, it's the sort of instant miracle we accomplish from the ship scores of times a day wherever we happen to be in the world. Arab oil sheikhs, Wall Street financiers and British business tycoons come aboard the *QE2* with the confident knowledge that their offices, their banks and perhaps their bookmakers are only as far away as the stateroom phone.

Towards the end of 1977, as I was flying across the Atlantic to spend Christmas at home, the *QE2* was starting out from New York on one of her shortest ever voyages, leaving her Manhattan West Side berth to sail the six miles to the Bethlehem Steel Corporation's dry dock at Bayonne, New Jersey. There the *QE2* began a seventeen-day overhaul costing around £2½m to make her ready for a rather longer trip. In mid-January 1978, I was to take her on a 39,000-mile, three-month round trip titled 'The Great Pacific and Orient Cruise'. And while the *QE2* was at Bayonne, two brand-new, superbly luxurious penthouses called the *Queen Mary* and *Queen Elizabeth* Suites were slung, already built, onto her signal deck – the ship's highest level. Weighing fifteen tons each and with a framework of all-welded aluminium, the suites were assembled ashore and then lifted by crane onto foundations already prepared on the deck just aft of the mast.

The going rate for a three-month tenancy of either one of the penthouses during our South Pacific saga was just under £1000 a day. For that sum, we were offering what was undoubtedly the

226

most luxurious passenger pad afloat anywhere. London designers Dennis Lennon & Partners had created the interior decor, which included a split-level bedroom-sitting-room equipped with a twelve-foot, suede-covered sofa. Each suite had twin bathrooms complete with gold-plated fittings, music centres featuring stereo radios and record players, infinitely variable Italian lighting combinations, plus the finest in overall furnishings from Europe and the United States.

Another major refurbishment programme that was carried out while the *QE2* was at Bayonne was the transformation of the 836-seater Britannia restaurant into a completely new dining concept titled 'The Tables of the World'. Dennis Lennon and his associates had come up with the idea of dividing the former Britannia into five separate eating areas, each based on distinctive national themes. The 'Londoner' evoked the atmosphere of a traditional English eating house, with a plentiful garnishing of old prints, a sixteenth-century Chaterlain wall map, some Spry cartoons and models of famous Cunard paddle steamers. The 'Florentine' had a white tile floor as a setting for dark blue, velvet covered chairs, and walls featuring Pucci hangings in silk as well as abstract designs based on the Duomo in Florence. The Spanish-style area was called the 'Flamenco', and here Picasso drawings of bullfights were a dominant influence.

A sun-drenched garden in Paris with a backcloth of scenes from the French capital formed the theme of the 'Parisienne' section, which drew traditional flavouring from the display of wall prints depicting Versailles. And perhaps the most dramatic sector of all was the 'Oriental', set right in the centre of The Tables of the World. Its central feature was a glittering pagoda, surrounded by a gold ceiling, silver walls, black carpeting and bamboo hanging lanterns. At the heart of this Oriental extravaganza was positioned my Captain's Table. Maybe some shipboard spy had whispered in Dennis Lennon's receptive ear how much I appreciate shark's fin soup, chicken chop suey, sweet and sour pork and lychees.

A team of British designers, craftsmen and technicians flew out to New York to co-operate with their American colleagues during the revolutionary, seventeen-day up-date on the *QE2*. New kitchens were added to match the demands of The Tables of the World and the ship's three other dining-rooms. An additional games room for teenagers was fitted, and staterooms for 300 passengers were given an attractive new look.

More than 3000 miles away from the Bayonne action arena, I was putting away impressive helpings of turkey, stuffing, Christmas pudding and white rum sauce, bolstered by hot roast chestnuts and mulled ale. The Arnott family festivities went merrily through into the New Year, which flashed into Fleetwood on a cheerful chariot of hospitality, powered by a palatable fuel of some eighty per cent proof. Then, two weeks later, I flew out to New York to join Cunard's pristine palace of the oceans for her first foray of 1978. Tonga, Tahiti, Fiji and the lands of the distant East were calling me again across the southern seas.

Chapter 26

Shimmering lights from the World Trade Center's twin towers danced out over the black swirling waters of the Hudson as I took the *QE2* downriver at the start of her South Pacific pilgrimage. It was just 7.30 p.m. on the evening of 16 January 1978. Weeks of warm sunshine were waiting for our cruise passengers, but as we moved out into the Atlantic, snow flurries flecked the bridge and a heaving, icy ocean mauled the *Queen*'s freshly painted hull.

New York's ten degrees of frost melted into just another winter memory as we cruised southwards along a Florida coastline basking in mid-seventies sunshine. Joan was starting to recover from the cumulative effects of jetting to New York and then facing an ocean contorted in spasms of white-topped wrath. She joined me on the bridge to watch the normally routine docking at Port Everglades, but this time there was a submarine blocking our approach. This turned out to be an entirely friendly member of the United States Navy, but her ominous black bulk didn't altogether help the delicate manoeuvre of installing the *QE2* at her allotted berth.

Fully laden with passengers and provisions, the last great monarch in Cunard's line of ocean queens moved away from the Everglades quayside just four hours later. I set course through the north-east trade winds to Curaçao and after a day among the Dutch colonial comforts of Willemstad with its floating markets and Queen Emma pontoon bridge, we sailed on the evening tide for the Caribbean, and the crossing to Cartagena on the Columbian coast.

Joan went ashore with friends for a tour of the old Spanish city under the guidance of a local travel agent whose far-sighted parents had obligingly christened him Marco Polo. He took our own explorers through the elaborate cathedral, to the Governor's palace and through winding streets to the San Felipe fortress, whose sixty-foot-thick walls once protected the local people from successive raids by French, English and Spanish pirates. Apparently the Cartagenans themselves weren't too fussy how they disposed of prisoners, and Joan inspected their execution 'chamber', a simple hole in the wall where condemned miscreants were fed to the sharks. A more salubrious spot of sight-seeing was a visit to the lovely old hotel where Princess Anne stayed on her honeymoon, and then it was back to the ship for the passage across the Gulf of Darien to the Panama Canal.

The verandahs on the canal's lock houses were duly collapsed so that the *QE2* could get through safely without tearing them from their metal mountings. She is still the largest liner to use the ocean interchange, and on the 1978 trip I was making an inaugural call at the port of Balbao at the southern end of the canal. More than sixty official guests came aboard for my official reception in the Q4 Room, including the lieutenant-governor of the Canal Zone, Richard L. Hunt, British Ambassador Robert Michael John, the US Ambassador William Jordan and the Indian Ambassador Cheddi Lal. If the assembled diplomats were looking forward to a heavyweight harangue from the Master of the *QE2*, they were disappointed. I simply said how pleased I was to bring my ship into their fine port for the first time, and then handed out a number of glass goblets embossed with the ship's motif. The cause of friendly international co-operation, I feel, is far better served by informal chats over drinks rather than by a long agenda of speeches, and that's the way I play it whenever I can.

'Our Man in Acapulco', Derek Gore, was waiting to meet us when we anchored off the Mexican resort. Derek runs the British consulate within the fabulous Las Brisas hotel-and-convention-centre complex, and his caseta there has its own private swimming pool. Joan and I were whisked up to Las Brisas in one of the hotel's pink jeeps, and Derek took time off from daily diplomatic chores to present me with a commemorative plaque for the ship. After lunch with him, director of the hotel Jack O'Hara and a group of *QE2* passengers, we all strolled along to the palm-shaded beach club. There, an afternoon of sea swimming and sun soaking was jollied along by lashings of the favourite local potion. Rejoicing in the colourful but accurate name of '*cocos locos*' (crazy coconuts), this high-octane Mexican mixture contained tequila, gin and vodka served in scooped-out coconuts. It was a men-only drink, and most of the girls cooled off with non-alcoholic, chilled fruit punches sipped from huge balloon glasses. That included such high fliers as Esther Kosmala, who has been known to dance on the roof of her white Rolls before joining the ship at the home port of Everglades, and her friend Trese Hollerich, one of America's first woman bank presidents, who hails from Chicago.

Some passengers took coaches to the cliffs at La Quebrada to watch the divers leaping into the seething Pacific. This time the Mexican divers escaped unscathed, but Mark Shorrock, one of the *QE2*'s waiters, went for a swim when the party called at the famous Princess Hotel in Acapulco, struck his head as he dived in the hotel pool and was killed. He was just twenty. Our two ship's padres, Father Billy Mills and the Rev. Hec Morphet conducted a moving memorial service for Mark as we cruised northwards across the Gulf of California towards Los Angeles.

While we docked at California's largest city, some of our passengers went on the traditional tour of Beverly Hills and Hollywood. They made the required stop at Grauman's Chinese Theatre to goggle at the stars' footprints set in concrete, then climbed aboard their coach to see the Hollywood Bowl. Another passenger tour went off to Long Beach for an advertised '81,000 tons of fun' aboard the *Queen Mary*.

I glanced through the programme on the fine old dowager on which I had first sailed in 1952. It promised that 'Charming hostesses will guide you through her promenade deck, her magnificent main lounge, the bridge – a panorama of polished brass – and her luxury suites. You'll also see Jacques Cousteau's *Living Sea*, the largest specially created marine show in the world, including a tidal pool with more than thirty varieties of live sea creatures.' I wondered what some of the finest creatures of the sea I had ever met, the old Masters of the *Queen Mary*, would have thought about it all. Not very much, I guessed.

At around seven on the evening of 30 January, the *QE2* left the lights of the California coastline for the vast ocean blackness of the Pacific. Five days and thousands of sea-miles away lay Tahiti, largest of the Society Islands. It was to be another 'first' call, and my steward polished up the decorative goblets that I was to present to government and port officials.

Four days out into the blue vastness of the Pacific, King Neptune and his Court performed their foaming rites on the

231

innocent initiates in the line-crossing ceremonial. Meanwhile, the president of the Chamber of Commerce and Industry at the Tahitian capital of Papeete was appealing for all shops, restaurants and tourist centres to open up specially on the day of our arrival there, a Sunday, when everything in the island would normally be closed down.

Two days after the *QE2* crossed the equator, I headed her into the narrow channel through the coral reef guarding the approach to Papeete. The traditional Tahitian silent Sunday, dating from the London Missionary Society's incursion there in the eighteenth century, had been abandoned in honour of our visit. As soon as we were alongside the quay, a bevy of dusky Polynesian beauties, led by the reigning Miss Tahiti, boarded the ship to bring flower-crowns, hugs and kisses to our 1700 passengers in a fashion that probably differed little from the way their ancestors received Captain Bligh and his ill-fated *Bounty* back in 1788.

After I had extricated myself from the amorous attentions of the two Tahitian dancers who were planting liberal kisses on each of my cheeks, I took refuge on the bridge and looked out over the harbour. Our escorting tugs were still dazzling the packed quayside crowds with a display of water-jet fireworks which broke into a million rainbow droplets as they fell through sunlight onto the white-sailed yachts and crowded motor launches milling around the ship. On the landward side, I could see the bungalows of Papeete (pronounced pap-ay-tay) almost hidden by a lavish profusion of bougainvillaea blossoms, and beyond ranged a succession of lush, vine-covered tropical ridges, climbing to the great black volcanic peaks of the central highlands.

With one of the biggest ordeals of the whole cruise safely over – my speech in French when I presented the goblets – our agent Monsieur Clement took Joan and myself, our Chief Engineer Bill Farmer and Chief Radio Officer Don Butterworth out to Faaa airport for an hour's flight around the islands in a Piper Aztec. From 3000 feet I could see the narrow strait in the coral reef where I had just squeezed the *QE2* through to her berth. No wonder our pilot Monsieur de Caill had said that it would be a close thing. The reef shone through the blue Pacific waters in a shimmering galaxy of turquoise, yellow, red and golden reflections, but the sublime splendour of the coral necklace strung around the island merely masked the ability of any one of its jagged gems to tear the heart out of an errant vessel.

Our Piper pilot swung the little plane out from the fertile island paradise of Tahiti across the broad Pacific rollers towards the smaller but no less lovely island of Moorea. It's also called, said our agent, the Bali Hai of the South Pacific. We swept in over pink coral strands, vine-filled slopes and coconut plantations, climbed over the pointed, volcanic central peaks, then out again across the reef-fringed lagoon on which stood the Bali Hai hotel, and back to Tahiti.

Practically every one of our passengers had been ashore for the day. They had eaten at Polynesian feasts, had been decorated with flower leis and regaled with rum punches. They had driven along the coast to Point Venus at Matavi Bay where Captain Cook landed in 1769, and they had inspected the artistic treasures of the Paul Gauguin museum on the east of the island. Paulina's professional dance group, Tiare Tahiti, swayed to the ancient native rhythms in a farewell quayside dance display as I took the *QE2* out into the crimson wake of the setting sun, and cries of '*Manuia*' (good luck) trailed away as we reached the deep blue waters of the open ocean. We had been in the remote Tahitian world only eleven hours, but the wonderful warmth of our welcome there would be remembered by everyone on the *QE2* as one of the more memorable experiences in life.

Another 'memory', but a slightly more tangible one, occurred in the waters around Tahiti. Suddenly our radio-room received a signal prefaced by the letters GBTT – the call signal of the *Queen Mary*. The message had apparently been sent during the Second World War, had travelled to outer space and then, some forty years later, returned to earth to be picked up by the *QE2*'s receivers. The incident surprised our radio officer, but it wasn't totally unique; similar phantom radio messages, plunging back to earth, from who knows where, are occasionally reported, but never before had one come back across the years bearing the royal call signal of RMS *Queen Mary*.

With the *QE2* speeding effortlessly across the broad vastness of the Pacific towards Tonga's Friendly Islands, I looked in at the Shrove Tuesday party organised by our cruise director Brian Price. Through clouds of champagne bubbles, I spotted Ben Lyon with his wife, Moira Anderson and her husband,

Alan Whicker and his girl friend Valerie, Lillian Gish, Moira's musical director Robin Stapleton, my wife Joan and Joe Loss with his wife Mildred.

'Come inside, Bob,' said the Hollywood veteran Ben Lyon. 'We trust you've left the ship on auto pilot.' I joked with him about his own days as a movie pilot in the classic film *Hell's Angels*. 'Do you know, Bob,' he said, 'I've been living off gags about that role for half a century. What'll ya have to drink?'

'Nothing, thanks, I have to go back to work.'

'Sure,' drawled Ben, sipping his champagne, 'me, too.'

Ben Lyon OBE was paying his way on the cruise by talking to passengers about his career in films and in the long-running British radio comedy show, *Life with the Lyons*. A question his shipboard audiences invariably asked him was 'How did you discover Marilyn Monroe?' 'With no trouble at all,' Ben would answer. 'It was just part of my job as talent director for Twentieth Century-Fox. Now if you want to hear something really fascinating, I can tell you about the greatest aviation film ever made.' No prizes for guessing the title of that one.

February the 8th, the day after Shrove Tuesday, didn't officially exist for the *QE2* because we were crossing the international date line, and immediately found ourselves into February 9, the day of our arrival at Vava'u in the northern Friendly Islands. A native feast of roast suckling pig, chicken, fish and Lu Pulo – corned beef, onions and coconut cream all baked in taro leaves – awaited our passengers on the lovely beach at Keitahi. I didn't join them, thinking it was far too hot to tackle such a banquet. I glanced at my bridge thermometer; the mercury level stood at 104 degrees Fahrenheit. In that sort of heat, Tonga's most attractive feature for me was undoubtedly the air-conditioning on the *QE2*. Joan, tireless as ever, went ashore to buy black and white coral necklaces in the native market. While she was away, a group of local dignitaries came aboard for drinks in my cabin, and then in the cooling early evening breezes I took the *QE2* out of Vava'u's cliff-lined bay into the Pacific for the short haul to Suva, the capital of the Fijian islands.

It was give-away goblet time again in Suva where I had the privilege of entertaining His Excellency the Governor-General, Sir George Cakobau, the Hon. Tomasi Vakators, Minister for Tourism, His Excellency James Stanley Arthur, British High

Commissioner, our agent Jack St Julian and several other Fijian VIPs. As my guests sipped their chilled gin and tonics, a call came through to the ship from a Melbourne radio station, and for a few minutes I chatted live on the air with presenter Bob Rogers across thousands of miles of Pacific ocean.

That afternoon Jack St Julian took Joan and me on a tour of Suva and then to Orchid Island where we were met by Gwyn Watkins and his wife Ivy, who had literally dredged the island out of jungle swamps and transformed it into a combination of botanical garden, menagerie and Fijian Cultural Centre. Dominating the scene was the Spirit House, an exact copy of the ones that used to be in every village a hundred or so years ago when cannibalism contributed extensively to island menus. Then, people were killed and eaten in ceremonial feasts when the supporting posts of the Spirit House were completed and again when the thatched roof was finished. Now Fiji is totally peaceful and Mr and Mrs Watkins assured us there was no fear of an unwary visitor ending up as the dish of the day. We walked through the gardens where 160 varieties of orchids bloom and to the museum where there was gruesome evidence of Fiji's violent past – fearful looking brain piercers, clubs and spears, and an authentic cannibal cooking-pot.

Mr Watkins told me that he had been in the tropics for thirty years. 'I'm convinced, Captain,' he said, 'that the native witch doctors here have the secret of rainmaking or rainstopping. Don't ask me how it's done, but these fellows have the power and certainly do it. Their gods too, I feel, are far more than sheer superstition.' Seeing my look of disbelief he turned up some photographs of the Spirit House. 'Look at these,' he said. On some of the frames there were mysterious markings on the thatched roof and beside the door. On others taken at the same time there were no marks. 'Those wraith-like shapes,' said my host, 'are in the exact places where the old gods entered the temple.' He added that the photographer swore he saw a strange entity going in, that his film had been checked by Kodak, and that in no way had it been 'doctored'.

There was no denying the unusual power Ivy Watkins had over the animals on the island. She knew all the flying foxes by name and usually had one clinging to her arm, or had young banded iguanas creeping over her arms as she showed visitors round the miniature coffee, cocoa, tea, vanilla and sugar plantation.

'Would you like to hold Erasmus here?' said Mrs Watkins, offering Joan a furry flying fox.

'No thank you,' said Joan. 'I'm not really keen on bats.'

'Oh please,' said our hostess, 'don't let him hear you calling him that or he'll be hurt, won't you Erasmus?'

'Oh sorry,' said Joan, 'but he just looks like a B–A–T to me. He can't spell, can he?'

Before leaving Orchid Island, Joan and I were chosen to be guests of honour at the drinking of yaqona, a potent concoction made from the powdered root of the pepper plant. All the visitors from the *QE2*, whom we were representing, gathered in a long native house to watch as we performed the ceremony. Half coconut shells of the liquid were passed to us and with due solemnity and respect we had to drain the bowl in a single draught. Our farewell potion was fiery but harmless, which was just as well because I had a ship to drive that evening.

I took the *QE2* into New Zealand's territorial waters through the Bay of Islands. Apparently, in prehistoric times the sea had rushed through the valleys on New Zealand's northern tip, surrounding the low hills to create a sudden and quite beautiful crop of islands. A flotilla of small craft buzzed us as we did a slalom in and out of the island waterways, and I noticed one of my navigating officers, John Carroll, waving joyously to a man in a small yacht. 'What's the semaphore signal?' I asked.

'Oh, didn't I tell you, sir?' said John. 'I was brought up around here and that's my uncle in that little boat out there.'

'Fine,' I replied. 'Please carry on waving.'

I was up at five the next morning to take the *QE2* into Auckland at precisely 7.30 a.m. on St Valentine's Day. It seemed that the whole population of Auckland had turned out along the waterfront to shower us with greetings, many in small launches which repeatedly came around the ship carrying cargoes of sightseers. I gave an early morning press conference to newspaper and radio journalists, then welcomed aboard a phalanx of local dignitaries including the mayor, the town clerk and harbour officials.

The day before we arrived in Auckland, the *New Zealand Herald* had reported that 'A name that conjures up visions of majesty, size and luxury will glide into Waitemata Harbour tomorrow.' When I had actually delivered the object of their graphic description into port, the *Herald*'s journalist wrote: 'It was like Regatta Day all over again. Auckland's citizenry stormed down from the hills to the sea and clogged the roads with their cars.'

While the leading members of that citizenry were aboard I presented to the Harbour Board, on behalf of Cunard, a model of the *QE2*, and received in return a framed picture of the fine harbour painted by the Auckland artist David Barker. I also handed over to R. W. Carr, chairman of the Board, a silver salver which the harbour authority had originally given to the ship *Port Auckland* in 1948, which had the signatures of all the Masters who had commanded her engraved on the back.

While the ceremonials went on aboard ship, the New Zealand Navy Band, augmented by musicians from our own ship's orchestras, gave a two-hour concert to big crowds in Auckland's *QE2* Square. When I had completed the presentations, Joan and I went ashore with our friends Bernard and Lorna Crisp for the traditional 'challenge to invaders' offered to me in the square by a talented group of Maori dancers. The band concert had built up a wonderful carnival atmosphere for the exciting challenge and for the enactment by the Maori group of a pageant depicting their tribal history in New Zealand. The fine voices of the Maoris softened the awesome effect of their fierce and practised hostility.

That evening, the four of us went along to a cocktail party organised by the New Zealand Tourist Board in an all-glass conference area overlooking the harbour. I drank whisky and water and took in the fine view of the *QE2* across the harbour waters, still surrounded by little pleasure boats drawing in their dollar windfalls. The party was a very friendly, informal affair, and Joan and I received scores of invitations to 'stay with us next time you're in New Zealand'. One knowledgeable fellow told me that the 'largest mussels on earth' were served at a nearby French restaurant – a temptation I couldn't resist. Joan and I left the party early and, with Bernard and Lorna, strolled along to the restaurant. Sure enough, the mussels that arrived on our plates were bigger than any I had seen anywhere in the world. We had ordered steaks to follow the mighty molluscs, but by the time I had eaten a dozen mussels, each well over six

237

inches long and with massive girth to match, I felt further food would be an anti-climax.

We hurried back to the ship just twenty minutes before we were due to sail. I changed from my flannels and open-necked shirt into a white tropical uniform, and went quickly up to the bridge. Coloured streamers trailing in the sea, car horns blaring, ships' whistles hooting and a rising swell of farewell songs from the crowded wharf followed us out of Waitemata in a crescendo of fraternal warmth. An hour later, as the *QE2* surged southwards towards Wellington, Joan and I drank a midnight cup of Horlicks in our quarters. 'What a super St Valentine's Day,' I remarked.

'Yes, it was,' said Joan, 'but whatever happened to the lovely old custom of sending Valentine cards?' I made a mental note to try to remember that aspect of 14 February the following year, but I don't think I did.

A chilling drizzle greeted the *QE2* as I manoeuvred her into Wellington's Port Nicholson harbour. The Prime Minister of New Zealand, the Rt Hon. R. D. Muldoon, came aboard with his Minister of Transport, the Hon. C. A. A. McLachlan, along with Sir Harold Smedley, the British High Commissioner, H. A. James, chairman of the Wellington Harbour Board, together with a distinguished array of national and civic heads. I welcomed everyone to the ship, and then the usual round of presentations began. I handed out my own gifts, including a model of the *QE2* to Mr James, and next it was the turn of Nigel Broackes, chairman of the Trafalgar House Group, to present one of the *Queen Elizabeth I* brass pens to the Prime Minister.

The drill was that, as Mr Broackes got to 'Here is a pen made from the porthole brass on the first *Queen Elizabeth*', I would hand him the pen from the cushion perched on the corner of the piano, where my gifts were laid out. I searched the cushion. No pen. I groped around under the piano stool. No joy.

Our Chairman bravely soldiered on by going into the detailed historical pedigree of the Parker pens. I put out a broadcast call for the young navigation officer in charge of my gift collection. I surmised, correctly, that he had removed the pen for safety, not knowing it was destined for our chief guest. It seemed like an age, but was in fact about eight minutes before a red-faced youngster appeared with pen in hand. There was relieved applause all round as Mr Broackes finally handed the memento to Mr Muldoon.

I quickly closed the ceremonials and led my guests off to a champagne lunch. Stiff protocol softened in the tides of bubbling solvent, and in mid-afternoon, surnames forgotten, I showed the party through the splendours of the *Queen Mary* penthouse suite, and afterwards took them on the bridge. The Prime Minister and his friends headed ashore in mellow mood around half past five that afternoon, leaving us with sincere and pressing invitations to 'Come back again as soon as you can.' I promised we would.

I went to my cabin for a couple of hours' rest before I took Joan on a drive round the city and up the beautiful slopes of Victoria. As we set out, Joan said 'You look a little tired, Bob. Did you have an exhausting time with your government friends?'

'Well, yes, in a way,' I began cautiously. 'It all started when one of *Queen Elizabeth*'s pens went adrift . . .'

After a day cruising in the spectacular but rainy Milford Sound, we crossed the Tasman Sea to dock at Hobart's brand-new MacQuarrie Wharf. It was yet another inaugural call for the *QE2*, and around eighty Tasmanian worthies assembled in the boardroom of the Hobart Harbour Board for the civic reception. In my speech, I welcomed the Hon. D. A. Lowe to the gathering, saying, 'It's very pleasant to see you here, Mr Prime Minister.' This brought loud guffaws and shouts of 'Has he been promoted, then?' since Mr Lowe, Minister for Industrial Relations and Health, was only the Deputy Premier, standing in for his chief. All was forgiven when I told the lads – it was an all-male assembly – how much I enjoyed the Great Cascade beers brewed in Tasmania. 'A marvellous pint,' I said. This brought cries of 'Top 'em up, Captain' from the politicos, waving their depleted glasses in the air.

While I lent my willing support to the shipboard civic beer festival, some of my passengers went off to Tasmania's Derwent Valley to see the 'Plenty Salmon Ponds' where, in 1864, the first brown and rainbow trout were successfully raised in the southern hemisphere. All current stocks of these fish in Australia's and New Zealand's lakes and streams originated from these Bush Park ponds. Other tourists from the *QE2* travelled by coach to see the old convict settlement at Port Arthur, dating from the 1830s. Now, they reported, the mental hospital building at the heart of the penal ruins has been restored to house a reception centre, a museum, a photographic display and an audio-visual theatre. I promised myself a visit to Port Arthur 'one of these days', but so far the time to make it has eluded me.

I headed the *QE2* into Melbourne Harbour before breakfast on 22 February. Reporters came aboard for a morning Press conference, then I held an inaugural reception for the Lord Mayor, Alderman Rockham, the Chairman of the Harbour Board A. S. Mayne and dozens of other Melbourne notables. Every inch of space along the quayside was jammed with people who had come along to see the ship, and my guests told me that traffic was snarled up for miles around the docklands.

I had already accepted an invitation from Melbourne TV's *Tonight* presenter Peter Couchman to appear on his show, and I wondered how Joan and I would get through the traffic jams to the studio. The simple answer was – by helicopter. The first chopper the TV station sent for us broke down on the way, but the second one made it and we arrived at the studio with minutes to spare. The theme of Peter's interview was 'How does it feel for the Master of the *QE2* to return to the land of his birth?' My answer was: 'It's marvellous. Wish I could stay longer here in Melbourne.' But the *QE2* was due to leave at ten o'clock that night for Sydney, and I didn't even have the time to accompany Joan on her quick visit to the Captain Cook cottage museum in Fitzroy Gardens, and to the gracious old Como House in South Yarra.

A solid mass of people stretching for miles along and behind the waterfront gave us a memorable send-off as the *QE2* moved out into the waters of Port Phillip Bay. As we rounded the coastline towards Sydney, one of that city's newspapers phoned me to say, 'We've heard they gave you a great welcome in Melbourne, but we're going to beat them hollow.'

Sydney undoubtedly did its best to fulfil that promise. The moon was just leaving the skies to make way for the red fire-ball of the rising sun as I took the *QE2* through the misty approaches to the queen of the world's harbours. We approached the circular quay in a fairly leisurely fashion, for the splendid waterway was seething with small boats which, with their owners, I had to be careful to leave intact. Traffic on the steel-arched Sydney Harbour Bridge came to a standstill, in defiance of the city's bye-laws, and vehicles at the end of the sightseeing queue smashed into the bumpers of those in front. Afterwards, lots of letters chased me half-way round the world accusing, 'You made me late for work on the morning of 24 February', or 'You completely disrupted my business that day.' I was also in hot water for allegedly pinching the cruise liner *Oriana*'s berth on the circular quayside. She arrived after us, and had to put in at an out-of-city mooring.

Apart from such negligible details, Sydney exploded with enthusiasm at our arrival. The Lord Mayor, Alderman Leo Port, arrived on board with his civic entourage for my reception, which closely followed a 10 a.m. get-together with the city's journalists and cameramen. Both meetings were conducted with rather more decorum than the Great Cascade convention with the city fathers of Hobart.

The next morning Joan and I set out by car with our Operations Director John Bown and his wife for a sentimental journey to Hamilton and the house where I was born. As we drove into Boreas Road, a young man stepped out into the road and I heard the familiar TV camera cry, 'Action'. We'd been ambushed by a television team only yards from my old house, and for half an hour or so I reminisced before the cameras about the days when my parents and I delivered mineral waters by horse and cart along the old Hamilton dirt-tracks.

We escaped from the TV men into the sanctuary of the old white house. It seemed not to have changed at all, since the earliest days I could remember there. Old Man Taylor and his wife Lizzie had died, but my mother's cousins Joyce and Merle Taylor made cups of tea and brown bread sandwiches, while friends from every nearby house came in to cram against the white wooden walls until I thought they would burst from sheer body pressure. They didn't. Old Man Taylor, who built the house with his bare hands, had done a sturdy, long-lasting job.

We drove back to Sydney through forests, then into steep cuttings between hills splashed with the greenery of gum trees, and followed the road across miles of orange grove plantations. I caught sight of the massive oyster bed on the Hawkesbery River, and wondered whether we should stop for samples, but the seven o'clock sailing that evening didn't allow the time for outdoor oyster feasting.

From the bridge I counted more than 200 vessels matching our progress out of the harbour. 'A great and joyous armada'

241

was how I heard one Sydney radio commentator describe the scene. He added, 'And yet there's a touch of regret that the first lady of the oceans is leaving the scene of her southern conquests for the far lands of the north.'

On the morning of 27 February we were at sea on course for Port Moresby. Apart from the fairly rare sight of four albatrosses floating effortlessly together in our wake, there was little to record of maritime interest, but on the *QE2*, it was a very important day for Joan and for Joe and Mildred Loss. Flowers were stacked knee-deep around my cabin from dozens of people who had heard on the ship's grapevine that it was Joan's birthday, and there was a similar floral assault on the quarters occupied by the legendary Joe and his wife, who were celebrating their fortieth wedding anniversary. A constant flow of greetings cards, bottles of champagne, and a day and night of parties marked our progress towards the Papuan port.

Unfortunately for some of the celebrants, the tail end of Tropical Storm Gwen lashed across the *QE2* as we neared Port Moresby. Seasickness ganged up with hangovers to disseminate widespread discomfort, but this had largely vanished by the time I was giving the order to let go the anchors in the harbour of the port named by Captain John Moresby in honour of his father, the British Admiral Sir Fairfax Moresby. It was the *QE2*'s first call at the Papuan capital, and the country's Prime Minister, the Rt Hon. Michael Somare joined me on board for cocktails, together with the Superintendent of the Pilot Authority, Bob Turner. Bob is a former Cunard first mate who sailed with my present staff captain Harvey Smith and is, in fact, one of Harvey's closest friends. Joan went ashore by launch with Bob's wife Jill who took her on a rapid inspection of the young nation's Parliament, the University of Papua, the National Museum and the native Koki markets.

Some of our passengers, meanwhile, had flown ahead of us from Sydney to the Papuan hinterlands. They returned to the ship with strange tales of the grotesque 'mud men' who live in the jungle village of Kominufu, and are supposed to be able to summon up their ancestors' spirits in a ghostly dance ritual. Our tourists had also seen 'spirit houses' reaching hundreds of feet into the jungle sky along the banks of the Sepik River, and they had brought back fine paintings by the Sepik natives who are among the greatest exponents of native primitive art.

More exotic art forms were awaiting our travelling connoisseurs in Bali. At the island's cultural centre of Bedula they watched the 'Kris' dance in which the 'Barong', a huge mythical creature representing the forces of good, battle with the 'Rangda', the Queen of the Witches. Joan and I missed that cultural treat and instead took a quiet drive around the island's lush green paddy fields and through the banana and coconut plantations. Pigs, ducks and chickens roamed the roads freely, and cows on long leads grazed the roadside verges. With native buses claiming the central section of the narrow highways at speeds of around sixty miles an hour, the Balinese roads were no place for the faint-hearted.

I took the *QE2* away from the vivid greenery of the Bali coastline out into the Java Sea on course for the City of the Lion, or 'Singapuru' in Sanskrit. A fleet of Rolls-Royces arrived at the dockside there, carrying the royal passengers who were travelling on the next stages of our voyage. I welcomed aboard Malaysia's Supreme Head of State, His Royal Highness Sultan Yahya Putra Ibni-Marhum, with his consort Queen Zainib and a retinue of eighteen courtiers from the State of Kelantan. The Sultan was occupying the throne for five years under the royal rota basis practised by the Malaysian sultans. He and his Queen proved to be among the more reserved of the royal personages who have travelled with me on the *QE2*, speaking little English, and mostly staying in the luxurious seclusion of their deck suite.

That evening, Joan and I went out for dinner with Chia Chong, General Manager of the Straits Shipping Company, and his attractive wife Dorcas. Our venue was the Tropicana, where we enjoyed an extensive Chinese meal before watching the ballet featuring nude male and female dancers. 'Well danced, not at all offensive' was Joan's verdict on the show, but for me, the Chinese roast duck was much more memorable.

Singapore also brought to the ship a second Malaysian royal family, the Sultan of Selangor and his wife, who were travelling with their two teenage daughters. The Sultan, ruler of more than a million people in Western Malaysia, was much more extrovert than his royal compatriot the Sultan of Kelantan. When Joan and I chatted to the Selangor schoolgirl princesses at one of my cocktail parties, they were both unanimous that they didn't want 'Daddy' to be the next head of state. The elder girl said, in excellent English, 'We've spent a lot of time at school in England, and we love the freedom girls have in London. If Daddy becomes king, it will be like going back into purdah for us.'

Later that night I talked to the Sultan of Selangor in the ship's casino, where the pleasant, cultured gentleman from Kuala Lumpur was happily trying his luck on the dollar one-armed bandits, without too much success. 'Don't let my daughters worry you about their future,' he said. 'No one will force those two independent young ladies to do anything they don't want to, whether they're in London, in a royal palace, or on the moon.'

Next day I mentioned the gist of what their father had said to the young princesses. With a wisdom beyond her years, the younger girl remarked, 'What is spoken on your lovely ship, Captain, and what happens in an eastern palace are truly worlds apart.' Fortunately for the girls' peace of mind, my Malaysian friends tell me that, so far, 'Daddy' hasn't been elected to the supreme throne. I trust the Selangor princesses are still enjoying their emancipation.

The city of Manila came up with a congenial new slant in welcomes as the *QE2* sailed into the capital's broad and beautiful bay. A helicopter cruised overhead, showering our decks with thousands of small white, sweet-scented flowers, and as we approached the quayside the skies were suddenly dotted with clouds of multi-coloured, helium-filled balloons.

While I was making presentations to Filipino VIPS – it was the *QE2*'s first visit to Manila – more than 1000 of our passengers hurried ashore to take a closer look at the capital and its three and a half million citizens. The *QE2* tourists inspected and photographed Intramuros, the ancient city whose thick walls were built to defy pirate raiders. They saw Escolta and Rizal Avenue – Manila's top shopping thoroughfares – and walked round the American War Memorial and cemetery, where thousands of marble crosses mark the graves of allied service-men who died in the great Philippine battles. Some intrepid passengers penetrated the hinterland as far as the old Spanish town of Pagsanjan and shot the river rapids there in dug-out canoes – fourteen rapids and nineteen waterfalls in fifteen minutes. 'Exhilarating and quite dangerous,' one middle-aged lady passenger from Boston told me when she returned. 'I got drenched to the skin,' she added, 'but it was the sort of thing I've seen done so many times on the films, and I just had to try it.'

That favourite comedian of Britain's Prince Charles, Sir Harry Secombe, joined the ship in Manila with his wife Myra. I listened to Harry's superb tenor voice and laughed uproariously at his unique style of humour when he gave his first performance in the *QE2*'s Queen's Room, and afterwards Joan and I had drinks with the famous Welshman and his lady.

'Nice little theatre you have here, Bob,' said Harry. 'Reminded me tonight of a seasick Swansea Empire. It wasn't only my singing that sent the audience rushing for the doors, you know.'

'Well, the seas were a bit rough during your show,' I admitted, 'but the South China Sea is always unpredictable this time of the year.'

'What are you saying, boyo?' said Harry in mock alarm. 'My agent told me this concert was being given in Cardigan Bay. Have you checked your compasses recently?' A most generous trouper, Harry offered Joan and me the use of his holiday villa in Majorca. We recently took advantage of his kindness, and spent a pleasant holiday on the Mediterranean sunshine island.

Meanwhile, in mid-March 1978, our absolutely reliable and totally sophisticated navigational equipment told us we were right on course for Hong Kong. It was there that Joan was due to leave the luxurious comforts of the *QE2* to explore the secret world of the Communist way of life on the western side of the Chinese border. Mrs Joan Arnott and party were bound for Canton.

Chapter 27

A churlish South China Sea plagued the progress of the *QE2* until she reached the haven of Hong Kong's superb harbour. Warships of the world's navies, cargo boats, bat-winged junks and cradle-like sampans were already bustling about the teeming waterway as I took the *QE2* across the harbour bar soon after first light on Monday, 13 March 1978. Two days later, Joan was one of a large group of passengers who crossed the border bridge joining the New Territories to the People's Republic of China. Along the bridge, a huge mural proclaimed 'Long Live the Great Unity of the People of the World', and the Union Jack and the red flag of Communist China fluttered only a few yards apart.

The denim-clad citizenry of the Chinese People's Republic couldn't have known that they had been infiltrated by one of the Western world's more compulsive diary chroniclers. Joan emerged from her travels behind the Bamboo Curtain on the afternoon of St Patrick's Day, 17 March, with a diary bursting with Chinese chit-chat. Here are some of her observations.

15 March
Taken to Tung Fang hotel. No room service, but flask of boiling water and mimosa tea in cupboard. No central heating, and very cold. Told to report back to bus in an hour for visit to Culture Park where 'You will enjoy yourselves.' We didn't. Art exhibition there unfortunately pathetic. Few pictures, plastic toys, basket work, cotton goods, fireworks and posters showing happy workers with Chairman Mao.

The people smile whenever we speak to them. Everyone seems cheerful, but there's an awful sameness about the smiles and the people. Blue uniform of sorts worn by everyone, and bicycles – without lights at night – are universal transport. Back to the hotel by 8.45 p.m. No bar, no coffee lounge, no nothing. Some wiser souls had brought bottles. Foregathered in a bedroom for nightcap. Going to sleep now at 11.20 p.m. Reveille at 6.45 a.m.

16 March
Mr Yuong, our Chinese leader, very helpful young man with good command of English, but unfortunately his pronunciation is terrible. Fully half of time can't understand what he's saying. All his instructions end with 'You unnerstan?' He took us to Pingchow People's Commune. It has 17,000 households. Went into village hall, big, lots of windows with lace curtains and pictures of Chairman Mao, Chairman Hua, Marx, Lenin and Stalin. Only other decorations framed sheaves of corn. On to farm, where every pig has its own little sty. Lots of hens, ducks and every kind of vegetables. Every inch under cultivation. One communal waterway where people washed clothes, others washed mud from paddy fields off their feet and legs, some were rinsing lettuce, while lots of folk carted water away in bucketsful, presumably to make more China tea.

Showed us old straw 'oppressed' peasant's house, kept to recall bad old days. Visited peasant woman's new home. She looked eighty, but we're told she's forty-one. House about twenty feet square, with flower posters on wall. Interpreter said it was owned by family, paid for by earnings. 'Can they sell it?' we asked. 'No, but after family all die relatives sort it out between them.' Peasant lady very friendly, served tea, but did not speak. Her daughter, twenty-three, worked at nearby rattan-ware factory. Floor there was of stone and the women sat on blocks of wood and worked at an incredible speed. Asked interpreter what they do with their earnings. 'Buy furniture, pay for wedding, or help socialist government better the people.'

Only toilets in village holes in ground, and only privacy walls two feet high between them. No luxuries such as doors, or water flushing. Just bucket for soiled paper. Some passengers said, 'Nothing on earth would make us use those.' Before day was out, they did.

Went into kindergarten school. Children clapped us in, then sang and danced for us. They were delightful, like little dolls in brightly coloured costumes. Did long routines without a single hitch. Ended with usual flowery tribute to Mao. These people all seem to think in the same way, behave in the same way, yet they know they're going places. They believe in themselves.

247

They're not envious of us, indeed one almost felt they were sorry for us because in their eyes we don't think and live 'on the right lines'.

After excellent lunch, went to zoo. Saw two giant pandas. On to antique shop where, I presume, they're selling off things taken from decadent middle-class during revolution. I took fifty dollars with me and brought back forty as didn't think much of goods on offer.

Supper at 5 p.m! Then told: 'You will be on bus at six o'clock, see acrobats, and you will enjoy. You unnerstan?' Went to 4000-seater theatre, sat near front behind four rows of soldiers. They applauded only the comic, a slip-on-banana-skin exponent. Acrobats very clever, so were conjurors, trapeze artistes. Only the Westerners clapped. Apparently not done. Got back at 9.30 p.m. exhausted. Had hot bath then climbed into bed under mosquito nets, but no self-respecting mosquito would be seen dead here. No heating at all, and temperature in low fifties, but beds comfortable.

17 March

Our group leader Mr Yuong is having time of his life. He eats up whatever we leave at meals, and tosses back glass after tiny glass of plum wine, saying 'Bottoms up.' That's what we now call him. He smokes everyone's cigarettes, non-stop.

Visited 32 Middle School at Kwanchow. I went into English class. Textbook started out: 'To learn English is a weapon for our future.' In physics class children were making torch bulbs. Eventually they go out into factories and farms two days a week to prepare for working life on leaving school. Everyone works at something. Went to school gym, invited to play table tennis against pupils. They were sensational players. Children gave us concert, with dancers and orchestra. Very good, but all school windows wide open, stone floors and no heat. Yet everyone looked well, perfect teeth, and only saw two people wearing glasses all time in China. Asked our guide what happened if people don't work. 'First show him error of ways.' 'But what if that doesn't work?' 'Then, we stop his food. That make him work.' Must be a moral there for the Western world.

Back on train from Canton through countryside more intensely cultivated than any I've seen anywhere in world. Mile upon mile of rows of cabbages, lettuces, greens of every kind, orange groves, banana plantations, sugar cane, oats, wheat, barley and, of course, paddy fields. Water buffalo wandering in fields with ducks and geese all over. Everyone was busy digging, hoeing or collecting crops, mostly working barefooted. Little mechanisation, saw only two farm machines in two hours' rail journey.

Pleasant to leave the Red Flag and walk across to the Union Jack. Everyone's spirits immediately lifted. Yet Hong Kong's New Territories seem tatty compared with tidyness and neatness of Chinese countryside. But it's lovely here to see children running about just for fun.

Got to gangway of ship, but couldn't get on. King and Queen of Malaysia coming ashore, and we weren't allowed on until they came off. But then it was nice to be back in lap of luxury, particularly a lovely warm bed. But my thoughts were still across the Red Bridge and I just couldn't sleep. Bob had to be up at 3 a.m., because ship sailing at 4 a.m.

With Joan and her fellow researchers safely back on board, I headed the *QE2* towards Japan. Around 170 Japanese gentlemen had joined us in Hong Kong for the fairly short cruises to Kōbe and Yokohama. They felt their tickets entitled them to be photographed with the *QE2*'s Master throughout the day and night, to have constant access to his services as a signer of autographs and to shake his hand whenever they cornered him in public rooms, in companionways or even in the ship's lifts. Of course, I did everything I could to humour their whims, but there were times when I simply had to retreat into the privacy of my cabin to escape the friendly attentions of the ever-smiling posse of pursuers. I even tried to switch their allegiance to comedian Dickie Henderson, who was playing to appreciative audiences in the ship's theatre as we headed for Japan.

'Mr Henderson very clever English entertainer,' I pointed out to my Japanese friends as Dickie was turning one of his famous somersaults. It didn't work. 'Captain sir big star on this ship,' said a bilingual member of my Nippon fan club. I gave up. And no doubt Mr Henderson, whom I later told of my ploy, was mightily thankful that it didn't succeed.

I'm told that, each year, more than 10,000 ocean-going ships call at Kōbe, the great port-city on the north shore of Japan's Osaka Bay. On the morning of 20 March 1978, the *QE2* increased this substantial statistic by just one, but it was apparent from the furore accompanying our berthing at the Port Terminal that our particular arrival was one that all Kōbe had turned out to see. Light aircraft and helicopters flew over us at mast height as we entered the bay, and when we drew nearer the quayside, fireboats shot streams of water aloft in a triumphal welcoming arch. The terminal building itself was jammed solid with more than 10,000 spectators. Pacific storms had delayed us a couple of hours, but the solid mass of sightseers had been entertained in the meantime by lively music from the Band of the Kōbe Fire Brigade.

Seven Kōbe 'Queens' – beautiful girls clad in traditional kimonos – came aboard with city officials soon after our tugs had nudged us against the quay. Then Yukio Torii, director of Kōbe City's Port and Harbour Bureau, handed me a glass-encased Samurai helmet on behalf of the mayor, Tatsuo Miyazaki. I wondered what the 'Queens' were going to do, but their task, I found, was to hand out bouquets of flowers all round as well as thousands of colour picture postcards of Kōbe to our passengers and crew, accomplishing this job in a delicate yet totally effective fashion.

Kōbe, said the mayor, is anxious to promote itself as a tourist centre as well as being Japan's second largest port; the number one port – Yokohama – was to be our next call along the coast. Kōbe certainly has a lot going for it in natural and man-made attractions. It's built at the foot of pine-clad hills which range upwards to Mount Rokko, a cable car resort looking out over the beautiful Osaka Bay and Kōbe city, home to more than a million purposeful, prosperous Japanese ladies and gentlemen.

Two of them were travelling as passengers on the *QE2* – Mr and Mrs Toyoka Iwata, owners of The Hook, one of Kōbe's more exclusive restaurants. Joan and I popped in there for lunch with our agent, Mr Agawa of the Swire Shipping Group. This super meal started off with smoked salmon that had been cured in one of the factories owned by the Toyokas, followed by French onion soup, then moved on to the main course featuring the renowned Kōbe beef; we finished off with luscious strawberries and cream and Irish coffee. The wines were served in glasses with rather unusual stems. These were naked ladies, and I mean naked. 'They're symbolic,' said Mr Agawa, but didn't explain what the shapely stems were symbolising.

Yokohama, our next coastal call, was almost destroyed by Allied non-nuclear bombardment during the war, but today it's an impressive cosmopolitan city with a fine seafront promenade. Yokohama's residents turned out by the thousand to greet the *QE2* when I brought her through the chilling rain to the quayside at lunchtime on 21 March. The civic fathers didn't quite match up to Kōbe in their numbers of beauteous emissaries, for only four flower-laden 'Miss Yokohamas' came aboard. They covered everyone in sight, including myself and my chief executive officers, with sweet-smelling blossoms and planted equally fragrant kisses on our startled cheeks.

Many of our passengers climbed on board coaches to make the twenty-two-mile drive north to the Japanese capital along the Third Keihin Expressway, which is Tokyo's equivalent of an American freeway. Others who weren't in the mood for the capital's frantic bustle went on a tour to the ancient seaside city of Kamakura to see the massive 750-year-old bronze Daibutsu, the Great Buddha, then drove along the pine-fringed Pacific shore road to the hotspring mountain resort of Hakone.

'We were amazed that there were so many religious shrines around the city, in the countryside and even in amusement parks,' was a comment I heard more than once when our tours returned that evening. Passengers had been surprised to find that Japan, with its outward worship for the gods of commerce, still draws heavily on an ancient and powerful religious tradition. Perhaps, I reflected, that's the secret power-base for the Japanese people's phenomenal energies.

Cold, cutting rain showers pelted the *QE2*'s bridge and decks as I manoeuvred her out of Yokohama Harbour and set course for Honolulu, some 3500 miles away on the other side of the ocean. Two days out into the Pacific, the King of Malaysia sent his secretary Dato Mohsin round to my cabin with the message that 'Their Royal Highnesses the King and the Queen of Malaysia will be calling upon you for cocktails at 12.15 p.m. today.' It was just five minutes to mid-day, and to anyone other than his royal personage, the answer would positively have been 'Not at such short notice.' But what can you say to a king? My reply was that I would be delighted to receive their majesties. Joan, my steward and myself set a new speed record tidying up my day quarters.

251

It was the first time I had talked at any length to the Yang di Pertuan Agong, which, he told me, is a shortened form of his full Malaysian title. I found him a tremendous advocate of all things British. When I handed him one of my *Queen Elizabeth* pens, His Majesty said in his halting English, 'You know, Captain, I shall really treasure this.'

'This also will have an honoured place among my shipboard souvenirs,' I assured the king as he presented me with a silver-framed photograph of himself in full royal regalia.

The next day was Saturday, 25 March, and so was the following day: we were traversing the international date line, where time behaves in bizarre fashion. On the 'first' Saturday, a group of Japanese passengers headed by a Mr Yamada gathered on the afterdeck with bared heads and tossed a wreath into our foaming wake. Mr Yamada, a former naval officer, told me the little ceremony was in remembrance of all their countrymen who had died in the Pacific war. As the bright blossoms faded from sight, I too remembered war-time shipmates who had been resting in the Pacific's eternal black fathoms for more than thirty years.

The Sultan of Selangor, his wife and two schoolgirl daughters came to my cabin for pre-lunch drinks on the 'second' Saturday. 'Please take care of this for me until we reach New York,' said His Royal Highness, as he handed me a superb, solid gold statuette of a racehorse set on a fine jade plinth. He explained it had been made by a British jeweller and presented to him by some of his Chinese racing friends in Hong Kong, where he owned and raced a string of thoroughbreds.

I noticed the golden steed's saddlecloth bore the number 35. 'Everyone knows that's my lucky number,' said the Sultan, 'or should I say everyone except your croupiers. Would you mind speaking to them on the matter?'

I promised I would do what I could, which of course was precisely nothing. However, the Sultan made me a double presentation of his own personal shield and a Malaysian pewter clock, while his wife gave Joan a lovely rose bowl made from metal mined in the King of Malaysia's state of Kelantan. My gift to the Selangor royal couple was one of my rapidly shrinking stock of *QE1* pens.

'Oh, Daddy, please can we take that back to England to show off in school?' pleaded the younger princess. His Royal

Highness didn't say anything, but from the frown that crossed his normally cheerful regal brow, I imagine the ultimate answer was negative.

Our arrival in Honolulu was scheduled for lunchtime on Easter Monday, 27 March. As we surged through the dark waters of the Pacific on the night of Easter Sunday, the cruise ended for a fabulously wealthy Swiss widow named Iris Bodmer, who vanished into the ocean depths. Why or how we still don't know for sure, but I believe that Mrs Bodmer, who was sixty-nine, simply jumped into the sea. It's impossible to fall off the *QE2* accidentally unless you're fooling around climbing the handrails, which is hardly the exploit of an elderly lady. Mrs Bodmer had been a lonely old soul, who seldom mixed with the other passengers. She was due to leave the ship in Honolulu, but I'm sure she decided to opt out of life before the warmth of the 'Aloha' waiting there for everyone on the *QE2* had the opportunity to melt her melancholia. It was a strange decision for Mrs Bodmer to take because the old lady left behind jewellery worth more than $3 million dollars in the ship's safe.

While we were tied up in Honolulu Harbour, a favourite outing from the ship was the cruise to Pearl Harbor. Our passengers had boarded the pleasure launch *Adventure V* in the Kewalo Basin and, following the coastline past our mooring near the Aloha Tower, went on to Hickam Field and into Pearl alongside Battleship Row. I didn't hear how our Japanese sightseers reacted to the guide's narration of the events on 7 December 1941: he titled his talk 'The Day of Infamy'. Afterwards *Adventure V* took our tourists to the huge Arizona Memorial which stands across the hulk of the sunken USS *Arizona*, the great warship that is the tomb of more than 1000 sailors of the United States Navy.

That sort of doleful day out wasn't everyone's idea of fun, and many passengers joined a tour to inspect the natural delights of the Kalihi valley on Oahu island, Waimea's awesome Grand Canyon, and the Kilauea volcano and Halemaumau fire pit on the big island of Hawaii. Joan and I popped out for dinner with shipboard friends to the Kahala Hilton where I made the acquaintance of Hawaiian mai tais, a potent concoction of rum, cointreau and fresh pineapple, recommended by the Hilton's Polynesian barman as a 'dreamy mixture'. I think he really meant to say that it was a swift passport to slumberland, but happily, we weren't leaving Honolulu until the following evening.

After four days of swift sailing across a fractious and freezing cold Pacific, the *QE2* entered San Francisco harbour under the splendid and spectacular span of the Golden Gate. The ever-faithful fireboats were waiting with their welcoming water-arches and a mini-navy of coastal craft swirled around the ship's massive black hull as I directed her gently towards her berth at Pier 35. From far below on the crowded quayside, the strains of 'Sweet Georgia Brown' came wafting up to the bridge from a jazz band giving an early morning concert to celebrate our arrival. Nearby a gleaming line of limousines, many with uniformed chauffeurs, waited to meet passengers ending their cruise at San Francisco. As one of the local papers reported next day, 'It was like a scene from the era of *The Great Gatsby*, when liners carried the rich and unhurried from continent to continent.' But 1978 was, in fact, the first year that the world's largest passenger liner had ever been to San Francisco, and a party of local VIPs came on board to celebrate the event. I opened up my stock of *QE2* models and goblets to hand out mementos.

One of the cars lined up on the quayside was a Cadillac which had been ordered by Joan's friend and our very regular passenger, Mrs Kathie Bainbridge. Kathie took Joan to lunch at the Fairmont Hotel, then on a sightseeing tour of the city, taking in Fisherman's Wharf, Chinatown, Twin Peaks, Golden Gate Park and the Seal Rocks, where scores of baby seals were taking the April sunshine. By mid-afternoon, I had completed my handshaking sessions, and when Joan returned from her Cadillac joyride I drove her across the Golden Gate Bridge to relax for a couple of hours in the quiet beauty of the yacht harbour at Sausalito.

We returned in our little hire car half an hour or so before the *QE2* was due to leave for Los Angeles. In an evening paper I bought on the quayside I spotted an item headed '*Queen Mary* for sale – Price is $30m.' The report claimed that, since the City of Long Beach had bought the grand old lady of the Atlantic in 1967 for $3m, she had been losing an average of $1.8m a year. It added: 'Local critics have been trying to torpedo the *Queen Mary* – something the German Navy was unable to do between 1940 and 1946 when she carried 765,000 troops between the United States and Europe.'

'Poor old lady,' I mused to myself as we climbed the *QE2* gangway.

'Did you say something, Bob?' asked Joan.

'Not really. I was just muttering to myself about a very dear old friend who's in trouble.'

'Can you do anything to help?' queried Joan.

'Not a thing,' I replied. 'She's way beyond my help.' Leaving Joan wondering what on earth I was talking about, I went up on the bridge to direct our departure.

Through the night we cruised southwards along California's old Spanish galleon trail past Santa Cruz, Monterey and Santa Barbara to reach Los Angeles on the morning of 2 April. That evening we edged out into the Pacific, still heading south, then curled into the Gulf of California for an inaugural call at the Mexican port of Mazatlán. While I was handing out a couple of *QE2* goblets to the representatives of the local mayor and the governor, motor coaches were trundling our passengers to Concordia, a former Spanish colonial centre established in 1563. My own sightseeing was limited to gazing out from the bridge over Mazatlán's glistening turquoise harbour, dotted here and there with tiny green islands. White-painted launches were speeding out from their berths for a day of big game fishing, while the traditional, gaily-coloured Mexican trawl craft ambled along leisurely in their white-foamed wakes.

Later in the day, while our shore excursionists, including Joan, were enjoying their Mexican meanderings, a strong south-westerly wind came gusting in from the Pacific to interfere seriously with the operations of our own transit launches. Fit young passengers were able to climb up the pilot ladder onto the ship, but many returning elderly folk were finding it quite impossible to leave the launches as they bounced around against the *QE2*'s shell doors. Finally, with two hours' sailing time already lost, I ordered the last two launches, crammed with passengers, to be winched directly aboard ship. I'm sure that finding themselves swinging up the side of the *QE2* in an open-air elevator wasn't the pleasantest of experiences for our passengers, but it was far safer than our manhandling them across a few feet of malignant ocean. The launches were dented in the airlift, but their occupants arrived on the liner's deck totally intact.

That evening, cruising along the Central American coast towards the Panama Canal, our still-shaken adventurers were soothed by tranquil tunes from our illustrious resident violinist Max Jaffa and his pianist Vincent Billington. Max always draws an attentive, faithful following when he performs on Cunard vessels, and his Grand Hotel 'Palm Court' style, blended with his wife Jean's relaxing songs, provided a pleasant melodic medicine for our aging travellers.

Still out in the Pacific the next night, I developed a slight cramp in my right hand from having shaken hands with 600 of the passengers who had come aboard in San Francisco and Los Angeles. Colour shots are taken by our ship's photographers of each individual greeting, but this time the films had been ruined while being processed, so most of these good folk turned up the following night for a second 'shake' while I was saying hello to yet another 600-strong block of passengers who had joined us at the two Californian ports. The substantial Arnott right fist had lost its usual supple shape by the time I finally reached the last of the line.

It was as much as I could do to grip a large whisky and water a few minutes later when I joined a group of guests who had been patiently waiting for the end of my gargantuan greeting parade. The golden soothing spirit was a balm to my aching digits, and I enjoyed a relaxing half hour chatting to the Archbishop of Caracas, Ester Kosmala and 'Lulu' Edwards, as well as John and Ann Riley, who were among the wealthier residents of the North Manchester dormitory suburb of Prestwich.

John Riley told me that, just a few years earlier, he had lost his job as a Glasgow bus driver and decided to take a seasonal job in Blackpool selling leather goods from a seafront stall. After his first season on Blackpool's Golden Mile, he had gone into partnership with an Indian gentleman; they took over a disused mill and began to manufacture goods for other traders. The business prospered and soon John was able to open a massive wholesale trade warehouse in Manchester, selling everything from television sets to skate boards. Hence John's presence with his wife in one of the more expensive suites of the Canal-bound *QE2*.

The Canal area was at its April loveliest as the *QE2* made her way through its locks into the Caribbean. The yellow blossoms

256

of the Guayacan trees (identified by my personal softwood specialist, J. Arnott) spilled out over the lush greenery of canal banks refreshed by the first showers of the region's rainy season. However, things weren't quite so salubrious in the town of Cristobal at the northern end of the canal. We were warned by police that there had been a spate of recent muggings, and one of our French passengers who went ashore was immediately seized by thugs near the main shopping area and robbed of $450 in cash plus all his travellers' cheques. Joan was in a nearby arcade when the attack happened, but I had made sure that several beefy companions from the ship went with her on her shopping trip.

With the predatory perils of Cristobal fading over the horizon, the *QE2* moved out into the sparkling waters of the Caribbean for a leisurely half-moon circuit of the Colombian and Venezuelan coastlines to La Guaira, port of Caracas. The white-hulled *Cunard Countess* was already berthed in the spacious, sultry harbour and her Master Doug Ridley came over to join me at lunchtime for a cooling tumbler of gin and iced water. We sailed away from the verdant Venezuelan coastal strip in the late afternoon, but not late enough for the nine revellers who had failed to rejoin the ship in La Guaira by quite a wide margin of litres. Appropriately, they hired a fast liquor launch to overtake the *QE2*. I noted with some relief that the launch's decks were clear of contraband as it drew alongside. How much of the liquor load our belated boarders were carrying was strictly their own affair.

Lots more liquor, in duty-free kegs and bottles, came aboard for our passengers when we reached Charlotte Amalie, capital of St Thomas in the Virgin Islands. We spent the hot hours of 12 April moored in the picturesque and historic harbour, whose waters were also adorned by the presence of the latest entrant to our company's cruising fleet, the elegant *Cunard Princess*. When the dreamy white *Princess* headed out for the cooling breezes of the open seas in the late afternoon, her Master, my friend Captain Peter Jackson, ordered hundreds of helium balloons to be released as she passed our bows. Soaring skywards to the cheers of passengers crowding the decks of both Cunarders, the baby blimps brought a dazzle of reflected colour to the waters where the notorious Captain Edward Teach – alias Blackbeard – had sailed his pirate craft nearly three centuries ago. Earlier in

257

the day, a group from the *QE2* had driven out to Blackbeard's Hill to take a look at the solid stone tower where the old villain planned his marauding missions across the Caribbean, returning by way of Drake's Seat, a look-out point perched high above the magnificent Magens Bay Beach. Sir Francis reputedly climbed the steep hillside there to get a bird's-eye view of his own pirate-chasing fleet, moored more than 1000 feet below.

Our Great Pacific and Orient cruise was drawing towards its conclusion as I headed the *QE2* on a north-westerly course across the Caribbean to Port Everglades. As we cruised past the familiar coastline of Puerto Rico, a white-haired old lady from Dallas came up to me on the promenade deck. 'I do hope, Captain, that you're not taking us through that awful Bermuda Triangle,' she said anxiously.

'Well, madam,' I replied, 'I'm afraid we're already in it. But don't let it worry you, because I don't think there's a word of truth in all the tall tales you hear about it.'

The Dallas dowager's worried face relaxed. 'Do you mean that, Captain Bob?' she persisted.

'Of course I do. The Triangle has made a lot of authors rich, but as a seaman I believe it's a load of codswallop.'

I wasn't just saying that to pacify an old lady's anxieties. Obviously, with hundreds of ships and planes entering the Triangle year in and year out, there are going to be a number of accidents, but that equally applies to scores of other busy shipping interchanges throughout the world. Perhaps when somebody thinks up similarly scary titles such as the Bombay Barrier, the Sicilian Square, the Tasmanian Trapezium or the Manx Circle, those neglected arenas of maritime mystery may also achieve profitable literary recognition.

We emerged unharmed from the alleged perils of the Triangle to reach Port Everglades on 14 April. A blinding thunderstorm hit the Florida coast as we were leaving for New York, cutting visibility to near zero. With the *QE2*'s sophisticated array of electronic instruments, our exodus posed no navigational problems, but we missed our usual massed valedictions from wellwishers on shore. I sent out a couple of hoots on the ship's whistle just in case anyone was waving to us through the wet blackness.

Weak, early sunshine filtered over the *QE2*'s decks as we headed up the Hudson River to our New York terminal on the morning of Sunday, 16 April 1978. The Great Ocean Adventure was over for most of our passengers. Beaming through tropical tans, they embraced their kinsfolk who had been waiting, pale-faced and patient, on the quayside.

That evening I took the *QE2* out into a heaving, still wintry Atlantic. A howling westerly followed us across to Cherbourg, where we docked on the afternoon of 21 April. A few hours later the *QE2* was churning her way through a choppy Channel to her home port of Southampton, and not long afterwards, Joan and I were cruising up the north-bound motorway to our own home port of Fleetwood. We docked safely, and for the next four weeks the nearest approach I made to any sort of ocean action was tossing a few pebbles into the breakers of the Irish Sea just a few hundred yards from our front door.

Chapter 28

If I had to choose one Cunard skipper who had taught me more than any other, that man would be Captain Joe Woolfenden, DSC, RD, RNR. Our paths first crossed in the early 1950s when I served as chief officer under Joe's command on the *Andria*, and in the years that followed I always regarded the inimitable Joe as my maritime mentor. When he died, his wife Marion asked me to scatter his ashes at sea, and to this sad request I readily agreed.

Soon after dawn on the morning of 7 June 1978, I walked to the afterdeck of the *QE2* with my staff captain and stood, bareheaded, in the chilling headwind. We were just about half-way from Southampton to New York on the ocean crossing that Joe Woolfenden knew so well. When Joe commanded the *Carmania*, his ship's signal letters were GSJS, which everyone in Cunard knew meant 'God Save Joe's Ship'. Now, in mid-Atlantic, I whispered a quiet prayer to the Almighty for Joe himself as I consigned his last remains to an eternal tranquillity in the cool green depths. I replaced my peaked cap, gazed for a moment over the *QE2*'s swirling wake at the red-streaked eastern skies, then hurried back across the still-deserted decks to a day's duties and the steaming hot coffee awaiting me on the bridge.

On my next voyage to the United States, we carried two passengers I had hoped to dine with, show around the ship and introduce with filial pride to guests at my VIP parties. But dense midsummer fog blacked out my plans for Fred and Elsie Arnott. I saw little of my parents either going to or returning from New York, but, with their chum Harry Hayes, they called in at one of my parties to talk with some of the people enjoying cocktails while I stayed on the bridge peering into Atlantic murk. I made the last ten minutes of the party in time to see Mum – crossing the Atlantic for the first time – chatting with Harry Broccoli, of James Bond film fame. 'Glad to see you're enjoying yourself,' I said to her.

'Well, I am now,' she said, 'but earlier on I was talking to a man who said you'd run your ship into his.'

'He said what?' I gasped in surprise.

'He said you'd crashed into his ship,' replied Mum. 'But I told him his ship must have got in the way.'

'Well, thanks for your confidence in me, but I still can't think what on earth you're talking about,' I told my loyal mother. I glanced around the groups of guests in my cabin, and spotted Mr Lanzoni, of the Costa Shipping Line. I had a sudden vision of a sunny Caribbean quayside, the *Cunard Adventurer*, the Costa Line's *Carla C* and a gentle collision.

'Some sort of mechanical failure on your ship, I seem to recall,' said Mr Lanzoni, when I chatted with him a few moments later. 'I was just having a little joke with your mother about the incident.' That may have been his impression, but my mother certainly hadn't seen the funny side of the crash. Yet the bouncing of *Adventurer*'s bows into the Italian cruise liner had had an amusing sequel. As we had traipsed around the Caribbean with our pranged prow, I had sent a signal from *Adventurer* to the *QE2*: 'You may be the Queen of the Seas, but we're a little bent too.'

As the *Queen* of the oceans cut through the shimmering waters of The Solent, I saw the serene and elegant shape of Her Majesty's royal yacht *Britannia* steaming towards us. Was the Queen aboard, I wondered. My binoculars searched *Britannia*'s decks as she came to her closest point to us a half a mile distant, and my glasses caught a glimpse of someone walking on deck whom I took to be Her Majesty, looking out towards the *QE2*.

Minutes later, my supposition was confirmed. A signal from the flag officer of the royal yacht to the Master of the *QE2* was handed to me on the bridge: 'I am commanded by Her Majesty the Queen to say how pleasant it is to meet you at sea and how nice you look. Bon voyage.' I sent an immediate reply, saying, 'Thank you for your kind message. All the passengers and the ship's company send their loyal greetings. Arnott, Master *QE2*.' I learned later that Her Majesty and the Duke of Edinburgh had been on their way to the Channel Islands when they sent us their friendly felicitations.

Coincidentally, around that time I received an invitation from Buckingham Palace to attend my first garden party there. Joan and I and our youngest daughter Kate enjoyed a really

261

pleasant summer afternoon in the Palace grounds and enjoying Her Majesty's cups of tea and cucumber sandwiches.

Summer fog again shrouded the *QE2* on my next voyage to New York, and I had to postpone for twenty-four hours an interview I was scheduled to give to George Morrill of the *Reader's Digest* magazine. The following day, the mists lifted sufficiently for me to leave the bridge and talk to George. His feature, entitled 'Golden Days for an Ocean Queen', appeared in *Reader's Digest* the following May on the tenth anniversary of the *QE2*'s maiden Atlantic crossing. Quoting from *The Observer* newspaper, George reported that the first *Queen Elizabeth* and the *Queen Mary* had lost money 'like dowagers on a drunken spree', and when the *QE2* set out for New York the first time, the pessimists were again shaking their heads. But ten years on, in the words of an un-named but remarkably articulate *QE2* steward, 'Now this monarch of the oceans scoops up gold the world over.'

Reading through the advance copy of the magazine which *Reader's Digest* sent me, I wondered, like the article, about the *QE2*'s future. Is she indeed the last of her breed, whose like will never grace the world's oceans again? George Morrill had concluded that she was. I reflected that the ship would be reaping her golden harvests at sea long after my retirement, for George quoted her Chief Designer Dan Wallace, whose expert view was that the *QE2* was 'virtually ageless' and would be roaming the oceans at least until the end of the 1980s.

There is no certainty, I must point out, that the oft-repeated statement that the *QE2* is the 'last of her line' is necessarily true. In that summer of 1978, when Trafalgar House chairman, Nigel Broackes, was presented with the 'Young Businessman of the Year' award by the then Prime Minister, James Callaghan, he declared, 'There is little doubt that a *QE3* would make sense for Britain,' adding that whether it would make sense for Cunard to introduce a competitor to the *QE2* was quite another matter.

Accepting his award at London's Mansion House, Mr Broackes told his distinguished City audience: 'There may indeed never be another *QE2*, but sometimes I wonder if it wouldn't be better for Britain to subsidise the construction of another rather than subsidise still more foreign orders for low-technology cargo ships which will bring us no continuing revenues, and are bound to jeopardise British employment at sea as they inevitably compete with our own vessels. The subsidy for another *QE2* would be very large, but the ongoing yield to this country in foreign exchange and employment would be extremely high.'

It seems, then, that the chairman of the group that owns Cunard, has by no means written off the idea of another super-liner that could be cruising the world's oceans well into the twenty-first century. Amid such exciting speculation, one thing is already certain: regrettably, the man in command around the year 2000 will definitely not be Captain Robert Arnott.

But back on that foggy crossing in 1978, I also had another fine writer travelling to New York with me, the travel and cookbook author Carol Wright, who presented me with an autographed copy of her best-selling *Cunard Cookbook*. This records, in highly readable fashion, the famous recipes created and prepared by Cunard's legendary chefs on vessels ranging from the paddle steamer *Britannia*, through the golden Atlantic days of the *Berengaria*, *Mauretania* and *Queen Mary*, down to the *QE2* and the magnificent menus served at her Captain's Table, where I've entertained Carol more than once during her blue riband researches.

I liked the story Carol told me about the illustrious Cunard chef, Bill Ransom, who had catered for most of the world's top political, sporting and celluloid celebrities in his forty-plus years with the company, and persuaded many of them to sign his now priceless autograph book. Among the master chef's famous signatories were Jack Dempsey, Field Marshal Lord Montgomery, Billy Graham, Leopold Stokowski, Yehudi Menuhin, Stirling Moss and Benno Moiseiwitsch. But Chef Ransom's favourite autographed message was from the well-liked British, 'common man's' comedian Arthur Haynes. After putting away a gigantic mid-ocean gastronomic feast, all that Arthur wrote, feelingly, was: 'Thank God for Alka-Seltzer.'

Ocean skies were clearer on the return voyage from New York to Southampton, and I was able to spend a little more time on the ship's social scene. At one of my mid-Atlantic parties I entertained the forthright Senator George McGovern and his wife, Gordon Booth, the British Consul in New York, and US science-fiction writer Ray Bradbury. A prince of the Saudi royal household and his entourage had also been invited, but didn't show up. Passengers rarely turn down an invitation to the

Captain's party, but the occasional exceptions tend to be Arab princes, although I'm sure they don't intend to be discourteous. They're naturally shy people and don't like to turn their pleasantly private Atlantic crossing into any sort of an official occasion, but they sometimes pop quietly into my parties well after they've started, invariably as private individuals and not as royal statesmen.

A final midsummer party on the *QE2* was, for me, a somewhat sadder occasion. This time I was the principal guest, for I was leaving my command after two years and two months. The ship's officers presented me with a fine decanter in Waterford crystal, now a much-used memento at my Fleetwood home. Thanking my wardroom colleagues, I told them, 'To paraphrase another gentleman with close Pacific connections, whom I admired very much, "I've travelled the oceans with you, and I'll be back." ' And I was, just over a year later. But first I had to keep a date in the Caribbean with a Danish-born countess.

On 27 July 1978, I flew out to Miami, and the next day went on to St Thomas to join the blue-blooded, creamy-hulled *Cunard Countess*. Officially, I took command of her on the next day, when she had crossed the shimmering inter-island strip of Caribbean to the familiar but always breathtaking beauties of Puerto Rico's San Juan Bay. As *Countess* docked there, I scanned the harbour suspiciously, but happily, the *Carla C* was engaged on her voluptuous Latin voyagings elsewhere.

Outgoing Master of the *Countess* was Captain Doug Ridley, who now left his gentle jaunts around the Caribbean for the harsher realities of the North Atlantic, where he had been appointed relief master of the *QE2*. I inherited from Doug a 17,586-ton liner custom-built for Caribbean cruising, and as I took her out of San Juan harbour that evening, the *Countess* responded sweetly and swiftly to the finger-tip control system operated from the bridge. She surged smoothly through the broad blue rollers fringing the bay of San Juan and effortlessly attained her 20-knot cruising rhythm as we reached the wider waters of the open Caribbean.

My new command had the distinction of being built in two different countries. Her hull, superstructure and engine installation had been completed in Denmark at the Copenhagen shipyard of Burmeister & Wain, and then she had sailed under her own power to La Spezia in Italy for the fitting of the splendid staterooms, lounges, theatre, shops and convention centre under the supervision of internationally renowned Italian architect Carlo Bertolotti at the workshops of Industrie Navali Mechaniche Affine.

As a velvety tropic darkness swathed the seas, I left the *Countess*'s bridge to make my own initial tour of inspection. I chatted to some of my 700 passengers in the spectacularly spacious Galaxy Lounge, and peeped into the plush intimacy of the Club Aquarius. I looked in at the 500-seat Gemini dining arena, then climbed to the panoramic heights of the sun deck to make a non-playing incursion into the green-baize world of blackjack, roulette and jingling jackpots in the Starlight Casino. Appropriately, I ended my first-night star trek in the Splash-down Bar next to the swimming pool, where I re-fuelled with a heavenly hooch bearing the Cunard code name, Apollo Punch. It certainly carried one.

Sailing on my first Caribbean circuit with the *Countess* was a fellow-Australian, from Tasmania. Austin Fitzgerald, managing director of the celebrated Cascade Brewery, was enjoying Caribbean calm in contrast to the wilder delights of Hobart's Storm Bay. He came to my cabin to offer a friendly word of thanks for my spontaneous promotion of his company's fine brews when the *QE2* put into Hobart.

'You gave us a great boost, for free,' said Austin. 'That reception of yours was the talk of the island for weeks afterwards. When are you coming again?'

Suddenly remembering that pleasant afternoon in Hobart, I was relieved to be able to answer quite honestly, 'I haven't the remotest idea.'

A couple of days later I took the *Countess* into the deep-water harbour of Bridgetown, capital of Barbados. Although the island's name comes from the Portuguese '*los barbudos*', meaning bearded fig trees, it's as British as bacon and eggs and is often called the Little England of the Caribbean. The centre point of Bridgetown is Trafalgar Square, with a statue of Lord Nelson that is fifty years older than the one in London.

On the sheltered west side of the island is Cunard's Paradise Beach Hotel, celebrated for its water ski-ing, snorkelling and sailing. Trafalgar House group director, the Marquess of Tavistock, had been paying a commercial visit to the hotel, and that evening he came aboard the *Countess* to join me for dinner, along with Trafalgar financial director Gerry Kinally and his wife. After-dinner table talk ranged from the state of the British and American stock markets to the political dispute brewing up on a nearby Caribbean island. 'Oh, they're always at loggerheads over there,' said one of my locally based guests.

'You mean they're throwing hot pitch over each other?' I asked innocently. My seven table guests looked at me blankly, and I explained that the loggerhead was an old-time sailing-ship tool used for spreading pitch between the hull's wooden seams. It was warm, wearisome work, and fractious sailors occasionally used the loggerheads to paste each other with hot pitch. Hence the phrase 'being at loggerheads'.

I don't know how much my guests appreciated having that little slice of sea-lore tossed into the conversation, but at least it deflected the talk away from the effervescent issues of island politics. 'Any more language lessons, Captain?' smiled one of my brandy-sipping companions.

'Well, you would be amazed just how many of our every-day terms come straight from sailor-talk,' I replied. 'Most of them are pretty obvious, such as "high and dry", "under the weather", and "taking the wind out of somebody's sails". But did you know that the word "buccaneer" evolved out here in the Caribbean?' Shaking heads indicated they didn't, and I went on to recall the swashbuckling days when the islands sheltered an assortment of pirate rogues. These lads had huge appetites, both for the cargoes of gold that sailed past and for the meat of the islands' wild cattle. The fighting Frenchmen among the pirates used a '*boucan*' – French for a 'grill' – to barbecue the unfortunate beasts, and thus the term 'boucan-eer' came to mean a sea pirate.

By way of a final encore, and to bring matters right up to date, I mentioned that the long-running sequence of British film comedies in the *Carry On* series drew that part of their title straight from the mentionable portion of bosuns' language on the old square riggers. In those days, when a spanking wind-powered clip across the oceans was all important, 'carry on' was a specific order not to shorten sail, but to carry as much canvas as the vessel could safely bear. Stars of the fantastically success-ful *Carry On* series such as Barbara Windsor, Kenneth Williams, Kenneth Connor, Jim Dale and Joan Sims perhaps never knew, or even cared, that they were the modern beneficiaries of a linguistic property created by sailormen more than one hundred years ago.

At this point I felt that my marine instruction period had lasted quite long enough and I called my steward over to bring another round of liqueurs by way of reward for my after-dinner friends' forbearance.

The Marquis meanwhile invited me to lunch the next day in the island of St Lucia, where his wife was staying with their two young sons and their nanny. The Marchioness came aboard when the *Countess* reached the palmy haven of Castries harbour, and I took the whole Tavistock family and the nanny on a ship walkabout. When the Tavistocks arrived back at their ducal family seat at Woburn Abbey, Bedfordshire, they sent me a note of thanks saying how much they had enjoyed visiting the *Countess*. As I read the little handwritten message in my cabin, I felt its sentiments were reciprocated by everyone who had met the family during their brief shipboard interlude.

On my first leave from the *Countess*, I flew out to the Mediterranean to stay with Joan, my son Roger and youngest daughter Kate at Harry Secombe's beautiful villa on Majorca's eastern seaboard. When we flew into the holiday island's Palma airport, waiting to meet us were Harry's friends Cyril Mitchell and his wife. 'Mitch' is a former Epsom jockey and racehorse trainer who retired to Majorca when his son took over his racing stables. Cyril drove us out to the villa on the eastern coast of the island near Son Servera, and for two weeks I simply stretched out in the sun, or pottered round the island in the Morris 1300 which Harry had generously left, along with a short note pinned to the dashboard which said, 'Welcome aboard, Bob. Hope you all enjoy your holiday, and my little Morris. Next time, I'll leave you the Rolls.' The four Arnotts indeed enjoyed the holiday magic of Majorca, and as an amateur astronomer, I was pleasantly and completely surprised on the evening of 16 September 1978 when a gradual darkness began to black out the bright moonlight. Sitting back in a comfortable chair on Harry's verandah, I watched a total eclipse of the moon, set against crystal-clear, velvet skies.

Back in England, I persuaded our friends Bernard and Lorna Crisp to travel north to stay with us and take a tour along Blackpool Promenade to see 'The Greatest Free Show on Earth' – Blackpool's autumn Illuminations. After driving

Bernard and his wife along the spectacular miles of fantastic seafront lighting effects, Joan and I took our friends to Blackpool Opera House to see the summer show featuring lovely Scottish songstress Moira Anderson. Afterwards, we went backstage to talk to Moira, whom I had last seen on the *QE2*'s South Pacific cruise.

'You've been my host at so many Captain's Table dinners on the *QE2*,' said Moira, 'but tonight it's my turn.' Midnight found us tucking into roast beef at Ashley Hall, a lovely house set in spacious grounds in the Fylde countryside near Blackpool. Moira rented a cottage there for the summer season from Jimmy Porter, local property magnate and owner of the Hall. To celebrate the end of Moira's Blackpool season he laid on a fabulous early morning dinner for us, rounded off by fresh cream and strawberries served from a giant silver bowl. Amazingly, Moira's eyes still sparkled after two lengthy shows that evening. 'Have you noticed, Bob,' she said, 'that we're eating on Ashley Hall's finest Royal Albert crockery. That's because here the floor never ever jumps up at you half-way through dinner. How is our beautiful ship?'

The *QE2*, I told Moira, was temporarily under new management, but would wait out there on the oceans until we returned. On that promissory note, Joan, Lorna, Bernard and I bade a 4-a.m. farewell to Ashley Hall and Miss Moira Anderson.

But the *QE2* didn't wait. She came out into the Caribbean to meet me in Barbados on a balmy Wednesday morning in January 1979. For the *Countess*, it was her usual weekly cruising call at Bridgetown, but when her royal sister made her grand entrance into the holiday harbour, Barbados suddenly became Cunard carnival-land. More than 1000 passengers from the *QE2* and perhaps half that number from the *Countess* flooded into Bridgetown's already bustling waterfront streets, and a rollicking boarding party from the *QE2* invaded my quarters on the *Countess*.

These cocktail pirates included Vic Arbuckle, first captain of *Cunard Ambassador* and his wife Muriel, former *QE2* captain Bill Law and his sister Eleanor, 'Lulu' Edwards, our friends Elgin and Helen Brooks from Toledo, Ohio, the *QE2*'s social director Bryan Vickers, Bill Summers of Garrards, the royal jewellers, and his wife, and Liverpudlian Father Billy Mills, probably the most popular chaplain ever to serve on the *QE2*, who dispenses a judicious blend of cheerful friendship and spiritual comfort to his Catholic flock and everyone else.

'I have a request from Her Majesty over there,' said Father Billy, sweeping his priestly arm in the general direction of the *QE2*. 'When, she desires to know, are you coming back?'

'Well, Father,' I smiled, 'I'm afraid I can't manage it today, but I'll be along later in the year.' And I was.

In their regular rounds of the Caribbean islands, the men and women who work on the Cunard cruise ships build up friendly and rewarding relationships with the local folk. The crew of the *Countess*, for instance, took a particular interest in the poorer children of Barbados, and not long before her Bridgetown rendezvous with the *QE2*, the *Countess* had been transformed into a Christmas wonderland party for some one hundred youngsters from Barbadian children's homes.

For months before the big day, veteran *Countess* barkeeper Bob Fitzgerald had spent all his free time in Barbados, visiting various charity homes with Olga Lopes-Searle, a local radio personality, to find out just what was needed most by the island's impoverished children. The answer turned out to be clothing, shoes and toys, in that order. Bob and the whole *Countess* crew then set about raising cash by holding raffles, bingo parties and direct collections, and by Christmas of 1978, we had accumulated $6000. That bought one hundred youngsters a full set of clothing and a pair of shoes each, plus dollies and dress-making sets for the girls and train sets or model kits for the boys.

On his rounds of the homes, Bob Fitzgerald had asked each youngster just what he or she would like, and at the *Countess* party Father Christmas handed over the exact items requested on each little list. That human touch was achieved only after Bob and his crew helpers made dozens of searches of island shops in off-duty hours, seeking bargains, not only in Barbados but also in Venezuela, Grenada, St Lucia, St Thomas and Puerto Rico.

On party day Mrs Lopes-Searle came aboard with the youngsters, and we also welcomed Lady Ward, wife of Governor-General Sir Deighton Ward. In her 'thank you' speech, Mrs Lopes-Searle made everyone on the ship feel it had all been very worthwhile, declaring 'Of all the things that have happened to these children in the past, and whatever might become of them in the future, they will never forget this day of happiness on the *Cunard Countess*.' It didn't end there. With cash left over from the presents, we were also able to buy radio and stereo equipment for the children's homes.

After Christmas, it was the season of charter cruises around the Caribbean. We had the American Grocers, who brought tons of fresh fruit and vegetables on board, the American Floral Society, who arrived with trucks full of flowers and shrubs, and the Spanish Roca ceramic sanitary-ware company who brought only their brochures. Roca were setting up factories to manufacture toilet sets, baths and washbasins in the Dominican Republic, and although the country's capital Santo Domingo wasn't on the *Countess*'s usual itinerary, I took her there for a first-time visit. President Silvestre Guzman and his wife came aboard with members of their government and with diplomatic representatives from the United States and Britain. I brought out my stock of gift goblets for the occasion and received an impressive national plaque from the President.

Later that week, I welcomed a second President to the *Countess*. Jean-Claude Duvalier, otherwise known as 'Baby Doc', the President of Haiti, joined us in the harbour of Port-au-Prince, and I took the amiable young President on a fast tour of the *Countess* before he got down to business with the Roca chiefs on the matter of founding factories on his island. A black, tropical rainstorm burst over the *Countess* as Baby Doc walked with me round the ship. Chatting mostly in French, the language of the island, the President told me, 'Two years ago we had a massive famine here, and lost many of our population through starvation and thirst. Now we're getting back to normal, and I'm anxious to restore our industry. Already, we make baseballs, brassières and electronic goods for export, as well as growing coffee, sugar, cocoa and cotton. Now, we have this fine chance to make pottery. I'm delighted you brought these gentlemen to my country.' My French wasn't quite up to explaining that the planned pottery wasn't of the Wedgwood variety, but no doubt my friends from the Roca company went into that delicate aspect when they entertained the President later that evening.

Back to the regular cruising rounds of the islands, I was invited out to lunch in Barbados by Paul Foster, who looks after our tour requirements there. We ate at the Bridgetown Gentlemen's Club, one of the few male hideaways in the western world still not penetrated by women. The house rule of 'men only' means what it says, and the club's rich, timber-panelled walls enclose one of the last shrines of peaceful masculine dining, wining and gossip. Tom Castledine, the new manager of the island's Paradise Beach hotel, Paul Foster and I enjoyed a fine lunch of turtle soup, flying fish roes with vegetables, and fresh strawberries. Even the simple male pleasure of quaffing a pint of cold beer is steeped in tradition at the Bridgetown club. The bar tankards are solid silver, presented by the officers of British warships that called regularly at the island up to the end of the last century. Each tankard bears the name of one of the men o' war on its base, but the beer arrives so chilled that a fine frost completely covers the embossed motif and, before the name can be read, the white masking has to be wiped away. Naturally, you can't do this safely without first drinking the beer. I reckoned the whole elaborate ritual had been evolved as a thirst-inducer among a club membership with a powerful naval tradition. The system still works admirably.

Just a week later, the *Countess* arrived in Barbados again. My own cricketing days were virtually over, but I still enjoyed watching a good game and was thrilled to be invited to the one-day international between the West Indies and Kerry Packer's Australian side. I had lunch in the Bridgetown pavilion with the players, and chatted to the Chappell brothers, Viv Richards, Clive Lloyd and Andy Roberts. It was a magnificent, closely fought match with Australia just failing by seven runs to catch the West Indies total of 240 over 45 overs.

Towards the end of May 1979, I delivered the *Countess* to the Curaçao shipyards for the fitting of a new engine and the replacement of part of her sun deck. Some months earlier, a connecting rod in one of the four diesel engines had decided to make a break for it, and had crashed right through the side of its engine casing. Now the shipyard was completely replacing the seven-cylinder engine and, while the *Countess* was in dock, her Number One deck was being extended and switched from a metal surface to wooden plank decking. During the first two years of her voyages, as sunbathers stretched out on the deck in sizzling Caribbean sunshine, the decking beneath their brown bodies – originally constructed of steel and covered with composition – had gradually started to crack. Our experience had shown that traditional wooden planking handled the hot sun

271

better, and so the *Countess* was going back to timber. I stayed in Willemstad's Intercontinental Hotel while the work was under way.

On the night of 21 May a call came through from Joan to tell me that our first grandson had been born. Our daughter Gill presented her husband John with the 7lb 11oz Andrew Phillipson at a nursing home in Kilwinning in Scotland. I promised Joan that I would try to be home for the christening, and managed to get leave to travel to Ayrshire for little Andrew's baptism day.

On my first cruise from San Juan after I joined the ranks of happy grandfathers, British comedian Les Dawson and his wife were among the first people taking the Caribbean airs on the *Countess*'s new sun deck. Les wasn't doing a shipboard show; he and his wife were paying passengers. Prophetically, Les said to me one morning, 'Now don't forget, Captain Bob, if ever you write your memoirs, say that Les Dawson bought his own ticket when he travelled on your ship. You can also say he's a jolly fellow off-stage who makes no charge for the clever, sophisticated and totally original jokes he tells his fellow sufferers, er, passengers.'

At the beginning of September 1979, Hurricane David swept across the Caribbean and tore up buildings, smashed island piers, and flattened crops. A heavy, oily atmosphere followed by a freshening wind and torrential rain had warned me that trouble was heading our way at nearly one hundred miles an hour, but I had had even earlier omens from our radar and from satellite photographs. David was tearing over the whole of the West Indies, but fortunately I was able to sail the ship well behind his furious frontage and so avoid the sort of damage to the *Countess* that was being inflicted on the hapless islands.

Our next cruise was a positioning voyage to Port Everglades for a series of charters by the Motorcraft Division of Ford Motor Company. We were due to embark from St Croix in the American Virgin Islands, but Hurricane David had flattened the embarkation area at St Croix, swiftly transferring much of the island's landing pier out into the Caribbean. So we switched our passengers to St Thomas, also somewhat devastated but with landing facilities intact. Damage round the islands was so comprehensive that I wondered if our next port would be open, but then we received a radio message from a private yacht moored in the harbour of Puerto Plata in the Dominican Republic that dashing David had forgotten to call there. 'No problems at all here,' reported the yacht's skipper, so I decided to head the *Countess* there. Remarkably, Puerto Plata harbour was undamaged apart from a few flattened hoardings, yet Hurricane David had shown no mercy to other major population centres throughout the entire island of Hispaniola.

Hurricanes are no recent innovation in the West Indies and, within days, the resilient island folk had bounced back into business. For most of the remaining months of 1979, the *Countess* operated around the Bahamas as a floating incentives centre for Ford dealerships in the United States. Each week, three dealership districts selected from the whole country came out cruising with us. Naturally, the first winners came from Texas.

All of the Ford cruises were between Port Everglades and Freeport and Nassau in the Bahamas, and this gave me the opportunity to visit Freeport's Lucaya Country Club with our shipping agents Malcolm and Valerie Goodyear. Val challenged me to a round of golf, and I decided I would be easy on her and not beat her too harshly. It didn't happen that way. I was thrashed. Next time I called in at the Bridgetown Gentlemen's Club on Barbados that was one golf game I forgot to mention to my cronies of the silver tankards.

In October, I found myself selling the Cunard Company at the Travel Age West trade show in San Diego. Cunard were running an exhibition stand in the city's huge convention hall, and as company salesmen handed out leaflets to the thousands of visitors thronging around, I talked about life at sea on a Cunarder to anyone who cared to listen. I also reached a rather wider audience in a series of radio interviews. Some of my interviewers took the line that the duties of the Master of a modern liner are rather like being the mayor of a travelling city, and they asked me to describe my 'marine mayoralty'.

'Well for a start, I'm no politician, I wasn't elected and I hate windbag speeches' seemed a reasonable sort of initial response to that analogy, although I did admit that there are some parallels particularly in the United States where the mayor usually has more feudal powers than his counterpart in Britain. In addition, each evening after a hard day on the Cunard stand, we ate in a different restaurant, and the excellent dishes served

273

up in San Diego hotel restaurants reminded me that ocean liner captains can generally take their pick of the world's eating spots, a privilege not usually enjoyed by land-based mayors.

To prepare the way for my own return to the world circuit of centres of gourmet delight, I ordered my faithful old trunk to be shipped from the *Cunard Countess* in San Juan to the Passenger Terminal Building on New York's Hudson River. On 21 December 1979, the *QE2* was due to leave her familiar West Side berth to transport more than 1500 fortunate fugitives away from winter shivers and out to a Caribbean Christmas. The day before the *Queen* was due to make her exotic exodus, a New York cab drove me to the Hudson quayside. I looked up at the splendid silhouette towering across the skyline, acknowledged salutes from a couple of young officers who almost collided with me on the gangway, then took an inter-deck lift to the Master's quarters of the *QE2*.

Chapter 29

The proud and patriotic citizens of Venezuela will tell you unhesitatingly that their country, including its Caribbean islands, covers 570,000 square miles and that it has more than 1000 rivers, including the great Orinoco. But the inhabitants of the coastal strip fronting the capital of Caracas occasionally have problems with simpler statistics.

For instance, when I took the *QE2* into La Guaira harbour on her Christmas cruise around the palm-fringed islands of the Caribbean, I suspended my healthy suspicion of on-board open-house hospitality in the interests of the festive season, and agreed to a VIP reception for the members of local high society. The alleged reason for the party was the opening of a new liner berth in the harbour. Port authorities had told us sixty '*convivados*' would be along. Guests and gatecrashers were indivisible in the 165 who showed up. The spacious Q4 Room bulged with voracious Venezuelan aristocrats stripping our stewards' trays of canapés, cheese straws and chicken legs, long before their bearers could reach and replenish the blitzed buffet tables. Cargoes of drinks were similarly decimated. I blamed the whole happy shambles on two fateful factors: we were down South American way, and I should have known better.

In contrast to the tumult in Q4, the cheerful chit-chat among guests at my Captain's Table seemed almost taciturn. The American couple, Mr and Mrs Charles Pecker, spoke blithely of their fashion fad of always dressing exactly alike, often in fabulous outfits. If Mrs Pecker wears a bright, flowered dress, Charles puts on a dinner jacket made of identical material; a vivid red tartan on Charles evokes an identical response from his wife. 'It's our particular thing in life,' Charles told me. 'We get a hell of a kick out of wearing a oneness in clothes. And why shouldn't we?'

'I can't think of a single reason,' I assured my duplicated diners.

275

More than once I caught another of my table guests staring at me over dinner, but he wasn't behaving badly. Bearded royal painter Bernard Hailstone was casting his professional eye over my features for a proposed pastel portrait. His commissioned paintings of Her Majesty Queen Elizabeth II, Sir Winston Churchill, Sir Laurence Olivier, Princess Anne, Prince Charles, Lee Remick as Jennie Jerome, President Carter and many other international celebrities had already brought him world acclaim. During the Second World War, Bernard Hailstone had been one of Britain's Official War Artists, with the rank of captain, and he had painted Lord Mountbatten and the Allied Chiefs of Staff. But portraits in pastels were a comparatively new medium for Bernard and I was among the first of his pastel subjects. As well as sidelong glances over the hors d'oeuvres, Bernard managed to fit in one or two proper sittings with me while he was on board, and the finished portrait now hangs in my Fleetwood home.

On a subsequent cruise, Bernard overheard Joan say that she didn't feel the picture was quite 'me'. 'Well, Joan,' said Bernard firmly, 'you must accept that those of us who haven't known Captain Bob since he was a boy, as you have, are quite likely to view him in a totally different way from yourself, particularly in the matter of character interpretation.' The point must have hit home with Joan, for she has already completed her own preliminary portrait sittings with our prestigious pastellist.

On the run-up cruise to the *QE2*'s 1980 world circuit, two other gold-braided captains joined me on the bridge. Captain D. Thorbjorn-Hauge, Master of the *Norway* (formerly that Atlantic leviathan, the *France*) and Captain Lingess, vice-president of the Norwegian-Caribbean Line, came along on our West Indies cruise in early January to see exactly how Cunard's ocean queen went about earning her living. The two master mariners showed up on the bridge for the *QE2*'s arrivals at and departures from Curaçao, La Guaira, Grenada, Barbados, St Thomas and New York, essentially to take notes on just how these were accomplished with a vessel as massive as the *QE2*.

The three of us got on famously. One result of Cunard's hospitality to the two Norwegians was that Captain Thorbjorn-Hauge, senior master of the line, extended a standing invitation to me to join him on the bridge of the *Norway* which, as the *France*, had been the last of the Gallic giants to operate a regular transatlantic service. As with many of the hundreds of other invitations that have come my way on the *QE2*, I haven't yet been able to accept.

I had a pleasant drink with my Norwegian-Caribbean Line guests just before we docked in New York. Then it was time to go ashore to meet Joan, who had just flown in from Britain for the start of an adventure ranging across the waters of the world. A tranquil desert meeting with the Sphinx of Giza in Egypt and a sea-battle with the Russian Bear were destined to be entered in my Captain's log along the way.

I took the *QE2* out of New York on the icily clear evening of 17 January 1980 and asked my steward to make sure that my white tropical uniforms were ready for our arrival at the warm-water, paradise ports of the Caribbean, the Pacific, the Indian Ocean, the Red Sea and the Mediterranean. As we followed the sun from Port Everglades towards South America, my Chief Officer John Hall reported: 'Sir, there's a dangerous stowaway at large on the ship. It's a boa constrictor.'

It appeared that one of our crewmen had decided to treat his pet boa constrictor to a world cruise. He called the huge serpent 'Basil' and smuggled it into the *QE2*'s crews' quarters complete with a live white rat intended for Basil Boa's first Sunday lunch out at sea. Our investigation revealed that as soon as Venezuela's offshore breezes wafted over Basil, he sensed he was within hissing distance of his native South America, and he at once made up his mind that he would rather go tree-climbing with his cousins ashore than snooze around the world in a *QE2* cabin. He made a break for freedom, taking with him the white rat with whom, in defiance of serpentine standing orders, he had become firm friends.

But Chief Officer Hall's ruthlessly efficient snake sleuths tracked down first the white rat and then his fleeing buddy, and both Basil Boa and his albino accomplice were taken into custody and sentenced to immediate banishment from the *QE2*. They did a dual dive into the blue waters of the Caribbean and struck out strongly towards the not-too-distant Venezuelan coast. I hope they made it.

A Caribbean princess waited in enforced attendance on the *Queen* of the oceans when we made our second grand entrance within a month into the sunny harbour of La Guaira. The cruise liner *Sun Princess* had arrived earlier that morning, but had been kept out in the bay until the *QE2* had docked before she was allowed into her own berth.

'Sorry the port people kept you waiting,' I apologised to Captain John Young, Master of the *Sun Princess*, when he came over for lunchtime gin and tonics.

'Don't apologise, Bob,' he replied, 'because watching the most famous ship in the world sail so serenely into harbour was a sight my passengers won't easily forget. It was worth the wait.'

At sailing time that afternoon, I headed the *QE2* smartly out of port towards the Dutch Antilles. As I vividly remembered the recent mass Venezuelan visitation onto the *QE2*, I felt it prudent to make a prompt exodus. After a day at Curaçao, we were scheduled to make the tight transit through the Panama Canal out into the Pacific. The President of the Republic of Panama, Dr Aristedes Royo, came aboard with his wife and children and a host of government ministers as we entered the canal. 'Do you know, Captain,' said the remarkably youthful head of state, 'this will be the very first time I have been the whole way through the canal?'

'It's appropriate, then,' I said, by way of boosting Britain, 'that your Excellency's inaugural crossing of one of the world's most vital waterways should be in the most celebrated ship afloat.'

That was my only speech of the day, for as the *QE2* edged her vast hull through the canal locks, often only inches away from the sides, I stayed on the bridge with my Staff Captain Harvey Smith to oversee the delicate and demanding operation. Below, Joan and Harvey's wife Christine hosted a luncheon party for our government guests and senior canal officials. This was an apt illustration of how officers' wives at sea can effectively take over some of their husbands' ever-expanding range of social duties.

On this occasion the girls were rewarded on the spot for their services: President Royo handed them each a silver 20-Balbao coin as a memento of his visit to the ship. 'I thought silver would be more practical than a plaque,' said the smiling young president. 'If you need to, you can always spend my gift. This is one country where we don't issue paper money.' So far, Joan hasn't needed to spend her presidential souvenir and neither, I believe, has Christine. Both Harvey and I are still regularly earning British paper currency.

Just 470 passengers were making the whole world cruise, including Americans Mr and Mrs Guiser who had paid around £100,000 to watch the panorama of the planet from the sumptuous comfort of the Queen Elizabeth suite. On my deck walkabouts and cabin parties I came across many of the faithful *QE2* world cruise *habitués*. Mrs Gladys 'Fashion Queen' Solomon had installed a vast and varied wardrobe in one of her two round-the-world suites, and in residence at their favourite staterooms were the regular world rovers 'Lulu' Edwards and Ann Brooks. Marjorie Tomayo had missed the ship in La Guaira, perhaps because of our prompt departure, but she had flown out to join us in Curaçao. Joe Loss and his band were nightly putting our passengers 'In the Mood' (Joe's famous signature tune) and Joan was already fighting a running battle with seasickness. I got the feeling that I had seen the whole show in the same fabulous theatre just about a year earlier.

Yet each year's performance was different. This time, our annual bomb scare happened in Honolulu. A phone-in maniac threatened: 'There's a bomb right underneath the *QE2*. It will blow her out of the harbour.' Someone suggested we should send for Jack Lord from *Hawaii Five-O*, but the port coastguards ruled that divers were a better bet. They sent a team of frogmen down to the ship, but with grateful thanks I turned down the services of those rubber-suited gentlemen. Holding up a ship the size of the *QE2* is a mightily expensive business, although of course that wasn't the main reason I decided to sail on schedule. Perhaps through a Master's sixth sense, I was convinced we were dealing with a Honolulu hoaxer. Thank goodness I was right.

The Pacific wasn't at all anxious to make our passage from Hawaii to Japan a tranquil transit. For thousands of miles, massive, spuming water-mountains smashed across the bows and decks of the ship as she ploughed resolutely across the heaving ocean towards Yokohama. Three days out into the Pacific I went along to the storm-tossed birthday party of one of our more obsessive world cruisers.

White-haired widow Hilda Bishop, from Brighton, England, isn't one of the wealthy dowagers who float around the world on the *QE2*. Since her husband died, Hilda has had to think carefully before taking even a single £1 note out of her old leather purse. How, then, has this likeable lady managed to make several world cruises on the most luxurious liner of them all? She's played the market with her sole asset – the house in which she lives.

Hilda's husband had left her the quite handsome property where they had shared their lives for many years, and when she had emerged from her grief, Hilda decided to turn the house into cash and see something of the world. She sold her home astutely, bought a smaller property, and used the surplus from the sale to buy herself a ticket on the *QE2*. She had repeated this fiscal ploy several times with the help of a generally rising British property market, and now, after her newest coup, she was sailing with us as far as Sydney, then flying back to her latest house.

'Oh, do come in, Captain Bob. I am glad you were able to make my party,' said Hilda when I arrived at her cabin. 'We thought the storms might keep you on the bridge.'

'Fog, yes, but I don't call this a storm,' I replied.

'But where's Joan?' asked Hilda, disappointed. 'I was looking forward to giving her a piece of birthday cake.'

'Somehow, I don't think at this moment she'd be able to eat it,' I said. 'Let's just say she's confined by the storm to her cabin. Joan sends her warmest wishes to you all for a very happy birthday celebration.'

Later, I recorded a message which Hilda now uses as an introduction to her charity slide lecture based on her *QE2* world cruises. She has raised hundreds of pounds for cancer research by putting on her travel talks at fifty pence a head (including a cup of tea) in Brighton community halls. Recently, a letter from Hilda arrived at my Fleetwood home. 'Dear Captain Bob and Joan,' she wrote, 'I've just had an audience of 150 at Rottingdean Red Cross headquarters. They were thrilled to hear your voice, but I'm afraid I won't be hearing it myself any more on the *QE2*. I've not been too well, but also property values seem to be static. But we've had some great times on your wonderful ship, haven't we?'

The Pacific hurled its worst waves at the *QE2* for another twenty-four hours. A note from Joan's diary for 9 February 1980, reads: 'Fourth day at sea on way to Yokohama. Weather appalling. Ship goes up and down like a perpetual seesaw, and every so often does a sort of corkscrew twist. Whole vessel shudders as though in anguish. We certainly are.'

Some of the *QE2*'s senior officers were seasick for the first time in their lives under the non-stop pulverising inflicted by the ocean. Pale green faces packed my morning service on Sunday, 10 February, but prayers anxiously whispered for the Pacific to be urgently restored to sanity achieved no instant answer and strong winds still howled across the seas. But that evening the *QE2*'s battered bows broke through into quieter waters. Hundreds of our passengers and crew were suddenly stricken with attacks of appetite. With faces restored to healthier shades of white, they mounted ravenous invasions of the *QE2*'s recently depopulated dining arenas.

Our agent in Yokohama, Michael Lewis, laid on a fine sukiyaki meal for Joan and myself on the evening we docked in Japan. We took along Christine and Harvey Smith, Chief Engineer John Grant and his wife Dorothy, our vice-president of operations Ian Borland, while Mike Lewis brought his American wife Ci Ci. After days of dancing the 'Pacific bounce', we really relished the delicious Kōbe beef slices stir-fried with fresh vegetables in a sort of wok right on our table. Saki flowed freely in the Suehiro Steakhouse – the oldest in Japan – as we rediscovered the joys of dry-land dining.

Before we sailed for Manila next day the Mayor of Yokohama came aboard. He told me, through an interpreter, 'We're going to build a bridge across the harbour, but we've made sure it will be high enough for your excellent ship to pass through. We are telling you this so that you will come to see us again.' I promised him that we would be back, and asked him to make sure that the city engineers realised that the *QE2* was the height of a thirteen-storey office block. 'You bet' was the short translation of Mr Mayor's answer, but so far I haven't returned with the *QE2* to check out that he passed on that statistic.

On the peaceful Pacific passage to Manila, Joan gave me an unexpected hug when I returned to our quarters for lunch. 'Bob, darling,' she said, 'this year you remembered St Valentine.'

I looked blankly for a moment, then saw the huge card and box of chocolates displayed on the central table. 'Why, er, yes,' I murmured in appropriate embarrassment. Later, I discovered the identity of Joan's anonymous admirer. Cunard was the name. I can keep a secret.

Switchback seas again hit the *QE2* on the cruise strip between Manila and Hong Kong, but by now most people aboard were becoming reasonably immune to the Grand National flavour of our ocean course. Ship's shows, exotic eating, disco and quick, quick, slow dancing, flirting, loving and playing the wheel all flourished in luxurious safety from the stormy world outside the *QE2*'s steel plating. I made a broadcast to the British sector of that world with a satellite-link phone call direct to TV's *Onedin Line* Captain Peter Gilmore, who was opening the Birmingham Boat Show. In picture-postcard style, I told everyone at the vast exhibition centre: 'We're having a wonderful time out here in the China Sea. Wish you were here. Have a very successful show.' Across the planet, reception was loud and clear.

It was Chinese New Year when the *QE2* moved through the still-sleeping denizens of Hong Kong harbour to reach the quayside at five o'clock on the morning of 18 February 1980. The occasion was something like Hogmanay in Scotland, and there were lots of private celebrations with many Chinese-owned offices, shops and restaurants staying tightly closed.

That evening Joan and I had to eat Korean style since the Chinese restaurants were still closed. With Harvey and Christine Smith we drove through dark streets of shut-down eating houses to the bright lights of the Korean House in Kowloon. It was a CIY (cook-it-yourself) meal – the fashion in many Korean establishments. We sat round a candlelit table with a hot grill plate sited in the centre, while Joan and Christine cooked up splendid barbecued pork, shrimps, tripe and half a dozen succulent Oriental vegetables. It was hard work for the girls, but a refreshing change from more formal shipboard menus. Harvey and I sipped cold beer as the colourful platefuls came our way. Such impromptu excellence on the part of our cooks deserved a grateful liquid recognition. 'What will you have to drink?' I asked.

'Well, I think a gin sling would go down very nicely after all that,' said Joan.

'And one for me, please,' added Christine.

Our waiter brought the strangest-looking gin slings I had ever seen. 'Tastes like cough mixture,' complained Joan. 'Ugh,' was Christine's comment. My on-the-spot enquiries showed that our Koreans didn't understand what we meant by 'gin-sling';

they thought we meant a nauseous nectar based on a liquid tincture of their famous ginseng root.

'You ask for two ginsengs – we give you them,' said the Korean House's slightly affronted manager. Our complaint collapsed into floods of laughter.

For its size, Hong Kong must be one of the most intensely covered territories in the world in the realms of newspapers, magazines, radio and television. I spent much of our second day in the colony giving interviews to a pleasant succession of journalists seeking new angles on the ship and its interesting itinerants. I talked about the *QE2*'s role as the world leader in passenger shipping, and discussed one or two of our world travellers.

Comedian Dickie Henderson, son of the famous music-hall monologue specialist Nosmo King, was now a regular *QE2* passenger and performer who merited media attention. So, too, did our American couple 'Happy' Franklin and his wife Frances. Happy's main pastime outside his flourishing commercial enterprises was buying his wife breathtakingly beautiful jewellery, and she had almost as many permutations of jewellery as Gladys Solomon had with clothes.

'Is the famous Gladys with you again this cruise?' asked the reporters.

'Would we come without her?' I replied. 'She's probably waiting to talk to you right now as you leave the ship.' I always try to maintain that sort of friendly informality between the gentlemen and ladies of the Press and myself. Far better, I believe, than handing out a mass of hackneyed statistics.

Having talked to journalists for most of the day, I was delighted when Ann Brooks invited Joan and me to one Chinese restaurant that had stayed open for the *QE2*'s visit, and that evening we took the Star Ferry across the bay to the Mandarin Hotel. Our fellow guests included Gwynneth and Dickie Henderson, the Franklins, and Christine and Harvey Smith. Frances Franklin's off-boat jewellery was decidedly subdued. 'It's only on the *QE2* that it's safe to wear a fortune in diamonds,' declared Frances – a comment I've heard from many of the world's wealthiest ladies.

The meal, in the Man-wah room at the Mandarin, was memorable. We started out with shark's fin soup, followed by Peking duck wrapped in petalled spring onions, duck meat with ribs of Chinese cabbage in a subtle sauce, crab claws in vinegar and ginger sauce, plus minced quail rolled in lettuce with plum sauce, chicken in edible rice paper, beef with taro root, fried rice and noodles – and for those whose stamina was still holding out, a delicious dessert of hot almond cream. I estimated the *QE2* took on a sizeable extra tonnage when our group, lavishly laced with Moet Chandon, returned aboard at around half past midnight. Fortunately, we were not due to sail for another thirty-six hours.

The next afternoon Joan, Christine and Jean Vickers, the ship's social director's wife, drove out on a sightseeing tour of the island. They ascended the sharp slopes of Victoria Mountain to the Peak area, where the wealthier residents of Hong Kong pay upwards of a million dollars for their naturally air-cooled houses, where average temperatures, at 1300 feet above the bay, are some seven degrees cooler than on the sweltering streets below. And the layers of hill houses are a fair measure of social standing in Hong Kong – the higher the residence, the more substantial is the owner's wealth and importance.

From the Peak, the girls drove to Aberdeen, the village of the boat people on the ocean side of the island. Scottish sailors gave Aberdeen its distinctly un-Chinese name, and it's the site of the original Hong Kong, where 60,000 Chinese fisherfolk live out their whole lives on the water. An old superstition among them is that they will become sick if they move ashore, but a more cogent reason for living afloat is that there's no rent to pay out on the boats. The cheerful, hospitable boat families may not be the richest of Hong Kong's residents but the *QE2*'s tourists often tell me that they feel that the carefree, fish-fed way of life of the Chinese Aberdonians has a uniquely attractive escapist appeal.

Out at sea the next evening on the way to Singapore, Joan wore a matching set of diamonds priced at £110,000 for a Queen's Grill dinner party. I know the exact figure because, as she was dressing for dinner, Joan handed me the price ticket and said, 'Take care of this, please, Bob.' Even forty years at sea doesn't offer any sort of training against such shocks. It was only when Joan explained that she meant me to look after the price tag and not pay it that my face recovered from an instant attack of anaemia. Apparently, Bill Summers, jeweller to Her Majesty Queen Elizabeth, had asked Joan to 'model' the diamonds for his company during the evening.

Before dinner, at a Queen's Room reception, I welcomed all the passengers who had joined the ship in Hong Kong, and then Joan and I went on to the Q4 Room where the ship's 'The Shop on Board' together with Mr and Mrs Summers were giving a cocktail party, the shop girls also modelling some of Garrard's jewellery. Someone at the party remarked, 'Look how Bob gazes at Joan after all their years together. It's a nice tribute to marriage.' Perhaps it was, but actually my eyes were sharply focused on the glittering display adorning my beloved. I'm sure my solicitude had something to do with Joan's request that I should 'take care' of the price tag reposing in my pocket.

As the *QE2* skirted the warm seas at the southern fringes of Asia, a new team of lecturers, singers and dancers came on board to interest and entertain our passengers between their shore explorations of Singapore, Colombo and Bombay. Arthur Schlesinger talked of his days of destiny as adviser to John F. Kennedy. Peter Gordeno and his dazzling dancers kicked their way through the Indian Ocean, and piano duettists Rostal and Schaefrer provided a feast of keyboard artistry. Max Jaffa, Jean Grayson and Vincent Billingham recreated musical moments that brought youthful magic to the *QE2*'s mature majority. Joe Loss and his orchestra beat out their own distinctive blend of dance band rhythm, and a fabulous young singer, new to the *QE2*, soothingly swayed appreciative audiences towards the view that world cruises held more subtle pleasures than sun, sea and fine food. Demure and completely delightful, Iris Williams enchanted her listeners, including Joan and myself, with tones as deep and warm as the exotic ocean through which we were sailing.

While the *QE2* was making her first voyage through the Gulf of Aden and into the Red Sea, I visited the Princess Lounge birthday party of one of our more frequent world cruisers, ninety-year-old American Mrs Sudie Magette. 'We've been waiting until you arrived before we cut the cake,' said the lively nonagenarian, 'but first you must have a drink, Captain Bob. Young Susan here will see to that. Whisky and water, isn't it?'

Young Susan, Mrs Magette's daughter, would soon be celebrating her own seventieth birthday, she told me blushingly as she poured my drink. 'Well, then, I trust I'll be getting another birthday invitation,' I said. 'Meanwhile, here's to your Mum. Happy birthday, Sudie.'

When we reached the harbour of Djibouti, I entertained thirty or so of the new nation's government chiefs in my quarters. We had no planned inland tours for our passengers, mainly because of recent fighting in adjacent Ethiopia. Britain's man in Djibouti, a local bank manager named Hopkins, told me that the former French colony had eighty per cent unemployment and that the economy was maintained largely by the spending power of the 5000 French Foreign Legionnaires permanently stationed there. A sergeant, for instance, said Mr Hopkins, drew more than £1000 a month.

With Joan, I took a brief look at the Beau Geste territory. Goatherds ushered their scrawny charges through streets lined with ornate buildings, shimmering white in the mid-day sun of one of earth's hottest territories. Shopkeepers had laid out their rugs, hand-woven African fabrics and ornamental, fearsome daggers across the pavements for the benefit of the *QE2*'s eager shoppers. 'This is a golden day for our local economy,' said Mr Hopkins. 'Try to imagine a country without agriculture, with no fishing fleet, and most of its territory burning up day by day in desert desolation. Well, that's Djibouti.' Nevertheless, I formed a powerful impression that the young country, formerly French Somaliland, would make its own way in the world, powered by a fierce mixture of national pride and youthful idealism.

Another commodity that wasn't too abundant in Djibouti was dockside skill in casting off moorings. The *QE2* should have been tied up at the quayside with the usual wire hawsers, but local limitations meant we could use only ropes and just one steel cable. Understandably, the local lads didn't have too much experience in handling a vessel the size of the world's largest passenger ship, and they tied themselves in something of a tangle with the sole hawser. We were slightly behind our scheduled departure time because of this, but at least the dockside rope tricks kept up everyone's interest in the *QE2*'s first visit to the independent Republic of Djibouti.

After a smooth, 1400-mile passage through the sultry waters of the Red Sea, the *QE2* arrived at Port Suez shortly before midnight on the evening of 7 March 1980. Although she was the most illustrious vessel afloat, we still had to queue up with dozens of other ships of lesser fame for the privilege of transitting the 104 miles of the Suez Canal – the world's longest – to come out into the Mediterranean at Port Said.

At the stroke of midnight, an official Egyptian launch drew alongside. I was on my way down from the bridge, heading for a good night's sleep to be ready for an early morning start on our canal transit. It wasn't to be. Egypt's Minister of Tourism, Ali Gamal el Nazer, led an excited, laughing boarding party of twenty of his fellow countrymen straight to my cabin, and for the next couple of hours, I talked to my Moslem guests over glasses of orange juice and Coca-cola.

'Our apologies for the midnight intrusion, Captain,' said Mr el Nazer, 'but we just couldn't wait till morning to meet you and your fabulous ship.' I recognised the touch of the true diplomat in the way the minister phrased the remark.

'It is an honour, sir, to welcome you and your friends to the *QE2* no matter what the hour,' I replied. I began to regret my own diplomacy a little later as my voluble guests talked their way well into the next day.

It was ten o'clock next morning before the sea-way was clear for me to take the *QE2* on her first transit of the Suez Canal. Unlike the Panama, there are no locks and no overhanging buildings trying to make their mark on the side of the ship. At times, though, our designated channel was fairly narrow, while at others it was broad and free, and we steamed along steadily to reach Port Said before nightfall.

Since her schooldays, Joan had always wanted to see the Great Pyramid of Cheops and its neighbour the Sphinx. We went ashore by launch to Alexandria, and were then driven down to Cairo in an ancient Peugeot. Here are one or two extracts from her diary for the day:

'Up at 5.45. Breakfast, then down to 5 deck where queued up ages for a launch. Got over to Alex. at 10 minutes to eight. Driven down towards Cairo. Land well cultivated, but methods archaic. Oxen pulling ploughs, children leading cattle to pasture and looking after small flocks of sheep. Women carrying baskets on heads and camels snoozing at roadside. Water-wheels all over and irrigation channels criss-crossing the land.

'Flat-roofed houses with things like beehives on top. Not for bees, but for storing grain and fodder for family's oxen. Many orange groves with fruit for sale at roadside.

'Arrived Cairo 10.40, reached pyramids 11.20. Our excellent driver got us tickets to go into Great Pyramid. Terribly steep, dark and narrow. People trying to get down as we went up. Had to bend double most of time. Most claustrophobic. Glad to get out. Went on to Sphinx, then escaped from guide to dash into nearby restaurant for much needed gin and tonic. Looked in at Papyrus museum on way back along desert road. Notices say "No foreigners to leave main road." Who wants to? Sand, sand and still more sand for miles. Also lots of military installations. Back to ship at 6 p.m. Dinner, then listened to Max Jaffa and Jean in theatre. Later judged passengers' talent competition. Great little show. Collapsed into bed 12.30 a.m.'

It's obviously not easy being the Master's wife on the *QE2*, but by the time we reached Haifa, Joan was ready for another Marco Polo act ashore. Although it had been snowing there the week before our arrival, the morning was bright and sunny, an ideal day, according to Joan, to walk up the historic slopes of Mount Carmel. In the interests of saving time, we compromised and took the funicular railway up the hillside to look out over the wide blue waters of the Mediterranean from the Carmelite church at the summit.

I stayed aboard the next day while my tireless travelling partner took a coach to Jerusalem. The Damascus Gate, the Wailing Wall, the Via Dolorosa, the Mount of Olives and the Church of the Holy Sepulchre all came under Joan's industrious and reverent scrutiny. From the cradle of the Christian faith, I headed the *QE2* towards Istanbul, the Black Sea and the lands of the hammer and sickle.

Chapter 30

Ever since Joan and I had drifted round Fleetwood's Marine Hall at the Saturday dances a few thousand nights before, a moderate waltz, quickstep or even the odd samba have been more or less within my reluctant Astairean abilities, and occasionally Joan coerces me into taking a couple of turns around the *QE2*'s ballroom to the rhythms of Joe Loss and his sea-going swingers. But none of this proved to be any sort of effective preparation for the Friday lunchtime in the Presidential suite of Istanbul's Hilton when Miss Topkapi, 'the world's greatest belly dancer', commandeered me as her partner in an alarming routine of gyrating, jelly-wobbling spinal undulations.

My conscription into the Turkish cabaret came a few hours after I had brought the *QE2* into Istanbul harbour at eight o'clock on the morning of 14 March 1980. Waiting to meet us on the quayside was Leo Caouki, one of the three sons of Istanbul international businessman John Caouki, an Anglo-Maltese, who has straws dipping deeply into many rich commercial brews. He had sent Leo along to collect Joan and myself and the *QE2*'s Hotel Manager John Sawyer and his wife, Joan, for a morning tour of the city before going on to the Hilton to a luncheon party which John Caouki was holding in my honour.

In his speech of welcome, John, who is intensely proud of his British ancestry, said nothing about my having to earn my meal by cavorting with a belly dancer. I suppose he didn't want to ruin my turbot and roast lamb. Before lunch, I had been talking over navy days with Captain John Tate, of HMS *Cleopatra*, which was moored in the Bosporus with two other frigates, HMS *Avenger* and HMS *Amazon*. Captain Tate had come to the Hilton with Britain's naval attaché in Ankara, Commander Brian Gresham.

Said John Caouki, 'The arrival of the magnificent *QE2* makes this a wonderful day here for the British. I'd like to express a special welcome to our guest of honour, the super-liner's Master,

Captain Robert Arnott, whom I happen to know holds the rank of Captain in the Royal Naval Reserve.' Then, to demonstrate his pride and pleasure, John produced the amply endowed belly dancer. I didn't quite follow his logic, but not wishing to offend local protocol, I took the floor. More accurately, I was hauled onto it by the magnificently muscled Miss Topkapi. Joan, I was relieved to note, laughed as much as everyone else at my hot-browed contortions at the hands of the curvaceous piece of Turkish delight.

The next morning, a couple of hours before the *QE2* sailed for Yalta, I went down to the gangway to escort aboard Captain Tate, Commander Gresham, Commodore Sam Dunlop of the Royal Fleet Auxiliary supply ship *Fort Grange*, and Commander Robert Woodard, of the frigate HMS *Amazon*. Knowing we were having Royal Navy officers as guests, my steward had laid out the Booth's gin, jugs of water and angostura bitters in my cabin. Sipping his pink gin, Captain Tate asked, 'Don't you ever wish you'd come over to the Senior Service, Captain? After all, you've been a full Captain with the Reserve for nine years. Maybe you'd have been an admiral by now if you'd opted for the Royal Navy when you were first commissioned.'

The rank of Captain is, of course, as far as an RNR officer can go. I told the frigate flotilla commander, 'I've never wanted to be anything other than Master of the finest ship in the world, and here I am. But I do wish I'd been able to spend more time with the Navy on my reserve duties. If I'd had to choose an alternative way of life, the Royal Navy would have been right at the top of my list. But destiny and Dad steered me into the merchant service.'

Tactfully, my guests didn't rib me too severely in the matter of my short spell of service with the belly ballet the previous day. As I took the *QE2* out through the cold waters of the Bosporus later that afternoon, I lowered her fluttering flag as we passed first the *Amazon*, then the *Avenger* and finally, the flagship *Cleopatra*. My gold-braided friends dipped the ensigns of their frigates in acknowledgment of my salute and fire hoses from the three warships sent farewell salutes spouting sky high. The *QE2* cruised calmly through the busy channelway between Europe and Asia on her way into the ominously named Black Sea and its Crimean port of Yalta.

So far as I remember, Franklin Roosevelt and Winston

Churchill fought a battle as tough as any in the Second World War when they squared up to the greying, grizzly Joe Stalin at the Yalta Conference in February 1945. For a start, the Western allies were taking on the Russian dictator in his own lair, and the great American president was already a mortally sick man. Neither he nor Britain's legendary leader could match Stalin's peasant cunning when the conference reached the item on the agenda broadly headed: 'sharing the spoils of war'. Perhaps the Russian officials on duty at the Crimean resort on the morning of 16 March 1980, had inherited a substantial slice of old Joe's implacability.

But probably more significantly, the United States boycott of the 1980 Olympics in Moscow was picking up steam as President Carter reacted angrily to Russia's blatant invasion of Afghanistan, and British Prime Minister Margaret Thatcher was also busily trying to persuade Britain's athletes to stay away from the Games. As I dropped anchor half a mile off Yalta, the Russians must have been wondering if their investment of millions of roubles in the Olympics was destined to be decanted down the Moscow drains. And the worried Soviets were well aware that eighty-five per cent of our passengers were from the United States, with most of the others carrying British passports.

These matters are worth mentioning by way of background to the remarkable reception awaiting us in Yalta. Invariably, the tourists from the *QE2* and other cruise liners are allowed onshore without special visas at Russian ports, provided they don't wander too far outside the city limits, and I had no reason to think that this trip would be any different. But it was. The subsequent story of the *QE2*'s Yalta incident was scooped by the British *Daily Express*, and then rapidly flashed to other media outlets throughout the world.

It was around eight in the morning when the *QE2*'s anchors hit the bottom of Yalta Bay. Passengers who came out on deck early to photograph the Crimean coastline were assailed by icy blasts sweeping down from the snow-topped heights stretching away towards Balaclava. The 'balmy spring' of Yalta mentioned in the state tourist bureau's promotional blurb hadn't yet managed to oust the coldly entrenched Russian winter. No matter. Seven hundred of the *QE2*'s passengers showed they hadn't come along only for tropical sunshine and, wrapped up warmly in thick overcoats, they crowded into the Queen's Room to pick up their tickets for the shore launches. Forty other adventurous folk had booked an Intourist-organised trip to Moscow, and had left the ship much earlier. Another couple of hundred passengers had bought tickets for coach tours around the Crimea, and the rest of our shore party intended to potter round Yalta for the day under their own pilotage.

I looked out from the bridge shorewards and spotted a beamy launch clipping across the white-tipped waves towards the ship. The English-speaking Russian pilot had already come aboard, and the launch now deposited on our decks a small army of money-changers, their black briefcases stuffed with roubles for exchange into dollars and pounds sterling. Our latest arrivals also included immigration officials and a corps of bulky men in immense overcoats. The KGB? I couldn't be sure.

The Russian money men quickly set to work in an office I had assigned them below decks, switching tens of thousands of dollars and pounds sterling into roubles. Our first launch load of day excursionists left the ship for Yalta, planning to spend their newly acquired local currency in Iron Curtain seafront shops and cafés.

The March morning sunlight splashed down across the Crimean mountains onto the *QE2*'s still shivering decks. I began to feel uneasy. The men in dark overcoats were moving among my passengers, and carefree queues waiting to board the shore launches were being transformed into red-faced, angry men and women. The Russians were insisting that everyone going ashore should produce a passport for on-board inspection, a process that was likely to cause immediate chaos.

I put out an urgent announcement over the ship's loudspeaker system. 'I apologise for the delay in disembarkation today,' I said. 'The authorities are insisting on checking every passport, which, as you can imagine, is a slow and tortuous process. All efforts are being made to get you ashore as soon as possible.' That broadcast went out at exactly 9 a.m. Then I set out on a rapid walkabout. The Russians, I saw at once, were now being even more bloody-minded. Their uniformed officials were demanding that every shore-going passenger should hold a full Soviet entry visa or a pre-paid tour ticket, effectively banning half our people from disembarking. I summoned the Russian official in charge to the bridge.

'What's the game you're playing?' I asked.

The sallow-skinned Russian looked at me sourly. 'You have many Americans and Britons on your ship,' he said in hesitant English. 'We have decided no one enters Russia without paper documentation. If that causes delays, so be it.'

I turned to the Russian pilot standing by my side. 'Order the launch heading inshore back to the ship,' I demanded. The man looked startled. 'Do it now, please,' I insisted. The pilot spoke into his radio telephone. The launch, crowded with nearly one hundred passengers, was approaching the Yalta quayside, but in seconds, it had put about to return to the *QE2*.

This was the *QE2*'s tenth anniversary world cruise, and it had been a particularly pleasant voyage for everyone – until Yalta. If I'd given in to the Russian demands, there would have been mayhem on board. How could I explain to my passengers that the Russians had suddenly changed the long-standing rules, that some people could go ashore immediately, others would have a long wait and many more would probably never reach the Red quayside at all.

At 9.50 a.m. I made another broadcast: 'Since my last announcement the authorities are insisting that anyone disembarking must have either a visa or a tour ticket. This is an impossible situation. I have recalled the boat that has already left the ship and, when its passengers are back on board, I am sailing.'

The Russians gaped; they hadn't anticipated such an outcome to their actions. The stirring strains of 'Rule Britannia' rang out throughout the ship – our patriotic DJ had obviously been keeping in close touch with the mounting crisis. I bore the Russians no ill will. They were attempting, in a typically ham-fisted fashion, to rub our British and American noses in Soviet mud, but I had no intention of allowing that. As the remarkably apt lyrics 'Britons never, never, never shall be slaves' rounded off 'Rule Britannia', I heard a swell of cheering surging through the ship. It didn't come from the Russians, who left the *QE2* shame-faced, to the accompaniment of 'The Stars and Stripes' belting out from the ship's amplifiers across Yalta Bay.

That evening, when Joan and I entered the restaurant, the diners rose to their feet clapping, cheering and singing 'For he's a jolly good fellow'. I had left masses of flowers behind in my cabin specially ordered by passengers from the ship's florists.

One New York couple had sent me a dozen red roses with a card inscribed; 'Good for you! Now you can see red pleasantly.' A basket of daffodils had a card saying, 'Hats off to a Great Master!' and there were dozens of other blush-bringing messages in similar vein.

Aaron Binenkorb, of Jamesbury, New Jersey, came up to my room with his wife Marion, to say thank you on behalf of my grateful passengers. A retired wholesale paper merchant, Mr Binenkorb said that he intended to write a letter to the *New York Times* on the Yalta incident. His letter was subsequently published and reported:

'One launch was already loaded and on its way ashore when Captain Arnott was informed of the new Russian requirements. With no hesitation the *QE2*'s Master challenged the arbitrary demands, insisting that all passengers should be able to go ashore without either a Cook's tour ticket or a visa. The Russians would not budge. Captain Arnott responded by recalling the outgoing launch to the *QE2* and demanding again that every passenger should have the right to go ashore – or he would cancel the whole Yalta call. To the obvious disbelief of the Russians, this he did.

'Captain Arnott's gutsy decision was overwhelmingly applauded by the passengers, representing many nationalities. One can only guess the impact of his reaction on the Russians waiting in Yalta. They had made elaborate preparations for the visit ashore by 1500 passengers and hundreds of crew. It is too bad the West does not have more leaders like Captain Arnott to protect its rights when negotiating with the Russians.'

As we cruised towards Constanta on the coast of Romania, stewards delivered hundreds of letters to me from British, American, Dutch, German, Italian, Swedish and French passengers. From Cabin 3021, Margaret Viauh wrote: 'A good decision. We support you 100 per cent in sailing from Yalta. There's nothing they have there that we need.' But I don't think that I'll ever take another ship to Yalta. An Intourist official told officers of a cruise ship that called there soon after us that they had assembled seventy coaches at the port, complete with seventy English-speaking guides, 'all at great expense to the USSR', for the *QE2*'s visit. I know that lots of our passengers would have loved being shown round the house where Chekhov lived and wrote, as well as the Lividia Palace, venue of the 1945 summit. But the price of admission was far too costly.

We were still in Communist territory when we arrived at Constanta, but our reception couldn't have been more different from the frigid fiasco at Yalta. The Romanians laid on the warmest of welcomes for our shore party. After showing our tourists round the archaeological museum, the opera house, the local aquarium and the Genoese Lighthouse, the Romanian guides led the way to the Casino Restaurant for baked chicken, veal, cabbage, *crêpes suzettes*, cognac and coffee. The restaurant's resident equivalents of our own Max Jaffa ensemble serenaded our diners with romantic Romanian airs, then moved on to 'God Save the Queen' and 'God Bless America'. It was 17 March, and the lunchtime concert ended appropriately with a St Patrick's Day rendering of 'When Irish Eyes are Smiling'.

As we neared the entrance to the Bosporus the Royal Navy frigate flotilla joined us in line ahead. Her Majesty's ships *Cleopatra*, *Amazon* and *Avenger* steamed proudly in close convoy formation and executed various manoeuvres to the delight of our passengers while escorting the *QE2* through the Sea of Marmara as far as the Dardanelles.

One of HMS *Amazon*'s surgical staff had been travelling with us for several days. A young naval orthopaedic specialist, Lieutenant Leicester had come aboard in response to my plea to his commanding officer for help after one of our elderly American lady passengers had fallen and broken her hip. The surgeon performed the urgently needed operation in the *QE2*'s operating theatre, working with our own medical staff, and now I returned the naval surgeon to his ship, with my appreciative gratitude. As we cruised into warmer waters, we acquired a new escort. A school of pro-British dolphins took over convoy duties on each side of our bows and matched our progress precisely until the *QE2* was safely within sight of Piraeus, the gateway to the Greek capital.

On our second day in Athens, Joan and I went as guests of Peggy Carr, one of our American passengers, to lunch at the Royal Hellenic Yacht Club, where Peggy is a member. I didn't ask Peggy how she had come to join one of the world's most exclusive yachting fraternities thousands of miles from her home, for I was far too busy admiring the teak and mahogany decor that I've come to love in yacht clubs all over the world. Meanwhile, the *QE2*'s coach-tour explorers were soaking in the historic airs of Corinth, where St Paul once tackled the sinful influences of 1000 heathen prostitute priestesses. Our tourists saw the Acropolis, the Theatre of Dionysus, the Parthenon and the Agora, a market-place where Socrates once taught, and at night, they bought plates from the tavern waiters of Athens to smash at the feet of Zorba-style dancers. I'm glad to say that this ancient Greek custom had not yet reached the hallowed halls of the Royal Hellenic Yacht Club.

The world cruise ended for Joan and myself when the *QE2* reached Naples. Although the ship was going on to take an 'in-depth look at the ports of the Mediterranean' – the words of our brochure – Joan and I were leaving to take our own in-depth look at our home port of Fleetwood. We caught a tea-time DC10 from Naples Airport to Gatwick, along with some 200 of my crew who were also going on leave. It was snowing heavily when we reached Fleetwood early the next morning after driving up the M6 with our Blackpool friend Don Butterworth, the *QE2*'s chief radio officer. Joan and I were pleasantly surprised to find our home was warm, well polished and flower-fragrant, our youngest daughter Katy having driven over from her Yorkshire home to prepare the long-deserted house for our homecoming.

A week later, I travelled to Southampton for the *QE2*'s triumphal return from her world travels, and afterwards joined Lord Matthews at London's Bristol Hotel for his end-of-cruise Press conference. That evening I was invited to the London Rooms in Drury Lane, very much a Cunard occasion, and I was asked to say a few words after dinner. 'I had two invitations for this evening,' I joked. 'One was for this splendid occasion, and the other was to call at the Soviet Embassy. Naturally, I chose this one.'

A few days later, Joan and I attended a memorable big-band evening at Preston's Guild Hall in honour of Joe Loss's fifty years as a band leader. It was Easter Sunday, and busy traffic on the way from Blackpool made us late. Joe's dance-concert was well under way as we walked into the Guild Hall, but as he saw us, he immediately switched from the disco number his band was beating out into the martial music of 'Rule Britannia'.

'This is my great friend Captain Robert Arnott, Master of the

QE2 and also, incidentally, Master of the Russians at Yalta,' announced Joe over the stage microphone. Embarrassed at the thunderous applause, I shrank into my seat at the edge of the dance floor. Afterwards, the Mayor of Preston, Councillor Dennis Kehoe, presented Joe with a piece of the Lancashire town's historic plate, and handed Joan and myself souvenirs bearing the crest of 'Proud Preston'. We then joined the packed dancers in singing to Joe, 'For he's a jolly good fellow'. With a sunburn heightened by his crisp white suit, Joe was, at seventy, a fine advertisement for the healthy efficacy of cruising the world on the *QE2*.

'See you back on board,' called Joe as Joan and I left Preston for the half-hour drive back to Fleetwood, but for the next couple of weeks the only attention I paid to matters of navigation was in steering round the eighteen holes of the fine golf course on the seafront near our home. My partner at the nineteenth hole was one Fred Arnott, who in his eighty-first year still spent much of his spare time acting as treasurer for Fleetwood Golf Club. My father has just retired from that post, but he's still one of the club's official pros in the matter of whisky tasting. 'It's the malt that keeps me going,' says Dad, now eighty-two.

'I'll drink to that,' say I.

Chapter 31

Six hundred readers of Britain's *TV Times* invaded the cabins and decks of the *QE2* for the first cruise after my return from leave. We were bound for the ports of Madeira, Tenerife and Lisbon, and as well as the readership of the television magazine, we carried on board quite a few of their idols. At one of my cruise director's parties. I talked to *TV Times* Editor Peter Genower, and to British TV favourites Patti Boulay, Dana, Lennie Bennett and Derek Batey. Quite a few of the *QE2*'s own show personalities came along too, including the girls of Sweet Elegance, and Roy and Jackie Toaduff whose immaculate song-and-dance act would, in my biased opinion have swept them to TV stardom long ago if they hadn't spent so many years treating the passengers of the *QE2* to nightly exhibitions of their glittering talents. But the Toaduffs are not totally dependent on stage work, since they own the busy Chantry Hotel at Dronfield, near Sheffield, which keeps them busy outside the calls of cruising. It's not that unusual for Cunard folk to have prosperous shore businesses. I know a captain who has made a killing from his property interests, while one of our ship's doctors owns a successful farm where, when he's around, the delivery of breech-birth calves presents no problem at all.

With our *TV Times* readers safely delivered back in Britain, I took the *QE2* across the Atlantic to New York and then out into the Caribbean. In Southampton before sailing, decorative supernumeraries on the bridge were contestants in the *Daily Express*'s 'Nurse of the Year' competition, being filmed for the televised presentation of the contest final. In the previous year's event, one of the *QE2*'s own nurses, Michelle Gunter, had been a finalist. Now, she left her below-decks hospital duties for a few minutes to watch some of her shore colleagues being filmed in the *QE2*'s Tables of the World restaurant, where our head waiter had obligingly set up a flambé sweet at the request of TV producer Jean Moreton.

'It's so glamorous here on the ship,' said one of the nurses to me. 'Not at all like working in a hospital ward.'

'It may look glamorous,' I replied, 'but caring daily for the every need, every whim, and the total well-being of one and a half thousand passengers has one very important thing in common with hospital service.'

'What's that, Captain?'

'They are,' I said, 'both extremely hard work.'

Arriving back from the Caribbean on 16 May, I looked out across New York Harbour at around 6.30 a.m. and saw another ocean giant looming through the river mists. I called out 'Bon voyage' to the Master of the *Norway* as our ships swished by. So far as I know, it was the only time that the *QE2* has met her former French rival in the Hudson, and there probably won't be another meeting between the great ships, for SS *Norway* no longer visits New York.

At the beginning of July, I switched the *QE2* from the sunny shipways of the West Indies eastwards across the ocean and into the chill waters of the Norwegian Sea. Joan joined me in Southampton for the cruise to the Arctic Circle, the North Cape and the lands of the midnight sun.

Before setting course for Norway, I took the *QE2* into Bremerhaven to collect passengers from West Germany. Line-handling arrangements in Bremerhaven are remarkably efficient. Two small mobile winches are each handled by two men to carry out the handling of the ropes and wires, and I was told that twelve men had been needed before the exercise was handed over to private enterprise.

American Independence Day saw us docking in Bergen. The Norwegian weather was so brilliantly warm that it was hard to believe that we were within a short sail of the icy Arctic. Girls lay sun-bathing in bikinis on the *QE2*'s top deck as Joan and I left the ship for a few hours ashore. Bergen, we learned, was the former capital and had been one of the most important cities in Europe some 500 years ago. We saw finely preserved fourteenth-century Hanseatic warehouses and walked through the banquet halls where kings and warriors had gathered for gargantuan feasts. Then we took the funicular railway to the top of Mount Floien, the closest and fiercest of the seven hills surrounding the ancient city. We looked down from the peak at the multi-coloured contours of Bergen, spread out far below like a 3-D relief map at the edge of the fjord.

Our next port of call was Trondheim and then we cruised up Holandsfjord to see the spectacular Svartisen Glacier shimmering blue-black in the hot sun. As we sailed further northwards along the wild mountain-fringed coastline, the temperature dropped sharply, but the friendly people of Hammerfest warmly welcomed our fur-coated shore excursionists. Situated five degrees inside the Arctic Circle, and the most northerly town in Europe, Hammerfest had been razed by the Germans as they pulled out in 1944. On our trip ashore Joan and I found that it's now a thriving fishing and tourist port of some 8000 hardy souls, who have perpetual daylight during their short summers but seemingly endless darkness in their long winters.

Later the same evening, the *QE2* dropped anchor still further north. We had reached the North Cape. Reindeer looked at us curiously through clouds of their own steaming breath as our ship-to-shore launch reached the barren beach, yet buttercups were blooming on the harsh landscape as we drove from the fishing village of Scarsväg, near our landing point, to the top of the Cape. It was completely shrouded in mist. We had hoped to see the midnight sun dipping to the horizon but we couldn't even see the sea – visibility was about five yards and it was bitterly cold. Joan said, 'This must be the edge of the world. I'm frozen.' We hurried back to the *QE2*, warm comfort and a cold-weather feast of hot tripe and onions.

Most of our passengers, including Joan, went on coach tours overland to Merok when we reached the little port of Hellesylt on our return voyage along the Norwegian coast. Joan told me later: 'It was so sunny that we were really hot until we reached the glaciers. It was wonderful to see so many wild flowers in bloom. There were harebells, fireweed, knapweed, cotton grass, monkshood and buttercups. Merok's houses were all flower-bedecked and beautifully painted. There weren't many animals around – we saw only a few cows and a dozen sheep all day – but there was lots of hay hung out to dry over wire fences.'

While my reporter on Norwegian rural life was swanning across the glacial countryside, I took the *QE2* up the Geiranger fjord to pick her up with my other tourist passengers at Merok.

300

That evening we cruised back down the breathtakingly lovely fjord, surrounded by rugged, mile-high peaks rising starkly from the water. Cameras clicked away furiously as I took the *QE2* close alongside the cliff face where the Seven Sisters water-fall usually descends like seven vertical rivers. But on that trip, water was apparently in short supply and only two 'rivers' were in action.

At Stavanger, our next south-bound call, Joan and I popped ashore to look at the twelfth-century St Swithin's cathedral, the fruit and fish market, and the sardine-canning factories. As we walked back to the ship, a mother duck from a pond alongside the main street joined us for a few hundred yards, along with her half-dozen fluffy ducklings. With a few gentle 'shoos' I dissuaded the adventuresome mum from joining the *QE2* and she quite happily returned with her little flock to rejoin the swans and gulls paddling around on the city-centre pond.

Our thirteen-day voyage to the lands of the Far North ended on 12 July, when I brought our floating luxury hotel back to a late-night arrival in Southampton. Joan departed for Fleetwood, and the next day the *QE2* and I set out for New York. Travelling across the Atlantic with me was one of the more wealthy inhabitants of this planet, who appeared on the passenger list simply as 'Mr K. Abdullah – and friend'. But at sea I quickly discovered that our black-haired, immaculately dressed passenger was His Royal Highness Prince Abdullah of Saudi Arabia. He was visiting America with one of his friends, Azim Bassam, and a couple of male secretaries.

The Prince told me that this was his first ocean voyage. He said, 'I didn't really know what to expect at sea, and half expected to be bored. I brought along a multi-channel TV receiver, and dozens of films on video tape. I'm glad to tell you, Captain, that I've never even switched the set on. I've been far too busy exploring your ship.' The Prince and his friends had dined in the *Queen*'s grill, they had watched all our shows, looked in at the casino, and sipped orange juice in a dozen of the ship's bars. 'I've had no time to be bored,' said His Royal Highness, 'and next time I'll leave all my cassettes at home.'

With his excellent command of English, the Prince was a

popular figure with his fellow passengers. His appearance was eminently Western, but I suspect many of our passengers and crew knew that the pleasant, dark-skinned gentleman was, in fact, the scion of one of the Middle East's more dazzling dynasties. Prince Abdullah was on his way to the Kentucky Horse Sales to look for new blood to strengthen his superb racing stable. 'Do you own any horses, Captain?' asked the Prince.

'Well no, although I often used to have a little investment in one or two,' I replied.

'Ah yes,' said the Prince, nodding his head, 'a good way to invest considering the rise in bloodstock values these days.' I don't believe the royal interpretation of 'invest' was the same as mine, but no matter. I switched our little chat to matters of oil. The *QE2* burned it night and day, and His Highness's country produced it on a similar basis. Not such an interesting topic as racehorses but, I believed, less open to misinterpretation.

That Atlantic crossing coincided with my birthday and Val Groom, my managing director's wife, invited me to her cabin for a surprise birthday party. She produced a beautiful decorative basket fashioned entirely from baked pastry, bearing a single candle, and filled with caviar and smoked salmon canapés. 'We thought this would be a change from the usual sort of birthday cake,' Val said.

Among the other friends at the party who had turned up to wish me well were Lord and Lady Robens and author John Maxtone-Graham and his brother. John's book *The Only Way to Cross* is a fascinating and authoritative work on the world of North Atlantic liners. Before I left the party, I was given two fine Waterford crystal brandy goblets, and to go with them a bottle of Napoleon brandy. As a final and totally unexpected gift, John, whom I've known for many years, handed me a birthday poem. He explained he'd had problems finding words to rhyme with Arnott. This is how he coped:

> *Many happiest returns to the Master*
> *Who drives the* QE2 *faster and faster,*
> *Through five days of fog*
> *While cooking the log,*
> *If* France *had been here, we'd have passed her!*

Having searched through all English argot,
There seems absolutely no rhyme for Bob Arnott –
Wherever we seek
This nomenclature unique
Defies save invention of words that are not!

But nevertheless we're content
To offer a rhymeless present
Two snifters of crystallery,
With liquid distillery
Come with our love and esteem and intent.

So – All hail to Arnott
Don't close the bar – not yet!!

That evening, my officers had arranged a full birthday blow-out in the wardroom. Atlantic fog cancelled my attendance.

As we sailed again to New York at the end of July, the *QE2* passed the royal yacht *Britannia* moored off Cowes for the start of the annual regatta. Her Majesty was not on board, but Rear Admiral H. P. Janion sent me a signal from *Britannia* saying, 'How nice to see you again. Best wishes to you and your passengers.' I answered the admiral's thoughtful between-ships courtesy with the signal: 'Thank you for your greetings. I hope you have a successful Cowes week.'

My eldest daughter Jan was making the trip to the United States with her husband David. He's a college lecturer and she teaches English – both in Cheshire. Jan hadn't been on the *QE2* since the 'shakedown' cruise, and on this latest trip she became firm friends with Diane Coles, wife of Trafalgar House personnel director Peter Coles. Diane, a successful book- and record-shop owner and a publisher in her own right, had come aboard to sort out and rationalise the *QE2*'s library operations. She did an efficient, razor-sharp job on our book systems – a vitally necessary task as most of the *QE2*'s passengers are avid, late-night paperback readers.

Also crossing to New York were a certain 'Mr and Mrs Cummings'. My 'tiger' tipped me off that the Christian name of the tall, lean gentleman certainly wasn't Robert. 'It's Henry Ford, travelling incognito,' My steward whispered.

If the automobile millionaire wished to be known as plain Mr Cummings that was OK by me, but I still invited him to one of my cocktail parties. I shook his hand, and was about to say, 'Mr Cummings, I presume,' when my lanky, hard-eyed guest announced, 'I am Henry Ford.' Simple anonymity, I'm afraid, never lasts long on the *QE2*. But it's not often the incognito person himself throws away the cloak so quickly as did Henry II.

Her Majesty Queen Elizabeth the Queen Mother has always enjoyed a close association with the Cunarders that bear the names of her family, and on 4 August, I sent a 'Happy Birthday' signal to Buckingham Palace: 'The Master and Ship's Company of the *QE2* including many ex-*Queen Elizabeth* personnel send their loyal greetings and wish a very happy eightieth birthday to Queen Elizabeth the Queen Mother.' A couple of days later Her Majesty's reply arrived in our radio room: 'I am extremely touched by your telegram of good wishes for my birthday. My sincere thanks to you and all who joined in your kind message. Elizabeth R, Queen Mother.' I broadcast that gracious message over the ship's loudspeakers, for Her Majesty is held in great esteem and affection by Cunard men and women – as indeed are all the royal family.

I wasn't able to lay on a helicopter in New York for my daughter Jan and her husband, as I had done for Katy, but by way of consolation I drove them on a tour of Chinatown, Greenwich Village, Wall Street and Broadway. At lunch-time we met up with Jody and Bob Swearingen, President of Moritz Travel in the States, and with my Staff Captain Harvey Smith. We all talked travel trade shop over a steak lunch, and then the magnet of Macy's giant department store drew Jan irresistibly inside. Her husband and I could do little else but follow.

That evening we were returning, laden with Macy presents, across the Atlantic. I was due for leave, and drove Jan and Dave back to Fleetwood, where they joined Katy, Joan and myself at a dinner in celebration of their seventh wedding anniversary. To a seaman constantly crossing the oceans of the world, such family get-togethers are a powerful link with home, and the pleasurable anticipation weeks ahead of the actual anniversary is an effective antidote to loneliness.

Half-way through my leave, I flew back to New York to join

the *QE2* as a passenger. I was taking part in Cunard's first on-board management seminar, which had been scheduled to take place in the exotic atmosphere of a Caribbean cruise. My own part in the business exercise was completed by the time we reached the Virgin Islands, so I took a small plane from St Thomas to San Juan, picked up an Eastern Airlines jet to New York, then flew home on Concorde to take up my leave where I had left off ten days earlier. On the splendid supersonic flight I sat next to Mr Rayne, Her Majesty the Queen's shoemaker, who often crosses the Atlantic in more leisurely circumstances on the *QE2* when he has frequently been a guest at my parties. This time, like myself, he was in a hurry, and we reached Heathrow, after a champagne and caviar lunch, in exactly three hours and forty minutes. On the way, Captain Myers, pilot of Concorde, invited me up on his flight deck. 'This will give you a new slant on the Atlantic,' he said. It did. I much prefer the view from the bridge of the *QE2*, whose crossing speed is 28½ knots against Concorde's 1300 miles an hour.

When I returned to the Atlantic, my son Roger crossed with me, and on board he became firm friends with Admiral and Mrs Moran, who run the Moran Towing Company, one of the largest of its kind in the States. When we reached New York, the admiral took over my usual role as guide and showed Roger the sights of the city. I met them both for lunch in the restaurant of one of the World Trade Center's twin towers, the first time I had ascended New York's tallest building, although I had flown over it with my daughter Katy in a port helicopter. As the admiral, Roger and I sank our teeth into succulent steaks, we had a fine view of the river and of the familiar shape of the *QE2* moored there, some 1350 feet below, that reminded me silently that I had better hurry back, for we were sailing to Europe only a few hours after docking in New York. Swift turn-arounds at both sides of the Atlantic have been one of the vital economic factors in keeping the *QE2* afloat through the Eighties. I left the sweet trolley to Roger and Admiral Moran, and caught the express elevator to plunge back to earth, and to work.

Two days out into the Atlantic, I talked over the radio telephone to the latest bearer of one of the most famous names in maritime history. Lieutenant Commander Francis Drake, temporary captain of the reproduction of the *Golden Hind*, was opening the Southampton Boat Show, and I wished him and the show every success from me, my passengers and crew, one of whom reminded me that it was 400 years almost to the day since Sir Francis completed his three-year voyage round the world in the original *Golden Hind*.

A Force-10 storm blasted the *QE2* on my next voyage to New York. Our electronics told us the roaring disturbance was 600 miles in diameter, and with a barometric reading of 972 millibars, I decided that we would be safer keeping a low profile until the worst winds had scudded by. In fact, we were nine hours late in arriving off Ambrose Light, which meant an even swifter turn-around than usual.

For two of my passengers, the delay meant more hand-holding time at sea. Soprano Lorna Dallas, a glittering star on both sides of the Atlantic and a firm favourite with the *QE2*'s shipboard audiences, said 'Yes' when the *QE2* theatrical agent Garry Brown proposed marriage in mid-ocean. Lorna had just said 'Not yet' to Yul Brynner when he had offered her the role of Anna in *The King and I*. 'I'm really too busy just now,' Lorna had told Mr Brynner.

'I meant my showbiz commitments,' she explained to me, 'but a girl simply has to find the time to marry, don't you think, Captain Bob?'

'Of course, Lorna, but remember that the time to marry will have to be found ashore. I'm all for love and marriage, so long as I'm not asked to perform the ceremony.'

'Well, I must admit we were thinking of asking you to officiate,' said Lorna, 'but if you can't, you can't. I know you would if you could.' True enough, for Lorna and Garry are two of the most popular people in the *QE2*'s brotherhood of show folk.

After a short cruise to the Caribbean, I returned with the *QE2* to New York to take on board two Hollywood immortals. James Cagney and Pat O'Brien were crossing with their wives for the filming of 'Ragtime'. It was to be Cagney's first screen appearance in twenty years. He had been cast in the role of a New York police commissioner of the Teddy Roosevelt era. After the Press men and women had completed their interviews with the legendary veterans, I visited them in their penthouse suites. Mr Cagney, as tough as they came in black and white films, said 'Come in, Captain. I never shook like this in the old days. Those Press youngsters have got me all of a dither. They think they're still talking to the old screen toughie. I guess I'm luckier than most of the gang I used to work with. They're just not around any more, and here am I off to Britain a couple of months after my seventy-sixth birthday.'

'Well, perhaps you'll join me in my cabin later for a belated birthday drink,' I suggested to Mr Cagney. 'What date is your birthday, by the way?'

'July 17,' the old fellow replied without hesitation. 'A great day for Hollywood,' he added modestly.

'It certainly was,' I agreed, 'and also a great day for me. I too was born on July 17.'

'Well then,' said the superstar, 'I'll surely have to come up to celebrate.'

But he didn't. His agent Mrs Zimmerman told me: 'The poor dear was quite overwhelmed with all the excitement in New York. He's decided to stay in his suite and just take it easy until he gets to Britain.' I didn't mind. I was more than grateful to have met and talked to James Cagney just once.

I'm afraid poor Pat O'Brien spent most of the voyage lying in bed suffering from seasickness. I suppose one of the two most sumptuous suites afloat is as good a place as any to be ill in, but I had hoped to be able to talk to the fine actor I had first seen when I was eight. His film, *The Front Page*, hit Britain's north country screens around 1932, and since then I had seen many of Pat's movies right through to his appearance with Marilyn Monroe in *Some Like It Hot*. I sent him my best wishes for a speedy recovery but didn't see Pat again until he was leaving the ship in Southampton.

Travelling on the same trip as the Hollywood doyens was famous American lawyer Robert Mihlbaugh. A most likeable guest at my dinner table, Robert invited me to get in touch with him at once 'if ever you get into any sort of trouble in the States'. Fortunately, I haven't needed to take advantage of the offer, but I did promise to pay a social call one day on Robert and his wife Barbara at their home in Lima, Ohio.

An elegant and splendidly opulent affair of the heart aroused intense interest on our return crossing to Britain. The tall, lean and archetypal young Englishman Jeremy Irons boarded the *QE2* in New York along with two lovely young companions, the actresses Diana Quick and Jane Asher. Their mission was to recreate in mid-ocean the romantic pages of Evelyn Waugh's *Brideshead Revisited* for the film cameras of Granada Television. The TV people had decided that, with a deft line in disguise, the decks and lounges of the *QE2* could masquerade as those of the ornate ocean liner of the Thirties on which Waugh had set his Atlantic action.

Derek Granger, producer of the £4m, thirteen-hour television serialisation, came to me, and I poured him a drink in my cabin as he told me of his troubles. 'First of all, Captain,' said Derek, 'we want some extras to move around in the suits and dresses of the Thirties that we've brought along.'

'No problem,' I assured Derek. 'With 2000 or so amateur television stars on board, you'll have to fight them off once I put the word out.' And so it proved. A senior American diplomat, a Chicago millionaire's wife, and lots of fellas and flappers from the *QE2*'s crew strolled nonchalantly before the cameras as the ship made her anachronistic progress eastwards. They were the lucky few who hadn't heard the fateful words 'Next, please' at our crowded shipboard audition.

But Derek Granger's second request wasn't so easily satisfied. 'We need a roustin' rollabout Atlantic storm,' he told me quite calmly. 'Comes in the book, you know.'

I took a deep draught of my whisky and water. 'Some things I can guarantee happening on this ship if I give the order. A storm by special request isn't, I'm afraid, within my powers.'

'Why not?' asked Derek straight-faced. 'You're the Master around here, aren't you?'

Fortunately for Derek's touching trust, his scripted storm duly hit us on the third day out of New York. 'Thanks, Captain,' he murmured, when I met him later for cocktails with Jeremy, Jane and Diana. 'We all knew you could do it.' Jeremy Irons nodded approvingly, and Misses Asher and Quick laughed deliciously. I decided not to spoil the joke by pointing out that in the tempestuous transition from autumn to winter, violent outbursts by the unpredictable Atlantic are by no means rare. Instead, I assumed my professional air of maritime mystique.

A few weeks afterwards, the television company sent me a 'thank you' note. 'We are grateful,' they said, 'that you were able to supply the every need of the stars and production team

308

of *Brideshead Revisited.* Your ship – and storm – will feature in Episode Eight.' When Brideshead's magnificent adaptation reached Britain's television screens in the autumn of 1981, I was, of course, away at sea – sailing the *QE2* through another of those occasionally opportune Atlantic upheavals.

As autumn of 1980 drifted away across the Atlantic horizons, I took the *QE2* into the ocean's more southern waters on a series of sun-chasing charters to the islands of the Canaries and the Madeira group. A note in my cruise diary for 8 November 1980, records: '635 handshakes with incoming passengers in 34 minutes.' That speedy session took place at the entrance to the *QE2*'s Queen's Room, where my chief deck steward Bob Woodhouse introduced the embarkees, counted their numbers on a hand-held counting device, and also timed the whole exercise. We weren't trying to set a record; urgent matters of navigation were awaiting on the bridge, and I duly paid for the rapid-fire handshakes with a squashed right hand.

Towards the end of the year, both the *QE2* and her Master were ready for a respite from our incessant ocean wanderings. The ship entered dry-dock for her well-earned winter resuscitation, and I headed home to Fleetwood for an old-fashioned Christmas at the family fireside. Then, in early January 1981, I flew out with Joan from Gatwick on a Laker Airways DC10 bound for New York. With a choice of seven different radio channels and a double feature film programme of *Fawlty Towers* and *Close Encounters of the Third Kind*, the flight across to Kennedy, against strong head winds, passed pleasantly enough.

Flurries of outsized snowflakes swirled through the evening air as our sixteen-seater Cunard crew bus ferried us from the airport to the ocean passenger terminal. Desolate automobiles, abandoned by their owners in the blizzard that had swept the city earlier in the day, were scattered alongside the cross-town roadways. We stepped down from the bus onto a snow-patched quayside, and quickly climbed the gangway into the warm, exclusive world encompassed within the *QE2*'s vast contours.

Relief Master Doug Ridley handed over the comprehensive range of documentation involved in a changeover of captaincy. I flipped through the passenger lists, checked over the recommended table seatings and, one by one, called in the ship's departmental heads to report on their planned operations. Conferences completed, I moved out onto the bridge. Outside, the night air was shedding its moisture into instant icicles that clung to the *QE2*'s decks and superstructure. I glanced at the exterior thermometer reading, ten degrees below zero. Time to cast off moorings and set sail for the sun.

Chapter 32

Our first major sun search of 1981 achieved early success when we reached the Florida coastline after two days of cruising southwards along the eastern seaboard of the United States. Furs gave away to cool summer fabrics as the *QE2*'s deck temperatures edged upwards through the sixties. Hundreds of world cruise passengers came aboard at Port Everglades, and many of those who had started the voyage in New York went ashore during our seven hours in port. They explored Miami twenty miles south, shopped in Fort Lauderdale or flew in the Goodyear Blimp over the coastal strip's criss-cross of rivers, sea inlets and man-made canals. I was still busily occupied with a multitude of planning details for our voyage, but Joan and a couple of friends slipped ashore to watch the dolphin show at the Ocean World Seaquarium. They also had an invitation to watch a display of alligator wrestling at a nearby Seminole Indian village, but the girls chose friendly mammals rather than belligerent reptiles.

Just after seven o'clock on the evening of 20 January the *QE2* left Florida and headed for the Windward Passage between Cuba and Haiti, and then moved into the sun-splashed waters of the Caribbean. Two of the guests at 'Lulu' Edward's going-away party in Room 1030 had missed the final 'all ashore' calls in Everglades, and they were now taking an unexpected and costly short cruise to Curaçao. On top of full shipboard charges, they also had to pay air fares from the Netherlands Antilles back to the United States.

While our accidental stowaways enjoyed their enforced trip, I began the mammoth rounds of handshakes with some 1500 ticket-holding passengers. Although the latest greetings sessions in the Queen's Room went on at a more leisurely pace than on the recent Atlantic isles cruise, I still ended up with a stiff neck, aching back muscles and a numb right hand. Fortunately, such minor discomforts were quickly banished by a scotch in the Midships Bar before going on to dinner.

Curaçao's Director of Tourism, Rafael Hato, led a party of his officials on board as soon as we reached the island, and they presented me with an etched copper picture of Willemstad mounted over a wall clock. It's a nice addition to my cabin furnishings, but I still haven't any idea what prompted the gift, apart from the universal South American ingenuity in dreaming up excuses for parties.

On the evening we left an unusually wet and dull Curaçao, I looked in at a party that was being held for more understandable reasons in the *QE2*'s Queen's Room – our 'Travelling Alone' get-together. Cruise director Brian Price had invited along everyone without a travelling partner – some hundreds of our passengers – to drinks and snacks and, more importantly, to all-round introductions. Due to various frailties of the human state, women always outnumber men at these parties. We have wealthy widows, glamorous divorcées and liberated wives seeing the world while husbands are hard at work back home. These days, on world cruises we carry a dozen or so chatty, handsome and well-educated gentlemen whose specific function is to make the *QE2*'s unescorted feminine majority feel that they're no longer alone. Inevitably, critics label these heroes 'gigolos', but the description isn't merited. 'Must be able to dance well', is really the only vital qualification the cruise director insists on for his industrious gentlemen.

Steamy South American sunshine sent temperatures soaring into the mid-eighties as the *QE2* neared Cartagena on Colombia's Caribbean coast. Once one of the richest ports in the old Spanish colonial empire, just before our arrival Cartagena had acquired one of the crowning hallmarks of modern sophisticated tourism – a Hilton International Hotel. It had been open for business only a couple of weeks when our friend Ann Brooks took Joan and Christine Smith, wife of my staff captain, to lunch in the attractive open-air restaurant where they were joined by the hotel's public relations director, Sonia Gedeon. Fresh Colombian fruits, seafood kebabs on rice and tuna fish salads were their simple, and they hoped, safe choices as persistent Colombian flies invaded the still unfinished hotel. But at least the swimming pool was completed and, after rounding off lunch with delicious local pastries, coffee and potent iced drinks, Joan and Christine plunged into the tingling, refreshing water. Miss Gedeon then whisked them off on an hour-long car ride round the sultry city, where high-rise flats, opulent offices of the platinum, coffee and oil companies, and dazzling white hotel developments were rapidly challenging the mediaeval Spanish baroque splendours.

Waiting at the quayside for a launch back to the anchored *QE2*, they met Mr Marco Polo, Joan's guide on her Cartagena travels three years previously. 'I see today you're with Miss Gedeon. 'Very wealthy young lady and daughter of our mayor,' confided Marco. 'Hope she looked after you as well as I did.'

'Yes, she did,' replied Joan, 'but she didn't tell us she was the mayor's daughter. She's a charming and very modest young lady, obviously.'

'I'm modest too,' sighed Marco. 'It isn't easy with a name like mine.'

As we approached the Panama Canal, our agents prepared a cheque for $82,000 – the one-way canal transit charge when the *QE2* crosses from Atlantic to Pacific, and the highest toll ever paid by any vessel using the canal. By contrast the lowest, a sum of thirty-six cents, was paid by one Richard Halliburton who swam through the entire length of locks, channels and man-made lakes in 1928.

As the *QE2* went through, some 52 million gallons of fresh water from the canal's locks were spilled out into the sea. Overall, it is reckoned that the water needed for canal operations for just one day would keep the city of Boston, Massachusetts, amply supplied for two weeks. No pumps are used in emptying or filling the lock chambers; the water simply runs downhill from the Gatun Lake, which is eighty-five feet above sea level and, with an area of 163 square miles, is one of the largest artificial bodies of water on earth.

After nine hours of meticulously monitored progress along the canal, we reached Balboa at the Pacific exit. Britain's chargé d'affaires Barry White and his wife Sheila came on board for early evening drinks in my cabin. The Panamanian President Royo couldn't make it, as he was getting ready for a six-country trip to Europe, taking in Britain and some of the Iron Curtain countries. The amiable president sent his regards, and an hour before midnight we left his territorial waters in the

313

Gulf of Panama to swing northwards to our next shore stop at Acapulco.

We dropped anchor in Acapulco Bay and I looked out at the harsh, mountainous tracts surrounding the Mexican resort. The airborne 'sails' of para-skiers floating gracefully across the blue waters shared some ancestry with the billowing topsails of Spanish galleons that had once brought silks, ivory and perfumes from Manila to Acapulco, and then returned to the Philippines heavy with Mexican silver. Our own tourists went ashore by tender to trade their dollars and pesos for handmade Mexican shirts, onyx ware, bark paintings and oceans of tequila.

Joan and I caught a bus along the curved, palm-shaded bay – an oasis on a particularly barren strip of coast – and up to the headland overlooking Puerto Maquez, a beach and lagoon that had occasionally been used as settings for Tarzan movies. It wasn't just a sightseeing trip, as we had remembered the lobster and 'coco-loco' at the Las Brisas hotel, perched high on the hillside. The luncheon lobsters were glorious, and so were the rum and fruit punches, the avocado dips and the ice creams laced with a lethal coffee sauce. Over the coco-locos, Joan and I chatted to astronaut Scott Carpenter and his attractive young wife. When I had been cruising the Pacific on RMS *Caronia* in 1962, Scott had been swishing high overhead in *Aurora 7* during Project Mercury, but now, like me, he makes his living from the seas, as a respected and successful oceanographer.

The pleasantries of that sunny afternoon were somewhat marred when Joan slipped as she entered the pool for a swim, bruising and grazing her arm and back, but that didn't stop her diving in immediately and giving a fair imitation of Esther Williams. My Weissmuller act, I decided, could wait for another day, and I sipped fruit punch and talked of stars and satellites with Mr Carpenter.

At Los Angeles 500 passengers and fifty or so journalists came aboard. I met the Press boys and girls in the Doubledown Bar, where they stood around eating snacks and canapés and firing and odd question at me above the general din. 'How much are the top two suites costing this time around the world, Captain?' My shouted answer of 'Around a quarter of a million dollars each' scarcely reached beyond the nearest talkative group of hungry, thirsty journalists, but I didn't worry. Informal, friendly meetings with the Press I like. Stuffy, presidential-type official question-and-answer sessions I don't. The Los Angeles meeting with the Press on Sunday, 1 February 1981, was a most pleasant and mutually productive affair. We produced answers, food and drink, and our Press friends produced a fine crop of stories and photographs.

The north-easterly trade winds that had scudded sailors of centuries past across the vast blue reaches of the Pacific now blew steadily across our own swiftly broadening, white wake as the *QE2*'s 110,000-horsepower engines surged us towards the islands of Hawaii. The ship is often billed as a floating resort that follows the sun. Most of the time that's just about right, but it didn't happen in Honolulu. Rains driving across the *QE2*'s bridge drenched me as I took her into the hazy waters of the capital's harbour.

Undaunted, hundreds of our passengers poured ashore to head for Waikiki, Diamond Head and Pearl Harbor. I had a reconnaissance mission to perform on the island of Maui, half an hour's flight away, to see how it was shaping up as a possible calling anchorage for the *QE2*'s 1982 world cruise. By the time Joan and I boarded the white Cessna of the Royal Hawaiian Air Service to fly high over Oahu's green-topped mountains and across the Pacific rollers to Maui, the morning's rainstorms had taken off in the general direction of Japan, but the skies were still heavily overcast and far from ideal for our pathfinder patrol.

Our pilot clipped the little eight-seater along the mist-shrouded coast of Molokai island, crossed the straits to Maui, and went in low over Kaanapali. Our ship's chief photographer Tony Sekker busily clicked away as Cunard's Hawaiian agent Ken Bowman pointed out the proposed 1982 anchorage. 'The *Canberra*'s launches should be somewhere around taking passengers ashore,' said Ken. 'That will give you some idea of what's involved.' The SS *Canberra*, P and O's cruise liner, was, alas, nowhere to be seen, and when we landed on Maui I wasn't surprised to find that it had been too rough for the *Canberra* to send her passengers ashore. She had upped anchor, and set out for Honolulu, where she was due to take over the *QE2*'s berth when we departed for the Friendly Isles.

Meanwhile, on the flight back to Oahu, our pilot swept low over the north-west corner of volcanic Molokai for us to see the leper colony where Father Damien had lived and worked in the latter part of the nineteenth century. Our knowledgeable agent told us that Damien was the religious name of the Belgian priest Joseph de Veuster, of the Fathers of the Sacred Heart, who had asked his superiors to send him to work at Kalaupapa leper settlement on Molokai, where he remained until his death in 1889. 'And for the last four years,' said Ken, 'he truly knew what it felt like to be a leper outcast. He caught the disease in 1885, and was only forty-nine when it killed him. Father Damien cared for his fellow lepers' souls and bodies single-handedly right to the end.'

A voice from the back of the aircraft cried, 'Oh, what a sad and wonderful story.' It was Joan. We had had to install her in the tail seat because she was the lone non-heavyweight among our reconnaissance party. From her rear-guard vantage point, Joan watched, almost tearfully, as Father Damien's domain slipped away over the eastern skyline.

More than 200 replacement crew joined the *QE2* in Honolulu to effect a smooth changeover with ratings and officers due for leave or re-assignment. Among the new passengers who also joined us was Wilma Costello who had flown out from Sydney where, by courtesy of airline baggage, most of her clothes still languished. But Wilma had carried her jewels in her handbag on the flight, and when she came down to dinner at my table she was sparkling, not with the standard sets of diamonds worn on the *QE2*, but with brooches, pendant, ear and finger rings mounted with pale blue, finely cut opals. Her husband, she explained, had an opal shop in Sydney's city centre. 'I suppose,' said Wilma, 'That I'm what you might call a floating advertisement for my husband's business.'

King Neptune, his sea courtiers and attendant mermaids performed their ancient rites of tossing travellers into the quarter-deck swimming pool when we crossed the equator during the six-day Pacific stretch from Honolulu to Tongapatu. Elderly passengers, invalids and friendly following whales were the only ones with effective certificates of exemption from the 'big dip'. Shouts of 'But I've crossed the line before' afforded no defence to a ducking for passing officers, ratings and even the ship's doctors. Joan and her friend Christine Smith, wisely avoided the blandishments of King Neptune's court by pleading that they were needed for a special assignment – sunbathing – on a distant deck.

I was roped into the festivities that evening when the Clerk of Neptune's Court read out a rhyming citation from a scroll: 'The Great Ocean Master Bob, who, we're relieved to say, really knows his job, in leading us all the way, across the Pacific. We think he's terrific!' I listened, laughing, to the comic stanzas during a brief break between dances at the Neptunian Ball in the Doubledown Room, reasoning that being harangued beat getting thrown in the drink.

February 9, 1981, didn't officially exist because we were crossing the international date line, and the 10th, surprisingly, saw me again attending Hilda Bishop's birthday party in the Princess Grill. This time Joan was on sufficiently good terms with the Pacific to go along with me, and we both sang 'Happy Birthday' to our friend from Rottingdean, Sussex. I had thought that Hilda had been marooned ashore because she had no more money to pay for her yearly *QE2* world trip. I was absolutely accurate, but this time the irrepressible Hilda had sold her car to raise the 1981 ticket money.

At eight o'clock in the morning of 11 February, I anchored the *QE2* off Queen Salotte's wharf at Tongapatu. The British High Commissioner, His Excellency Bernard Coleman, came aboard with his wife and daughter. 'How many for tennis?' he enquired. 'I've had our local tennis courts specially prepared for your visit.'

'I'm afraid, Your Excellency,' I replied, 'that in this heat there won't be anyone for tennis.' The temperature reading in Nuku'alofa Harbour was around ninety degrees Fahrenheit, and I wasn't about to invite heat strokes for either crew or passengers.

As I talked with the High Commissioner and his family, the harbour master and a group of local bank managers, Joan was making a swift exodus ashore. Her diary entry for 11 February tell more Tongan tales than I could, for I didn't leave the ship on the 1981 call.

'Christine and I got the launch about 10 a.m. Very rickety bus to Oholei beach, no windows, just tatty blinds in case of rain. But it was lovely as the air came through them, fresh and warm. Countryside interesting, bananas, coconuts, tara, lush tropical vegetation. Passed umpteen immaculate white churches, many of them Latter Day Saints.

317

'Took about an hour to get to beach but well worth it. Beautiful blue sea, white sand and palms. Had a coconut milk drink with a tot of rum in, then Christine, Jean Vickers and I quickly into water. Bathed in lagoon with huge waves coming in over coral reefs. Afterwards had a super lunch of pork, lamb, red snapper (fish), taroroot, sweet potatoes, bananas, yams, plantain, and salad with peppers, all served on "boat plates" made from split palms – no washing up!

'After lunch, sat under a palm for a while, then sailed on outrigger canoe. Fantastic, but Jean, sitting at back, was washed off by big wave and had to swim ashore. Not hurt, but an elderly man swimming was carried out to sea and taken back to ship's hospital, apparently with a heart attack. We came back to ship on launch, wrote some picture postcards, and then got ready for evening round of parties.'

My own routine shipboard duties were far more mundane than that 'Day in the Life of Joan Arnott', but the pace quickened towards early evening when the time arrived to take the *QE2* through the narrow jaws of the reef guarding Nuku'alofa Harbour and out into the open Pacific. Our passengers, many wearing souvenir clothing made from the beaten bark of Tonga's mulberry trees – called tapa – lined the decks to wave reluctant goodbyes to the friendly lands ruled by that gentlest of giants, King Tupou IV.

Sailing through the zig-zag date line on the way to Fiji caused its usual quota of calendar confusion. The line deviates to take in the remote Pacific island groups, where generally time doesn't matter as much as it does on a tightly scheduled ocean liner. We successfully cracked the calendar code to reach Suva's King's Wharf exactly at our expected arrival time of one o'clock on the afternoon of 12 February. Warm showers were tumbling into the harbour from clouds bursting over the surrounding high peaks, but raindrops running down gleaming cornets, bugles and flutes didn't deter the Fijian Police Band from blasting up to us from the quayside a damp but stirring rendition of 'On the Quarterdeck', followed by a rainswept 'Rule Britannia'. Eleven thousand miles from home, the *QE2* was being accorded a traditionally British brass-band welcome, complete with seaside summer showers.

Joan and I drove out to Orchid Island with Christine and

318

Harvey Smith. Since our visit there three years earlier, floods had swept away much of the life's work of curators Gwyn and Ivy Watkins. Many of the animal enclosures and their occupants had vanished in black floodwater, but Mr and Mrs Watkins with their son Keith had managed to save some of their pet flying foxes and iguanas. They were currently successfully breeding more iguanas, a somewhat slow process because, as Mrs Watkins told us, each egg of the lizard-like creatures takes eight months to hatch. Her husband remarked that he was now more than ever convinced of the reality of native spirit powers, but fortunately for everyone's equanimity we came across no tangible confirmations of Mr Watkins' assertions during our Suva sojourn. Our shore guides and hosts, agent Jack St Julian and his wife Kay, came aboard for farewell drinks just before we sailed out into the midnight waters of the Pacific, bound for the Arnott homelands of New South Wales.

An immense trans-ocean marathon lay ahead between Fiji and our Australian berth at Sydney Harbour's Circular Quay, but the watery wastes of the Pacific presented no opportunities for tedium for the 2500 people living, loving, working and playing within the *QE2*'s steel-walled city. The crew and hotel staff were totally committed to their disciplined duties, and all day through most of the night, our stateroom residents were assailed with an avalanche of ship-board attractions.

Those people unaffected by fragility from the previous night's festivities could tune in to *Bobbin' with Robin*, DJ Robin Hargreave's breakfast show broadcast from 8.15 a.m. on the *QE2*'s own radio network. Nine o'clock was time for prize quizzes on *Famous People* or *The World of Medicine* – a fine exercise for hypochondriacs but one which holidaying doctors were on their honour not to enter.

The ship's linguist Dorothy Hughes coaxed passengers up the first steps to success in Spanish from 10 a.m. in the Double Room, while along the boat deck Eric Mason was leading a gentle jog before switching to swimming coaching at the Seven Deck pool. In the Queen's Room, Social Director Candy Boyd was introducing a talk by passenger Mrs Desai on 'How to wear a sari', and at 11 a.m., golf pro Mel Martens was starting free lessons at the Upper Deck lido. A similar mission for bridge enthusiasts was under way in the Q4 room led by Serry Naugle.

In the theatre, world cruise lecturer Sheridan Garth was talking about 'MacArthur's Sea Trail to Victory'.

For amateur navigators fancying a flutter, the Tote on the ship's mileage was picking up bets in the Midships Bar, while for serious music fans the ship's Channel Six was broadcasting Beethoven's piano concertos No. 1 in C major and No. 3 in C minor played by Wilhelm Kempff and the Berlin Philharmonic. Then there is always a break in the passengers' pastimes as the clocks reach mid-day – cocktail time, a crucial hour from the days of Britain's Empire that survives honourably on the *QE2* today.

With lunch and liqueurs satisfyingly despatched, Dinah Sheridan welcomed the mid-Pacific afternoon by reading *The Railway Children* over Channel Six. From 2.30 p.m., Richard Naugle taught duplicate bridge in the Queen's Room, and at 2.45 there were card parties, painting lessons and electronic video matches. A financial seminar, starting at 3.15 in the theatre and titled 'Winning the Stock Market Game' was conducted by Don Mead and Howard Skaug, vice-presidents of Shearson, Loeb Rhoades. Classical music recordings, trap shooting, dancing classes, a yoga retreat and cash bingo rounded off the afternoon's athletics of body and mind.

Night-time entertainment began at 8.45 p.m. in the Double Room with the songs of Scotland's Stuart Gillies, the Sweet Elegance dancers and the orchestras of Rob Charles and Joe Loss. Bill and Lisa Manning supplied cocktail music in the Theatre Bar, and the Jeff Wraight Four set the Queen's Room swinging, while George Corderoy was offering his smooth pianistry in the Double Down Bar. When most of our shows were taking their final applause, the Sportsman's Club casino was starting to spin into late-night action. For non-gambling night owls, astronomer Ted Pedas was pointing out the 'Wonders of the Skies' from the Helicopter Deck observation station. And so to bed, or maybe to the Q4 nightclub for more dancing and an early morning nightcap.

The pleasurable permutations of the Pacific crossing were truly infinite and probably matched favourably any entertainment scene currently available in most of the world's more static resorts. And the parties in bars, cabins, staterooms and grills provided a round-the-clock setting for the ship's always fascinating, social strategems.

Sydney's skies were already hot, heavy and humid as I stood on the *QE2*'s bridge at six o'clock on the morning of 16 February to take her past the Heads and into the Circular Quay. Shafts of gold shone through the mists as we reached Bennelong Point, reflecting tumults of light across the harbour from the sail-like roofs of the still-muted Opera House. After four days and nights crossing the Pacific from Suva, we were just five minutes ahead of our arrival target of eight o'clock when we tied up at our city centre berth.

An hour later I was talking to Carol Thatcher, daughter of Britain's Prime Minister, on Channel 7 TV. Carol, in her early twenties, reminded me strongly of her mother in speech and mannerisms except that her hair was chestnut in contrast to her mother's golden hues. Carol spared me political questions. 'What does it feel like for a native-born Australian to command the British-based world's greatest passenger ship?' was the sort of undemanding query she threw at me. I pointed out politely that the *QE2* probably spends less time in British ports than most other ships in the country's maritime fleet, and answered, 'Yes, it's a fabulous feeling for an Australian to command the finest ship afloat.' Indeed it is, but even if it hadn't been, I was hardly likely to say so in Sydney with the *QE2*'s engines switched off.

Apart from Miss Thatcher's interview, I put in several radio and TV spots that morning, including a twenty-minute 'This is Captain Arnott' profile feature for Radio Australia with Eric Waite.

The next day, my old chum from Blue Funnel days, Radio Officer Dave Alcock, came down to the ship with our mutual friend Margot, one of the former Geddes girls who served us many war-time Sunday lunches. Dave brought me a fine photograph of my first ship, SS *Antilochus*, plus a well-polished brass button of the Blue Funnel Line. My memories of Sydney in the war years were sharply restored as the three of us breathed again the forgotten air of the Forties, and nostalgia still gripped the *QE2*'s Master's quarters an hour later when my mother's cousin Joyce Taylor phoned me from her Manly home. She had been hoping to get down to the ship, but was entering hospital later in the day and couldn't make the trip.

More relatives, including Margaret and Phillip Rudder whom we had met in Britain on their recent holiday there, came to visit us later in the day, and Joan took them on ship walkabouts. By early evening, the Australian associates of the Arnott clan had all departed ashore, and the massing of thousands of folk on the quayside reminded me that it was time to leave memories and homeland once more. Buzzing flotillas of little boats escorted us away from the lengthening shadows of the Sydney Harbour Bridge out towards the darkening waters of the Tasman Sea.

Boisterous transfusions of Australian passenger blood livened our shipboard scene as we headed towards Papua New Guinea. One of the livelier members of the group I had at my table in the Tables of the World restaurant was one Harold Killick, who told me that 'Cunard had better watch it. My son and I are going places in the luxury cruising business.' But Trafalgar House didn't have to start worrying yet, as Harold's main business was operating a chain of Australian wine and spirit shops. However, with his son Bob, he also ran the Port Hacking 'Daytripper' cruises for 'up to forty people at a time'. Harold showed me photos of one of his tripper-craft: it had a canopy-topped 'sunbakers' deck, a 'water-bike' for lagoon lounging, a small fleet of windsurfing craft and 'his and her amenities right down to showers'. 'We're just getting our marketing approach right,' said Harold modestly. I also liked his sales slogan, 'Come and Relax with Us', and Harold and I relaxed on the *QE2*, with the help of some choice Australian clarets he had brought on board from his shops' stocks.

A radio-phone call from the Australian police ended my anxieties about a missing passenger, an eighty-one-year-old retired professor from Sydney who had disappeared from the ship. It turned out he was the original absent-minded academic, and had gone ashore in Sydney without telling anyone, promptly forgetting about the *QE2* and the small matter of his wife being aboard. The professor was found by police meandering through a Sydney bookshop. His wife's only comment, when I told her he had been found, was 'I knew he'd be all right. God always looks after children, drunks and old people.'

Our next port of call should have been Port Moresby, but the *QE2* developed a leak in the starboard boiler. Immediate repairs were begun, but they slowed up our schedule and I cancelled the Papua New Guinea call and instead, took the *QE2* through the Grafton Passage into the coral kingdom of the Great Barrier

Reef. For hundreds of both passengers and crew, this was an unexpected visual bonus. They had never before been inside the vast labyrinth of reefs and cays – roughly the combined area of England and Wales – that forms a natural breakwater for Australia's north-east coast. Of course, the *QE2*'s builders hadn't anticipated that we would be making a close inspection of the Barrier Reef, or they might have fitted some of the glass bottom viewing panels that are standard equipment in the fleets of tourist craft that explore these cloudless waters.

From the *QE2*'s high decks, our eager crowds of observers had magnificent overhead views of a bewildering wealth of coral forests spangled in shimmering crusts of blue, purple, flame and gold. A giant green turtle, weighing around 400lb, flippered herself gracefully alongside, matching our meandering progress for a few furlongs, and then dived swiftly from our sight. Battalions of yellow-banded hussar fish retreated indignantly as the *QE2*'s bows crossed their seabed frontiers. Disturbed by the commotion, a massive grey reef shark surfaced briefly, glared at us and vanished. And on the coral islands fringing our seapath, angry honkings from terns, shearwaters and booby birds warned us to steer clear of their desolate strands.

Our friendly reef pilot told me that the largest structure on earth fashioned by living creatures isn't Australia Square in Sydney, London's Houses of Parliament, New York's World Trade Center or even Moscow's Kremlin. It's the Great Barrier Reef, built by a labour force of astronomical numbers of coral polyp workers, and the latest generation of more than 400 coral species is still hard at work on the 2000-kilometre length of the Great Barrier project, providing homes for more than 1500 different species of fish and for wide varieties of crustaceans, and is the biggest turtle-breeding grounds on earth.

The whole 207,000 square kilometres of the reef waters, said our pilot sadly, had long been plundered by man for 'sport', greed and gain. So-called sporting fishermen had scoured the reef waters, killing the colourful underwater residents with explosive spearheads, the once beautiful coral islands had been desecrated for their mineral wealth, and excavations for oil and coal had left their scars. But now, huge areas of reef territory were being declared protected national parks, giving new hope of survival for their ravaged residents.

At 3.15 on the morning of 24 February, after passing through the Torres Strait, I landed our Barrier Reef pilot at Thursday Island, off the Queensland coast. Half an hour later, with the *QE2* still in Australian territorial waters, I conducted the burial at sea of a seventy-five-year-old Australian who had died after a heart attack only hours after coming aboard in Sydney. As the poor fellow's body was plunging through cool waters to an eternal darkness on the deep sea-bed, I whispered a final silent prayer for the repose of his soul. I replaced my peaked cap and left the quiet peace of the afterdeck, returning to the bridge. Where I ordered 'full speed' across seas already streaked by a red tropic dawn. I glanced at my bridge clock. It was 4.30 a.m. I set course for bed.

Six days and twenty-two hours from leaving Sydney, I gently eased the *QE2* into her berth at Pier 15 in the broad beautiful bay of Manila. We had sailed 4047 miles across the Pacific, which made our Australia–Philipines voyage the furthest and longest in terms of time ever accomplished by the *QE2*. A brass band blazing away on the quayside noisily applauded our arrival as our mooring hawsers were secured.

After such an epic odyssey Joan and Christine decided they deserved to go ashore, spending the afternoon sight-seeing, shopping and dodging attempted assassination by drivers of the city's jeepneys. These are brilliantly painted jeeps, left behind by the American forces and now operating as highly customised mini-buses. Their interiors have stereo music, hand-made cushions and pictures of Rudolph Valentino, Elvis Presley and the Pope. Jeepneys, a vital and colourful part of Manila's transport system, are usually driven in a style that reminds me of hostile fairground dodgem cars. However, Joan and Christine got back on board safely and did a quick change before going out for dinner with Harvey and me. Our hostess was one of the *QE2*'s most faithful travellers, Mrs Trese Hollerich, and our venue my favourite hotel, the elegant Manila.

The Filipino capital is a city of hotels. Fourteen superb, international-calibre establishments were opened there in 1976 for the World Banking Conference and the tourist people tell me that there are more than 4000 top-quality hotel rooms in the central area alone. But in my opinion the Manila Hotel is the finest of them all. Built about seventy years ago in Spanish Mission style, its famous marble foyer leads to exquisite restaurants and lounges unsurpassed anywhere in the world for sheer excellence in service, food and traditional care. President Marcos and his wife are said to dine there often. As we went into the beautiful Champagne Room, each lady was given a lovely orchid and a section of the country's national philharmonic orchestra provided 'palm court' background music. In this tranquil atmosphere, we sat in the high-backed cane chairs, sipped chilled white wine and sampled the day's delicacies of snails, crayfish and frogs legs. We drifted through exotic main courses and into the delicious realms of fresh strawberries and cream, followed by the hotel's mellow, soothing Gaelic coffee. The meal was superb and the service unbelievable. As we drank our final liqueurs, I watched the aromatic grey clouds from nearby cigars curl up towards the top of the roof-high crystal tree and almost regretted being a non-smoker. Perhaps, I reflected, General Douglas MacArthur had also found the sedate attractions of the Manila irresistible when he chose the hotel for his living and working headquarters during World War II. My reflections were brought to an abrupt finish when I glanced at my watch. It was almost sailing time.

We made it back safely to the *QE2*, and I set course northwards from the pleasantly warm Pacific into the chilly, rainswept stretches of the South China Sea. I turned out of my blankets at quarter to four on the morning of 26 February to take the *QE2* through the dark, crowded waters of Hong Kong harbour to her berth at the Kowloon Ocean Terminal. We were finally tied up around eight and, guessing that Joan would have emerged from slumberland by that time, I joined her in our quarters for my invariable breakfast of a glass of milk and a glass of fresh orange juice.

Press conferences, radio and television interviews and ship's business ate away at my daylight hours, while those of Joan were spent shopping at the Ocean Terminal near the quay, and at the remarkable Nathan Street shops where the clothes range from Paris models to snappy jeans and cost considerably less than they would in Europe. After years of patriotically inspired resistance, I've even acquired my own Hong Kong-based personal tailor. Known simply as 'Sam' of Kowloon, he comes aboard as we dock, takes orders for hand-made shirts, suits or dinner jackets, and delivers the finely tailored garments – all made from British materials – before we sail two days later. It's the sort of service that would be difficult to equal in London.

The Duke of Kent has obviously found this too, for he's one of Sam's regular customers.

On our first night in Hong Kong, Ann Brooks invited Joan, myself, Harvey and Christine, and Captain Ian Borland, vice-president of Port Operations in New York, out for a Rolls Royce drive to the Mandarin Hotel, where we again had as fabulous a meal as we had had the year before. Amazingly, we were still able to enjoy a few dances before we caught the Star Ferry back to the ship. The following evening, 'Lulu' Edwards – from Tallahassee – took us on a similar mission of waist expansion to Gaddi's Restaurant in the Peninsula Hotel. Nigel Roberts, the ship's doctor, joined the party but we all exercised such restraint during the delightful *à la carte* feast that his professional services weren't once needed.

At sea the next night, I shook hands with all the people who had joined the *QE2* in Hong Kong, my last official function on my section of the 1981 world cruise. When we reached Singapore, I handed over command to Relief Master Doug Ridley, who had flown in with 250 change-over crewmen. Joan and I caught a Laker airways charter flight to Gatwick with a couple of hundred leave-hungry officers and ratings.

Our DC10 roared into Singapore's midnight skies and as the big jet burst through the final thickness of cloud cover, the bright stars of the Southern Cross twinkled at us reassuringly across the heavens. Half an hour later my jolly jacktars were tucking into steaks, sprouts and chips at 35,000 feet. Our stewardess, Jill Woods, turned out to be the daughter of some old friends of ours, Bill and Margery Woods, from St Annes. She warned us when we left the aircraft for a twenty-minute break at Sharjah, near Dubai, that the price of a cup of tea would amaze us. It did. It cost us one US dollar a cup. The views across the desert from the new airport terminal were breathtaking, the sands beyond our parked plane glistening in red and gold which deepened through the distance to a blue and mauve infinity. Perhaps, mused Joan, it all came inclusive in the price of our teas.

As we crossed the snow-topped mountains surrounding Damascus, I stepped onto the flight deck for a taste of navigation at more than 500 miles an hour. I got a visual 'fix' over Beirut, then looked down at the Mediterranean whose waters I knew so well at a much more intimate level. We flew across Greece,

326

Yugoslavia, the Austrian Alps, Luxembourg and then descended over Dungeness to Gatwick.

I picked up a Godfrey Davis hire car at the airport, drove through a wet and cold London, and headed up the M6 motorway at a steady seventy miles per hour. I decided to take a break from the incessant swishing of the wiper blades, and left the motorway at Cannock for a steak and kidney pie pub lunch. 'Wud yer loik sumfink to drink whell we woit fer sum fresh chips?' asked our pleasantly buxom Staffordshire barmaid. Hardly the champagne service of the Manila, and I'm not even sure my phonetics are accurate, but that cheerful Black Country voice added a homely, welcoming flavour to our first meal back in Britain and, just two hours later, our hired Cortina deposited us in the driveway of the Arnotts' English habitat. I helped Joan to unpack, then we drove in convoy to Blackpool's Imperial Hotel to return the car to the Godfrey Davis office there. Our drive back along the cliff tops to Fleetwood, alongside Britain's only remaining tramway, was the breezy finale to our 1981 world adventure. The *QE2* was still at sea, making for Sri Lanka, and I was due to rejoin her a month after she had completed the world cruise.

Chapter 33

Some of the celebrities featuring in the latest *TV Times* 'Meet the Stars' cruise were lugging their own luggage aboard when I returned to the *QE2* in Southampton. Clodagh Rogers, Les Dawson, Lennie Bennett, Barney Colehan and lots more British television favourites invited along by the magazine were victims of a port dispute; even our ship's stores had to be taken out to Lisbon in containers. We collected them there, then cut across to Tangier and called at Gibraltar and Madeira before heading home to Southampton. But we couldn't enter the port due to another dispute, or perhaps the earlier one still going on. It didn't matter which. I took the *QE2* into Cherbourg and arranged for our 600 TV fans to be taken back to Britain in three charter aircraft and a ferry boat. At that moment, the glamour of the 1981 world cruise seemed a million miles away.

But the fragrant magic of the southern oceans wasn't altogether lost. My friend and world cruise passenger Jeraldine Saunders, writer of TV's *Love Boat* series, sent me a clipping from her syndicated travel column, regularly published in sixty-five cities throughout the USA. The lovely Jeraldine wrote: 'Whatever the *QE2* does stir in your imagination, she truly brings you the royal way of life, a glittering fantasy land. You run your own slice of that kingdom just as you choose. Her Majesty The Ship and Captain Robert Arnott, his crew and hotel staff, are there to help you to make memories you will treasure for the rest of your life. I believed I had sailed in the best of the world's luxury liners, but little did I know the joys awaiting me in the most resplendent of them all – the Cunard monarch *Queen Elizabeth II*.'

Somewhere in the Pacific, Jeraldine had presented me with a copy of her latest book, *The Complete Guide to a Successful Cruise*. She wrote on the fly-leaf: 'To Captain Bob. I am certainly enjoying your *QE2*. You are truly a *Love Boat* captain. Happy sailing, from Jeraldine Saunders.' Jeraldine's husband, who is

328

in the aerospace industry, was with her when she handed me the book, and he smiled. 'I suppose giving the Master of the *QE2* this book is, as you say in Britain, like carrying coals to Newcastle.'

I glanced at Jeraldine's autographed message, and immediately showed it to Joan. Perhaps it was a self-defence reflex action, but Joan merely said, 'Jeraldine has only written what I've known for years. Now what else is new?'

In the early summer of 1981, not a lot was. I took the *QE2*, her famous folk, her business tycoons and her thousands of ordinary people seeking the last great thrill of ocean travel, between Britain and the United States, to the Atlantic isles, the Caribbean, and once again up to the North Cape.

The Scandinavian cruise was quite a family gathering for me as Joan, my cousin Douglas Brooks and his wife Muriel from Turton, and a golfing friend from Fleetwood, Ernie Barron, came on board in Southampton for the trip to the 'Land of the Midnight Sun'. Regrettably the midnight sun again eluded us at the North Cape, but the fjords, waterfalls and glaciers were as spectacular as ever and more than atoned for the indifferent weather.

Then, after a foggy transatlantic crossing to New York we embarked 1823 passengers, mostly Americans, for the *QE2*'s inaugural trip to Canada. It was moonlight as we went up the St Lawrence, but the first rays of a summer dawn broke through as we tied up at our berth in Québec at four o'clock on the morning of 20 July. Even at that early hour there were 200 or so carloads of people on the quayside watching the *QE2*'s arrival. We moored right opposite the Heights of Abraham which looked as stark and challenging as I remembered them from 1967 when I first saw them from the decks of *Carmania*. Probably, I reflected, they hadn't changed very much since General Wolfe and his men scaled them in 1759.

Radio, Press and TV people arrived on board at the noon cocktail hour for a party in the Q4 room, as well as many of the people who had helped to organise this first-ever visit to Canada. I chatted to British Consul General Murray Simons, to the American Consul General and his wife Mr and Mrs Jaeger, and to scores of other visitors eager for their first on-board view of the ship. The pleasantries and a quick lunch completed, Joan and I went ashore. The Canadian summer air was amazingly hot and our ship's agent had thoughtfully provided an air-conditioned car, but this blew such cold air on us that often we had to open the windows to keep warm.

On Québec's streets, men walked around in shorts and the girls wore thin, sleeveless dresses, as if to soak up whatever warmth and sunshine were around in their short summer. Our French-Canadian driver took us to the Wolfe-Montcalm monument, to du Tresor Street – the artists' quarter where the walls are hung with pictures for sale, Paris-style, and to the Citadel. From the battlefield of the Plains of Abraham, now a national park, we looked down over the 525 steps leading up the Heights, and at the *QE2* lying far below, looking like a toy ship left behind on a thin silver ribbon.

Our brief Canadian shore tour ended at the Château Frontenac, and soon afterwards I was back on the bridge for sailing. Sudden summer rain swept over the thousands of people lining the quayside as we moved away, and small boats buzzed around the *QE2*'s vast quarters like so many happy harbour flies. And as darkness fell, cars on the river banks hooted and flashed their lights as we sailed by.

Our old grey enemy caught up with us before we reached Halifax, and when we docked there, the fog billows were as dense and menacing as have ever blown over me in forty years at sea. But when Joan and I went ashore, the Halifax skies suddenly became blue and sunny, and we toured the fine white old Colonial buildings and then looked in at the brand new Barrington shopping complex. That afternoon I had the pleasure of welcoming aboard Admiral Fulton of the Royal Canadian Navy, and later several ex-Cunard colleagues now based in Nova Scotia dropped in to talk about the old days before the *QE2* sailed for Maine later in the evening.

Shortly after seven the next morning, we dropped anchor in the lavishly beautiful Frenchman Bay, off Maine's Mount Desert Island. The big tender *Arcadian* arrived to ferry passengers ashore to Bar Harbour, and on board I gave a cocktail party for local dignitaries in the Q4 room. I presented Mrs Patricia Curtis, chairman of Bar Harbour Council, with a picture of the *QE2* and she handed me a fine New England pictorial plaque. Governor Brennan of Maine brought on board his nine-year-old daughter Tara, and the little girl was so thrilled to be on the *QE2* that I gave her a picture of the ship, too. After thanking me, she turned to her father, and asked wistfully, 'If I do without a birthday present for two or three years, can I have a trip on the *QE2*?' That seemed to be a good moment for me to leave the local VIPs and talk to the Maine television, radio and Press people. Interviews completed, I joined my civic guests on the quarter deck for a recital by the local pipe and drum band.

Then, at last, Joan and I were free to go ashore for lunch with our agent Bill Leavitt and his wife Rho, who introduced us to Maine's speciality – lobsters. They were superb. In the afternoon, we drove to the top of Cadillac Mountain and looked out over the magnificent panorama.

Our Canadian adventure now ended, I headed the *QE2* back to New York, and then across the Atlantic to Southampton. But before we reached our home port, a Very Important Happening was to take place on 29 July.

Almost without exception, the passengers from Britain and the United States who travel on the *QE2* are staunch supporters of the British monarchy, and the Master, officers and crew certainly are. So there was massive disappointment aboard when we were still out at sea at the end of July on the day that His Royal Highness Prince Charles married Lady Diana Spencer in St Paul's Cathedral. Television broadcasts don't yet reach out into mid-Atlantic, even for royal occasions.

Of course, we were able to tune into the live BBC radio commentaries, and relayed them over the ship's own broadcast system. Passengers sipped free champagne in lounges bright with red, white and blue decorations while they listened to the Royal couple making their wedding vows. As I proposed the toast 'Charles and Diana' in the crowded Queen's Room, our ship's bandsmen struck up 'God Bless the Prince of Wales' and 'God Save the Queen'.

As I walked back to my cabin I met my old cruising friends Phyllis and Tom Botting of Tonbridge. 'Doesn't it all make you feel proud to be British on a British ship?' said Phyllis.

'Indeed it does,' I replied. That evening our Executive Chef John Bainbridge put on a special Royal dinner with such appropriate items as 'Cocktails of Crabmeat Claw Duchy of Cornwall', 'Potage Caernarvon Castle', 'Tenderloin Steak Lady Diana', and 'Spring Lamb from the Cotswolds Prince Charles'. These were all very moving moments on Britain's Queen of the Oceans, but how much more enjoyable would the whole occasion have been for my passengers if they had been able to watch as well as hear the St Paul's nuptials.

The next day, a yellow helicopter flew in from the east and hovered over our sun deck, while the ship's fire and safety crews stood on alert below as a precious package was winched down to eagerly waiting hands. Then, as the whirring blades lifted the machine high over our bows and away towards Bishop's Rock, the package was rushed to the *QE2*'s theatre-cinema. Ten minutes later our projectionists were screening the first of four full-house showings of an hour-long colour film of the Royal Wedding Day. And it wasn't only the ladies whose cheeks felt salt tears as Lady Di declared 'I do'. Better, I had decided, to see the film twenty-four hours after the event than not at all.

On the Royal Wedding Day, a telegram of greeting that I had sent to the Prince and new Princess of Wales at Buckingham Palace proclaimed: 'The ship's company and passengers of RMS *Queen Elizabeth II* send their congratulations and wish you many years of happiness together. Arnott, Master.'

My own years of happiness with the ocean queen are now, inevitably, drawing to a close. They will soon be interrupted when I take over command of *Cunard Princess* for a sunny spell of Caribbean cruising, and then I may be back on that magnificent bridge to spend the last months of more than forty years at sea as Master of what is the last great ruler in the illustrious dynasty of British ocean monarchs. In such a position of absolute power, I've always tried to keep things simple, doing my job without any fancy frills or titles. The thousands of friends who've sailed with me over the years know me – affectionately, I hope – simply as Captain Bob, Master of the *QE2*. And that's how I would like them to remember me.